THE STAR OF AFRICA

Colin D. Heaton

"In *Star of Africa*, Heaton has produced the definitive biography of Hans-Joachim Marseille, the unconventional Luftwaffe super-ace who dominated the North African air war....The text is superbly augmented with rare photos and numerous appendices that will keep readers and researchers busy for decades to come."
—Barrett Tillman, *Forgotten Fifteenth: The Daring Airmen Who Crippled Hitler's War Machine*; Former Secretary, American Fighter Aces Assoc.

"Great story of a German war hero who opposed his brutal government and displayed chivalry and compassion towards his enemies, maintaining his honor, and becoming a legend."
—Maj. Gen. James E. Livingston, Co-author of *Noble Warrior: The Story of Maj. Gen. James E. Livingston, USMC (Ret.), Medal of Honor*

"What Colin Heaton has written is the Magnum Opus of the Marseille phenomenon....a 125-pound killing dynamo that broke and then rewrote the rules of fighter-to-fighter combat, allowing him to dominate the North African skies for almost 18 months. There is simply no better book on this topic."
—Lt. Col. Robert Tate, USAFR (ret.), AWACS Pilot and WWII Historian

"Heaton has created a very well-written, meticulously researched triumph of a biography with interviews from men who knew the amazing Marseille—a German, anti-Nazi Swing Kid and highly decorated fighter pilot—who threw away the rulebook but proved that he indeed ruled the skies in WWII."
—H. P. Shreve, Author of *The Secret Diaries of a POW: COL Arthur L. Shreve, Jr.*, (adapted to film *Once a Colonel*)

"Having read other biographies of Marseille...I was surprised to find that this gracefully written new work adds fascinating details and accounts from extensive interviews with Luftwaffe *Experten* that make it worth reading no matter how deeply immersed in Marseille lore you might already be."
—*Aviation History* magazine

"His loss was a bitter blow to his compatriots in JG-27 but a blessing to those of us on the other side."

—Ron Cundy, Royal Air Force, North Africa

"Watching Marseille in the air was like watching a deadly aerial ballet. He looked like he was twelve years old, and often acted like it."

—Major Werner Schroer, Knight's Cross, Oak Leaves and Swords, JG-27

"Marseille was perhaps the best that the Luftwaffe had. His record was only surpassed by his immature unprofessionalism."

—Col. Hajo Herrmann, Knight's Cross, Oak Leaves and Swords

"Men like Marseille captured the public imagination, and rightly so. They played a dangerous game, and Marseille was perhaps the best to ever fly a fighter."

—Lt. Gen. Gunther Rall, Knight's Cross, Oak Leaves and Swords with 275 victories

"Marseille may not have been the perfect officer, but he was the perfect fighter pilot."

—Gen. Adolf Galland, Famed German Ace

"*The Star of Africa* shares Marseille's journey from marginal young pilot to 'virtuoso of the fighter pilots' (the title given to him by Adolf Galland)...with close attention to detail throughout. An excellent book."

—Trevor J. Constable, Coauthor of *The Blond Knight of Germany: A Biography of Erich Hartmann* and *Fighter General: The Life of Adolf Galland*

"Heaton expertly portrays Marseille as one of history's great fighter pilots, as well as a man who lived life to the full and who fought with honor."

—Dennis Showalter, Pritzker Prize for lifetime achievement in military history writing

"...there is no better book to acquaint a reader with this extraordinary fighter pilot and man."

—Chuck Oldham, *Defense Media Network*

Also by Colin D. Heaton

THE GERMAN ACES SPEAK
THE GERMAN ACES SPEAK II
ABOVE THE PACIFIC
THE STAR OF AFRICA
FOUR-WAR BOER
THE ME 262 STORMBIRD
NOBLE WARRIOR with James E. Livingston
NIGHT FIGHTERS
GERMAN ANTI-PARTISAN WARFARE IN EUROPE
ABOVE THE REICH
OCCUPATION AND INSURGENCY

THE STAR OF AFRICA

THE COMPLETE STORY OF HANS-JOACHIM MARSEILLE AS TOLD BY THOSE WHO KNEW HIM AND THOSE HE FOUGHT

Revised Expanded Unabridged Edition

by

Colin D. Heaton

WARRIORS PUBLISHING GROUP
LOCKHART, TEXAS

Star of Africa
Copyright © 2025 by Colin D. Heaton

A Warriors Publishing Group book/published by arrangement with the author

PRINTING HISTORY
Warriors Publishing Group edition/November 2025

All rights reserved.
Copyright © 2025 by Colin D. Heaton
Cover art copyright © 2025 by Gerry Kissell (gerrykissell.com)

A previous version of this book was published by Zenith Press.
All photographs are from the author's collection unless noted otherwise.

This book may not be reproduced in whole
or in part, by mimeograph or any other means,
without permission. For information address:
Warriors Publishing Group
310 North Commerce Street
Lockhart, TX 78644

ISBN: 978-1-944353-86-5, 978-1-944353-87-2
Library of Congress Control Number: 2025944342

The name "Warriors Publishing Group" and the logo
are trademarks belonging to Warriors Publishing Group

PRINTED IN THE UNITED STATES OF AMERICA
10 9 8 7 6 5 4 3 2 1

This book is dedicated to the men of the *Luftwaffe,* especially the airmen of *Jagdgeschwader* 27 and their Allied counterparts from Australia, Great Britain, New Zealand, Canada, South Africa, and the United States who fought with courage. They were all young men thrown into the greatest war in history, and many did not survive, but their legacy of service lives on as long as we remember them.

Introduction

WHEN ANNE MARIE LEWIS and I wrote *The Star of Africa: The Story of Hans Marseille-The Rogue Ace Who Dominated the World War II Skies* I did not choose the title. I was also restricted to submitting a manuscript below 100,000 words, which meant that much of the information that I had acquired had to be left out—especially interviews with people who knew him well and those who fought against him—along with many of Marseille's practical jokes and personal issues. Also, when I received the galley for review, there were a few errors and a few spelling issues in the format transition and publisher's edit that I addressed in my corrections list to the editors. However, these were not all corrected before they released the hardcover.

When the book was released in 2012 it was well received, and over time it has been translated into French, Polish, Swedish, and Finish. There have been several good books on Hans-Joachim Marseille by English, American, and German historians, and I had read them all. The most glaring difference between my book and all the others was the simple fact that I had dozens of interviews with the people who were involved in Marseille's life, both in the military and in his personal life, friends and enemies alike. I felt that the lack of all this additional information reduced the value of the previous books and diminished the quality of his remarkable story.

However, I always regretted the word-count limitation as there was so much information that I wanted to include from the interviews that provided a greater overall picture of the air war from both sides, not just the Germans. This new edition hopefully corrects those issues, adds more information about Marseille by expanding the information gathered from the many interviews that I conducted, both Allied and German, while those people were still alive.

Another reason for updating the book was when I was contacted by Richard J. Carthew of Melbourne, Australia in 2015. Richard is the nephew of Graham George Buckland, Marseille's 65th victory. Over the years of my many emails, phone calls, and Zoom meetings with Richard, I gained more insight into Graham as a person, and as to what the Buckland family knew, what they did not know, and what they learned from the book. I was pleased to learn that the information gave the family closure and cleared up a mystery that had lingered for many decades after the war. He sent this email which was a follow up to the initial contact:

Message dated 7/10/2015 2:54:24 A.M. Eastern Daylight Time writes:

Hi Colin,

The parcel post has just arrived. I ripped open the envelope and went straight to the index and then to page 106. The only person home was Max, my daughter's boyfriend who is over from Rome for four weeks. His occupation is a pilot. I sat down and read him the page and couldn't believe events like this had been recorded. He said Italians only think of history if it is over 2,000 years old.

I will phone Emily at the R.A.A.F. Museum on Monday. I am sure she will be delighted with the book that details Graham's last minutes.

Please find attached the pictures of Graham's watch we found at my mother's home.

Thank you very much for the dedication in the front of *The Star of Africa*.

Kind Regards,
Richard

Hopefully other families may find answers to their questions given the additional content. I believe the reader who is familiar with the previous book will find this a far more engaging, interesting, and well-rounded publication that answers many of the questions that were not addressed previously. One of greatest benefits of writing these types of books is discovering that sometimes a family learns something about their loved one that remained a mystery, such as Richard J. Carthew and his family, and he provided this letter:

> Since my boyhood days I have wondered: whatever happened to my uncle, Graham Buckland? My sisters and I were regular visitors to my grandparents' home in James Street, East Ballarat. There were no photographs, mementos or even medals of Graham. The small bits and pieces I did know came from my father and mother.
>
> Dad told me Graham was shot down in North Africa and that he flew a Kittyhawk. Mum told me that Graham, 11 years older would play the harmonica to her in the bath. Years later I found out that my wife's auntie had applied for and received the medals of an uncle that who had been shot down over Berlin whilst seconded to RAF Bomber Command. Hearing about this I asked my mother, Graham's closest living relation to apply for his service medals. This was a small step into finding out more about Graham. These medals have been worn proudly by various members of the family at ANZAC Day services since.

Pilot Officer Graham George Buckland (center) in flight training (Richard Carthew)

More insight was gained a few years later when my mother showed me items that came from my grandmother's home after she had passed away. There were photos, certificates from the Boy Scouts and YMCA and most importantly letters sent by Graham from North Africa. Later, Mum found Graham's logbook and a group photo of RAAF personnel but no details of who, when or where.

Graham George Buckland, Marseille's 65th victory (Richard Carthew)

I took the photograph to the RAAF Museum in Melbourne to see if they would like to have it. At the same time, I took the logbook. Curator Emily Constantine looked at it and instantaneously came up with two observations. That Graham had gone from Australia to North Africa without going to training school in Great Britain and she was amazed at the amount of hours Graham spent in the air.

The RAAF were happy to receive the logbook and photo, it was then decided to donate other photos and letters that Graham had sent. Then came the big day, Sunday 31 May 2015 when Senator the Hon. Michael Ronaldson, Minister for Veteran's Affairs accepted the 'Buckland Collection' on behalf of the RAAF Museum. In attendance were Graham's surviving sister, Barbara, six nieces and nephews and partners and eight great nieces and nephews. It was a great honour to have the Senator at the presentation, because the Senator and Graham's families both come from the same town, Ballarat.

Happy with what we had achieved and to have honoured Graham in this way, this felt like the ending. Then by chance I was reading a Wikipedia entry about a Luftwaffe Pilot, Hans-Joachim Marseille. It mentioned that he had shot down an Australian pilot Flight Sergeant Graham Buckland, and the reference for this fact was from the book The Star of Africa by author Colin Heaton. I immediately sent an email to Colin in the States, and the reply was very quick, and this started a new chapter of discovery.

What I learnt from Colin about the events on 30 May 1942, two days before Graham's 21st Birthday, amazed me. Such detail of what Colin had researched almost felt like a minute-by-minute description on what was happening in the skies over North Africa that day. Two things that I really took note of was that there had been talk within the family that Graham's Kittyhawk was shot down, he bailed out and injured himself when landing. Then for three days he was cared for by Berber tribesman, this was simply not true as Colin had interviewed Luftwaffe pilots and ground crew and knew exactly was happened.

The other matter of what Colin had described was that Graham was given the Last Rites. My nan, a religious woman but not Catholic, had she known that it would have made her grieving a little less painful. These facts are all thanks to Colin Heaton, my American mate. I am pleased that he is writing the expanded revised edition, providing more insights and details from not just the Germans, but also from their opponents, the Allied Commonwealth pilot who fought a brave war against an equally determined enemy. Colin is giving these men their voices from his interviews, in order to provide the reader with a comprehensive perspective of the war without bias or purpose. This is especially true of the men who represented the Australian fighter squadrons, and there were none braver.

It is well beyond time to let the old propaganda and prejudices of the past go. Both sides had young men, like Marseille and Buckland, who were simply young men fighting for their respective countries. Men of honour flew on both sides. This is truly their collective story.

As a result, I no longer wonder what happened to my uncle Graham George Buckland. I only wonder what could have been had he lived.

Richard J. Carthew
Melbourne, Australia

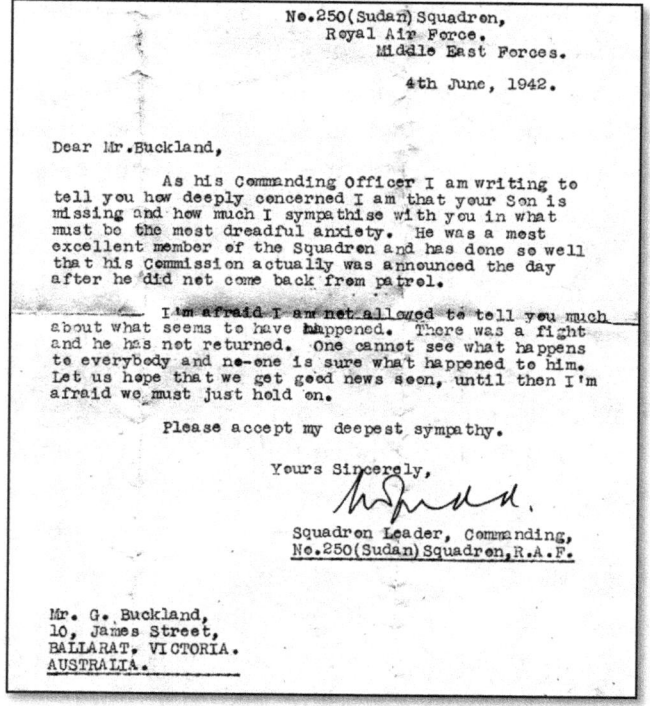

Letter written by Michael Judd to Graham Buckalnd's family. Interesting to note that the letter did not disclose the details of Marseille or the circumstances, per orders. p. 5 (Richard Carthew)

I wish to especially devote this work to the memory of all those young men who fought in the skies over North Africa, but especially Edu Neumann, a mentor to many and a good friend to all. He was critical in gathering the men around to help do the interviews who flew with Marseille. A special recognition to my late friends Col. Raymond Frederick Toliver, USAF (Ret), and Trevor James Constable, as their works introducing the world to the *Luftwaffe* fighter pilots sparked my interest decades ago. They were extremely helpful over the years with information and hard to reach contacts for interviews.

I also need to thank all those who wrote blurbs and endorsed the first version as the manuscript was developed over the years, who have now left us: Dr. Dennis Showalter, Col. Walter J. Boyne, USAF (Ret), Brigadier General Robin Olds, USAF (Ret), Jeffrey L. Ethell. Also, thanks to my attorney, historian and friend, Albert H. Wunsch III. Special thanks to Robert Tate and Nick Hector for unselfishly providing documents from their own research to help complete the complicated career of Hans-Joachim Marseille and some of his fellow pilots, and their contributions are so cited.

Also, a very special thanks to my agent Dr. Gayle Wurst at Princeton International Agency for the Arts for once again doing the heavy lifting. If not for her belief in this and previous works, this book would not exist. I also wish to thank the extraordinary team of Captain Dale Dye and Julia Dye for believing enough in this story to publish the expanded and revised edition. I must give kudos to my friend Marilyn Walton, a wonderful editor on this and many projects.

I sincerely hope that people read Marseille's amazing story and reflect upon this young man who maintained his honor and humanity, while fighting for a regime that he learned firsthand was evil, yet still served his country and his comrades to the best of his ability. On that note he was not unique. Many Germans who learned of the horrors their nation was perpetrating had their own demons to deal with. Marseille was no different. What I find astonishing about him was his ability to overcome so much personal loss in his life, becoming disillusioned with his national leadership, and still maintaining his sense of personal honor, which was even extended to his enemies.

On that note he truly was "The Star of Africa."

—Colin D. Heaton, 2024

Forewords

OVER THE YEARS IT has been my privilege and pleasure to meet many World War II fighter pilots from both Allied and Axis countries. Their number includes Sir Douglas Bader, Adolf Galland, Günther Rall, Walter Krupinski, Gabby Gabreski, Johnny Johnson, Saburo Sakai, Chuck Yeager, and many more. I can say unequivocally that none of these fine airmen, as deserving as they were, had the great good fortune to have biographies written of them that compare in quality, accuracy, or tone to Colin Heaton's superb book on Hans-Joachim Marseille.

This stems in equal parts from Heaton's research and Marseille's mystique. His astounding victory record, phenomenal shooting accuracy, and less than Prussian demeanor were written about for years, most often in a questioning way. It just did not seem possible that someone so young, with such engaging characteristics, could also be an ace of such legendary skills.

As the author reveals, Marseille did in fact differ from almost every other fighter ace, particularly those of the *Luftwaffe*, in many significant ways. He rose above the traditional German officer's strict military regimen, just as he rose above the super-nationalistic and racist precepts of the Nazi regime. Only a man of Marseille's ability could have done this and escaped the usual political repercussions.

Marseille's blazing combat career was made possible by his unbelievable skill. Heaton has captured this. Perhaps even more important, he has also captured the many incidents in which Marseille revealed his humane nature. He was a young man who cared both for his comrades and, when the fight was over, for his enemy.

—Col. Walter J. Boyne

The enigma that is Hans-Joachim Marseille is not easily deciphered and seldom discussed. This Knight of the Reich personified all that was taboo to the Fatherland. In many ways, he was a typical Berliner youth—rebellious, Bohemian, and juvenile. Yet, he also possessed the tenacity and discipline necessary to achieve aeronautical excellence. This dichotomy clearly frustrated the German High Command and made him the idol of the rank and file. This quintessential "bad boy," however, was a chivalrous and brave warrior. He amassed 158 victories and was dead by 22 years of age.

Certainly, this inherent contradiction can be attributed to his upbringing, surroundings, and Huguenot heritage. Each, I believe, contributed to his essence as well as his success. It provided a duality not often found in a German military man.

The Huguenots, a term originally used in derision, were traditionally known for their harsh and pointed criticisms of the doctrine and worship traits of the Catholic Church. Living in France, they denounced the Pope as a tyrant. These controversial views provoked persecution culminating in the St. Bartholomew's Day massacre (August 24–October 3, 1572), wherein approximately 30,000 Huguenots were killed, forcing mass exodus from France or conversion to Catholicism. Many Huguenot refugees found safe haven in Germany, and a good number settled in Berlin. By 1700, one-fifth of the city's population was French speaking. The use of French in their Church services lasted until the early 1800s.

Clearly, this heritage promoted individuality as well as a conscious appreciation of those who suffer persecution. Among the faithful, there must be a subliminal recognition of the plight of the refugee as well as an advocation of tolerance.

Berlin, in Marseille's formative years, was a well-known mecca for artists. Jochen, as he was known by his friends, hailed from the Berlin-Charlottenburg district. This was also home of the famous Romanisches Café. This café-bar was a hot spot for the intelligentsia, a place at which leading writers, painters, actors, directors, journalists, and critics of the day met. The youth of Berlin were offered the opportunity to consort with Billy Wilder, Bertolt Brecht, Otto Dix, Sylvia Von Harden, Arthur Kronfeld, and Erich Maria Remarque, to name a few. These left-wing intellectuals discussed politics and listened to American swing and jazz music.

Jochen's family life can be characterized as unstable. His parents divorced when he was very young. Siegfried Georg Martin Marseille, his father, was an army officer during World War I. He would rejoin the military in 1933 and would rise to the rank of *Generalmajor*. Siegfried would be killed on the Eastern Front in 1944.

Jochen had a difficult and distant relationship with his father. The divorce further drove a wedge between father and son. He did share his father's penchant for the nightlife but had little else in common. They were never close.

Charlotte, his mother, remarried a local police official, and initially Jochen took his last name, Reuter, for school purposes. Jochen would change back to Marseille prior to entry into military service. During the war, his younger sister, Inge, with whom he was very close and protective of, was murdered under mysterious circumstances. This loss left Jochen with deep emotional scars.

It is my opinion, after reading this book, that these factors left a profound impression and deeply motivated Jochen. They affected his lifestyle and outlook. He wore his hair long, loved to play practical jokes, partied, enjoyed jazz and swing music, womanized, and yet was sensitive.

He was not a typical Aryan fighter pilot. Jochen was a true individualist who did not blindly follow or march lockstep with the German High Command. As demonstrated superbly by Dr. Colin Heaton and Anne-Marie Lewis, Jochen was not a racist. He was not a follower. Moreover, the authors accurately portray Jochen as a man not fazed by bigotry or narrow-minded thinking. This informative book portrays this overlooked historical figure as a benevolent, enlightened, and inspired warrior. This "Star of Africa" was a star indeed.

—Albert H. Wunsch III

Preface

THE FIRST AVIATION HISTORY book I ever read was Raymond F. Toliver and Trevor J. Constable's *Horrido! Fighter Aces of the Luftwaffe*, and the men they wrote about intrigued me. What was even more fascinating was that during this period in the early 1970s, most of these men were still alive. I read this book many times, then I began reading any other books I could find about aviation history, air combat, and stories about—and preferably by—the aces.

The tales of their accomplishments and their humanity struck me as solidly as their aerial skills. Sometimes a few of the *Luftwaffe* aces would come to America and hold symposiums with American and even British aces, and I longed to attend. I finally managed to attend one while in high school, then others later, and I was able to briefly meet Adolf Galland, James H. Doolittle, Robert Stanford Tuck, Walter Krupinski, Johannes Steinhoff, Johnny Johnson, Brian Kingcome, Günther Rall, John Cunningham, W. Dennis David, Dietrich Hrabak, W. Dennis David, Erich Hartmann, Wolfgang Schenck, Dietrich Peltz, Hajo Herrmann, and many others.

As I came to know them better in later years, I realized at some point I was going to write about these men. Fortune smiled upon me when I received letters from James Doolittle, Ray Toliver, Adolf Galland, Edu Neumann,

Johannes Steinhoff (Jahannes Steinhoff)

Wolfgang Falck, Gunther Rall, Erich Hartmann, Hajo Herrmann, Josef Kammhuber, Johannes Steinhoff, and Walter Krupinski, and many others who sent along addresses and contacts for more of these men I had read about. In the early 1980s when I was stationed in West Germany, I was fortunate enough to meet most of these men on several occasions and was able to expand my contacts to include many branches of the German military from World War II.

The greatest assistance came from Krupinski, Falck and Steinhoff, who were in contact with all of the former aces. As a result, a ripple effect followed. While meeting with dozens of pilots, I was able to gather not only interviews and signed photos, but also a great support network for my interest. I was very pleased that most of these men applauded my efforts to expand the literature and educate people further about their service. They are all gone now, and that leaves a void that hopefully this book—and other books that I have written and will write in the future—will fill.

One of these outstanding men was *Oberst* Eduard Neumann. I was able to visit him a few times in Munich and knowing I had read of the exploits of the "Star of Africa," Hans-Joachim Marseille, Neumann suggested that I speak with a few of the men who also knew him. Following these meetings, I must admit that I, too, fell under the spell of the "Marseille Magic." Johannes Steinhoff and Herbert Ihlefeld were less than enthusiastic about Marseille's personal character, but they acknowledged that he did possess a gift envied by all fighter pilots. According to Steinhoff, "his greatest gift was luck."

Several books have been written about Marseille: Franz Kurowski's work is very good, but Robert Tate's is still the best in my opinion. However, after discussions with Neumann in 2000 and 2001 and conversations with Steve Daubenspeck at Zenith Press in 2011, I decided that the time was right to do a book on the "Star of Africa" using the personal data I had collected. I already had several of the veterans read the various manuscripts in progress, and I gained some great advice and input.

The end result is this book, which I hope is received with an understanding that the intention was not just a resurrection of well-known facts (these will be covered of course) or a chronicle of the short life and meteoric career of a gifted pilot, but a portrait of a very charming, tortured, and complex person whose life outside the cockpit was just as exciting, tragic, and adventurous. Marseille lived a fast life, and he left his mark upon history. He remains held in high esteem by both his friends and former adversaries. He has beyond any doubt earned his honored place in the pantheon of young warriors who would never come home.

For simplicity and easier understanding of the designated matrix regarding the Messerschmitt 109, we have chosen to use the prefix "Me" throughout the book, as opposed to the early war prefix "Bf" (for *Bayersicheflugzeugwerk*), which is more historically accurate until Professor Willi Messerschmitt took personal control of the company in 1944. "Me" was how the Allied pilots identified the 109 so we will use that method.

Times posted in this book will use the 24-hour military clock. In addition, when comparing posted times, such as the time for a victory by Marseille, it must be remembered that the British used Greenwich Mean Time (GMT), which was one hour behind Berlin time. Therefore, 18:00 hours GMT would be 19:00 Berlin/Central European Time (CET), or 6:00 p.m. GMT and 7:00 p.m. CET respectively.

—Colin D. Heaton 2023

Acknowledgements

Writing this book would not have been possible without many years of close association with the *Luftwaffe* members and the many authors and historians who contributed their experiences, works, and personal memories regarding Hans-Joachim Marseille. This is especially true of the men who flew with Marseille and knew him best. These primary *Luftwaffe* personnel, and subsequent German military and civilian personalities who knew Marseille and also passed on their recollections of him, are probably the greatest assets that this project provides. The men and women mentioned are listed in appreciation for their contributions. Military personnel are listed with their last active-duty ranks, whether from World War II or service in the *Bundeswehr* or *Bundesluftwaffe*.

Although many listed here have left us, they will always be remembered and thanked for their contributions and those who consented to giving interviews: Col. Raymond F. Toliver, Trevor J. Constable, Jeffrey L. Ethell, *Generalleutnant* Adolf Galland, Lothar Löwe, *Oberstleutnant* Kurt Bühligen, *Oberleutnant* Franz Stigler, *Brigadegeneral* Friedrich Körner, *Generalleutnant* Günther Rall, Major Professor Dr. Ludwig Franzisket, *Generalmajor* Kurt Kuhlmey, *General* Josef Kammhuber, *Oberst* Eduard Neumann, Leni Riefenstahl, *Oberst* Bernhard Woldenga, *Generalleutnant* Johannes Steinhoff, SS-*Obergruppenführer* Karl Wolff, *Generalleutnant* Hans Baur, *Hauptmann* Ernst Börngen, *Major* Werner Schroer, *Brigadegeneral* Gustav Rödel, Anton "Toni" Weiler, Jon Guttman, Ambassador Franz Elles, Barrett Tillman, *Hauptmann* Emil Clade, *SS Oberführer* Artur Axmann, *Oberst* Herbert Ihlefeld, *Generalmajor* Hannes Trautloft, *Generalmajor* Kurt Kuhlmey, and Lt. Col. Robert Schmidt, USAF, Col. Walter J. Boyne, USAF (Ret); *Leutnant* Jorg Czypionka, RAD Wing Commander (Ret) Professor Geoffrey Morley-Mower, RAF Group Captain

(Ret.) Michael Thomas Judd, *Oberleutnant* Kurt Schulze, historians Robert Tate and Nick Hector.

Special thanks to Steve Daubenspeck for suggesting the book topic and to Erik Gilg for believing in it. Once again thanks to Norman Melton for his continued assistance with sources and support; and my co-author on the first edition, Anne-Marie Lewis. All of these remarkable people were there every time it counted.

Certain proceeds from this book will be delivered to the Wounded Warrior Project and Tunnel to Towers for their great work in assisting our disabled veterans return to as normal a life as possible We as a nation, and the world owe them a great debt.

Table of Contents

Introduction	i
Forewords	viii
Preface	xi
Acknowledgements	xiv
Chapter 1	1
Chapter 2	19
Chapter 3	41
Chapter 4	67
Chapter 5	95
Chapter 6	123
Chapter 7	163
Chapter 8	203
Chapter 9	253
Chapter 10	291
Epilogue	333
Tables	353
Bibliography	371
Index	375
Notes	386

Chapter 1

Unlikely Beginnings

> *Marseille was the ultimate role model for German youth—until he opened his mouth.*
> —Artur Axmann

HANS-JOACHIM "JOCHEN" WALTER Rudolf Siegfried Marseille was born to a strict military family at BerlinerStrasse 164 in Berlin, Germany, on December 13, 1919, at 11:45 p.m. While a young child, he became one of the hundreds of millions of victims of the Spanish influenza and was one of the lucky survivors, although he would always be a thin and sickly boy, prone to illness.

His mother, Charlotte Marie Johanna Pauline Gertrud Riemer Marseille, and his father, then *Hauptmann* Siegfried Georg Martin Marseille, were a typical German military couple, but divorced when he was still young. The rigid lifestyle imposed by his father, as well as the subsequent divorce, were probably the catalysts that forced him to rebel, disdain discipline, and challenge authority—traits that he would carry throughout his life.

His mother later married police official Carl Reuter, and while at primary school, Marseille initially carried the name of his stepfather at his mother's insistence. He never cared much for this, although their relationship developed into a copacetic one. He later retook the name Marseille before he finished gymnasium, or high school.[1]

Siegfried Marseille (Bundesarchiv)

Marseille became a teenager during the tumultuous events that formed a gathering political storm in Germany. The Reichstag's passage of the Enabling Act in 1933 provided a legal foundation for Adolf Hitler's dictatorship, giving him, as chancellor, the power to create laws without the consent of the Reichstag. Hitler soon abolished all other political parties and trade unions and integrated the roles of president and chancellor. The National Socialists followed up with the Nuremberg Laws on racial distinctions in 1935. Like all young Germans, Marseille was constantly inundated with the racial laws and propaganda spewing from the Propaganda Ministry, and his years in the Hitler Youth were undoubtedly a disturbing period. Marseille's best friend while in grade school was a Jewish boy, a neighbor whose family had simply disappeared by the time Marseille returned from advanced flight training. His family physician—the doctor who had delivered him—was also gone, along with his entire family, as were all Jewish families in his district. Their homes were occupied by strangers.

Marseille's early character development revealed traits antithetical to the expectations of a young German officer, or even a good German citizen. He played on his school's soccer team as well as on another youth league team and was quite skillful. He was placed on a team with boys two and three years older than himself, and often played against another Berlin team that had a player with whom he would become friends, a future war hero and fighter pilot named Hans Strelow.

Fellow Berliner and acclaimed journalist Lothar Löwe, born on February 9, 1929, was among the many young boys in the Hitler Youth who wanted to get close to "The Star of Africa" after Marseille returned to Berlin in June of 1942. Löwe was fortunate to be able to walk and talk with him, as their families knew each other. His opinions on Marseille and his relatives are interesting:

> "His mother taught piano, classical music and he was himself also a student, but I would say that he was more self-taught He also played many instruments, not just piano. I knew his sister also, and she was a very pretty and nice young lady, but his mother was a special woman, and everyone thought a lot of her. I recall my mother meeting with her as Hans-Joachim became more famous and his face was in so many newspapers and magazines. I only recall seeing his father once, but I did meet his stepfather, Herr Reuter a few times, and he was a policeman and rather well known. I do not think that they had, how would you say, a very close relationship."[2]

Marseille with his mother in Berlin (Raymond F. Toliver)

Hans-Joachim Marseille was always in some kind of minor trouble, but being one of the swing kids' breaking curfew, pulling pranks, and perfecting his practical jokes gave him a questionable reputation. Marseille was labeled a juvenile delinquent and an outcast who never fit in anywhere until he climbed into the cockpit of a fighter. His lack of discipline gained him the reputation of a rebel while in school: a practical joker with a remarkable intellect but plagued by laziness.

He was supposedly charged with stealing a German soldier's motorcycle and crashing it while he was still in gymnasium. His policeman stepfather had no intention of assisting him, so his father had to intervene, destroying the motorcycle after he was bailed out of jail. Such events would not be abandoned later in his career. He was also quick to anger, as demonstrated while he was playing on his soccer team. The event was witnessed by a very young Lothar Löwe:

Marseille with classmates in Gymnasium (High School) (Raymond F. Toliver)

"Marseille was playing on the team, and this was in 1935 I think. I was about six or seven years old. There was a fight that began with the other team because one of the boys on that team made some comments about one of Marseille's friends who was Jewish. If I remember correctly Marseille knocked the boy down, and then the others all began fighting until the police arrived. The Jewish boy, whom I did not know was taken away and blamed for starting the fight. I knew that was not correct and I asked my father about it. He just said that "things were changing, and not for the better.' That was my introduction into how the Jews would be treated later. Three years later I would see the damage during the *Kristallnacht*. I knew it would be bad, but I never knew about the killing and the death camps until after the war. That was just not something that was told to us."[3]

After many teachers filed complaints about his grades, Marseille was given a stern lecture by his headmaster, Professor Dr. Poetzold.

Marseille finally corrected his approach to academics, graduating near the top of his class, while still never taking life seriously. Despite his slight build, he was a determined athlete with good stamina. Perhaps the lecture regarding his academic shortcomings and the physical training he endured on his own influenced his later competitive nature. He was a paradox, considered a lazy student, but he mastered French, English, Latin, and Greek, as he had a natural ability with languages, and excelled in history and mathematics.

Marseille in High School

Marseille was also part of the *Reichsarbeitsdienst* (Reich Labor Service), a compulsory duty for all young men not in military service, from March to August 1938. He then continued to basic infantry training that October at Quedlinburg. Marseille's laziness was a constant problem; he was always looking for the easy way out. Infantry training corrected this, and while his formal discipline did not improve, his military appreciation was enhanced. He failed to truly grasp the concept of teamwork, preferring to go it alone to accomplish his tasks, asking for no help, and often giving none in return. This characteristic would plague him early in his *Luftwaffe* career.

Throughout his life, Marseille had a difficult relationship with his father. He blamed his parents' divorce on his father's affair with another woman, and he refused to visit him in Hamburg for many years after. Just before he entered infantry training, his father, in an errant attempt at reconciliation, came to Berlin and introduced him to the nightlife that was to later damage his military career in the *Luftwaffe*. Despite the carefree atmosphere of women and alcohol, the relationship wasn't strengthened, and he rarely saw his father again.

Marseille was a notorious animal lover, and he had a lifelong interest in music. His mother, who taught piano, had hopes of her little Jochen becoming a prominent concert pianist, since he had been classically trained and was something of a musical prodigy. His fascination for American blues and jazz was manifested in an extensive record collection which he began as a boy, maintained while later stationed in France and continued to amass until his death, even though his favorite genres—swing and jazz—were banned by the Nazis. One of his passions during the war was listening to Allied radio stations, which was forbidden under German law, but Marseille did not care, and many Germans secretly listened in to the BBC for their music programs.

Marseille had always been enthralled with the stories of the Great War aviators, as his father had been one; his sense of high adventure was the main reason he was labeled a dreamer in school and not taken as a serious student. When asked what he wanted to do, the young Jochen told his father that he wanted to become a military pilot. Unlike many fathers of the day who balked at such an ambition, Marseille's father not only supported his son, but he also wrote letters to influential friends, securing him an examination and later an appointment to the ground school.

This is where Hans-Joachim Marseille was to stand out. He passed the rigorous four-hour entrance examination with a perfect score. As he would later transform from rebellious juvenile to dedicated pilot, he would not totally abandon his prankish nature, and his lighthearted devil-may-care attitude toward his superiors would endear him to some and enrage many others. This book is replete with the first-person comments of those who knew him, some may even say "tolerated" or "endured" him. According to one of his comrades in North Africa, fellow pilot Werner Schroer: "I think the Allies thought more of him than some of us did, because he showed them great respect. That was not always the case when it came to how he dealt with some of our senior leaders."[4]

On November 7, 1938, Marseille was accepted for flight training, just days before the horrific events of *Kristallnacht*, a series of attacks on Jews across Germany and Austria. He had witnessed the destruction of the Jewish houses of worship and businesses just before he shipped out for flight training. His opinions on this were remembered by his fellow flight school student and fellow fighter pilot in North Africa, Werner Schroer:

> "Marseille talked about this, and I also recalled the events being in the news, which seemed to downplay the actual problems. Marseille saw what had happened, and he simply despised the Nazis who allowed that to happen. I think that was probably the main reason he could never join the (National Socialist German Workers) Party. He was just not a politically motivated person, and he hated bullies. He saw the brown shirts as the worst kind of bullies. I agreed with him, as did many others we flew with."[5]

Despite his traditional and rigid militaristic Prussian upbringing, and his early years of intense National Socialist indoctrination, Marseille defied all conventions. His in-depth perceptions about what Germany was enduring under the Nazis during his youth are not well known. However, given his demeanor later in life, comments from those who knew him, and his penchant for flagrantly violating the racial laws and openly snubbing the upper echelons of the Nazi hierarchy, one may assume that he felt that it was an injustice. He never bought into the propaganda of Dr. Josef Göbbels or the rantings of Adolf Hitler.

He was completely apolitical, to the point of uncaring, as were most of the professional officer corps, especially within the *Luftwaffe*. Marseille refused to join the NSDAP, which stood for *Nationalsozialistische Deutsche Arbeiterpartei* (National Socialist German Workers' Party, also called the Nazi Party) and became even more disaffected with his national leadership as he discovered the truth behind the racial policy. Later in his career, questions would arise regarding a Jewish connection on Marseille's mother's side, possibly that his maternal grandmother was Jewish while married to a Protestant.

Propaganda Minister Josef Göbbels (Bundesarchiv)

According to Artur Axmann: "Regarding Marseille; there was even a rumor that she (his grandmother) was distantly related to the prominent Rothschilds of Europe, although there was nothing to support this assertion, and nothing came of it. Galland had the same accusation made about him by (Heinrich) Himmler, but I think all of this was just rumor and politically motivated."6

Hitler Youth Leader Artur Axmann (Artur Axmann)

One of the key factors about Marseille's character that emerged from the interviews was his deeply ingrained sense of right and wrong. Marseille was an idealist, playboy, and precocious young man, but he was brave enough to stand up to what he felt was wrong in his nation. Many first-person accounts show Marseille's blatant disregard for Nazi policy and his feelings of discontent, which plagued him. The only place he felt safe, secure, and above the political drama and polemic was in the air.

He never hid his mantra of chivalry, personal honor, living by a code of ethics, and treating all people as equal. He was a man living in the wrong time and place. His honorable conduct toward his enemies in battle proved it, as did his protectiveness of his best friend, a black South African Army conscript from the Transvaal, Cpl. Mathew Letuku, better known to the men of JG-27 as "Mathias." Marseille met Mathias in Libya, two months after the South African had been captured at the Battle of Tobruk.

Adolf Galland (Adolf Galland)

The Third Reich was not the place to be a rogue idealist, and Marseille was perhaps the most openly anti-Nazi warrior in the Third Reich. Mathias was his best friend; racial laws be damned as many high-ranking officers and dignitaries found out. Yet Marseille was not alone, all the men of *Jagdgeschwader* (JG)-27 became endeared to the black prisoner, as stated by Ludwig Franzisket:

> "When we first met Mathias, he had been captured by the Army, and then the prisoners were being separated. I do not know which one of us came across him first, but it was learned that he was a barber and also a trained auto mechanic, so we accepted him. He was not treated as a prisoner, as we did not feel that he was a threat. He only wanted to get through the white man's war. Well, we had him and liked him immediately, and he became one of us. When Marseille met him, they immediately became best friends. It was extraordinary."[7]

During an after-awards-ceremony festivity in Berlin in June 1942, when Hitler personally decorated him with the Oak Leaves and Swords to his Knight's Cross, Marseille overheard the truth about the fate of the Jews. This was confirmed by *SS-Obergruppenführer* Karl Friedrich Otto Wolff, Himmler's left-hand man and the last commander of the SS in Italy in 1945 and an early member of the Nazi Party, who was one of the early instigators of the Holocaust.

Marseille was the opposite of a racist in a society where racial superiority meant everything. He was a nontraditional junior officer, a nonconformist rogue in a powerful, professional military where such activity could, and often did, cost a man his rank, his freedom, and even his life. He was an intelligent, gifted, sensitive, gentleman warrior, a young knight born in the wrong century, a humanitarian living in the wrong society—yet above all else, Hans-Joachim Marseille was a reluctant, but consummate, practitioner of the deadly art of war.

Adolf Hitler aboard his Ju-52 (Hans Baur)

Marseille was the ultimate antithesis to the image of the German officer as commonly perceived in the postwar rhetoric, although he was not unique within the *Luftwaffe*. Regardless of their branch of service, most professional soldiers were not sadists; in fact, most of the German veterans that I interviewed hated the war. However, fighter pilots, as well as U-Boat commanders (perhaps above all others) inherited the virtues of chivalry from their World War I predecessors, and they maintained that standard until the last days of the war.

Marseille was loath to kill a pilot in a disabled plane unnecessarily, and as just one example, after a rather fierce fight over Gazala, he personally escorted one enemy aircraft to safety (the first of many), as Werner Schroer recalled:

"We had tangled with these Tomahawks, a lot of them, and we were quite happy. We scored, I think, six or seven victories in total. One of my men called out an enemy fighter, and then he said, 'Oh, no problem, a 109 has him.' I looked over and I saw the Yellow 14 pulling alongside this British fighter. It was Marseille, and I radioed him, asking what the problem was. His response was: 'He's wounded; I am trying to get him down.'

Werner Schroer (Werner Schroer)

"I was not sure that I heard him correctly, so I asked him to repeat that transmission. 'I am guiding him down, so he will not die.' I can tell you that this was a first for me, so I pulled more power and was followed by the rest of my *Staffel*. We watched, as Marseille gestured to the man, who was flying a P-40 that I could not believe was still in the air. We crossed our lines, and the enemy pilot dropped his landing gear, but only one wheel dropped, so he retracted, and bellied in. It was a good landing, in a very flat area that left the aircraft intact.

"We flew the rest of the seven minutes to our base. Jochen then jumped into his car, and I jumped in with him. I called for the medic to join us, and the poor medic, who was undressed, quickly took his trousers and medical bag and also joined us. He had to jump in as we passed by him, and he landed headfirst in the back seat. We reached the pilot after almost an hour. He was still sitting in the cockpit. There was no smoke or fire, but he had been shot through the shoulder, and a bullet had opened his skull. He was still conscious, but we saw that he had a broken left leg from the landing, probably.

"Jochen jumped on the wing, and I went over to the right side. We slowly lifted the man out, and Marseille spoke to him in English. I did not understand all that they were saying, but I heard Jochen say: 'I am glad you are alive; I was worried a bit you know?' We carefully placed a splint on the man's leg and used the rudder as a backboard stretcher to carry him. We laid him across the back of the car spanning the width of the backseat. The medic kept him talking and conscious while Jochen drove. We went to the field and Neumann had already prepared a field ambulance for him. Jochen rode with the man all the way to Derna, I think, and he came back the next day. The man lived, but what happened to him afterward I do not know.

"That was Jochen. Neumann and the others congratulated him on saving the man's life when he came back. He had a photo taken with the pilot, which he tended to do sometimes. Marseille was a great fighter pilot, but he was no killer. He was really too sensitive for something like infantry fighting. I think the cleanliness of combat in the air suited his personality. Once when he saw a dead enemy airman, whose body was mangled, he threw up, and could not eat."[8]

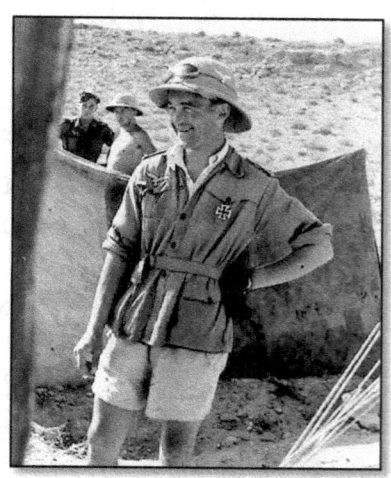

Eduard Neumann (1911-2004), as Kommodore Jagdgeschwader 27, wearing tropical Luftwaffe uniform in North Africa (Eduard Neumann)

Marseille started part of his legend after he shot down a Hurricane II of No. 451 Squadron, flown by South African Lieutenant Patrick Byers on September 13, 1941, who was flying with the Royal Australian Air Force. He then flew over the unit airfield of his downed enemy to pass on details, as eye witnessed by Byers's good friend and fellow Hurricane pilot, the late Wing Commander Geoffrey Morley-Mower:

*Geoffrey Morley-Mower
(Geoffrey Morley-Mower)*

"Pat Byers took off at about 6:20 p.m. for a sortie that should have taken half an hour at the most. The column was less than forty miles from our landing ground. Ray Hudson took off in pursuit a quarter of an hour later. By 7:30 p.m. neither had returned, and Wizard came to ask me to fly a backup sortie. The army commander was adamant that he must know the direction of the column at nightfall. When I landed, swung down from the cockpit, Hugh Davies, the Army liaison officer, was there with his staff car. 'Glad to see you made it,' he shouted. 'Is it still headed west?'

"'Yes. It is crossing the wire south of Capuzzo,' I replied. 'Did Pat get back?'

"'No,' Davies said. 'Ray Hudson couldn't find him. He returned back an hour ago.'

"Two days later, before the sun had risen, I was awakened by the sharp bark of a Bofors anti-aircraft gun situated a hundred yards from my bivouac. It was soon joined by the rest of the airfield defenses. I could hear the rattle of machine guns from the Australian machine-gun outfit across the strip and the whine of shells streaking across the dark sky. I scrambled out of my tent to see two Messerschmitts motoring into our field as if to make a landing. They were below 500 feet and flying slowly, then one broke away and climbed. Me-109s could not be mistaken for friendly aircraft. They were smaller than any plane we flew and typically screamed across the sky with a high-pitched engine noise that was quite distinctive.

"On this occasion their noise was muted, and the one lost altitude steadily. Gunfire petered out when he was too low to be attacked without risking damage to our parked Hurricanes. Halfway up the strip, a dark object fluttered to the ground. Then the Me-109 Yellow 14 opened up the engines and snarled off, weaving violently, followed by a pattern of Bofors shells whose white puffs curtained the dark sky.

"'You won't believe this, gents,' Wizard said. 'I feel like Mister bloody Chamberlain bringing peace in our time! I'll read it out to you. It is signed by the German flight commander.' When Wizard began to read out the message, however, his face became grave and his voice, more Welsh than ever, took on the cadence of a chapel preacher.

"'We are sorry to report that Lt. Byers was shot down by an aircraft of this squadron. He was badly burned while escaping the cockpit. He is now in Derna Hospital to recover. We wish to express the regrets of the *Luftwaffe*.' A cheer went up.

"Two weeks later, the same Me-109 made a return visit, as dawn was breaking. The Bofors guns and the Australian machine gunners made another serious attempt to shoot it down. Another message fluttered to the desert floor. This time it told us that Byers had died of his wounds and again offered the regrets of the *Luftwaffe*."9

Supplemental to this account as recorded in the book by Franz Kurowski, Morley-Mower had this to say:

"I was quite astonished to learn many months later year, after we learned who Marseille was, and that it was the same pilot on several occasions who had dropped his messages on Allied airfields. We had at least three visits from what I recall, others in the area also had visits. It was quite humorous in a way, because as soon as our forward ground spotter called in that we had unwelcomed company, he would identify the culprit by radio as Yellow 14. It was at that time the order was given to hold fire and see what the chap had to say. He never attacked our airfield, never shot up aircraft, just delivered his post as would any mail carrier, quite astonishing and the subject of great discussions afterwards, I can tell you."[10]

The record confirms that Marseille flew the mission to report Byers's situation on both occasions. In another act of chivalry, Marseille personally escorted another wounded pilot to a military hospital to make sure he would not perish in the desert. The man had safely parachuted despite serious injuries after Marseille had shot him down. Marseille carried the pilot's documents and personal family photographs on his own person for safekeeping until the man was safely in his hospital bed. He even filled out the pilot's Geneva Convention Prisoner of War Data Card for him.

According to Eduard Neumann, Marseille had a photo taken with the pilot, which he kept among his possessions. Unfortunately, that photograph and many others have been lost to history. The man's condition would later prompt another of Marseille's unauthorized flights to an enemy pilot's airfield.

One of JG-27's aces, *Oberleutnant* Franz Stigler, saw many sides to Marseille:

"When I first met Schroer he warned me about Marseille. He discussed many things, and he said that navigation was critical in the desert, where you did not always have defined landmarks, and instrument flying was very important. Then he said: 'If you follow Marseille, always watch his back, and make sure you also watch yours, because he will watch no one's. He just shoots things down.'

"Marseille was someone who everyone seemed to know, but no one really knew well. I guess that Werner [Schroer] perhaps knew him best. I was well aware of these flights to the British bases; it was greatly discussed in the unit. Everyone admired his ability as a pilot, but they really respected his sense of chivalry. Most of us, I think, were much the same in that regard. We never saw a need to kill an already beaten or wounded opponent."[11]

Marseille in his new desert uniform assigned to JG-27 (Raymond F. Toliver)

Marseille's unparalleled prowess as a fighter pilot turned him into a national hero, an icon in the public eye. His humanity did not set him apart from his comrades; it simply demonstrated how German airmen felt toward their enemies. The stories of his exploits became the equivalent of modern-day tabloid headlines, and he had a great following back in Germany. In one month alone he received over 600 pounds of fan mail. Yet, despite his being heralded as a perfect example of the National Socialist hero, featured in newsreels and magazines, Marseille maintained his rogue mentality. His conduct and dress in private life, and even in the presence of his superior officers, was in many ways opposed to everything for which the Third Reich stood.

Among his fellow soldiers and pilots, Marseille was more likely to spend time with enlisted men who were nearer his age than other officers of equal or senior rank, all much older than he. A born iconoclast with an intense sense of loyalty, he believed in the worth of the individual man, not in racial or political theories. He shared his quarters with Mathias, his black personal servant, confidant, and closest friend, whom he defended in defiance of all Nazi policy— and got away with it. His own policy was simple and absolute: "Where I go, Mathias goes."

Galland had his own thoughts about Marseille and Mathias: "I had also heard the reports from some senior officers about who were less than pleased with Marseille's lack of conformity to regulations especially regarding his friend Mathias. He was a black South African, actually Marseille's self-appointed assistant. He cooked, cleaned and did almost everything except work on his aircraft. Marseille taught him to play chess and speak fairly good German, and his servant taught him better English."[12]

Hans-Joachim Marseille was a legend in his own lifetime, a household name across Europe; the Germans called him "The Star of Libya," while Benito called him the "Star of Africa," and as such he would be forever known. Even his enemies read about him, perhaps hoping to be his victor, and possibly hoping they would never cross paths. However, in death he has earned the eternal admiration and respect of everyone, even his enemies, who considered him a worthy adversary and honorable warrior.

This is his story as told by those who knew him, flew with him, and those who fought against him.

Benito Mussolini (Author Collection)

GERMAN OPERATIONAL MAP OF THE NORTH AFRICAN THEATER

This was on Eduard Neumann's wall in his circus wagon.

West half of map, featuring Tripoli and Benghazi (Ben Ghasi)

East half of map, featuring Derna, Tobruk, and Cairo

Chapter 2

Marseille the Man

> *He looked like he was twelve years old, and he often acted like it.*
> —Werner Schroer

MARSEILLE'S FLYING CAREER STARTED in 1938 when he was 18 years old. He excelled at his academic work in ground school and was first in his class in aerobatics. He received his orders on March 13, and after a short leave and promotion to *Fahnenjunker*, he reported to the *Luftkriegschule* (Air War School) at Fürstenfeldbruck, where he met and trained with some of the men with whom he would later serve in combat. His problems with authority began here, and his reprimands for violations of the strict rules of flying went in one ear and out the other. Marseille managed to avoid being dismissed from basic flight school only through the intervention of his father, and everyone knew it, which created a lot of resentment.

Marseille was still one or two pay grades behind the men who had started flight training with him at the *Jagdfliegerschule 5* (Hunting or Fighter Flyer School) at Schwechat, near Vienna, on November 1, 1939. Schwechat produced the greatest fighter pilots, many of whom demonstrated their potential during training. Despite his irreverent demeanor and unmilitary bearing, Marseille was no exception. He excelled at gunnery and aerobatics, mastering the short takeoff, split-S, chandelle, and other maneuvers that many pilots found difficult. It was logical that he would be assigned to fighters.

Yet, despite his newfound passion for aviation and his extreme aptitude as a pilot, the strictness of his Prussian upbringing and indoctrination, and his father's high rank, Marseille continued to defy all convention. He was constantly in trouble. His escapades earned him many nicknames, such as "the Special One," "the Untouchable," and "the Bohemian Bandit." Werner Schroer and Kurt Bühligen just called him "The Idiot."

Kurt Bühligen (Kurt Bühligen)

Once, during a tight formation flight in basic flight school, Marseille separated from the rest of the group without orders and, without notifying anyone else in the formation of his intentions and began performing his own aerobatics. His fellow students watched in amazement as he began his own private dogfight. Upon landing, he was severely reprimanded by his commanding officer, *Hauptmann* Mueller-Rohrmoser, who restricted him from flying, and his promotion to *Gefreiter* revoked for "incompetence." His personnel folder was getting thicker by the week, and not because of his great success in following orders or stellar combat heroics.

Marseille's list of violations grew almost as fast as his list of casual girlfriends, and his "lone wolf" mentality meant that he had a tough time making friends, who did not want to be guilty by association. Werner Schroer, who flew with him in *Ergänzjagdgruppe* (Replenishment Fighter Group) at Merseburg, protecting the Leuna chemical complex, and later in North Africa with JG-27, was in advanced flight school with him.

Werner Schroer in his fighter (Werner Schroer)

Schroer stated: "Marseille was not the military type. He always seemed a somewhat shady character to us all. When he was noticed, it was always in a negative way. He was therefore often pegged for duty officer on the weekends and made to stay on post. Then I would find a scrap of paper that he left for me: 'Went out! Would you mind pulling duty for me?'"[13]

Marseille was also restricted to quarters many times, and on almost every occasion he violated that restriction, often managing to get back into the barracks without being discovered. He would return exhausted from entertaining some young lady, usually with alcohol on his breath. Drinking before flying was a dismissal offense. Marseille could not have cared less.

According to Schroer: "This guy was in trouble so often, and restricted, that it was a noteworthy occasion when he was not on restriction. Over six months, I can think of perhaps a half dozen times he was not restricted to quarters. We were in the mess hall having lunch one day and I asked him, 'Why do you do it? Do you not care that they will throw you into the infantry?' He said that before that happened, he would command a U-Boat. This guy was incredible."[14]

As part of his training, Marseille embarked upon his second timed cross-country solo flight from Magdeburg to Braunschweig. During the flight Marseille needed to relieve himself, so, seeing no traffic, he landed on the autobahn. Landing in any unauthorized location, unless caused by an in-air emergency, was a court-martial violation. As Marseille headed for the trees, some farmers ran to see if he needed any assistance. By the time they arrived, Marseille had jumped back in and started his takeoff roll. He waved as he lifted off. This landing was not a secret for long, and another punishment and negative entry went into his service record.

"Sure, we all heard about it," Schroer recalled. "Apparently there were not too many airplanes in the air on that route, and a policeman reported that a farmer reported a landing on the autobahn. He described the plane and gave the markings. It was all over for Marseille, and we thought that he was headed for the infantry, if not prison right afterwards. Well, we were wrong."[15] The antics did not stop when Schroer and Marseille were stationed together at Merseburg, and the young Berliner was transferred to the combat front on the Channel Coast just to get rid of him.

One of Germany's greatest fighter pilots, *Oberstleutnant* Kurt Bühligen, who scored 112 victories and received the Knight's Cross with Oak Leaves Swords (and ended the war in Soviet captivity until 1950), also attended fighter school with the future Star of Africa.

Bühligen stated: "In fighter school, we had very strict rules. Men were thrown out and sent to the infantry for even being late to a formation or failing an examination. There was very little room for error. One day we were up before dawn, which was usual. We always had the roll call and then breakfast. I heard the name 'Marseille' a few times and there was no response. Finally, this guy staggers in, and this was the first time I really ever saw him. He was obviously drunk, but he could stand and respond.

"Our section leader asked him where he had been, and he said something that I did not hear. Later, we found that he had slipped away during the night and met a girl. He managed to get back just as we joined morning formation. We were all puzzled how he got away with this, and other things, and then we learned that his father was a high-ranking officer. I remember saying, 'That explains it.'"[16]

Marseille excelled at everything that flight school had to throw at him. He had a photographic memory, an uncanny sense of bearing in the cockpit, and a situational awareness that was as critical as flying skill for a combat pilot. He knew where every aircraft was at any given time, enemy or friendly, and was able to carve a victory out of the most entangled melee. However, he was a slow learner when it came to discipline.

Following his posting to advanced flight school on November 1, 1939, Marseille's commanding officer was a no-nonsense World War I fighter hero, a *Pour le Mérite* recipient with 35 victories. *Generalmajor* Eduard Ritter von Schleich, the famous "Black Knight," commanded *Jagdfliegerschule 5* with an iron discipline. Von Schleich, who was not enthusiastic about the young Berliner's attitude but saw his potential, warned him that he was on thin ice. Marseille must have heeded the advice since he graduated with honors for gunnery and aerobatics on July 18, 1940. Schleich's friendship with Marseille's father since the First World War may have played a role in his not being dismissed.

Generalleutnant Eduard Ritter von Schleich, the famed "Black Knight" fighter ace of WW I and recipient of the Pour le Merite (Raymond F. Toliver)

On August 10, 1940, the war with Great Britain was less than a year old, and Marseille joined his new unit at Calais-Marck on the French coast. Poland, France, Denmark, Norway, Belgium, and Holland had fallen, and the Western Allies were quiet, apart from a few night-bombing raids. The war almost seemed to be over. On this day, just before the end of the Battle of Britain, Marseille was assigned to I *Jagd* (or "Hunting/Fighter") *Lehrgeschwader* (LG) 2. This was the original combat composite unit formed before the war based upon the matrix perfected during the Spanish Civil War and the Condor Legion.

Stab/LG-1 was formed in July 1936 and was a primary transition unit for the pilots joining the Legion Condor. On April 1, 1937, the *Stab Gruppe* was officially created, along with three *Gruppen*: I (*Leichte Jagd* or light fighters) with Me-109D fighters; II (*Schwere Jagd*, or heavy fighters) with Me-110 twin-engine heavy fighters; III (*Kampf* or "struggle, fight") with He-111 and a few Ju-88 medium bombers; and IV (*Stuka*) with the Ju-87 dive bomber. Marseille was assigned to the "light fighters," and he would see his first action, stationed at Leeuwarden, Holland, where his unit performed bomber-escort duties over England. With his record on the ground still questionable, Marseille had to distinguish himself in the air.

Marseille engaged in his first dogfight against the enemy on August 24, 1940, over Kent, England. He had abandoned his wingman to chase an enemy fighter, and the battle lasted a long four minutes. After several twisting, turning maneuvers, the Hawker Hurricane Mk I finally fell to his guns. The fighter began to fall apart, burn, and dive into the North Sea. Marseille had scored his first kill but violated four cardinal rules of aerial combat. Marseille was now in trouble.

His *Staffelkapitän* (Squadron Leader), *Oberleutnant* (later *Oberst*) Herbert Ihlefeld, who would end the war with 132 victories and the Knight's Cross with Oak Leaves and Swords, was not amused:

"When I landed, I told my executive officer to have that dumb bastard sent to my office. I told him to give me twenty minutes. I had to cool down. Marseille had peeled away from the *Schwarm*, never radioed his intentions—hell, he never even called out an enemy aircraft! Next thing I hear is, 'He's done it again' over the headset. I then decided that I would not dress him down; just remind him of his duties. He did, after all, get the victory, and brought his own aircraft back.

"When he walked in, I was still angry. He violated my specific orders yet again, but he had this smile on his face, holding up one finger. I really tried to hide the laughter I was feeling. He was like a young boy who had just caught his first fish. I sat him down, broke out a bottle of cognac, and poured one for both of us.

"I told him the kill was visually confirmed, and I would credit him with it. I then told him that if he ever broke formation in my unit again, if I could not shoot him down myself, I would shoot him when he returned, and I smiled as I said it. Then his smile disappeared. I then started to laugh, and told him I was joking, and after I stopped laughing, I told him that

I would throw him into the infantry. He smiled again after that, and promised he would not do that again. And he kept his word. He just found new ways to violate my orders, never repeating the same violation twice."[17]

Despite Marseille's unique solo mentality, Ihlefeld did give him high marks for airmanship and proficiency. It was his discipline that concerned the Spanish Civil War veteran. This first victory would also establish his attitude toward killing. As chronicled by Robert Tate, Marseille wrote his mother regarding this event:

"Today I shot down my first opponent. It does not set well with me. I keep thinking about how the mother of this young man must feel when she gets the news of her son's death. And I am to blame for his death. I am sad, instead of being happy about the first victory. I always see the face of the Englishman in front of me and think about his crying mother."[18]

As the evening progressed, Marseille was taken into the *Staffel* bar, where he was toasted for getting his first kill. He apparently displayed some regret at killing a man. Marseille was at a crossroads, one that many fighter pilots—or indeed any warrior—would face. Could he kill and live with himself? The following morning, Marseille woke, and remembering the conversations the previous night with his comrades, he decided that he could. He then wrote a letter to his mother and sister, part of which stated: "Now I am a fighter pilot. A harsh wind blows here on the Channel, but I will survive. Your Jochen."[19]

On another mission, he again left his wingman and attacked without support, chased an enemy without reporting his intention, failed to achieve altitude following the victory, and most important, failed to see if his victim had a wingman himself. The second Hurricane dropped from altitude, but luckily Marseille saw the fighter at the last second. He threw his throttle full open and slammed the joystick forward, heading for the ocean. The Hurricane closed in but fired from extremely long range; Marseille's rapid corrective action to a very bad decision saved his life, as his faster fighter hopped over the waves and escaped.

On September 2, Marseille put a second larger feather in his cap when he scored his second victory over a Supermarine Spitfire Mk I, again over Kent. He received some minor damage, but ran out of fuel and crash-landed, gear up, on the beach at Calais, flying Me-109 E-7 W.Nr. 3579. The aircraft was repaired and flew again. He also received the Iron Cross Second Class and another reprimand. Ihlefeld recalled, "I pinned the medal on him, he saluted, sort of, and I said congratulations on making it back. He admitted that he had lost focus on his fuel gauge, as the damage to his fighter from combat was minimal. I wrote him up for dereliction, and then praised him for the victory."[20]

On September 11, he scored his third kill over the French Coast as wingman to *Hauptfeldwebel* Helmut Goedert, a Hurricane at 17:05 while flying Me-109 E-7 W.Nr. 5597, but he took heavy damage when he broke from his flight leader to engage alone. The Me-109 was 75 percent damaged in his crash landing at Wissant and was written off. September 15 saw Marseille over southeast London, where he bounced a Hurricane over the River Thames for his fourth kill, with two Hurricanes being claimed by LG-2. Both Hurricanes were from No. 310 Squadron RAF, one flown by Pilot Officer A. Hess in R4085 and the other by Sergeant J. Hubacek in R4087. Both pilots survived. It is unknown which pilot may have been Marseille's victim.

Upon landing he had to report to Ihlefeld. "I was just on the phone to my friend Macky Steinhoff over at JG-52," Ihlefeld recalled. "It was his birthday on the fifteenth [September], and I had sent him a bottle of French champagne to celebrate it. He congratulated me for the Knight's Cross, and I thanked him. Then Marseille knocked on the door, and I motioned him in. There had been bad blood between Marseille and a few of the other pilots, who felt unsafe flying with him due to his independent nature, I could say. I told Macky that I would call him back, hung up the phone, and then it dawned on me.

"Steinhoff was short a few pilots, and I had a real problem standing right in front of me. I asked Marseille why he had failed to report for duty as the duty officer the night before. He said he did not know about it, but I reminded him that the day's rosters were posted in the operations room every morning. It was his responsibility to check. He apologized and said he would be sure to check every morning to see what the assignments were.

"I then asked him about the mission he had just returned from, and what had happened. He had become separated from the *Schwarm*, and even his wingman lost sight of him in the clouds. The one saving grace was that he radioed in, and then confirmed his flight leader's position and rejoined them. It took a couple of days to confirm his claim, but the kill was confirmed by a bomber crew that we were escorting part way. I restricted him to base for the night and the next three days, and he was to pull duty all three nights until 2100 hours after operations. That meant no drinking, just sit by the telephone. Well, he sat by the phone, but somehow, he had alcohol and smelled of it when his shift was over, so I grounded him again."[21]

In almost every mission in which Marseille engaged the enemy he brought back an aircraft that either was a complete write-off and cannibalized for parts or required extensive repair. During one bomber escort where no enemy was engaged, his engine died. He radioed that he was going in, and three hours later Air Sea Rescue picked him up in a Heinkel He-59 floatplane and brought him back, suffering from hypothermia.

"Marseille was not the only pilot to suffer this fate without being shot down," Ihlefeld recalled. "We had been investigating possible sabotage of our engine oil and fuel. The fuel was easy enough to check, but the oil was a different matter. Later it was determined that there was in fact some of the oil had been a lower grade than we required, but it was not sabotage. We learned a hard lesson, because even some of the planes that made it back had ruined engines, and many engine fires were the result. In most cases they just seized up and stalled. That was bad if you were engaged with the enemy."[22]

Marseille 19 yrs old in LG-2 (Raymond F. Toliver)

Victory number five was a Spitfire over Dover on September 18, 1940, and once again Marseille brought back a battered and damaged aircraft. On September 27 he shot down a Hurricane over London, although he lost his leader, *Staffelkapitän Oberleutnant* Adolf Buhl, when he broke off to attack alone, leaving Buhl unprotected. It was during this time that Marseille's "White 13" was changed to the number 14, as the men believed that 13 was unlucky for him.

"I told him to sit his ass down," Ihlefeld said. "I stood over him, and I used words that I had never used before. I had just written an evaluation for him, on his superior gunnery and airmanship, and I picked it up, along with a promotion consideration, and I tore them up in front of him. I asked him what in the hell he thought he was doing? A pilot never, and I mean never, leaves his leader, at any time, unless that leader is shot down. No victory is worth losing a fellow pilot and comrade. I wanted to choke him. I had my hand out, but something told me no.

"Then I looked at him. He was actually crying and apologized. I could tell that he felt really terrible about what had happened, and then I felt sorry for him. I told him, 'Marseille, you must pull your head out of your ass. You are not alone; this is not the Hans Marseille show. You will one day, perhaps, be a leader yourself. You must learn that your fellow pilots are the most important thing. What if someone left you all alone and you were shot down because someone failed you? I would suggest you think about that, and what you plan on doing with your career as a pilot. I can tell you this, one day your luck will run out if you keep this attitude. You are good to no one dead.' I knew then that if he did not come around, given the dissent from the other pilots that I would have to fire him. That actually turned out to be the case later."[23]

The following day, Marseille was wingman to the acting *Staffelkapitän*, who was probably the squadron executive officer under Ihlefeld. The eighteen Me-109Es were intercepted by around 40 Spitfires and Hurricanes. The leader, seeing that they were outnumbered at least two to one, ordered the unit to turn back, probably feeling that it was not worth engaging such numbers over the sea.

Johannes Steinhoff as Kommodore of JG-77 in Sicily 1943 (Johannes Steinhoff)

Marseille, always looking for a fight, was apparently upset at the order, but then he saw a Spitfire diving in and gaining ground on his leader.

As a wingman, it was Marseille's duty to protect his flight leader, and he wasted no time rolling over into a turn to intercept the enemy fighter. His seventh kill fell in flames into the English Channel. He had not had time to radio the warning to his leader. He was shot up and once again crash-landed on the beach. These were his first seven victories, at the cost of four of his own fighters written off, three others damaged, with four additional claims made without witnesses: not exactly a great record. His inability to follow orders was unchanged. His days in LG-2 were numbered.

Upon returning to base, the *Oberleutnant* in command during that mission, probably embarrassed, or perhaps feeling guilty for running in the face of the enemy, reported to Ihlefeld that Marseille had defied orders to join the squadron and take evasive action. Marseille was apparently stunned at the events that unfolded. He received credit and congratulations for the kill and then received a reprimand from Ihlefeld and three days confinement for disobeying orders.

Marseille's Me-109E crash 1940 (Raymond F. Toliver)

Not long after this Marseille was asked to perform an aerobatic display for a visiting *Luftwaffe* general, *Generaloberst* Hans Jeschonnek and he did a fantastic job. However, in doing his rolls, stalls, famous short takeoff and low approach, he violated the standing *Luftwaffe* order that low passes over an airfield must be made at or above the five-meter mark, or about 18 feet. This was to ensure that no one on the ground was injured in the process and that no aircraft or vehicles were damaged. Coming in low and slow, Marseille dipped his left wing and, with its tip, caught a white handkerchief tied to a one-meter pole, which also acted as his windsock.

Ihlefeld recalled the event: "I saw him coming in, and I knew immediately that this idiot was going to do that stunt. I felt like shrinking into my uniform so that I could not be seen when the spectacle was over. Then he did it."[24]

Chief of Staff of the Luftwaffe Generaloberst Hans Jeschonnek who committed suicide on August 18, 1943 (Josef Kammhuber)

Marseille landed, pleased with himself, and was immediately grounded for five days by Ihlefeld who said:

"Marseille had done a wonderful job of impressing the visitors, and especially so, given that he was not an old veteran with hundreds of flying hours, like many of us from Spain, or even from 1939. He was a naturally gifted pilot, the best at aerobatics in the unit in my opinion, hence my choosing him for this event.

"The *General de Flieger's* (General of Fliers) aide, an *Oberst*, was the person who remarked that my command 'must be very loose with the regulations, given the high numbers of damaged and lost aircraft for little gain. Now we see why,' or something like that. Then *General der Flieger* Jeschonnek agreed that we had to make an example. The punishment was minimal. In most cases a man could lose rank or be removed from flying altogether for a similar offense, but I could not see that as being appropriate."[25]

Reichsmarschall and Luftwaffe Commander in Chief Hermann Goering and Generaloberst Hans Jeschonnek (Josef Kammhuber)

The *Geschwaderkommodore* during this time of Marseille's participation was *Generalmajor* Alfred Bülowius, who received reports on all the pilots, and Marseille soon became a point of great interest. Bülowius was an old friend of Marseille's father, and it was perhaps this familiarity that saved the young Berliner from carrying a rifle or suffering a much worse fate. The reports written about him by his squadron leader, Ihlefeld, were taken seriously. It was at his discretion that Marseille be grounded, as opposed to any more serious punishment. However, the sensitive Marseille did not see it that way.

"I must say that Marseille was the greatest headache I had," Ihlefeld recalled. "He alienated many of the other pilots. He was somewhat arrogant, unapologetic, and always dragging others into his mischief. He was a bad influence on the junior noncommissioned officers. He was less than completely respectful to his superiors, and saluting was always an option with him.

"I had to make a choice. Keep Marseille and try to handle the discord in my unit, or send him elsewhere and pass on the problem, giving him to a unit that had the time to deal with him. I immediately thought of Macky [Steinhoff], and since I lost money to him in a card game, I felt this was my way of getting even. So, I cut the orders and sent Marseille packing. Three days later I had a phone call. It was Macky, and I had some explaining to do."[26]

Generalleutnant Johannes Steinhoff, then an *Oberleutnant*, was Marseille's new commanding officer.

"I was commanding 4./JG-52, and we were waiting on replacement pilots, which usually came from Schwechat, with a couple of hundred hours behind them. When I was told that I was getting this guy with seven victories and a lot of flight time, I was excited. I normally never received experienced pilots. But, as I always said, if you look a gift horse in the mouth, it was very often missing teeth, and so I learned with Marseille.

"I had requested his service record book, and I was very surprised to see that with his time in the service, and his experience, he had not been promoted. Then I received his record, and I could not believe it. I thought we probably had a real, unassuming hero. But these were not commendations and awards; these were reprimands, punishments, proficiency reports. You name it and it was in there. I also saw that he only needed to lose one more German fighter to be an Allied ace."[27]

After reading those reports, Steinhoff had questions. "I called my old friend and asked him about Marseille. He told me: 'Sorry Macky, but I had to send him somewhere; I did not mean to do that to you. Good luck, you will need it.' When I asked him what the hell he had done to me, he hung up. He showed up at my base later that week, landed on the airfield, and we had a good chat, or perhaps not so good. That was when I discovered how badly I had been screwed over."[28] Ihlefeld later admitted that he knew full well what he was doing to his old friend. He just did not want to warn him in advance!

Marseille finally reported to Steinhoff's squadron in France unannounced and late and was ordered to see his new C.O. (commanding officer) immediately. Steinhoff was holding Marseille's personnel record when the young Berliner walked in. Steinhoff asked, "What the hell is this? It's almost as thick as a telephone directory! Let's take a look." Steinhoff went through it, line by line, page by page, note by note, reciting every entry. This took over an hour. "What do you have to say to this?" Steinhoff asked. In typical Marseille fashion, he replied: "I never wrecked an airplane, *Herr Oberleutnant!*"[29]

Steinhoff explained further: "Marseille [had] walked in as casually as entering a *pilstube* [a bar], but once I snapped at him, he was locked up at rigid attention. I made him stand there, not because his folder was thick enough with violations for an entire *Geschwader*, but because he was a day late reporting for duty. You know why he was late? He was with a girl in a hotel, after being home for a few days, just before Christmas, and lost track of time. He admitted this. Marseille was many things, a drunkard, playboy, rebel, occasional idiot, but he was never a liar. He always admitted his mistakes. I could never tell him this, but even when I was at my angriest with him, I had to wait until he left before I often laughed silently to myself. It was just very hard to hate the guy. But the moment I met him, I knew he was trouble.'[30]

Once Marseille had left, Steinhoff got on the telephone again. "I called Herbert, and I asked him what in the hell had he sent me? His response was that he was overstaffed on pilots, and not enough fighters for the pilots. I told him that was because the man he had sent me had crashed all of them. Then he said, 'Macky, you are a great father figure, you know how to work with these men, you are a very good leader. I know my shortcomings, and I hope that you can help this guy. He does have promise.' Well, I had that telephone in my ear and looked at the thick folder on Marseille, and just said, 'All right, I will do what I can.' I had a bad feeling that I was making a huge mistake. I had no idea just what a bad decision that was until later, but I soon enough came to regret my decision.

"Most of us by this time who were squadron leaders or higher had a couple of years of flying combat. We knew our business, but the best of us knew that we did not know everything. Every mission, every encounter with the enemy provided another valuable lesson, all of which a good pilot learned, and quickly. Failure to do this would mean death, and there were many ways for a pilot to die: outnumbered, engine failure, bad weather, and bad luck. But dying due to being an idiot was unacceptable.

"Marseille had a natural flying talent, I guess you could call it a gift. He would pull stunts over the airfield, doing amazing things. He was good. That was not the problem. His problem was that he knew he was good, and his ego always got the better of him. During one mission we were flying, and I think this was the first mission I flew with him as the *Staffelkapitän*, we encountered Hurricanes over the English coast, and we flew the *Schwarm* formation, or 'finger four' as it was called by the

British. Each pilot had a wingman, and that wingman had only one job; keep his *Rottenflieger* (wingman) alive, clearing his tail if necessary.

"Once the enemy had been called out, Marseille disappeared. He left his flight leader all alone. No one knew where he was! Suddenly over the radio we hear 'got him' and it was Marseille [Author's note: Marseille claimed a "damaged," but did not confirm this or any victory while with JG-52]. Then we heard, 'Oh shit, he got me' and it was also Marseille. He had flown into a simple trap, lured in by a lone fighter and jumped by three others. Only his awareness and reflexes prevented him from being killed or having to bailout over England.

"We shot down three fighters on that sortie, and escorted Marseille back, as his fighter was leaking glycol and slightly smoking. He finally called out his fuel warning. He had to slide the fighter down on the beach at Calais, which was not his first crash landing. He was fine, and the fighter was later cannibalized for spare parts, but he was on my shit list. He broke the most cardinal rule of combat. He left the formation without orders, and even worse, without telling anyone. I grounded him for a week, to teach him a lesson.

"For that week he worked with the ground crews, pulled sentry duty, those kinds of things. It never occurred to me to restrict him to quarters, and that was my fault. He stole my car, went into town and came back drunk, with two girls in varying degrees of undress, also drunk, and one was driving the car. I was beyond angry. I restricted him to the base for a month, and after a week he was allowed to fly, and the only way out of his quarters for the rest of that month was to fly a mission. Once we returned, he was back under guard.

"That turned out to be another failure on my part. I did not nail the back windows shut. He managed to climb out. As the guard was posted at the front door, and there was not a back door, I did not know anything was amiss. In fact, early that morning I shaved and walked outside, and I thought I saw that my car had been moved. I asked the officer of the watch if anyone had driven my car. He said: 'Yes sir, Marseille left late last night. He just came back about an hour ago.' I was livid and could not understand how he did that.

"I asked the *Feldwebel* on guard duty at the door if Marseille had left, as he was not allowed to go anywhere. He told me that he never left the building. When I walked in my foot landed on a bottle that rolled out from under me. I fell on my ass and was very angry about it. I picked it up and saw that Marseille was sound asleep. I could smell the beer and liquor on him. I kicked his bed, and he tumbled out of it. I told him to get up, and just as I did, the order to form up was given. He jumped up, did not go to attention, and did not salute. He just fell over drunk. I just looked at him and told him to pack his bags. I said that I would tell him what I had decided to do with him after we flew our reconnaissance mission.

"I had him for over a month, when I finally decided that I had to get rid of him around later in January, early February. This guy had no concept of military bearing. He either respected you as a man, or not; your rank really meant nothing. The day he reported for duty, his only question had nothing to do with operations. He wanted to know which town had the prettiest girls. But things would get worse.

"Once when after a reconnaissance mission I was paid a visit by a *Gestapo Sturmbannführer* (Major), in fact it was the same day that I tripped over the bottle. This guy was an old Party type, Blood Order, Great War Iron Cross First Class, the works. This guy was looking for a pilot, name unknown, but he described Marseille perfectly. I thought quickly, and asked him what had this pilot done? He told me it was a personal matter, and he was visiting all the local air bases trying to find this guy. He simply said he would keep looking, and I offered him a drink. This was from the bottle of cognac that I had taken from

Marseille that I had tripped over that morning. I saw that it was very expensive, so I confiscated it. We spoke and he said that the man he was looking for had taken advantage of his daughter, who was visiting him from university.

"He also said that this *Luftwaffe* officer had the audacity to jump out his daughter's bedroom mostly naked, with his daughter throwing his clothes out after him. What he saw was the uniform and his best bottle of cognac in the intruder's left hand, and he named it. My blood began to run cold, I had just served him from that same bottle, so I leaned back as if stretching and turned the bottle around when he was distracted. That would have been damning evidence.

"That was when everything clicked in my head. Once when he [Marseille] returned, again with a partially dressed woman, I had to reprimand him. Then I had to cover for him, since she was apparently the daughter of the same local *Gestapo* officer. I felt as if I were more of a truant officer, or a probation officer as opposed to his commanding officer. It was at about this time I had to get him the hell out of the unit without making clear the real reason. He could have gone to prison. I assured the *Sturmbannführer* that I would help him best I could, so I gave him a long list of all the *Luftwaffe* units in the area, and he seemed satisfied, and then he left. I was sweating worse than if I had been in combat. I knew right then that Marseille had to go.

"Once Marseille was late for a pre-flight briefing. As I was finishing the meeting, I heard a car pull up outside. I opened the door, and saw him climb out of a car, and kiss the girl driving it. Then another girl climbed from the backseat and sat in the front. He was still getting dressed into his uniform as he walked in the doorway. At this time, I had some pilots who would become very successful fighter pilots and good friends. They did not want to fly with him anymore.

"I asked him if he had a good explanation for being late before I grounded him. You would not believe his answer: 'Yes sir, I was too drunk to get out of bed, and when I did, I realized I was too late for the briefing. Sorry sir, I will try to not let that happen again.' Well, it did happen again, so I dismissed him, and sent him packing to Neumann where he ended up in Libya. Quite ironic in a way if you think about it. He left France in disgrace and then became a living legend. If there had been a lot of girls in Africa, I do not think he would have had such success. Although he was a chronic problem, I actually liked the guy very much, but I think that in sending him away I actually saved him. I cut his orders the next day, and within a week he was gone."[31]

Walter Krupinski who later retired as a Generalleutnant in the Bundesluftwaffe. (Walter Krupinski)

Marseille left a lasting impression even on those pilots who never came to know him well, such as 197-victory ace *Generalleutnant* Walter Krupinski: "I had just arrived at the unit when Marseille was there, so I did not really know him personally, but we all knew about is activities, and they were worth much conversation. We just could not figure out how he got away with everything, and stealing Steinhoff's car was something I will never forget, as well as the girls."[32]

Marseille's cavalier attitude toward life, the war, his superiors, and even his own personal safety endangered the men around him. According to Steinhoff, many of the men quietly requested that he not be assigned to their *Schwarm*, which only echoed the reports while he was under Ihlefeld's command. A lone wolf, never a team player, he looked for personal glory rather than working with a unit to achieve a greater objective. This attitude explained his missing four claims while in 4./JG-52. He had no witnesses to verify the victories, despite his ammunition depletion proving he fired at the enemy, and the fact that he lost six aircraft in total while in France and Holland. Had gun cameras been available at that time, he would have had video confirmation of his missing claims, but without them, they could not be entered onto his record.

Marseille was also a marked man by the local military doctor, who treated him six times during his bailouts and crash landings. He was listed as a "reckless sort," labeled a shirker in his duties, unprofessional in his military bearing and attitude, noncompliant and disrespectful towards his superiors in violating his orders when grounded and confined to quarters. Marseille was headed for personal and professional disaster.

The moment that men do not want to fly with a fellow pilot, when they don't trust their comrade to cover them, then a commanding officer has a decision to make. Steinhoff did not have time to change Marseille's attitude and nurture the man. He had a war to fight against the best pilots in the world, and Steinhoff made the right call. This opinion was shared by Adolf Galland. Even Eduard Neumann agreed that, had JG-27 been based in France, with all its temptations, he would have probably passed Marseille off down the line.

Marseille the insubordinate clown was well known. It was time for Marseille the legend to emerge.

CHAPTER 3

North Africa and Glory

> *I could not believe this clown;
> his lack of bearing and audacity stunned me.*
> —Johannes Steinhoff

FOR A NEAR COMPARISON to Marseille's behavior, imagine a World War II American Medal of Honor recipient openly dismissing the wartime and political policies made at the Pentagon, outlining the stupidity of the racially segregated U.S. military, challenging the authority and competence of his superiors, and refusing to comply with national or military laws, customs, and courtesies. The great difference between this hypothetical American hero and Marseille is that in Nazi Germany such talk and actions could get a man shot or placed in a concentration camp and often did—of which Marseille was well aware.

Oberst and postwar *Brigadegeneral* Gustav Rödel (98 victories, Knight's Cross, Oak Leaves) a Spanish Civil War veteran with Galland and Neumann, had commanded II./JG-27 and also flew with Marseille and Schroer under Neumann. According to Rödel:

"Marseille was a real bastard to fly with, as sometimes my II./JG-27 worked with the first *Gruppe,* and I and others wrote him up many times for disobeying direct orders prior to, and even while in, combat. He just did not listen. He was like an excited dog, abandoning all logic once he saw the enemy, breaking formation without support. [Gerhard] Homuth was his flight leader a few times, and he and I had been great friends. He constantly bitched about Marseille, gifted or not. But then, once he was engaged with the enemy, usually outnumbered heavily, it was like watching a well-orchestrated ballet.

Oberleutnant Gerhard Homuth (Ludwig Franzisket)

"He almost danced with the aircraft, and you really had to be there to see him at work. I actually tried a few of his stall maneuvers when not in combat, just for practice, such as lowering the flaps, chopping the throttle, kicking the rudder, rolling the stick, everything. I practiced at 10,000 feet and was never able to complete the maneuvers. I lost half my altitude just recovering from the stall. Marseille never stalled; he managed to shoot down multiple aircraft this way, sometimes just a few hundred feet off the deck. I really have no idea how he managed this feat, to be quite honest. He did this all the time."[33]

Werner Schroer, who scored 61 victories in North Africa and 114 total victories during the war, called Marseille "the most amazing and ingenious combat pilot I ever saw.

"He was also very lucky on many occasions. He thought nothing of jumping into a fight outnumbered ten to one, often alone, with us trying to catch up to him. He violated every cardinal rule of fighter combat. High speed, attack from altitude, climb to escape, and attack again converting the altitude into speed, always with a wingman for protection, were doctrine. He abandoned all the rules.

"He would fly into a formation called a Lufbery, which was a large circle of enemy planes. These would form a large wheel for protection. The theory was that each plane could protect the plane in front of the other. Then, if an enemy fighter attacked one, the pilot behind could shoot down the attacker. Unfortunately, that did not work with Hans. He would fly in, lower his airspeed by cutting the throttle, lowering his flaps to almost stalling speed, slip into the formation, shoot down a plane, and then skid out of the line of fire from the enemy behind him. That enemy would usually overshoot, giving him the kill shot, then Marseille would then increase throttle, line up a third kill, take it down, and then go for another if he had ammunition, which he usually did. He was a fantastic if not foolhardy pilot, but he achieved the results.

"When I met the new guys, I would discuss their flying training, experience, and simply talk about what they could expect. The British were damned good pilots, but we had better fighters, and better tactics. The one thing I always told them was, 'Do not start acting like Marseille, or you will get killed.' Almost all of the new guys had heard of him, had heard of me and others with victories, but almost all of them would ask, 'Do you think I will meet him?' Such was his reputation."[34]

JG-27 had served on the Channel Coast during 1940 and participated in the Battles of France and Britain. One of the earliest members of the unit was also its most famous son, the future General of the Fighters, Adolf Galland. Following the problems Mussolini's forces were having in the Balkans, the unit was sent to operate and secure the airspace over Yugoslavia and Greece. The first year and a half of the war had produced highly skilled and competent fighter pilots. These were the men who arrived in Bucharest, Romania, on February 2, 1941, and once the ground personnel gathered, they relocated to Bulgaria.

The first week of April the unit flew over the ancient land of Greece, patrolling for British fighters that were supporting the ground forces of the Greek and Commonwealth forces as they were being pushed ever farther south toward the sea. Following the collapse of Greece and Yugoslavia, as well as the costly capture of Crete that May, the *Geschwader* was sent to the Eastern Front, briefly joining the bulk of the German fighter forces for Operation Barbarossa, the June 22 invasion of the Soviet Union. From there the *Geschwader* went to Africa.

JG-27 had started arriving in fragments in North Africa from Greece aboard the freighter *Reichenfels* after serving in the Balkans. Their relocation came at the urgent and repetitious requests of *Generalmajor* (later *General der Flieger*) Stefan Frölich, commanding the air assets of the *Luftwaffe* in Africa. The first arrivals at the port in Tripoli were the ground crew and many of the pilots while those remaining in Greece continued flying operations while awaiting orders.

The first air contingent was led by *Oberleutnant* Karl-Heinz Redlich commanding 1 *Staffel* on April 18, 1941, 2 *Staffel* under *Hauptmann* Erich Gerlitz (three victories), followed by 3 *Staffel* under the command of *Oberleutnant* Gerhard Homuth (with 14 victories on the Channel Coast). One of the outstanding officers in that unit was Condor Legion veteran *Oberleutnant* Eduard Neumann who had six victories, of which two were scored in Spain. He would become the *Gruppenkommandeur* of I./JG-27 on April 18, 1941, with a belated promotion to *Hauptmann* soon afterward, followed by a promotion to *Major*. He would then become the *Geschwaderkommdore* in 1942 following the promotion and transfer of his superior, *Major* Bernhard Woldenga.

The initial air bases were established in and around Benghazi, until the *Deutsches Afrika Korps* under *Generalmajor* Erwin Rommel achieved their objective and completed the encirclement of Tobruk, pushing further east past Ain-el-Gazala and then Derna by April 11, 1941. On April 15, I./JG-27 was established at Gazala by an advance party of primarily ground support personnel. They were widely spread out, remaining in and around Bomba Bay until November that year. The 1 *Staffel* under Redlich arrived at the new field at Ain-el-Gazala with already outdated and battle-worn Me-109E fighters on April 18, and the next day they took off on their first combat mission of the African campaign.

Major Joachim Müncheberg

The air war was intensifying as the British increased the numbers of their fighters to protect their bombers, and the Italians joined the Germans in increasing their presence as well. On that first mission *Oberleutnant* Eduard Neumann arrived at Gazala with 2./JG-27, while Homuth's group detoured and landed at the air base of 7./JG-27 at Gela, Sicily. This was commanded by *Oberleutnant* Joachim Müncheberg, and was awaiting its own transfer orders, while flying air cover for the German transports shipping troops and materiel to Libya. Homuth's group then refueled and took off to join the others in Libya.

Upon arriving at Castel Benito, the designated refueling point, the entire area seemed abandoned, although from the air it looked like an active base. Homuth's seven Me-109Es of 3 *Staffel* landed, and upon confirming the lack of any personnel, he chose a new pilot, an ill-adjusted *Oberfähnrich* named Hans-Joachim Marseille, to fly on to Sirte to find out what had happened. Assigned Yellow 13, Marseille took off, although he never made it and had to land on a dirt road with engine problems.[35]

The next day the group moved back to En Nofilia, and Homuth sent *Oberfeldwebel* Herbert Kowalski to Sirte after not hearing from Marseille. Kowalski also had to land short of his destination after he ran out of fuel. Later that day an aircraft flew over Homuth's encampment and dropped a message, informing the officer that neither Kowalski nor Marseille had landed in Sirte.[36]

This was Marseille's seventh damaged fighter written off with nothing to show for it, not counting the fighters he brought back slightly damaged or the one bailout where he actually managed to score victories. He did manage to hitch a ride with an Italian truck driver and arrive at Sirte, thus stating his unit's condition and location at the Scorpion Airfield. Just before the fuel truck departed, Kowalski also arrived under similar circumstances and updated Marseille and the Italians of the move to En Nofilia, so the trucks were directed there.

Before sundown, Marseille arrived at En Nofilia in a truck with a supply of food and water and let them know that a fuel truck was arriving just behind them containing Kowalski. The fighters were refueled, although Homuth told Marseille that since he damaged his fighter, he would have to find his own way to the front. Kowalski may have returned to Sirte with the fuel truck and then gone onto Gazala from there, while Marseille caught a ride with an Italian convoy, where he ended up in Via Balbia.

After several conversations with various ranks, he pled his case to a *Generalmajor* Hellman, stating the urgency of his mission and the need to be with his unit in Gazala by the next day. The

Pilots of No. 73 Squadron (Geoffrey Morley-Mower)

only price for allowing Marseille to have a car and driver was that he had to dine with the senior officer and tell him of his exploits over the Channel. He also told Marseille to score 50 more victories to pay back the debt, and Marseille agreed.

Marseille and the driver arrived at Benghazi in the early morning of April 22, and by noon they reached Derna, where they refueled the car at the airfield. While there Marseille also collected his back pay from the duty pay clerk. He arrived at Gazala at approximately 17:00, just two hours behind the entire *Staffel*, impressing Homuth. That completed the arrival of all three *Staffeln*, which were now prepared for action from their new base. Meanwhile, as Neumann was organizing his group, the air war was ongoing. The previous day Redlich shot down two Hurricanes, while Hans Sippel and Schroer also scored a kill each, with Sippel shooting down a Vickers Wellington on April 20, the first twin-engine bomber kill for the unit in Africa.

"We were outnumbered, as we had eight fighters in the air," Schroer recalled. "We saw these dots just ahead and slightly below us, so Redlich gave the order for one *Schwarm* to attack, and the other, being mine to stay top cover. We had another *Schwarm* following behind also at altitude, as a reserve force, catching any enemies that broke through. There was also an Italian *Regia Aeronautica* fighter unit operating as well.

Marseille speaking with a local Arab while inspecting one of his Hurricane victories. (Raymond F. Toliver)

"The first four aircraft attacked by turning hard right and diving. The first pass saw three Hurricanes smoking, and as I banked, I saw one going down. The next few Hurricanes pulled up to engage us and escape our fighters completing the pull out of the curving dive. That was when I nosed over and hit one of them head on. Sippel was behind me, and he got off a good shot also, covering my tail. I had also taken 20mm rounds from a Hurricane into my engine. He went down, and so did mine. Then I felt hits, and knew that I was hit, my victim actually hit me.

"I hit a second Hurricane, but nothing to talk about, and my wingman scored the victory, but I had to put down. I was too low to bail out, and the desert terrain did not allow for a landing gear approach. The rounds hit my 109 underneath, and the engine started winding down. The oil cooler was shot out, and the temperature started to rise. I was at about two thousand meters and headed back to our lines, which was not far, just a few minutes. The engine started smoking so I shut it down and went into a shallow glide. I felt a pain in my arm and left leg. A small piece of shrapnel had hit me, but it was a minor wound.

"As the ground came up, I saw a small hill that I did not want to hit, despite being wheels up. I pulled back on the stick, and my airspeed was about one hundred kilometers per hour, maybe a little more. I lifted up and over and then set the fighter down. I just managed to drift into a shallow descent and eased into a controlled crash. I managed to get out and look at my fighter. None of the enemy shells had hit anything near where I was, so I was lucky. It was a good landing. I did not burn or blow up. The prop blades had been stationary for a few minutes, so only one blade was bent under the aircraft. The aircraft was salvageable. However, best of all so was I."[37]

The unit added further laurels, yet also suffered a loss on the April 21 engagement when Sippel was killed, and in the same dogfight Schroer was shot down again and made a crash landing but emerged just slightly wounded.[38] *Oberleutnant* Albert Espenlaub shot down a Hurricane, apparently flown by a Sergeant Castelnau of No. 73 Squadron RAF.

This period of initial organization did not go smoothly. According to Ludwig Franzisket: "We more resembled a Gypsy tribe mulling around than a well-organized and disciplined German unit. It was quite comical. Neumann even had his medicine show wagon brought over, which became his command post. All we needed were a few exotic animals and we could have charged admission. We already had the clowns."[39] [Author's note: The animals would soon join the circus, when the unit acquired a lion cub and a black bear they named "Bobbi."]

Ludwig Franzisket after receiving his Knight's Cross (Ludwig Franzisket)

The *Staffeladjutant* was *Oberleutnant* Ludwig Franzisket, already credited with 14 victories, and *Oberleutnant* Gustav Rödel, with ten European victories, would arrive later. The first order of business was establishing water, fuel, oil, latrines, and ammunition supply depots, and protecting them from attack. The bleak landscape did not provide much in the way of assistance, so bunkers and aircraft revetements had to be dug into the sand and covered by tents and camouflage nets so that they could not be seen from the air.

Sanitation in the desert was, as in any field environment, a major concern. The standard method was to dig a hole approximately four to six feet deep, with an outhouse covering the hole. Once a week the outhouse would be relocated to a new hole far away, and gasoline would be poured into the foul mixture and burned then filled with sand. Disease was an enemy that was hard to combat once it appeared, and Neumann took great care to ensure that his men did not succumb to the many possible maladies that could erupt and ground a unit. Libya seemed as far from home as any place on earth. However, dysentery and malaria would still become a problem.

Ludwig Franzisket described the world they entered: "Flying over the sea and seeing the beach and clear blue water was like a vacation. Landing and seeing the barren landscape was as alien as the moon to us. I thought to myself that this could be a very good place to fight the war and probably survive, given that unlike in France say, or Crete perhaps, several engagements per week, even per day with the enemy was always the case. You tend to get very weary of watching friends die. You get exhausted. I thought it was paradise at first. Then as time settled, I realized that we had entered hell, a hot one too!"[40]

Marseille playing another practical joke (Ludwig Franzisket)

The wildlife was also hellish, and Marseille's frequent pranks didn't make things any easier. Franzisket explained:

"I always had this great fear of snakes. We had them there: asps I think, and even the occasional cobra. Scorpions were a real problem, and we had to check our shoes every time. I tied my shoes to the tent top to keep them off the ground. I was asleep, and I felt this movement under my blanket. It was cold at night in the desert.

"I thought someone was shaking me awake, until I felt this thing sliding across the back of my neck. I froze, eyes wide open. Then I could take no more and I jumped up screaming, and tore right through the side of the tent, running as fast as I could. My tent mates were laughing like hell, and I stopped and saw Marseille. He had taken a broken fan belt from a vehicle, and had rubbed it against me, as if it were a snake. I wanted to kill that guy, so I chased him around the compound, but I could not catch him. He was too fast.

"After a few days I calmed down. Then, one morning while at breakfast, which I hated, Marseille was sitting across the far table, and said loud enough for me to hear: 'Too bad some people don't like fan belts, really a shame.' I looked right at him, and with all seriousness, I told him that his pranks would land him in big trouble one day."[41]

Crashed Hurricane (Geoffrey Morley-Mower)

Gustav Rödel recalled his first impression of Africa:

"The beaches were not that unlike Greece or parts of Italy, even southern Spain, but the heat was the real problem. The constant dirt and dust got into everything. You could be completely drenched in sweat after a mission, but ten minutes standing outside you were completely dry. We fried eggs on the truck bonnets [hoods], and heated water for shaving by just leaving it in the sun. But that was not even the worst of it. The flies were incredible, fleas and even scorpions, and the occasional snake.

"Sometimes at night it was so damned cold, you could almost see your breath, but that was rare given the lack of constant humidity. It was dry heat in summer and during most days, and a dry cold, unlike back home, which made it more tolerable at night. It was a miserable place to be, nothing like the postcard pictures you would send home on holiday. And of course, there was the enemy, making things difficult. Sandstorms were not too common, but when you had one, sand got into everything, even inside the cockpits when the canopy was closed. The mechanics spent half their entire life cleaning sand out of the engines."[42]

When Marseille had first arrived at Gazala, he was met by his best friends at the time and his future constant *Rottenfliegern* Hans-Arnold "Fifi" Stahlschmidt and Reiner Pöttgen. They wanted to show him something. As they walked over to the ready line, Marseille was introduced to his new fighter, bearing the number Yellow 14. Schroer explained why Marseille's number had been changed:

"Marseille was like every other pilot. We are all superstitious creatures to some degree, and after all of his mishaps flying a '13' [just as in LG-2] it was decided that he would fly a '14' instead, just as he did in LG-2, as they changed his number from 13 to 14 also. This was as much as a morale boost for him as it was a way to show that he was valued. I think it was Gustav's [Rödel] idea, but I cannot remember.

"Marseille walked over as the unit emblem was being painted, and he said, 'I will make it famous,' and of course we were thinking 'Sure,' but he did do that. Then he said: 'But the rudder looks a little bare. I will have to fix that in time,' meaning that he would have to score more victories to add to the painted victory bars. We laughed."[43]

Few realized just how prophetic Marseille's words were or how his success would impact others, as Rödel recalled. "One day after Marseille had shot down over one hundred aircraft, Neumann said to me as a joke, that since he [Marseille] flew Yellow 14, and I was then flying Yellow 4 (later White 4), and the British knew him by name and number, that I should perhaps be even more vigilant as there may be a few enemy pilots who wanted to take that scalp, and I could get confused with him."[44]

The early Me-109Es were equal to or better than most of the British counterparts they faced on the Channel Coast the previous year during the Battle of Britain and in the Balkans, such as the Hurricanes, Spitfires, and Curtiss P-40s. However, once in Africa, the Germans found their fighters were relegated to second-class status against the newer Spitfire V being used by the British and Commonwealth forces by late 1942. Also problematic was the constant sand and dust that accumulated in the engine intakes, necessitating the introduction of the tropical filtration system.

The Germans in JG-27 were a combat-hardened unit, with gifted pilots who had a certain confident swagger about them, but nothing resembling arrogance. They were too experienced to believe their own propaganda. As Gustav Rödel noted: "The fastest way to die in combat was to think your enemy was stupid or not worthy of your attention. Treat your opponent as an expert, and that will keep you sharp. Graveyards are full of young pilots who failed to heed that lesson. That was what I told my new pilots without any combat experience."[45]

The newer Me-109Fs from the Messerschmitt plant in Augsburg were already being introduced to the *Luftwaffe* but these had gone first to the fighter units on the Western Front, then set aside for the units preparing for Operation Barbarossa on the Eastern Front. On the

Western Front the units (primarily JGs-2 and -26) received first choice; Africa was considered a third front and a backwater operation in Hitler's plans. According to *General der Flieger* Josef Kammhuber: "Hitler had Russia on his mind from the start. After Barbarossa it was all consuming. Only the Balkans and Crete disrupted his ambitions. The *Luftwaffe* in North Africa was really just an afterthought."[46]

The pilots who flew the Messerschmitt fighters in World War II all had their opinions of the various models. When the Me-109E was the mainstay fighter, nearly all the pilots were very impressed with the firepower of four machine guns (two wing mounted and two cowl mounted) and the single 20mm cannon firing through the propeller hub. These three centrally mounted weapons required little correction for long-range deflection shooting. The Me-109F abandoned the wing mounted machine guns but kept the two top cowling-mounted machine guns and the centrally mounted cannon, which came in both 15mm and 20mm varieties.

Most Me-109 pilots loved the F, which was known as both the "Franz" and "Friedrich" (the E model was called the "Emil" and the later G model the "Gustav"), with the F regarded as the purest form of the design. Without the added weight and drag of the wing mounted guns, the F model was a tighter, leaner, and more agile fighter. Such qualities were life insurance in a dogfight, and it was this model that Marseille exploited to the fullest. The later G model saw the return of the wing-mounted weapons, as well as keeping the two machine guns and cannon up front. Although it came with a more powerful Daimler-Benz engine and increased speed and firepower, it was not as agile as the F model had been.

Postwar *Generalleutnant* Günther Rall, 275 victory ace and Knight's Cross, Oak Leaves and Swords recipient, really loved the 109:

"It was the aircraft that I was most comfortable with; it felt comfortable. The 109E was the best fighter in the world at that time, only matched by the Spitfire, which was more maneuverable, but we had the firepower and speed. But their fighters caught up, with better speeds and placing cannon on them. We could not out-turn the Spitfire in the early days, and even later with better 109s that was a dangerous thing to try to do.

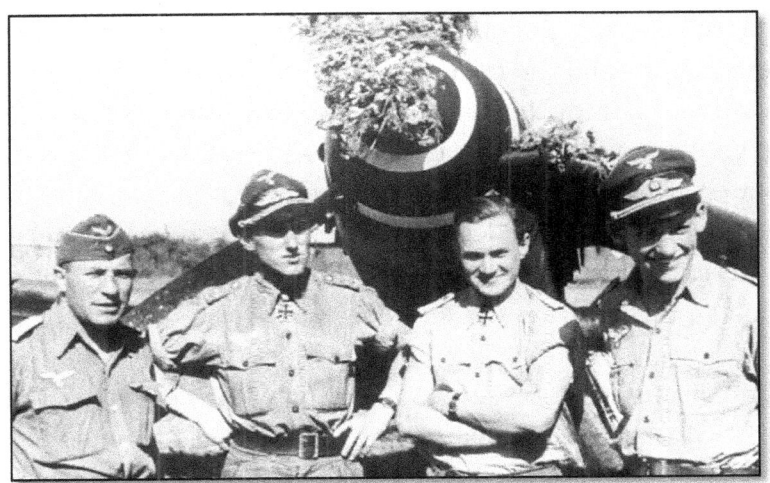

Günther Rall (2nd from left) and Walter Krupinski (3rd from left) in Ukraine August 1943 (Günther Rall)

"The E model was great, and when it was replaced by the F, that was even better. It had a better roll rate, could turn tighter, and later models of the F and the G were built with better control surfaces, a good leading edge that allowed you to maintain control in a tight turning fight. What I liked the best about the F was the fact that it did not have the wing guns.

"When you were in a high G twisting fight, sometimes the ammunition feed belt to these outside guns broke, as it was fed by a chain. If that chain broke, you only had central mounted weapons, and the extra drag of the wing guns did nothing for you. On my fighters when I later flew the G, I just took the wing guns out. At the very least, unlinking the ammunition chain was a good idea. If that broke, none of the guns would work. That was really bad in a serious fight. Besides, a good fighter pilot does not really need a battery of weapons. He should be able to shoot down aircraft with a minimum of ammunition, and two guns and a cannon in the front were plenty.

Perhaps a ground attack pilot might need all that rubbish, but not a fighter pilot.

"I found that with the wing guns removed I was really flying a more powerful F model. I had better roll, maneuverability, better climb, and the turning radius was a little better. Not to mention that reducing all of that extra weight extended your range, saving fuel, as it reduced drag. The F was the perfect fighter. If I could have had the F throughout the war, and had the engine of the later K model, I would have probably been a better pilot. But you must remember that the aircraft is only as good as the man who flies it."[47]

Remaining E models were sent to Germany's allies, especially Finland, Bulgaria, Hungary and Romania, and some to German units in Sicily. These older E model single-seat fighters of JG-27 were the first actual defense against the British bombers that had operated virtually unopposed, with fighter escorts, for months. Their operations had almost destroyed the Italians on the ground and were constantly interdicting supply convoys, hence Hitler's desire to support the cause with his newly created Afrika Korps. It did not take long for the Germans in Libya to see action.

The primary German target was the British garrison in the port city of Tobruk, which meant that *Generalmajor* (later *Generalfeldmarschall*) Erwin Rommel's Afrika Korps's lines of supply risked constant interdiction. The Royal Navy virtually controlled the Mediterranean Sea, and the Royal Air Force, in conjunction with the Australian, South African, and New Zealand Commonwealth units had free rein to strafe and bomb Axis supply columns at will, with their bases secured behind the lines in Egypt, and access to supplies through the Strait of Gibraltar as well as the Suez Canal. The Germans were hard-pressed to replenish and resupply on a similar scale. Marseille had arrived in time to join in the hunts, although his primary duties were escorting Ju-87 Stuka dive bombers, a job every fighter pilot hated—except Marseille. It was this escort role that he came to know Stuka pilot and Knight's Cross recipient Kurt Kuhlmey very well, at least over the radio.

On April 23, 1941, the day after his arrival, Marseille took off with Reiner Pöttgen on a Stuka escort to Tobruk. Flying very high, almost 15,000 feet, they could see the Stukas below and ahead. These Stukas belonged to 2, *Staffel* I./StG-3 (*Stukageschwader* 3) commanded by *Oberleutnant* Kurt Kuhlmey, who recalled his impressions of JG-27:

> "I always worried about when or if my fighter cover would arrive. Many times, a group would be enroute to rendezvous with my Stukas, but they would encounter enemy fighters and get engaged. That meant I had no fighter cover, and when attacking a target like Tobruk, with enemy fighters always around that was a nervous time indeed. But I knew what when I saw Marseille and the first *Gruppe*, my men would get home safe."[48]

On this mission Schroer's *Schwarm* was flying ahead at the same altitude. The German fighters saw antiaircraft fire bursting around the altitude where the Stukas had been, but they were below the preset burst altitude, diving in on their bomb runs. Once the Stukas released their payloads and banked away then climbed for more altitude, the fighter pilots turned on their heading to return to their base.

Oberleutnant Kurt Kuhlmey (Kurt Kuhlmey)

But then, as Ludwig Franzisket recalled: "We were also going home when someone called out enemy fighters below us. I called for confirmation, and Schroer confirmed it was

Marseille who had spotted them. I could not see a thing myself until I looked to my eleven o'clock. That was when I called my wingman [*Leutnant* von Moller] to join me, and we winged over to engage. As we closed in, I saw Yellow 14 and his wingman one behind the other, just below me, attacking. A couple of Hurricanes around me went down in flames and smoking.

"I fired at a Hurricane making a flash right past me, getting good hits, and I hit right rudder and threw the stick to bank over and get on his tail, and that was when I saw Marseille, on his back, going in for another victory. Once he locked on to a target, you knew it was going down. It was a real sight; I can tell you."[49]

Marseille had inverted to follow the Hurricane in its dive and pulled the stick back to increase the dive until he could line up the target. A quick burst from the guns and he shot down the Hurricane over Tobruk, bringing his total wartime score to eight. However, when Marseille decided to attack his latest victim's wingman, four other Hurricanes then locked onto his tail, and Pöttgen could not do much to help. Marseille had again committed a cardinal sin—what would

Stuka of StG-3 damaged by anti-aircraft fire near Tobruk that almost made it back (Kurt Kuhlmey)

become one of his signature maneuvers—breaking contact rapidly and leaving his wingman behind.

Marseille and Pöttgen managed to convert their dive speed into energy and climb up and away from the danger, escaping any damage. Marseille had just scored the first victory for the 3 *Staffel* in Africa. On the third and final mission of the day, 20 Me-109s were to escort a like number of Stukas for another strike on Tobruk. The unit again encountered the enemy and had the altitude advantage. Marseille saw the chance for another kill, and without radioing any intentions at all rolled over into a diving attack. The failure to inform his comrades of his intent, let alone his wingman, was to prove almost fatal. The Stuka flight leader, *Oberleutnant* Kurt Kuhlmey witnessed it all.

As Kuhlmey recalled: "We had radio confirmation that JG-27 was our cover, and then we saw them, but we also saw the enemy fighters. We knew Yellow 14, as Marseille and his *Gruppe* often protected us. I saw two 109s go into the attack from altitude, and they both fired on the Hurricanes; two Hurricanes were smoking, and the Yellow 14 flashed past me from the opposite direction. It was then that he climbed, reversed and attacked again, but he had company this time. Quite a display."[50]

Before Marseille could line up the shot, he had three enemy fighters on him. He took rounds in the engine and canopy and was almost decapitated, the protective armored headplate behind him absorbing the impact of a canon round, while more rounds shredded his fuselage. As the odor of burning oil and leaking glycol became stronger, he pulled away and headed for his airfield. He managed a gear-up landing without fire or explosion. Over thirty enemy rounds had hit his fighter.

According to Franz Kurowski, the pilot who almost killed the future legend was Sous-lieutenant James Denis, a French pilot with No. 73 Squadron RAF, who scored 8.5 victories during the war.[51] Writing after the war, Denis recalled:

"When we arrived near the target, I dived quite steeply and realized my wingman was following shyly. Pompei [his wingman] was a very good pilot but had never trained as a fighter pilot. Worried to see how he was following so far behind, I kept looking back and noticed a Me-109 attacking him. Having no radio, I could not warn him. He was hit and then the Me-109 flew in my direction. I acted as if I hadn't seen him, but never stopped watching, and when he was in range I throttled back violently and skidded to the left.

"Since I was going very fast, my Hurricane [No. V7859] reacted violently. I saw the hail of bullets pass on my right, and the Me-109 could not slow down and flew in front of me. We then started a dogfight, for which the Hurricane was quite good due to its maneuverability. At that moment my plane was flying nose up, hooked to its propeller, when I saw the Me-109 in the sun. I fired a burst so close that we almost collided. I noticed my bullets enter its fuselage."[52]

Marseille in the cockpit. (Raymond F. Toliver)

Marseille had almost been killed, and that close call awakened him to some degree as well. He was in very fast company, and the flamboyant, carefree devil-may-care womanizer had finally found his true calling. Without distractions, Marseille found himself more than up to the challenge at hand. The war was heating up, and throughout the blazing summer of 1941 JG-27 gave a great account of themselves. However, they were being drained.

Schroer recalled his conversation with Marseille after the day's mission: "I told him that he was very lucky, but then he said that he could not be killed by the enemy, still claiming that he was immortal. Then he told me a crazy story, but one which I believed. He told me that when he and his sister were children, they went to a carnival in Berlin and his sister wanted to go have her future read by this fortune teller. Well, their mother and father took them both in, and paid the five marks each. But then the old Gypsy woman handed the money back, and said they should leave, there was no charge. Apparently after being questioned as to why, the old woman told their mother that her children would not have long lives, which upset her. Marseille laughed at it. As we now know that old Gypsy woman must have had some insights. I still think about that conversation. Very strange it was."[53]

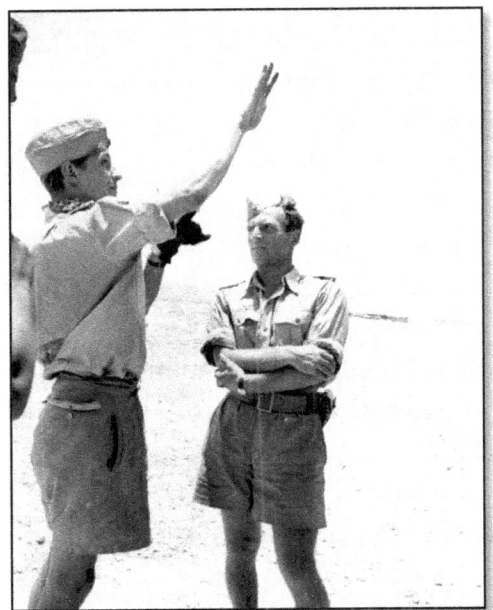

Marseille describing a combat action (Raymond F. Toliver)

The rest of April saw constant contact with enemy fighters, especially with the constant aerial bombardment of Tobruk. On April 28, Marseille and Pöttgen caught a Bristol Blenheim of No. 45 Squadron RAF over Tobruk. Pöttgen intercepted the bomber, which, upon seeing him approach, headed out to sea. Marseille wasted no time and closed rapidly and fired into it at close range, sending it into the sea killing all aboard.[54]

JG-27 was performing admirably, along with support from the Me-110 unit III./ZG-76, but they were seriously outnumbered, so the air contingent was augmented by the temporary arrival of I./JG-53, and a week later a *Staffel* from JG-77 was dispatched for temporary duty to assist in the air battles. Rather like the Gypsy tribe described by Franzisket, JG-27 and all of its *Gruppen* would find themselves moved around, almost as if in a mindless game of musical airfields.

On May 1, Homuth briefed his pilots on a new mission. They were to once again grind their teeth and escort Stukas, but Franzisket said, "Marseille liked the escort missions, even though we had to cut power and weave to stay with them. I asked him why he looked forward to these. He said very simply that Stukas were magnets for fighters, and the more the Stukas could draw in, the more victories he could score. It sounded logical to me."[55]

For this mission Homuth would lead the lower echelon while Marseille led the higher-flying group. Not long into the mission a scout aircraft was spotted, and then Marseille called out four enemy fighters (of No. 274 Squadron SAAF) at their altitude, 9,000 feet. Homuth gave the order to climb and then bank. He wanted his group to attack out of the sun, making it harder for the enemy to see their approach. The enemies were already within perfect strike range of Marseille's *Schwarm*, so Homuth told them to attack. Marseille agreed.

With Pöttgen in tow, followed by Stahlschmidt and his wingman, Marseille knifed into the enemy. Two Hurricanes in his sight gave him two options, so he fired at the leader, who fell away in flames. Then the enemy's wingman banked left, abandoning his fallen leader. Marseille followed him, and to cut the distance he gave full throttle, banked sharper left, lifted his nose after cutting inside the enemy's turn, and with a long-range deflection, he fired. The shells streaked far ahead of his target, seemingly into empty space, but the Hurricane flew directly into the path of the arcing projectiles and fell away to the desert floor. Gerhard Homuth also shot down two Hurricanes over Tobruk, which the Germans called the "Happy Hunting Ground."

The next day, Marseille was promoted to *Unteroffizier*. During this period, in addition to the previously mentioned units, 7. *Staffel* II./JG-26 was also transferred from Gela, Sicily, and sent to bolster the German air offensive, although its *Staffelkapitän* Joachim Müncheberg only had six Me-109Es with him.

Müncheberg had 43 victories at that time, yet he would also eventually become one of the legends of the air war, later commanding III./JG-53 and becoming *Kommodore* of JG-77 (sharing that distinction with Bernhard Woldenga and Johannes Steinhoff), only to die on March 23, 1943, over Tunisia, during the twilight of Hitler's grip on North Africa fighting against American flown Spitfires and P-38 Lightnings. At the time of his death, he had scored 135 victories and earned the Knight's Cross with Oak Leaves and Swords.

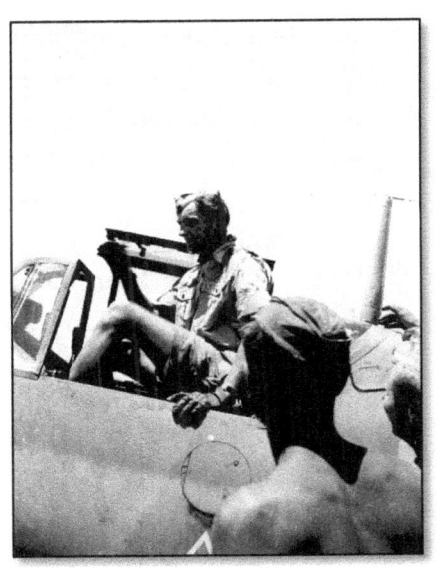

Marseille in the cockpit (Raymond F. Toliver)

Müncheberg had met most of the JG-27 men at some point, even Marseille, who during the first meeting was still an up-and-coming pilot, already notorious for his demeanor, infractions, and checkered combat record. Müncheberg had made some comments about the insubordinate Berliner and his lack of military bearing after meeting him.

According to Franzisket: "Müncheberg did not think a lot of Jochen, not at the first meeting anyway. I was there. Müncheberg had arrived in his staff car to meet with us all and introduce himself. He was already well known. He went down the line and shook our hands, speaking with us about Africa, what we thought, and the enemy condition. He really wanted to know a lot, but that was good.

"He steps up to Marseille, and I was only three places to the right, and asked him 'What do you think about Libya?' Marseille replied, and I tell you with a straight face; 'They should really bring some girls here, sort of boring and all that, and not even a *pilstube* in the area. At least the Italians have theirs.' Müncheberg, apparently expecting some comment on the enemy pilot situation and aircraft quality, weather, or some other innocuous response, seemed actually quietly shocked at what Marseille had said.

"Then Stahlschmidt, standing right next to him, and perhaps influenced by being around Jochen so often, said: "This is quite true sir, it would be good to have a few drinks after a flight. I think the Italian fighter squadron nearby has a refrigerated unit too.' Müncheberg said to them both something to the effect that 'you are here to fight a war, not expect the comforts of home.'

"Marseille then mentioned that 'the rear area officers lived quite well without taking any of the risk,' and at that time Müncheberg, who had already grown annoyed at both of them, smiled. 'You are correct; they do have it easy while we take great risks. That opinion I agree with. You, Marseille, still need a damned haircut.' That was our first meeting with Müncheberg."[56]

"Marseille had that effect on people," Schroer pointed out. "Once you walked away from him, you either hated him or you loved him, it was a matter of personal taste. However, nearly everyone who spent any real time with him learned that he was just himself. He hated no one, loved life, and despite his flamboyant and cavalier attitude, he was a really good fellow to be with. That was unless you were flying with him, at least in the early days. Then he was a real bastard."[57]

Marseille was coming into his own, and he was getting better as a pilot, but he still had a lot of work to do when it came to being a team player.

Marseille drinking one of his many gifts (Ludwig Franzisket)

CHAPTER 4

Learning the Ropes

One thing you had to say about Jochen; he never ran from a fight.
Friedrich Körner

The men of JG-27 were not very active during the first week in May 1941. Flying reconnaissance and a few short escort missions, the enemy fighters were few and far between. "It was strange really," Rödel recalled. "From the first days in April we were against large numbers of enemy fighters, and had some success, and we thought May was going to be a good one, especially after the first. But it was rather quiet, almost as if the war had been suspended. From what we heard there was not much ground fighting going on either.

"Müncheberg's small *Staffel* was assigned to us for operations, although they could plan and fly their own missions when not working with us on a larger operation. That is a dream for a fighter leader, to be able to plan and fly your own missions. I would not enjoy such liberties until later in the war. They did well though, as did we all."[58]

June was to see the war increase in momentum. The South African units had established their presence in Egypt in force, organizing in

Alexandria and then farming out into the desert frontier. The British RAF and Australian RAAF had also increased their fighter presence, including introducing newer Spitfires and the Curtiss P-40s, which they called Tomahawks and Kittyhawks, depending upon the variant. These were inferior in their aerodynamic capabilities and speed to the Me-109 or Spitfire, but far superior to the Hurricane and all other Allied types in durability and firepower until the Hurricane II armed with cannons arrived.

Curtiss P-40 K battle damage being repaired (Geoffrey Morley-Mower)

The late model P-40N also had better weapons, with six .50-caliber machine guns and well-made armor plating protecting the pilot and double self-sealing fuel tanks. Only the Me-109E could almost equal the P-40 with its centrally mounted 20mm cannon that fired through the propeller hub, supplemented by the two cowl and two wing-mounted 7.92mm machine guns. Not even the Me-109E model could match the protective quality of the P-40s armor plating and ruggedness, but it was more maneuverable and faster. In addition, the P-40 only had a range of 240 miles, which limited its combat time deep into German territory. Many times, the Germans saw the P-40s they were fighting suddenly run from the fight. They thought that it may have been new pilots afraid to engage, but it was usually due to their limited range.

June was to see the British launch several operations, such as Battleaxe and Tigercub, both small operations with a greater objective in mind. The first major Allied effort was the push forward with a heavy concentration of tanks and infantry through the Halfaya Pass to capture Capuzzo and Musaid, around Sidi Omar, thus extending the Allies' lines of supply and communication. If they held those gains, it would allow their fighter cover to advance closer to their forward elements, thus providing more time over the front to assist the ground forces with air cover and strafing attacks. This new British offensive would draw the men of JG-27 into the fight they were waiting for.

Marseille mounting for a mission (Raymond F. Toliver)

On June 12, the South African Air Force (SAAF) began its first missions in North Africa in support of the ground offensive. The Germans were outnumbered in tanks and men, but the British soon learned to fear their great equalizer, the dreaded multipurpose 88mm flak gun. The subsequent air battles would determine who controlled the airspace over the desert. The British would begin using their bombers and fighters in even greater numbers. This created a target-rich environment for the Germans, and Marseille would find himself in his element, at least for a while.

On the early morning of June 14, the first Hurricanes attacked in a steep diving attack on the airfield at Gazala, home of 3 *Staffel* JG-27, just after dawn. The German fighter base was a known location, hence a prime target for the bombers. If they could hit the airfield and destroy the aircraft of I *Gruppe*, and particularly 3 *Staffel*, in concert with other strikes, then a large part of their aerial problem would be neutralized. After their pass and strafing run, a few bombers followed the fighters, dropping their payloads, followed by a second wave of a few bombers. Then two Germans took off in pursuit, as Ludwig Franzisket explained:

> "In the few minutes between the first and second wave of bombers I jumped out of bed and, in my 109, started off from the southern edge of the field. As I was about to close the canopy, my crew chief shouted to me: 'There, a twin engine Herr *Oberleutnant!*' and pointed to the eastern sky, where a single aircraft was bound directly for the airfield.
>
> "I climbed upward and in a slow turn headed toward the aircraft and came under withering fire by our own flak in the process. Climbing, I reached an altitude of approximately 1,500 meters when I spied a Hurricane heading toward me at about the same altitude. Since my 109 climbed very slowly I had only one chance, and I pointed my nose at the nose of the incoming Hurricane.

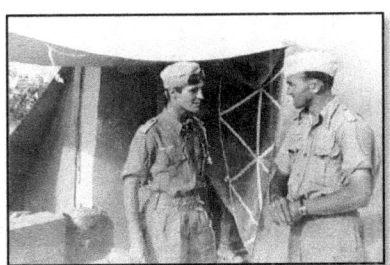
Marseille and Neumann at his tent (Eduard Neumann)

"I shot! My opponent fired also, but his aim was too high, as I could tell from his tracers. We fired continuously until the last moment. Our aircraft touched, but just prior to contact I had placed a bullet in the Hurricane's engine, as its pilot, Captain Kenneth Driver, later confirmed to me. My propeller clipped the right wing of the Hurricane. Driver's propeller, on the other hand, struck the forward edge of my 109's right wing. I saw my burning foe go into a steep dive and observed the pilot bailing out. The Hurricane impacted [a] few hundred meters south of our airfield and Driver landed not far away.

"As I turned back in the direction of Gazala I saw a Martin Maryland a few hundred meters north of the field and at an altitude of 1,500 meters. Although my aircraft was difficult to fly due to the damaged wing, I attacked the bomber. I fired, the Maryland began gradually turning to the right, and I fired again. My second salvo worked its way back from the right engine and along the entire fuselage to the empennage. The engine caught fire and the Maryland went into a flat spin towards earth. A parachute separated from the light bomber, which continued spinning until crashing a couple of hundred meters south of Via Balbia."[59]

Franzisket's first victory of that morning, Captain Kenneth Driver, was taken prisoner, and he asked his victor if his unit could be notified. Franzisket, who had taken over as *Staffelkapitän* from a dysentery-ridden Gerhard Homuth, flew over his opponent's airfield and dropped a handwritten note relating Driver's situation. "It was the right thing to do, and besides, we were not animals."[60] Marseille was not the only delivery man in JG-27.

It is quite possible that Franzisket's humane action toward a vanquished enemy—reminiscent of World War I when airmen battled as gentlemen, treated their enemy wounded and prisoners as special guests, and buried their foes with military honors—more than anything influenced Marseille, who was very impressionable. Despite his reputation as a lone wolf who never developed any close personal friendships until he met Stahlschmidt, he did learn quickly from the veterans and admired the more successful pilots.

Bernhard Woldenga (Bernard Woldenga)

Bernhard Woldenga's impression of Marseille was that, "There are many men you serve with and command. Some are good at their jobs; some are perhaps less so. Very few of them become chronic problems. Marseille was both; very good at his job and a major problem. His misfortune was being misunderstood, and his saving grace was that his success in the air protected him from very severe punishment."[61]

His gallant nature and personal struggle with killing another human being were probably the catalysts that drove him to be the man that he was. More important, under Neumann, Schroer, Franzisket, and Rödel, all of whom were very dismissive of the National Socialists, if not openly anti-Nazi, Marseille learned to be a team player, and so he felt free to express himself without fear of verbal retribution.

That morning of June 14 also saw victories for a few other lucky JG-27 pilots such as Redlich, Schneider, and Hoffmann, although Marseille once again found himself in trouble. He had taken off and engaged a light bomber, only to have no victory and his engine shot dead. He managed to crash land in German-held territory and the fighter was salvaged. Marseille rejoined the unit as 3 *Staffel* departed on a Stuka escort mission over Tobruk, with Marseille and Pöttgen in their *Rotte*.

Not long after the Stukas departed for their dive run, Marseille in a spare fighter spotted a flight of Hurricanes, as did Pöttgen as Marseille issued the warning over the radio headsets. Pöttgen decided to attack a Hurricane but then a second locked onto his tail. Marseille radioed his wingman of the danger as he banked and increased the throttle to lock onto the tail of the second enemy fighter.

On Marseille's order Pöttgen broke right, forcing the enemy fighter to follow. Marseille tightened his turn to narrow the distance, leaving his target only one hun-

Stuka flight (Raymond F. Toliver)

dred feet in front of him. An easy kill. Before Marseille could fire, his Me-109 erupted from bullets striking his canopy and engine cowling. He was losing power, the shattered glass allowed the slipstream to ravage him, and oil began to cover the windscreen as coolant was vaporized and circulated into the cockpit, along with smoke pouring in from the engine. He radioed Franzisket who recalled the event:

"Those two had gone in for an attack, and I saw a Hurricane begin chasing, one, and then another immediately turn onto him," Franzisket explained. "It was Marseille. But then another Hurricane dropped from higher altitude and got on his tail. I called out the threat, but it was too late. There was not much I could do as I was having problems of my own at that time, but I did hear him call to Pöttgen. He had also informed me of the event, and I told him to turn west. That was the last transmission he made that I heard. I knew that with his altitude he should be able to get close to our lines. I also radioed back to Neumann what was going on, as he always monitored the radio during our missions when he was not flying. Pöttgen turned to join him, and then that was all I knew until we landed."[62]

Marseille was in a smoke-filled cockpit, with no power, radio dead, engine burning, coolant streaming along with smoke up into his face from the floor, and limited rudder control. An old hand at a gear-up landing, he knew the drill. Fuel off, ignition off. Finally, he managed to slide across an open area where the Me-109 dug its propeller into the ground, swinging the fighter around, coming to rest over 90 degrees from the direction of the landing. Pöttgen flew overhead and radioed that he was all right, as Marseille leapt out of the smoking fighter, which still contained fuel and ammunition. Once the explo-

Marseille with Hurricane victory (Eduard Neumann)

sion did not occur, he returned to the fighter and collected his maps, papers, and the photo of his sister and himself taken at a carnival in Berlin when they were younger, one of his prized possessions. Not long afterward he was met by German soldiers and was returned to Gazala.

June 15 was a rare day in that Eduard Neumann managed to get in some combat time, shooting down a Hurricane for one of his modest thirteen total victories, while Franzisket, Hoffmann, and *Leutnant* Kothmann each scored a victory. Marseille was bedridden with chills and a fever, but he would be back the next day.[63] June 16 was a busy yet counterproductive day for Marseille. He dropped into an attack on three Hurricanes that were strung out a little too far away from their Lufbery formation, when a piece of flak hit his engine, spewing oil all over the windscreen. Once again Pöttgen was with him, and upon learning that Marseille could not see anything outside his windscreen, talked him down to the airfield. Marseille made a good gear-down landing, although the fighter was his fourth to be damaged, two of them written off in two weeks and his ninth damaged fighter of the war. Marseille was grounded for losing another aircraft with nothing to show for it.

The following day, June 17, the newly promoted *Leutnant's* grounding was terminated, due to operational necessity. On this mission Marseille shot down two Hurricanes over the Halfaya Pass during a Stuka escort for Kurt Kuhlmey. Italian fighters were operating as a close escort as well, but they encountered heavy antiaircraft fire, which blew up a Ju-87 in front and below Marseille and Pöttgen. They saw the two parachutes from the pilot and rear gunner of the Stuka, then Marseille saw and called out *"Indianer."* As he did so, he dropped his nose and screamed into the first Hurricane, firing a short burst. The aircraft fell away burning. Kuhlmey recalled the battle:

"We were bombing vehicles and troops on the ground when we heard the calls over the radio, 'Indians' which meant enemy fighters. Then we saw our fighters not hesitate to engage. Once we pulled out of our dives and banked away, I looked up to my left and there he was, Yellow 14. I always felt good when Marseille and his men were around me, as did my men. They were the best insurance policy."[64]

As Marseille began to pull back up, Pöttgen called out a warning to his right. Marseille, whose reflexes were legendary, immediately took evasive action, banking hard left as the streaks of enemy cannon shells passed close by his right wing and canopy. Had Pöttgen not called out the danger, Marseille would have probably been killed, or captured after being wounded, as they were well within Allied territory. Marseille had forgotten to check his flanks before engaging, a rookie mistake.

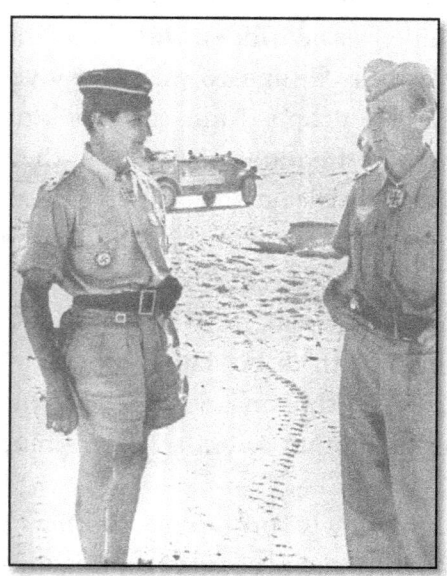

Marseille and Gerhard Homuth (Ludwig Franzisket)

Both pilots tried to out-turn the other. Whoever tightened his turn would win the battle. The Hurricane had a tighter turning radius than a 109, but Marseille knew that whichever of them could withstand the G-forces and not gray out would be the winner. As he pulled the stick into his stomach, wings vertical, the dim haze of gray must have been present. In the age before G-suits his extraordinary abdominal muscles would have been tightened, preventing the blood from draining from his brain and pooling in his legs. Again, enemy shells streaked past him. The Hurricane was closing in and Pöttgen couldn't help: he had his own problems.

Marseille rolled onto his back, cut the power, extended his flaps, and tightened the turn even more. This was considered foolish by many, including Neumann, as it brought the enemy closer for the kill. However, Marseille knew that a rapid drop in airspeed could cause the enemy behind to overshoot, or at least throw off his aim. The lower airspeed allowed him to tighten the turn, despite reaching stall speed, but by extending his flaps he remained level, and he was able to pull the nose up and aim his two 7.92mm machine guns and propeller hub mounted 20mm cannon.

The Hurricane pilot, now overshooting Marseille, either had to match his speed and maneuver or break off the attack and try again. He would not get the chance. Marseille found himself at a perfect 45-degree deflection shot angle. The Hurricane had crossed his predetermined line of fire. Marseille pressed the trigger without any visual contact with his enemy, then pulled away without seeing the Hurricane fly across the path of the shells. The fighter trailed a long plume of smoke as it plummeted into the desert below. The pilot did not escape, and Pöttgen confirmed the kill.

Marseille had just scored his second victory of the day, and his 12th and 13th of the war. Both of his victories were either from either No. 229 and/or No. 274 Squadrons RAF, as the Allies lost 13 aircraft in total while engaged. Other JG-27 men also had success, including *Leutnant* Heinz Schmidt, who shot down four Hurricanes, while *Feldwebel* Mentnich and *Oberfeldwebel* Förster each scored a victory.

The dangers of a high-G blackout cannot be underestimated, and every combat pilot in World War II had some degree of experience with the slow, enveloping dimness that came with higher speeds and more durable aircraft. A high, intense battle could see G-forces of five or six, increasing the weight of a pilot that many times, forcing the blood down the body, making it an almost superhuman event to move the arms and turn the head. Marseille managed to handle these factors while in combat and still score victories. One way he did it besides his physical exercises was that he carried a water bottle in his cockpit to always stay hydrated. The water bottles were how he managed to drop his notes, tied to the bottles and deposited on enemy airfields when he notified them about their pilots.

These exercises were perhaps the main reason, more than his marksmanship, for his great success. A man who could still see, move, and function in high-G maneuvers was a man who just might get home when the fight was over. The man who blacked out and did not recover was dead, as Schroer recalled: "These powerful G forces could cause any pilot to black out for periods of time. It happened to me one time, where I lost consciousness while in a dive, coming to only when my [Me]-109 was climbing again. I was shaking like a leaf."[65]

Hans-Arnold Stahlschmidt after a mission (Ludwig Franzisket)

Schroer's experience was not unique. In perhaps one of the most harrowing experiences of G-force blackout and recovery, 76-victory fighter ace and later Me-262 jet pilot Georg-Peter Eder described an event that still made him sweat in 1984 when he thought about it:

> "People see these films, and they think of the pilots flying combat, but they are not feeling the intense cold, or heat, and they are not understanding just how much strain and stress goes on. Blacking out has probably killed as many pilots as being shot down, we may never know. I can tell you the day I almost died after engaging B-17s. I had a lot of Mustangs on my tail and rolled my Fw-190 into a dive to get away. I do not remember what happened after that. I only remember waking up and my wingman screaming at me over the radio. I had dropped from over five thousand meters to just a couple of hundred meters from the ground. I only awakened after my fighter somehow leveled out, without my knowing about it. This allowed the blood to return to my head. After that I must admit that I was

a little hesitant to dive out of an entanglement later in the war."⁶⁶

Marseille had managed to master the threat of high G-force blackout, and continue the fight, when his enemies were probably unconscious. He had a physical exercise regimen of pushups and inverted sit-ups, tightening his abdominal muscles to assist in high-G turns. Tightening the muscles helped prevent a total blackout, since what pilots call a "gray out" was not completely debilitating. Initially after missions where he experienced this phenomenon, he often climbed out of his fighter, usually suffering none of the ill effects of exhaustion and dizziness that plagued his comrades in high G combat. Much later, the toll of combat and multiple missions began to wear even on him.

Ludwig Franziskez, who became a Doctor of Biology after the war, commented about Marseille's ability to recover rapidly from a very intense mission, often several in a day, with no ill effects: "He was truly remarkable. I, and I am certain everyone else, was exhausted after just one intense sortie, let alone flying two to four missions a day. I can only attribute his great ability to recover to all the alcohol he drank. Thinning the blood probably allowed for a more fluid and flowing vascular condition, easing the heart's ability to pump as he sucked in oxygen from his mask. It was an incredible thing to see anyway."⁶⁷

Marseille still occasionally fell into his bad habits and brought back a shot-up aircraft after jumping into another Lufbery circle, but he had just started his days of multiple victories, which eased the pressure of retribution he would have otherwise experienced had he not been successful. It would take some time,

Marseille pointing to 20mm damage from a Hurricane after he entered a Lufbery Circle (Raymond F. Toliver)

but he would soon master the rare art of entering an enemy defensive formation, scoring multiple victories then managing to get out. It would require great flying skill, every muscle, complete focus, excellent shooting, and a lot of luck. Marseille would become known as the "Lufbery Buster." However, that skill and the acquired nickname would be learned at great cost.

Emil Clade flew with Marseille on occasion and witnessed his skill in defeating the supposedly impenetrable Lufbery formation:

"He had two ways he did this: the first was to climb high and then dive, hitting one or perhaps two aircraft, creating great confusion. Once they scattered, he could then engage them at will. But his wingman would have a lot of work to do. Marseille thought nothing of jumping into a dozen enemies, with only a confused and often inexperienced wingman for protection. He would score victories, but he also brought back a lot of damaged aircraft.

"But then he developed a method that really was unique to him. I really never tried it to any large degree myself, so perhaps I was smarter, or perhaps less confident. Marseille's finally perfected method was to fly above the Lufbery, look for a space between aircraft, slip in, shoot one down, reduce his throttle, almost stalling, and extending his flaps to maintain altitude and tighten his turn, shoot down another, but managing to balance the delicate necessity of throttle control, propeller pitch, flaps, and still maintain his shooting eye. I do not think he ever worried about his six o'clock; I think he became too focused upon each target, taking his chances.

"This was why he was always getting bullets in his aircraft, and sometimes getting shot down. He took crazy chances, as Neumann once told him. I saw Marseille once shoot down four enemy fighters out of about ten in a Lufbery. The enemy fighters, who were supposed to protect their friend in front, were sometimes apparently unable to shoot him down, as they may have been less experienced pilots. Making those tight turns meant some G forces, and few fighter pilots would ever reduce flaps and cut power the way he did. It would be a great way to stall and crash, unless you had a great deal of altitude.

"However, Marseille often did this maneuver at less than two thousand meters, perhaps lower. It took almost two thousand meters of altitude to correct a stall and either restart the engine, or prepare for a powerless landing, as the aircraft would often tumble. He was a magnificent madman I can say."[68]

Gustav Rödel also described the challenges of attacking the Lufbery:

Marseille in the desert (Ludwig Franzisket)

"The only way we could score more than one kill was if one of us entered that 'idiot snake' as we called it, exposing ourselves. The best way to attack was in a *Rotte* or *Schwarm* formation, the *Schwarm* being best with four fighters.

"This allowed one *Rotte* of two men to attack, the leader's wingman to engage the enemy behind his leader's target, and the other two to interrupt the covering position of the two behind the targets being engaged. This would usually break the Lufbery open. Once that happened, it was a real game I can tell you, especially if we were outnumbered. However, remember that any *Rotte* or *Schwarm* attacking must have high covering fighters as a security measure. This prevented the enemy from breaking high and rolling or turning to get in behind you. Very dangerous business."[69]

Marseille's scoring run would come to a temporary end until August 28, when he returned from an enforced leave of absence. He fell victim several times to the "gut fire" of dysentery that always hovered around like an evil specter. A serious outbreak of jaundice also swept through the entire unit. He was additionally visibly suffering the strain of the multiple sorties on the days that they did fly.

Gustav Rödel and Marseille (Raymond F. Toliver)

However, despite Marseille's maladies, the unit would continue the fight while Marseille experienced his month-long scoring drought. It did not help matters that he still brought back damaged aircraft with nothing to show for it. Marseille's failures at scoring probably allowed him the opportunity to evaluate his personal tactics. Sometimes he would fly alone around the airfield, practicing maneuvers, combat stalls, hard low revolution banks and flap down turns. He would train as hard as he fought. Marseille may not have been scoring victories, but he was perfecting his craft.

During this period from May 2 to June 16, where he was bringing back damaged Me-109s but no victories, Marseille knew that he was in trouble for a number of other reasons, some having nothing to do with losing aircraft, but involving his attitude and complaints from superiors regarding his lack of bearing. The avalanche descended upon him not long after he and Stahlschmidt had a chat one day in mid-June, when one of their discussions was interrupted by a summons for Marseille to see the *Kommandeur, Hauptmann* Eduard Neumann.

Marseille went to his C.O.'s circus wagon and knocked on the door. Neumann had never had the opportunity for a one-on-one chat with the young Berliner before and barely knew him. But now, with his own superiors demanding answers regarding lost and damaged aircraft, and reports from army officers who encountered Marseille, something had to be done. Besides, he had not scored a kill in a month.

Franz Kurowski's book records Neumann's words on that hot day in June:

Marselle's chief mechanic Fritz Lettman and Marseille (Ludwig Franziske⁺)

"In the vast majority of our air battles the enemy has a superior numerical advantage, Marseille. It's therefore desired that a pilot would use a double-dose of prudence and thought. Only when you have come to the point to where you aren't frothing at the mouth and seeing only red, to where you not only see your opponent but you've completely mastered your aircraft, then maybe it would be possible to use your tactics and plunge into the enemy's defensive circle and score victories from any position.

"There's no shame whatsoever in going four weeks without getting a kill, Marseille. But it's simply punishable antics, the way you behave, risking yourself as well as valuable material. You'll only be a good pilot with many victories when you understand all this and keep your nerve in check with clear and calm thinking. So, when I consider what you've done on the latest missions then I must say that you've got more luck than sense. What you do is pure craziness! You are basically doing nothing more than cheating death. And as a bonus you're running our planes one after another into the sand.

"You are a good flyer, Marseille, I am aware of that. From your file I know of your numerous daring displays. But this is no air show, we're on the front and the Tommies can shoot. You can't play around with them as you like. I am ordering you to stop these breakneck aerobatics. It's better that you shoot down one enemy in four days than bringing us back a shot up plane every two days that we have a hard time replacing. You'll be in serious trouble if you do just one more of your crazy attacks, understand?"[70]

Marseille sheepishly acknowledged his errors. He knew that he was wrong, and he had been told before, but perhaps not quite with the fatherly approach that the more seasoned Neumann provided. The chat had also been overheard by a few of the other pilots, including Franzisket:

Marseille at the beach (Ludwig Franzisket)

"If I ever had to have a superior officer really angry with me, it would be Neumann. He could be very polite yet very upset at the same time. His gift was that he did not threaten or berate you; he pointed out your problems and explained how to avoid them. This was important with a person like Marseille, whose ego could be very easily bruised, and whose response was to rebel. Schroer had already told me about flight school and his silly ways there. Neumann would have none of it, not from any of us. The thing about Marseille was that he did not stop doing his crazy one-man air show, he just got so good at it, gaining victories, that Neumann let him continue on. Marseille later found his perfect method, and it only worked for him."⁷¹

Marseille was always marked for punishment, which he most often brought upon himself. Every commanding officer since flight school tolerated him to a certain point and then washed their hands of him. Neumann had served with Herbert Ihlefeld, Adolf Galland, and Gustav Rödel in Spain, and he also knew Macky Steinhoff very well. Both Ihlefeld and Steinhoff were more than willing to give the dirt on the problem child now under Neumann's command. Yet Neumann saw something special in him. Neumann the pragmatist always used punishment as a measured, last resort: "I didn't allow non-stop disciplinary action against him, because I was certain that once I had Marseille's trust and attention, I could mold him and do something with him."⁷²

During the period of increasing activity for the unit, and his own personal drought, Marseille was bonding ever closer to his part-time wingman Stahlschmidt. "Those two were definitely bound at the hip," Schroer commented. "You could not see one without the other close by, even in the air. The joke was that when Stahlschmidt flew, Marseille was also in the cockpit."⁷³

Marseille told his best friend of his philosophy of air combat: "Our aircraft are the basic elements, Stahlschmidt, which have got to be mastered. You've got to be able to shoot from any position. From left or right turns, out of a roll, on your back, whenever. Only this way can you develop your own particular tactics. Attack tactics, which the enemy simply cannot anticipate during the course of the battle, a series of unpredictable movements and actions, never the same, always stemming from the situation at hand. Only then can you plunge into the middle of an enemy swarm and blow it from the sky."[74]

Marseille with his Me-109E in Libya (Ludwig Franzisket)

Marseille had taken Neumann's discussion to heart, and he was also spoken to by the others in the unit who saw his potential yet needed him to be a team player. But Neumann saw that Marseille needed a break, and his illness needed to be addressed, so he authorized Marseille to go on home leave for a couple of months starting on June 18, 1941.

"Marseille had been very ill, stomach issues which we all had, and all of us lost a lot of weight being in the desert," Franzisket noted. "The food was terrible, and the heat made you sweat incredibly, but you could not see the sweat, it was so hot and dry it evaporated as it rose on your skin. You could say that the desert was a great weight loss program. But Marseille, who was already slight, perhaps weighing 150 pounds on a good day, had dropped to probably around 110 pounds. He looked yellow and much older than when he arrived, and several of us were very concerned about him.

"Our resident physician suggested that he be sent home, out of the heat, where he could rest and gain some weight. He also had raging fevers and chills, which was probably from malaria, which some of us got, but without a proper medical facility around, and with Derna being the closest, who knows? He was on bed rest for a few days for that. I was lucky. I know that he lost almost a third of his weight in two weeks or less, because his parachute harness had to be cinched in to make up for the loss of weight. His uniform just hung off of him. He was not a strong person to begin with, and in those days, you had to really throw some muscle around to fly the 109s. Putting him on leave was a good idea. In fact, when he came back, it was a different Marseille altogether."[75]

The one thing that his comrades noticed was his bragging about his female conquests. It was not to try to impress; rather that he was just very open about parts of his life (minus intimate details of course), to illustrate that, although he looked like a child, he was as much a man as anyone in the unit. Marseille was not idly boasting. Letters from many women, some quite famous, came to him. Many were perfumed. He was the idol of many whether in the air or not. Ludwig Franzisket came to know and respect Marseille after a rather tenuous first meeting:

Swedish actress Zarah Leander, one of Marseille's love interests (Hedy Lamarr)

"Marseille was the type who would have constantly taken a beating in school if he hadn't fought against it with everything he had. He was one of those rare people; always having to prove things the hard way. He was also like this in *Jagdgeschwader* 27. That he was able to succeed in the end says quite a bit about his personality, which to a certain extent consumed him."[76]

Franzisket had other additional observations:

Marseille's love interest singer Nilla Pizzi (Hedy Lamarr)

"He was a very competitive person in everything he did, whether it was combat, chess or card games. His loner mentality that he arrived with was not really due to his not liking or working with people. He really loved people; he was friendly and humorous, and he would have been a great social worker. His problem was that in having to prove himself, he took stupid risks, which was why Neumann wanted a word with him. This was also the reason so many of his previous leaders got rid of him. They just did not understand him; they simply saw a rogue pilot doing his own thing, risking others in the process.

"I think it was the competition, for him to be the best at something, whether chasing girls or scoring victories that drove him to be an individual. He wanted to be noticed, because his whole life he had felt like a failure. I think that this was due to his family situation, where I understood he had a great relationship with his mother and sister, but that he and his father had a very strange relationship. The whole time I knew him he would sometimes speak of his family. He never mentioned his father around me once."[77]

Marseille's greatest personal detriment and what garnered him unwanted attention was always his complete lack of military bearing and discipline. This set him apart from even the most anti-Nazi pilots in the unit, who themselves never hid their contempt for the national leadership and the polemic. At formations, when called to attention, Marseille stood as if he were at the beach, oblivious to the required posture. He once buzzed a ground convoy led by then *Generalmajor* Erwin Rommel, only clearing the general's halftrack by perhaps twenty feet. His aide, *Oberst* Fritz Bayerlein was right beside him, and he wanted the pilot court martialed. Rommel identified the pilot immediately as Marseille and told Bayerlein not to worry about it; "It's just Marseille Fritz, let it go."[78] Everyone who knew Marseille agreed that he didn't seem to take anything too seriously, and he was often the mastermind of some of the most childish pranks, as Emil Clade explained:

"There I was, assigned a new aircraft in 5./JG-27 and I was at the base. I had just finished my breakfast and walked towards my new 109F, when I looked up in the dim morning light. Someone was in my plane! I jumped up on the wing and looked in. It was a damned scarecrow, made from desert grass and old rags, complete with arms, legs, and a head made from a small melon with a flying helmet on it. The sign around the neck said *'Mein neues Rottenflieger'* (My new wingman). My anger turned to laughter when I saw that it was signed 'Jochen.' That was just the way he was. At some point everyone fell victim to him."[79]

The men around him always carefully checked their shoes and boots before putting them on, never knowing if the "Bohemian Bandit" had struck. Just going to the outhouse was fraught with danger, should one fail to locate a carefully placed trip wire that would drop foul-smelling liquids on those who entered. Even the highest brass were subject to attack. During one of *Generalleutnant* Galland's inspection tours of North African units, Marseille placed a special notice on an outhouse: "Reserved for the General of the Fighters." Another sign read:

Generalmajor Erwin Rommel arrives to greet Marseille. (Raymond F. Toliver)

"General of the Fighters Was Here." Marseille's lack of conformity was almost as legendary as his juvenile pranks, flying skill, and victory count.

One of the most embarrassing moments for anyone in JG-27 befell Werner Schroer, as he stated: "Jochen had become famous, and copies of *Der Adler* and *Signal* magazines were delivered in great numbers. You could not go anywhere without seeing his face on the cover. Well, such was the case when I went to the outhouse. I dropped my trousers, sat down, then grabbed one of the magazines used for such an event.

"Suddenly I heard this creaking noise, and then all four walls of the outhouse fell away, the roof folded back exposing me to God and everyone, sitting on the toilet. Everyone was standing around laughing like hell. I had never been so embarrassed in my life, and as I saw them laugh, what was I holding? A magazine with Jochen's face smiling back at me. How ironic."[80]

Ludwig Franzisket recalled that event, and he added another bit of humorous information on Schroer's misfortune:

"I felt sorry for Werner having been embarrassed like that. I can tell you that every man double checked to see if a rope was tied to any side of the outhouse after that. Jochen was told not to do that again, and he just smiled. But then he decided that he would do the same trick on Galland when he arrived, so he prepared the outhouse the same way he did for Werner.

"I saw him with the rope winding around behind the tent. I asked him who he was going to get next. Just then, the general entered the outhouse, and I said; 'No' not the general!' Marseille said 'yes' and before he could pull the rope I tackled him, while one of the mechanics took the rope away. I told him he was beyond insane to even think about it. He got up brushed himself off and said, "Maybe you are right. He could block my promotion.' I could not believe this guy."[81]

Adolf Galland was coming on another scheduled visit to meet the men of the various fighter units in North Africa, and he wanted to see Marseille:

> "I met Marseille for the second time in the desert during my first visit to the North African Front. I arrived in a Ju-52 and had to go to the latrine. Marseille and I met, and we spoke, and I also met others in the unit. I congratulated him on the award of the Swords as he was going to Berlin to receive them. I was the person as General of the Fighters who recommended him to Göring for the Diamonds award, after Neumann sent me the unit report, and after seventeen victories in a single day in Libya [author's note: It was actually over Egypt when that occurred].

General der Jagdflieger Adolf Galland with Major Eduard Neumann during one of his visits to JG-27 (Adolf Galland)

> "I found him very boyish and free spirited, but not completely immature, do not get me wrong, but he really marched to his own drum. He never even mastered the salute properly, but he was a very gifted pilot. I have to admit, he was not shy at all about his lifestyle. He played his banned American jazz music so loudly I was sure the British could hear it in Egypt. Marseille would have never had a great career in the *Luftwaffe*, or rose to great rank, but he could have cared less. He just

wanted to fly, and he looked at the war as a great sporting event.

"He also had a great hunting instinct, but this was tempered by a great sense of chivalry. He was known to have notified the British that one of their pilots was down and wounded, after he scored the kill. He did not believe that a man should die on the ground if he survived combat. That was the kind of man he was, and Neumann told me about that event during my visit. I read the entire after-action report about the whole affair. Göring even mentioned to me how gallant he must be to do such a thing, and then he banned anyone from doing it again."[82]

Marseille at the tail of his fighter (Raymond F. Toliver)

One example of his lack of military bearing was his personal appearance. One of the enlisted men served as the barber at that time. After looking at a few of his men, Neumann told him to make sure that after he returned from the mission, Marseille in particular was to get another haircut, since his hair was far too long. The barber, a new man in the unit, apologetically asked his commander who Marseille was. He had never given him a haircut since he had arrived in Africa almost two months prior. Neumann was not that surprised. (Marseille had never even had to shave until he reached Libya, and then only once or twice per week; Steinhoff said he looked like a 15-year-old, Schroer said a 12-year-old).

Marseille's misfortunes were just starting. *Oberleutnant* Gerhard Homuth's return from medical leave saw him resume his responsibilities as *Staffelkapitän*. Franzisket had been the acting leader of the *Staffel* and was far more tolerant and less rigid than Homuth, who was the consummate professional officer, right down to his tailored uniform and spit-shined shoes despite the desert conditions. Homuth was the exact opposite of Marseille, and for the rising Star of Africa that only meant trouble. For Neumann and Woldenga, it was a test of wills.

CHAPTER 5

Maturation and Success

Marseille had about three victories per mission on average. He could have been the top ace above Hartmann, if he had lived.
Hannes Trautloft

On June 1, while home on leave, Homuth received his Knight's Cross from *Reichsmarschall* Hermann Göring. He also had the opportunity to meet an old friend, Herbert Ihlefeld, with whom he had much in common, and in particular a certain pilot. Ihlefeld told Homuth all of the horror stories about Marseille that at first were simply believed to be careless gossip. Ihlefeld then said that he should contact Steinhoff in JG-52, who had his own stories about Marseille, but Homuth already knew them all. By the time he boarded the Ju-52 to return to Africa, Gerhard Homuth had a firm picture in his mind of his new subordinate, a man he barely knew when he left, but came to know better as he read reports and listened to others.

Upon his return to the unit, Homuth passed his time reading all the unit after-action reports, mission debriefs, and other data since his absence. One name kept coming up time and again: Hans-Joachim Marseille. The following morning, Franzisket was formally relieved of his duties and returned to being the *Staffel* executive officer. After Marseille returned from home leave on August 25, Homuth called Marseille into his tent for a chat, the specific details of which are unknown. However, Marseille was a much more dejected man leaving that tent than when he went in.

Marseille did confide in a couple of his friends that he thought that Homuth believed he was a bad example to others, good flier or not, and that he was waiting for the chance to throw him out of the unit. Marseille apparently felt persecuted once again, which he always called "the Huguenot curse," referring to the seventeenth-century persecutions of Protestants by the Catholics in France, forcing most to flee to neighboring countries. Marseille's ancestors had fled to the Lutheran region of Germany at that time.

However, Homuth did speak with Franzisket about Marseille after the meeting.

Marseille, Schroer and men at an Italian magic show (Raymond F. Toliver)

"Gerhard came to me, as we were friends," Franzisket recalled, "and told me that he was really hard on him [Marseille]. I told him that he probably needed it, and I also told him of the chat Marseille had just had with Neumann a few days before. Homuth admitted that he may have been a little harder on him than necessary, but that it was for his own good. Homuth saw the gifted pilot that Marseille was, but, like others before him, he also knew that a loner, a cowboy, was not good for the unit. He had to fly and fight as part of a team or be removed. Homuth said that he would rather see him in the infantry and alive, than see him die, or worse, get another pilot killed by doing something stupid.

"I understood where he was coming from, but I also told him that Marseille had improved in many ways. He just said; 'Well then I guess that we shall see in time.' Then I was informed of the long meeting he had with Ihlefeld, and the stories that were told, some coming from Steinhoff. We all knew Schroer, who knew Marseille from flight school, so we had also heard those stories. It all made perfect sense. I was shocked, and I laughed, and I was amazed at what Marseille had managed to get away with. 'That's what you get when you have a clown whose father is a general,' Homuth told me, and this information I did not know."[83]

Marseille was slowly developing friendships, such as his close bonds with Stahlschmidt, Günther Steinhausen and Reiner Pöttgen. Eventually everyone who came to know Marseille warmed up to him, clown or not, even the acerbic Homuth. "Marseille could only turn out to be one thing: either a disciplinary problem or a great pilot," Neumann stated. "At the beginning his stubbornness and lack of discipline kept his comrades away from him. Once they recognized his sincerity and camaraderie, his talent and abilities as a fighter, and saw the victories he was racking up, they too became convinced of his leadership abilities and were drawn by his magnetic charm. In the end they looked up to him like no other fighter pilot."[84] What was developing would become known as the "Marseille Magic."

Gunther Steinhausen (Ludwig Franzisket)

Marseille was back, but how he would perform was anyone's guess. On August 26, 1941, JG-27 took off on a mission and *Unteroffizier* Günther Steinhausen scored a victory over a Tomahawk, as Marseille (who had returned that day) again went without any success. Steinhausen's victim may have been British ace Sergeant Maurice Hards (and ace himself with seven destroyed, two probable and four damaged aircraft), who crash landed and was wounded in the leg on the Mersa to Matruh-Sidi Barrani road. JG-27 celebrated Steinhausen's victory upon his return. Marseille spent many hours lying in his tent, listening to his music, smoking his French cigarettes, sipping brandy, cognac, or wine, deep in his own thoughts after this mission where he still could not score a kill.

On August 28, Marseille's *Schwarm* engaged twelve Hurricanes of No. 1 Squadron SAAF while on an escort mission over Tobruk. Marseille and his *Staffel* were at higher altitude, always the preferred vantage point, when they saw the enemy fighters. Once spotted at a disadvantage, the Hurricanes formed into the protective Lufbery.

On this mission Marseille took the dive, climb, shoot, and roll-climb away option. When he saw that his rounds had scored lethal impacts, he scattered the rest of the Hurricanes, breaking up the defensive formation then pulled away. His victory was over Lieutenant V. F. Williams, who managed to evade landing or parachuting into enemy territory by crashing into the sea, suffering serious injuries, where he was later rescued. Marseille managed to bring his fighter back undamaged and was credited with his fourteenth victory. His confidence was growing.

The next day, August 29, the Germans again engaged, and Werner Schroer almost killed Flight Lieutenant Clive Caldwell of No. 250 Squadron RAF, who, although badly wounded, managed to shoot down Schroer's wingman. He also damaged Schroer's Me-109E, forcing Schroer to break off and crash land. Caldwell himself would be out of action until November, but he would collect a lot of scalps from JG-27 and earn the nickname "Killer Caldwell" and the Australian would become the subject of great moral debate among both the Germans and his own pilots for killing Germans under their parachutes. This was Schroer's account of the combat:

> "I recognized the markings on the Kittyhawk, I was not sure if it was the same pilot who killed our German airman under parachute, but that did not matter. We engaged in a fight that lasted about four minutes, as I shot one down, but the other

pilot [Caldwell] shot down my wingman and hit me after I hit him. I was losing oil pressure and the temperature was rising, but I saw the slight whisp of what I thought was glycol streaming from the Kittyhawk, so I knew he would be going down soon. I knew I hit him very good with the cannon, I could see the metal around the cockpit peel away, and rounds enter the cockpit."[85]

Damaged Hurricanes being salvaged (Geoffrey Morley-Mower)

In September, *Hauptmann* Wolfgang Lippert arrived in Libya with his II./JG-27, which included such outstanding pilots as *Oberleutnant* Gustav Rödel, now *Staffelkapitän* of 4./JG-27, and his often assigned wingman *Oberfeldwebel* Otto Schulz. This added punch and restructuring assisted the Germans immensely.

On September 9, Marseille flew with his impromptu wingman, *Leutnant* Hoffmann on a reconnaissance patrol near the Bay of Sollum, where they located a convoy, which they reported back. They jumped two enemy fighters, and Marseille scored one kill, Hoffmann the other. Later that day, in another mission, I./JG-27 sent up twelve Me-109s. They encountered seven Hurricanes from No. 33 Squadron RAF, who were flying cover for a ground convoy against potential Stuka attacks over Bardia. Marseille scored another kill to make two that day, his 15th and 16th victories to date.

Marseille was beginning to perfect his craft, and the days of multiple victories were to soon become legend. For his first kill he only used 22 cannon rounds, in the second fight about the same. Eventually he would be averaging 15 rounds per kill, three cannon and twelve machine gun rounds, and average three victories per mission during enemy engagements.

Erbo Graf von Kaganeck (Raymond F. Toliver)

September 11 saw 1 *Staffel* I./JG-27 with twelve fighters and six Italian G-50s engage twenty-four Marylands from No. 24 Squadron SAAF and their accompanying escort fighters. Not long afterward 2 *Staffel* had to take off and engage the incoming bombers. The result was one claimed kill each for Homuth (Maryland), Redlich (P-40), Steinhausen (P-40), Hoffmann (Maryland), Schroer (Hurricane), and *Feldwebel* Oswald (Hurricane). Marseille claimed a bomber, but without a witness, and no ground confirmation being over enemy territory, this was not confirmed in the unit victory record.

It was at this point that each *Staffel* began to rotate back to Germany and collect their new Me-109F models that most pilots believed was the purest, most true version of the 109 series. Every pilot loved it, with a far more powerful Daimler-Benz DB 601N engine, yet it maintained the nose cannon available in both 15mm and 20mm versions and two 7.92 mm machine guns in the cowling. *Oberleutnant* Gustav Rödel and his 4./JG-27 were the first to arrive with their thirteen new aircraft.

By September 30, the entire II *Gruppe* of JG-27 would be in Libya, under their *Gruppenkommandeur*, Knight's Cross recipient *Hauptmann* Wolfgang Lippert. They had been stationed on the Eastern Front, and they brought their Me-109F-4 models, as well as a lot of combat experience and 141 victories for the *Gruppe*. They also brought their two mascots, two lions named Caesar and Simba, which many thought would prove interesting, since Neumann already had a pet bear named "Bobbi." The rest of the Germans would have to wait to get the F models.

Lippert had scored four victories in Spain with the Condor Legion from where he knew Neumann, Rödel, and Galland. He had added another 21 victories during the Battle of Britain, flying with Neumann and Galland in JG-27 since the war began, and Galland transferred to JG-26. They had a long history together.

On September 13, I./JG-27 and the other *Gruppen* flew a multiple layered mission with their Italian allies, and they engaged Hurricanes over Sofafi from No. 33 Squadron RAF, which was on an escort mission for Marylands from No. 24 Squadron SAAF. Marseille shot down a Sergeant Leslie Blair Nourse in Hurricane I (W9298) of No. 33 Squadron, who safely bailed out but was slightly wounded.[86] The Allied forces lost three Hurricanes to the Germans, and Marseille had his seventeenth victory.

Curtiss P-40 Warhawk (Arthur Fiedler)

While 4./JG-27 was collecting their new aircraft, the rest of JG-27 continued fighting the war. The morning mission of September 14, 1941 brought Marseille nothing, but the late afternoon sortie saw him score his eighteenth victory, another Hurricane over Bardia, a lone pilot from No. 451 Squadron RAAF. This was the victory over Flight Lieutenant Patrick Byers, who had taken off on a reconnaissance mission and never returned, that prompted Marseille's first chivalrous flight two days later to report his condition (discussed in Chapter 1).

Two weeks later, after Byers died, he again flew to the enemy airfield, dropping the condolence message.

Marseille began what would be his trademark mission on September 24. The Germans from I./JG-27 were on a late-after- noon *freie jagd* (free hunt) when they encountered 18 enemy fighters, nine Hurricanes from No. 1 Squadron SAAF and nine from No. 112 Squadron RAF, which were coming back from an anti-shipping escort mission. A Maryland bomber from No. 203 Squadron RAF was also involved.

Two Allied pilots, Flight Lieutenant John Henry William Saunders and Sergeant Hiller, both of No. 3 Squadron RAAF, were on a separate patrol. They spotted several Ju-88 medium bombers, and Saunders shot one down, but was in turn shot down by *Oberleutnant* Homuth. He managed to bail out with a minor injury. The other Allied units were immediately engaged. Sergeant Hiller would survive this mission but would be shot down later on November 26, 1941, and bailed out of his burning Tomahawk (AM413) with severe head burns. His aircraft crashed near Sollum, Tobruk, Libya where he was taken prisoner and hospitalized, but he died of his wounds on December 2, 1941.

Marseille was flying with another impromptu wingman, *Oberfähnrich* Karl Kugelbaur, and he once again saw the enemy first, a Martin Maryland twin-engine medium bomber and fighters. Before they could even consider a Lufbery formation he gave full throttle and attacked the Maryland, diving in and setting it on fire for his 19th victory. The rest of the fighters hastily collected together into their protective Lufbery, so the bomber kill was an uncontested event. A dozen Hurricanes scrambled for the safety of the formation, but one was lagging.

Marseille dived on the last Hurricane, and it fell away in flames after he fired, burning and falling as it slashed through the loose staggered formation, becoming Marseille's 20th kill. The remaining aircraft finally formed their Lufbery, but as Marseille began his planning, a Hurricane caught Kugelbaur by surprise. Marseille turned around and cleared his tail, shooting down the Hurricane for kill number 21.

Marseille climbed for more altitude followed by Kugelbaur. He was ready to prove his theory. Marseille inverted his fighter and chose his entry point, then pulled the stick back, dropping the nose to gain speed. He sped into the Lufbery, picked a target, fired and pulled up without waiting to see what happened then chandelled away, and returned to altitude, knowing that the enemy below could not reach him. Kill number 22. The Lufbery was still intact.

Marseille dived in again, inverted, then rolled out and fired. His next target exploded. He then pulled out of the dive after scoring the victory and nosed upward again, gaining altitude, a textbook maneuver, and then banked around to convert that altitude into another speed dive. Kill number 23 dropped from the sky. He then flipped over and again started his dive and closed on another Hurricane that went down rapidly after he fired.

Franzisket saw the action: "It was really incredible flying. The speed with which he maneuvered and returned into the enemy after shooting aircraft was quite remarkable. I saw two of his victories, and the one enemy pilot was blown out of his

Pilots from No. 451 Squadron RAAF November 1941. Identified pilots are Harry Rowlands (top row far right), Ray Hudson (seated second from left), Paddy Hutley (seated fourth from left), Squadron Leader R.D. "Wizard" Willams (seated sixth from left), Geoffrey-Morley-mower (seated seventh from left), Patrick Byers is believed to be seated far left bottom row.

aircraft, and I banked over to see if there was a parachute. I never saw one. It appeared that the British pilots were almost frozen in their idiot snake, and it took losing at least three aircraft from their formation before they realized that they were in a bad position."[87]

JG-27 claimed six victories in this engagement, five of them for Marseille. No. 1 Squadron SAAF lost three fighters, including Captain C. A. van Vliet and 2nd Lieutenant J. Mac Robert, both uninjured, while 1st Lieutenant B. E. Dodd was reported as missing in action. No. 112 Squadron RAF lost Pilot Officer D. F. "Jerry" Westenra from New Zealand, who was shot down, but bailed out without injury.

Marseille returned triumphant and somewhat defiant. The tactics that he had devised had worked. He had violated most of the textbook rules but had one bomber and four fighter victories to show for it. On October 12, the men of I./JG-27 once again made an impact. The Allied pilots that day were at a great disadvantage as JG-27 was operating at full strength when they encountered both No. 2 Squadron SAAF and No. 3 Squadron RAAF. Marseille once again struck over Bir Sheferzan, shooting down two P-40s for his 24th and 25th victories.

Marseille called out the enemy aircraft, since as usual he was the first to see them, and again he was the first to start the attack. He started to dive into the enemy, choosing a target. However, this time Marseille was not alone. Two P-40s from No. 3 Squadron RAAF up top had followed him in his dive and were perhaps 500 meters behind him, soon to be well within killing range. What he was thinking at that point he never admitted, but what he did soon became a standard method of success and survival. Neumann called it luck. All agreed it was very effective.

Rather than pull up again into a climbing escape, he cut power to the engine, extended his flaps and nearly stalled. He raised his nose and fired as the two P-40s in pursuit overflew him, passing overhead at over 200 miles per hour faster than his Me-109, which was slowing down rapidly. One P-40 flew through his projectiles after passing just over his canopy, sending Flying Officer H. G. "Robbie" Roberts out of control. As the other P-40 tried to climb and turn away, Marseille gave full power, extended his flaps, turned tighter than his enemy, nose pointed skyward, and gave almost three hundred feet of lead when he fired.

Emil Clade recalled the event: "Marseille was being chased and someone called out the two Kittyhawks. Jochen said that he knew they were there. The first passed over him and he fired, and that was when I rolled over to get on the tail of the other one. But then my target pulled a hard turn, and I thought I would have him. Jochen then pulled tighter and fired. I thought he was crazy firing so far ahead of the Kittyhawk, but that fighter flew right into his cannon and machine gun rounds. It was a fantastic shot really."[88]

Perhaps three seconds passed while the projectiles headed seemingly into open space. The second pilot, Flight Sergeant Derek Scott, probably never knew what hit him. The British fighter started to break apart at the tail section including the rudder,

Sgt. R.G. Goldberg and his Hurricane of No. 451 Squadron (Geoffrey Morley-Mower)

and it smoked but did not burn as it fell to earth. These were Marseille's twenty-fourth and twenty-fifth victories. He had not simply rewritten the book on dog fighting; he had thrown the book away. Roberts survived any serious injury and made a forced landing inside Allied lines, and his aircraft was later repaired. Scott was also lucky and through excellent airmanship successfully crash-landed his badly damaged fighter back at his base. The fighter was a complete write-off.

As Marseille rolled away, he called out the kills, which were noted by his wingman Kugelbaur. Looking around, he again went in pursuit of more fighters. He caught another P-40 banking to turn inside him, a maneuver it was well capable of doing given the distance, but Marseille completed the turn in the opposite direction first. His cannon fired, and then jammed, but the remaining rounds from his machine guns found their mark. The rugged P-40 was only damaged and continued on its way. Marseille would have to wait for victory number 26.

Marseille leaving Neumann's wagon (Eduard Neumann)

After this mission, Marseille and I./JG-27 did not have any additional activity of note for the rest of the month of October. "His illness had also returned, and he was in bed for a few days at a time," according to Franzisket, who also suffered occasionally from bouts of dysentery.[89] The unit was preparing to receive new fighters and a resupply of ammunition and fuel.

The men of I and II./JG-27 rotated out of and back into Africa by *Staffel*. While in Germany, they were introduced to the new F model of their fighter. The men of the desert eagerly awaited their turn to get their hands on this fighter. Marseille also found plenty of time to continue his wayward ways, where the alcohol was as plentiful as the girls. This paid vacation gave him all the freedom he could have wanted, with the enjoyment of flying a new aircraft without the stress of combat. This gave I *Gruppe* a much-needed break and allowed the pilots to rest from almost constant operations. The rest and refit were welcomed, as was the knowledge of soon obtaining the new aircraft. Werner Schroer attested:

"We were low on parts, oil, fuel and even glycol for the cooling systems. Food was in short supply, drinking water was hard to get, and we had to boil what there was to make certain it was safe. The supply chain was in bad shape. The British had Hurricane IIs and new Spitfires, as well as a lot of the older American made P-40s, so we were not always outclassed, but we were also often outnumbered. Our aircraft were worn out, as were the men. Our skill and our tactics were all that kept us alive, but this arena was not for the faint of heart. The enemy was good, really good."[90]

However, in contrast to I *Gruppe,* II./JG-27 had been busy since October 3, where *Unteroffizier* Reuter of 5 *Staffel* shot down a Sergeant Lowty in his Hurricane; Lowty bailed out safely. A Lieutenant Lacey shot down a Me-109, while *Leutnant* Schlacht and *Oberleutnant* Rödel of 4 *Staffel* each scored a Hurricane. October saw II./JG-27 scoring steadily, with almost everyone adding white kill bars to their rudders. Despite a bombing raid on their airfield on October 17, II *Gruppe* maintained readiness.

November saw a few important events, such as Marseille being presented his *Ehrenpokal*, or silver Honor Cup, on November 3, citing his victories to date, a tradition dating back to World War I. This presentation could only be authorized by Göring himself, and from this point forward the *Reichsmarschall* would follow Marseille's every after-action report, since he kept files on rising stars. Worth noting, *Generalleutnant* Hans Baur, a World War I ace with nine victories and Adolf Hitler's personal pilot was often in Göring's company, when he discussed the pilots he followed:

"We were all sitting in the large living room in the Berghof, there was Hitler, myself, Bormann and others, and of course Göring. He was discussing some of the activities in Russia and Africa, and the name Marseille came up. I had not heard of him until that time and thought nothing of it. Then Göring began talking about his tactics as related in the reports, and I then took an interest. This Marseille seemed like a real loose cannon but one that was going to become famous, and little did I know that I would spend time with him later. I have to say that I was not disappointed."[91]

Upon returning to the theater of war, I./JG-27 went into the fight full fury, with several of its members making their presence known. One kill, a P-40, was claimed on November 12 and later *Staffelkapitän* Wolfgang Redlich scored seven of the *Gruppe's* 14 victories during the period of November 22–23, 1941. However, the *Staffel* did not go unscathed, as two of its own pilots were shot down and captured.

Most important, starting on November 17, a once-in-a-lifetime event began that would almost destroy JG-27 without a shot being fired. The Bedouin speak of a rare, legendary storm, known both as the "Wrath of Allah," when the waters come down in such a torrent it destroys everything in its path, and as the "Gift of Allah," since it provides life-giving water for people and allows crops to grow. Perhaps the interpretation depended upon one's perspective. For the Germans "Wrath" would be deemed more appropriate. But then again, the Allies were also in the same situation.

The storm originated in the deep Sahara Desert farther south. When the winds blow to the west across the Atlantic Ocean, and the conditions are right, this is where northern hemispheric hurricanes originate. However, once in a rare while those hot desert winds drive north and then stall due to a cold front. This was what the North African region was experiencing in 1941.

When the sky as far as the horizon turned dark gray, blue, and black, and the wind picked up, the locals knew to go for high ground, to get shelter from the wind and coming rain even though the last time this event occurred was six decades earlier, in the 19th century. The black sky gave way to incredible lightning shows, bolts that spanned hundreds of miles, the sound of their striking the earth rumbling like heavy artillery.

The men could feel the electricity in the air. By the next day the rain had started steadily, and then came down with such force tents were collapsed. Neumann and the other *Kommandeure* ordered drainage trenches to be dug to channel the water away from aircraft and sensitive areas. Self-preservation became the standing order. Officers dug with enlisted men, captains with privates, side by side. Moats appeared all over as the trenches were dug away from the camps.

Although not a perfect solution, it did later help save much of the equipment. Neumann and the other leaders also gave the order to remove all vulnerable equipment to high ground and for all tents to be moved and secured with long stakes. The dry wadis were in danger of flash floods. It was not long before the telephone land lines and radios relayed warnings all along the front.

Just after midnight the wind was near hurricane force, ripping anything not nailed down into the air. The aircraft had been covered by tarps that were deeply anchored into the ground, but almost nothing else would survive. Within three hours small rivers were formed and growing in depth, width, and speed. 3 *Staffel* was hit hard as the water rushed through, carrying everything away. Those who could do so gathered on the tops of small hills, normally 12 to 20 feet above the desert. They were now only half as high thanks to the rushing water. The rain reduced visibility to only a few feet and lasted

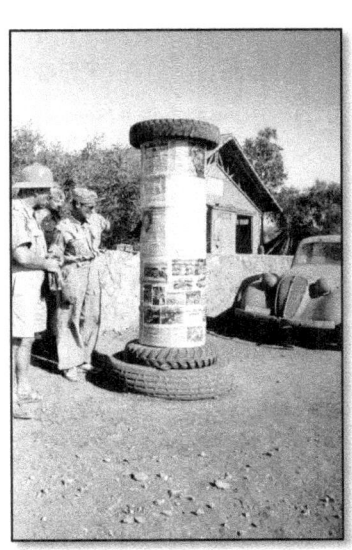

Marseille the men reading a news post in Benghazi, near the apartment he rented for his free time. (Ludwig Franzisket)

for over three hours before slowing to a drizzle. Then the real flood began.

Ironically, at the same time, the British had decided to attack, using the weather as a screen from aerial observation, since single engine aircraft would not fly in those conditions. Over 1,000 tanks, 1,000 aircraft (on standby), supportive artillery, and 1,000,000 infantry headed west. The first enemy the British engaged were the Italians, who to their credit fought gallantly, but could not hold. German forces responded: the 15th and 21st Panzer Divisions managed to halt the advance, and Rommel continued to battle the British through the end of the month, with sporadic small battles continuing through December. The weather and terrain played a major role in slowing down the British advance, as well as the German response.

The floods were something that the men would never forget. Schroer recalled the event with some levity: "Here we were, in the desert, where water was more precious than fuel, or gold: we never really had enough. We rarely had a shower, which was only possible when water was available. Suddenly, within a matter of hours, the ground you were standing on was under two feet of fast-moving water. Vehicles were being carried away, tents were gone, the bear disappeared, I heard. Someone said that Neumann's circus wagon had become an ark, floating on the water with the rescued bear, a lion and some refugees inside.

"The aircraft were safe as long as the water did not rise above two meters, or we would have ruined engines and the electrics would be shot. The generators we used were destroyed for the most part, but I think one was saved when a few of the men placed it in the back of a truck. That kept it above the water, but then the truck was washed away with the generator, so there you go."[92]

I./JG-27 fared better than the rest of the *Geschwader*, simply because they were already on higher ground, and Neumann wasted no time getting things prepared. They did, however, lose their water wagon. Derna had also been hit hard. II./JG-27 was established on lower terrain, requiring the equipment to be taken to higher ground a few miles away. Despite their best efforts, the tops of some tents were under water. As a result, neither unit had an airstrip capable of operations. The sand, normally baked hard, had become a quagmire. The only saving grace was that the coming sun would help dry the ground out in a few days. Parts of the airfield at I./JG-27 did dry out enough by later that afternoon to allow limited takeoffs and landings if required. The dry portion was marked with stakes and flags as a flight line perimeter guide, so that no one would stray and try landing or taking off in a bog.

By November 19 more of the airstrip was dry enough to use, and the ground gradually hardened once again in patches. 1 *Staffel* of I./JG-27 was almost fully operational by November 21, although the conditions may have explained the death of *Gefreiter* Paskowski, who died when his Me-109 careened on takeoff after digging a wheel in a soft spot and collided with the Me-109 of *Feldwebel* Kaiser, who was injured.[93]

On November 22, 1941, a few aircraft from 1 *Staffel* managed to take off and engage, with Redlich scoring two victories, and one victory apiece for *Unteroffizier* Grimm and *Oberfeldwebel* Albert Espenlaub. Once again circumstances prevented Marseille from getting in on the action. II *Gruppe* had been the hardest hit by the rain and subsequent flood, which delayed their participation, but Lippert and a few of his men managed to get involved. Lippert scored two victories himself and Rödel also shot down two. II./JG-27 had successes and losses, when *Unteroffizier* Reuter, *Leutnant* Scheppa, *Oberfähnriche* Waskott and Tarier tested their parachutes and survived without serious injuries and flew again. *Feldwebel* Hiller crash-landed after damage, as did *Hauptmann* Ernst Düllberg, who was wounded, but returned to Gazala and crash landed with his gear up.[94]

Allied activity increased to some degree with small incursions, forcing II./JG-27 to scramble several times when the alarm was given. Their response to these threats paid off with ten victories, of which Redlich scored three Hurricanes, Espenlaub two, and Lippert one before being hit and upon leaving his aircraft broke both of his legs against the tail section. Lippert's victor was Australian Flight Lt. Clive Caldwell, back on duty after having been shot up badly on August 29 by Schroer, when he had been wounded in the left shoulder, left leg, and back. When the British found Lippert, his injuries required a double amputation, which he did not survive. His final score was 29 victories.[95]

On November 27, 1942, *Feldwebel* Otto Schulz would have the distinction of taking off, shooting down a Bristol twin engine transport, and then landing, all within three minutes, near their air base at Ain-el-Gazala. This victory was important, as John Weal stated: "On this occasion the No. 216 Squadron machine was one of five carrying troops of the embryonic Special Air Service (SAS) on their first ever large-scale raid behind enemy lines. Their objective was to destroy the aircraft dispersed on the five *Luftwaffe* airfields in the Gazala-Tmimi area as the prelude to a major British offensive scheduled to be launched the following day."[96]

During this period *Leutnant* Marseille was still assigned to 1 *Staffel* although he usually flew with 3./JG-27, which was in action during the first week of December. On December 1, 1941, Eduard Neumann and *General der Flieger* Hans Geisler awarded Marseille the German Cross in Gold, which had been created as a decoration two weeks prior and was an award for merit or bravery that ranked just above the Iron Cross First Class and just below the Knight's Cross. The recipient had to have performed six actions that would have each merited the Iron Cross First Class. In Marseille's case, given that he already had both Iron Crosses and a couple of dozen victories, the award was welcomed, but a non-event. He wanted the prize: the Knight's Cross.

On December 5, 1941, twenty-one Me-109Fs from three *Staffeln* arrived at Tmimi: 7 *Staffel* (*Oberleutnant* Altendorf), 8 *Staffel* (now *Oberleutnant* Hans-Joachim Hennecke) and 9 *Staffel* (*Leutnant* Herbert Schramm, Knight's Cross) of III./JG-53 under the command of *Hauptmann* Wolf-Dietrich Wilcke were to operate to support the air umbrella contingent. Just as Wilcke (who had thirty-three victories and the Knight's Cross) and his men were getting oriented to their new station, I./JG-27 took off with twelve aircraft on another Stuka escort mission led by Homuth and soon engaged twenty Hurricanes, with the enemy aircraft divided between No. 274 Squadron RAF and No. 1 Squadron SAAF. Additional P-40s from undetermined units were also encountered. The German fighter pilots of III./JG-53 would not reach the Stukas in time.

Wolf-Dietrich Wilcke of JG-53 (Raymond F. Toliver)

The Stukas led once again by Kurt Kuhlmey were immediately engaged, losing 18 of the 40 dispatched to ruthless enemy attacks by the P-40s. According to Kuhlmey, "that was the worst day of the war for me, probably including the time in Russia."[97] Flight Lieutenant Clive "Killer" Caldwell of No. 250 Squadron RAF managed to shoot down five of the eighteen Ju-87s of I./StG-3 all by himself before the German fighters became involved. Caldwell would later add eight Japanese victories and finish the war with 28.5 victories, and he would be decorated by the British, Australian, and Polish governments. On this mission Caldwell would perform another one of his war crimes, as related by Kuhlmey:

"I saw three of my two man crews leave the aircraft that were smoking or on fire, and I banked over to see that there were six good parachutes. But then this Curtis fighter came up from below and fire, and destroyed the parachute of one of my men, and I must have been heard throughout the entire remaining squadron as I screamed and cursed. I called out the fighter to any of our fighters able to get to us and help. I dropped down to try and protect my men still in the air if possible.

"Then this P-40 came back, followed by three others, and he killed another man under his parachute, and I could not bring my Stuka around to get into a firing position. The other men were on their radios complaining about it. I was able to see the four remaining men hit the ground safely, but they would become prisoners no doubt as we were behind British lines. Then I saw what I believed was the same P-40 coming after me, my gunner called him out, but then I saw him break away, and Marseille had chased him off my tail. I had never been so angry in my entire life up to that moment. If I had fighter cover the entire time, I do not think that would have ever happened."98

Eduard Neumann's Me-109 escorting Kurt Kuhlmey's Ju-87 Stuka (Ludwig Franzisket)

Neumann explained what had happened to Kuhlmey's fighter cover: "The mission had III./JG-53 covering the Stukas inbound, we were to pick them up as they returned giving a total air umbrella for Kuhlmey's Stukas. I knew there was a problem when I heard Kuhlmey, call sign Albatross 1, screaming for his fighter cover, that they were under attack. I radioed the situation and their position to my men who were already in a fight, except Marseille's *Schwarm*. JG-53 had been enroute but encountered a large number of enemy fighters, and were unable to rendezvous with Kuhlmey, but my men were informed, and they vectored to assist the Stukas. When I heard Marseille over the radio that they had arrived I felt somewhat better."99

As Kurt Kuhlmey recalled: "We were really caught in a bad place, and there was little we could do. The enemy fighters were shooting into us, and we were loaded with bombs, so until we dropped them, we had no choice but keep flying. Then, as I saw several of my men going down, the German fighters appeared. At that time, I knew that we would be alright, but it was a very tense few minutes to be certain. I knew that JG-53 was supposed to be our cover, but Neumann explained and told me his pilots would try and help us.

Hauptmann Erich Gerlitz (Raymond F. Toliver)

"My rear gunner told me that an enemy fighter was going down smoking, and that we had another fighter closing on us from six o'clock. That fighter broke contact after being engaged, and the 109 flew past. I saw Yellow 14, and that was when I could breathe much easier. Marseille had saved our lives again. After this mission we were actually ineffective as a combat unit for some time."[100]

The fight lasted perhaps six minutes, although Marseille flying with 3 *Staffel* now equipped with the F model did confirm his 26th victory after clearing Caldwell off the Stuka flown by *Oberleutnant* Kurt Kuhlmey and then shooting down another fighter. Both Allied units confirmed one fighter lost each during the engagement, and no German losses were reported. Marseille had scored his only confirmed victory of the day, a Hurricane at 15:25.

The next day, December 6, saw I and II./JG-27 combine to again provide escort for nine Stukas from *Stukageschwader* 3 (StG-3) and conduct a fighter sweep, where they encountered 24 Hurricanes from Nos. 229, 274 (no losses reported by either unit), and 238 Squadrons RAF. The twisting, turning battle was one of the longest experienced in the African theater of operations, lasting 32 minutes. The Germans had intercepted the enemy on their way to hit Kuhlmey's Stukas, who completed their mission without loss. The Germans claimed four victories, with Marseille getting two Hurricanes for his 27th and 28th victories, both of which fell over El Adem at 12:10 and 12:25, respectively, although the two Allied units combined actually lost five instead of four aircraft in a rare circumstance of underclaiming victories on the part of the Germans.

On December 7, 1941, the world changed forever. III./JG-26 had arrived the day before at Tmimi, and the aircraft were readied for the next day's mission. That was just as the world learned of the Japanese attack against the American military bases of Pearl Harbor and Hickam Field in Hawaii. The news was yet to reach the men in Africa, since JG-27 was abandoning its bases to relocate. Gambut was in British hands, Tobruk had been relieved, and Ain-el-Gazala was being evacuated due to the advancing British infantry and armor. JG-27 was in full operation for a Stuka escort mission, protecting fifteen of the lumbering dive bombers when No. 274 Squadron RAF engaged.

Otto Schulz (Raymond F. Toliver)

It was on this day that two victories by Oak Leaves recipient and successful Eastern Front veteran *Oberleutnant* Erbo Graf von Kageneck elevated his personal score to 67 aerial victories, as he well represented III./JG-27. Otto Schulz scored a kill over a Boston bomber near El Adem, one of two engaged while *Leutnant* Remmer shot down the second, and observed one parachute.

When the bomber pilot, Lieutenant Kingon saw that his wounded crew could not bail out, he decided to crash-land. Upon coming to a stop he removed his crew personally, one by one before the bomber exploded.[101] The British Operation Crusader to break Rommel's siege of Tobruk was in full swing, and all three *Gruppen* of JG-27 were once again together, despite the reversal of fortunes, although Marseille had shot down a Hurricane at 09:30 adding to his score, standing at 29, as 2 *Staffel* under *Hauptmann* Erich Gerlitz shot down five of six unescorted SAAF-flown Douglas Boston bombers that they encountered. Marseille's victim was positively identified as Flight Lieutenant Hobbs of No. 274 Squadron RAF.

On December 8, Marseille scored victory number 30 at 08:15 when he flamed a P-40 from No. 274 Squadron RAF over El Ademat, which had become a hotly contested piece of airspace. Marseille had erroneously written up the victory in his *Abschuss* (after-action report) as a Hurricane, but later the identification was confirmed, and the victory stood. However, he still had collected seven additional "possible" victories up to this time that could not be confirmed, and never would be. The nature of air combat and the lack of gun cameras did not always support a pilot's claim. Much to his credit, the pragmatic Marseille never wrote these up in his reports as "claimed" victories—unless he saw a crash or a parachute—but as "probable victories, aircraft damaged."

Marseille on the cover of the French edition of Der Adler. (Author's collection)

After that mission the men gathered to hear the news of the Japanese attack the day before, and later the American declaration of war against Japan. All the Germans interviewed stated that the discussion was lively, and there were two camps of thought. The one camp was that it was believed the Americans fighting the Japanese would have little or no impact upon their fighting against them. The other camp was of a completely different opinion, as stated by Franzisket:

> "Many believed that the Japanese would occupy the Americans and that they would not be that involved with us. I did not share that opinion. On the contrary I firmly believed that eventually the Americans would probably focus on us at some point, since the British and Australians were also fighting the Japanese. Marseille shared my opinion, but his thoughts are worth noting. He said, and I remember this, that even if not one American soldier or pilot ever came to Europe, or Africa, that their industrial power could still supply the Allies far beyond our own capabilities, defeating us by attrition. He made a good point."[102]

December 9 saw I./JG-27 engage an enemy fighter unit strafing a German column, and the nineteen P-40s of No. 3 Squadron SAAF and No. 112 Squadron were attacked by Homuth's 3 *Staffel* with six Me-109Fs. Homuth, Schneider, and Grimm each scored a quick kill. A fourth P-40 crash landed, while another limped back to its airfield. One of those killed was a Sergeant Wilson, who had eight victories.[103]

Hurricane of No. 1 Squadron SAAF (Geoffrey Morley-Mower)

On December 10, No. 2 and No. 4 Squadrons SAAF suffered a major setback near El Adem. That morning I./JG-27 launched in strength and Marseille led a *Schwarm*, with his four aircraft formation being part of three *Schwarme* combining all the assets from 3 *Staffel*. Marseille's group flew high cover, above the thin clouds, with Marseille using his traditional half rolls left and right to see below. When he saw their opponents at a much lower altitude, Marseille called out the enemies and led his men into an attack.

Rolling over, Marseille hit the rudder and pointed the nose down. He closed in on the tail of a P-40, which never saw him, and a two-second press of the trigger secured the kill. He now had victory number 31. His victim was No. 2 Squadron SAAF pilot Lieutenant B. G. S. Enslin, who was uninjured after bailing out at 08:50. Meanwhile, 2 *Staffel* was also busy with the Stuka escort when they came across six Bostons. The Germans under the command of *Hauptmann* Gerlitz destroyed five of the six enemies, at a loss for one aircraft, when *Leutnant* Kothmann took defensive fire, and was uninjured landing his damaged aircraft at Tmimi field.

The day was full of activity for II *Gruppe*, as they also escorted their Stukas, and the fighter pilots strafed enemy armor and vehicles. During this mission Rödel was nearly killed when his rudder was torn away by his wingman *Unteroffizier* Heidel, who pulled up too close behind his leader. Rödel described the event:

"The strafing was always a dangerous game; as you were exposed to ground fire, they could easily hit you even with rifles. I had made my second pass when I felt this great loud grinding noise. I had absolutely no rudder or elevator control, so I just gave full power and flew southwest for a while. I looked back and saw a 109 just above me, the offender. I finally flew until I knew I was out of danger of being captured, as I was slowly losing altitude. I just set her down gently, and that was that. No great problem really."[104] After Rödel managed to crash-land uninjured, Heidel slowly lost power in the climb and managed to level out and fly behind Rödel and eventually bailed out at just over 50 feet altitude yet survived.

The next day, December 11, III./JG-53 *Pik As* (Ace of Spades) was full in the fight, minus three unserviceable fighters that they destroyed as they were in the process of moving from Tmimi to Derna. When the three *Staffeln* of III./JG-27 (7 *Staffel* commanded by *Oberleutnant* Hermann Tangerding, 8 *Staffel* under *Oberleutnant* Hans Lass, and 9 *Staffel* under *Oberleutnant* Erbo Graf von Kageneck, who had sixty-

Captured Me-109E7 *(Geoffrey Morley-Mower)*

five victories and the Knight's Cross with Oak Leaves) of III./JG-27 arrived, under the overall command of *Gruppenkommandeur Hauptmann* Erhard Braune, with JG-27 in total under *Major* Bernhard Woldenga, himself holding the Knight's Cross, the entire *Geschwader* was united once again after a year and a half of being dispersed.

On this day Marseille was able to shoot down a P-40. His 32nd victim was Canadian Flight Sergeant M. A. Canty of No. 250 Squadron RAF. His crashed fighter was found with him still strapped inside, and a single bullet hole was in his forehead from the shot that entered the windscreen. His remains were registered, and his family in Nova Scotia was informed on December 29. The Germans were now at full strength, but with the growing Allied air threats, they would need every plane and pilot just to survive. Retired Wing Commander Geoffrey Morley-Mower recalled the event:

"We had lost quite a few boys; some were never found and were listed as missing. But sometimes we did find a man, either with or without his aircraft. Long Range Desert Group would often be the men who found a missing pilot. They found Canty, poor man, his wingman confirmed that Yellow 14 shot him down, and damaged his own Kittyhawk. We had grown to know some of the Germans by their aircraft numbers, and in many after action reports, Yellow 14 was becoming more commonly mentioned.

"We also had a radio listening group, part of the intelligence corps at Tobruk. They monitored all German air, ground and sea transmissions. They had native German speakers, many of them Jews who left Germany years before, who listened and took notes on everything. It was a twenty-four-hour seven day a week operation. We found that the damned Germans were very talkative over the radio; they would not shut up. They seemed very undisciplined in that regard, calling out names in the clear, that sort of thing. Combining these notes gathered from the intercepts and the after-action reports and mission debriefings, we soon would gather a lot of information on our adversaries in the air and know who they were."[105]

Squadron Leader Michael Judd of No. 250 Squadron (Michael Judd)

Squadron Leader (later Group Captain) Michael Judd also mentioned these intelligence types and their knowledge being gathered: "You must understand that we had many sources of information, just as I am certain the Germans did. Prisoners while interrogated were fairly easy to get information from. We had an entire database of names of pilots, leaders, etc.

When combining all of this, with the propaganda the Germans put out, such as radio, newspapers and their propaganda magazines, we had a good picture of who we were up against. This was where we finally learned who some of the better German pilots were."[106]

CHAPTER 6

A Killing Winter

People think the desert is always hot. I can tell you that is not true. Men without blankets at night froze their asses off.
Franz Stigler

On Marseille's 22nd birthday, December 13, 1941, 1 *Staffel* of JG-27 was in the thick of it, losing *Oberfeldwebel* Albert Espenlaub, who had brought down 14 aircraft in his career before he was shot down near El Adem. Apparently forced to land with a dead engine, he radioed that he was going in. As he descended Marseille followed him down and reported that there were many enemy ground troops. Espenlaub radioed to his unit, "Going in. I guess I will see you after the war," and he was seen to crash land without much damage in his White 11 and was almost immediately surrounded by British troops.

Marseille flew very low and passed by overhead to see him captured but alive and well, and Espenlaub still in his cockpit waved to Marseille who waved back, but he was shot dead the next day in an unsuccessful escape attempt. In a *quid pro quo* an unknown Allied pilot flew to the German airbase and dropped a note informing them of Espenlaub's fate, with condolences. A telegram had also been sent. The news was taken badly by the men of JG-27, as Espenlaub was well-liked.

Neumann offered this information: "What was really tragic, was that his fiancé had learned that she was pregnant and had written him a letter that arrived the day he was shot down. I only learned of this because, after we learned of his death due to a very polite telegram from the Australians to our headquarters giving us the information, I read the letter. I had to know who to write the letter to, which I did whenever I lost a pilot. A personal letter to the family, parents or wife, what have you. Espenlaub died never knowing that he was going to be a father."[107]

That same day, on Marseille's birthday, the unit was flying high over Martuba when they engaged eight P-40s of No. 3 Squadron SAAF and he scored two victories at 16:00 and 16:10, respectively. Neither victory was spectacular. One of his victims was Flying Officer Thomas "Tommy" Trimble, who was wounded, burned, and survived the crash landing.[108] Marseille's second victory was either a Lieutenant Connel or a Lieutenant Meek from No. 1 Squadron SAAF, as both were shot down. These were his thirty-third and thirty-fourth victories. Lieutenant Meek would incredibly survive being shot down this time and return to his unit only to be again shot down by Gustav Rödel later.

The next day, December 14, *Oberfeldwebel* Hermann Förster of 2 *Staffel*, who had scored 13 victories, was overwhelmed in a fight with several Kittyhawks. He bailed out after losing his engine, but he was strafed in his parachute by Clive Caldwell. This horrific event was witnessed by several pilots, including Clade, Marseille, Franzisket, Homuth, Schroer and Rödel. It was not the first time that German airmen had seen this activity by Caldwell, although they did not know who he was.

"There were over five witnesses in the air," Rödel recalled. "This was really the topic of discussion for the entire unit, and not just my *Gruppe*, I mean the entire *Geschwader* was talking about this. Some pilots openly stated that, since the British had thrown away the Geneva Convention [of 1929], then we were clear to do the same. I stood my ground, and I told them that under no circumstances would any pilot under me intentionally fire upon a man in a parachute. I would shoot them down myself. Neumann and Woldenga backed me. Woldenga stated that 'this was not Russia, it is not a war with animals,' and he acknowledged that it was tragic, but not precedent setting for us.

"Marseille, Schroer, even Neumann and others gathered that evening, and we openly discussed this. Neumann made clear that anything can happen in combat, although it seemed pretty clear that the killing was very intentional. The law was laid down. None of us were to violate the rules of war, at any time, regardless of what the enemy did. I am certain that Neumann knew, as did I to some degree, that Germany was not going to come out of this war looking like the good guys. Once we heard that America had been attacked and had declared war, everyone knew it was over. We may have been able to hold Europe, but winning a total victory was out of the question. I think Neumann, and even Woldenga who was there, wanted our unit, as well as the *Luftwaffe* to be held with a clear record when it was all over."[109]

Espenlaub's Me-109 after he was captured by the British when he crash landed. He would be shot the next day. (Trevor Constable)

Schroer also commented on the event, which resonated throughout JG-27 and even stirred comments from the *Afrika Korps* commander as well: "We were told that under no circum- stances were we to follow the example set by that British (actually Caldwell was Australian) pilot, that it would be a court-martial offense. I understood this, and Marseille was very inquisitive as well, as such a thing was really unheard of to us, but the JG-27 men who had served in Russia said that it happened all the time. Those Soviet pilots always tried to kill Germans who bailed out. We were also reminded that Stalin never signed the Geneva Convention, but Britain and the Western Allies had. The whole event just put a bad taste in our mouths."[110]

It is unquestioned that the Allied pilot who killed Förster was Clive Caldwell; while not claiming a victory that day, he did claim a damaged aircraft, and he had admitted that he killed the German pilot. Even his own men saw him do it. Caldwell stated that he did not see any reason for the Germans who bailed out to get back into the war. However, in at least one conciliatory act of chivalry, he also stated that once they were on the ground, he would not strafe them. Opinions on Caldwell were quite clear as stated by Geoffrey Morley-Mower:

"Caldwell had this tendency, which I completely disagreed with as did others, and so did the men under him. Even his own wingman had complained that he did not want to fly with him due to the possibility that the Germans may be looking for Caldwell, and he would be there as a matter of circumstance. This was how he earned the name "Killer Caldwell", but despite this egregious character flaw he was a damned good fighter pilot, so our superiors looked the other way. I only felt disdain for him. It was almost a rude awakening later as we came to know who Marseille was and what he did for us."[111]

James "Stocky" Edwards who flew with No. 94 Squadron and later No. 260 Squadron had this view on Caldwell: "We knew what he had done, more than once, and it left a bad taste in my mouth for one and I was not alone. I saw no reason to kill a man already out of the fight. I guess that was where Marseille and I agreed. Once a man was out of his aircraft, he was no longer an enemy to kill. I was just disgusted with the entire affair, and I was very pleased that I did not have to fly with him. I spoke with a few of the men who had flown with him, and none were too pleased about this type of activity. I think the only reason why he was never brought up on charges was because he was a very effective fighter pilot."[112]

Caldwell knew that such an action would be violating international law, and his justification was that he had seen a German intentionally strafe one of his men in a similar fashion. Accidents do happen, but there is no record of any German pilot intentionally killing an enemy in his parachute in North Africa. There were incidents in Europe, one involving *Leutnant* Klaus Bretschneider in 1944 in the *Reichsverteidigung* (Reich Defense), and his commanding officer *Major* Walther Dahl ran him for court-martial, but Bretschneider was killed in action before the proceedings could begin with Galland's endorsement. It is hard to believe that no one would have reported a JG-27 pilot committing the act, given the standing doctrine and personalities who commanded the unit.

Michael Judd has his take on the situation: "This was not Caldwell's first indiscretion; he had a habit of doing it. The problem was that this time there were a lot of Germans who were witnesses to the event. Some of our men were worried that the sense of chivalry, let alone the written rules of war that prevented such a thing would be thrown away. I had to admit that I shared their concerns."[113]

Kurt Kuhlmey also saw Caldwell strafe his Stuka pilots and crews on at least two missions, which also created a great discussion: "This pilot, whom we later after the war learned was the Australian, had circled back and shot the parachute collapsing it, allowing one of my men to fall to his death. I was stunned into complete silence as I watched this. The rest of the men in my squadron jammed the frequency with shouts and curses. There was a lot of bad feelings after that, I can tell you."

On December 17, Marseille once again engaged No. 1 Squadron SAAF, a group whose pilots knew his Yellow 14, if not the name of the man who flew it, at least not yet. The eight South African fighters were escorting eight Blenheim bombers from both Nos. 14 and 84 Squadrons RAF when they were intercepted near Derna. The two enemy flights saw each other at the same time, as each group emerged from the clouds at the same time, head on, at almost the same altitude.

Australian Squadron Leader Clive Caldwell the "Top Gun from Down Under." Credited with 28.5 kills in 300 sorties and ace in a day. He served in the Middle East, North Africa, and the South Pacific. His victories included Germans, Italians, and Japanese. (Geoffrey Morley Mower)

Aerial combat was sometimes like gunfights in the Old West: the fastest man on the trigger was not always the man who walked away. However, the man who was the most accurate usually did. Marseille was fast and accurate. He destroyed the first enemy fighter at 11:10, as he aimed at eleven o'clock low, striking the fighter in the engine. His second victim fell with a kick of the rudder soon afterward, at 11:28, and he snapped a shot at another Hurricane that flashed past him, still murky and shrouded in the clouds. He did not claim a probable or damaged on this third aircraft, but he had shot down two Hurricanes, which he somehow misidentified as P-40s in the *Abschuss*.

When the battle was over I./JG-27 claimed five victories. Allied records show that three Hurricanes never returned: one crash-landed, one was shot down, and another limped back to base damaged. Marseille had scored numbers 35 and 36, but according to the new criteria, he was still four victories short for his coveted Knight's Cross.

Ludwig Franzisket also scored two victories on that mission. "We were flying in the clouds, which were unusually low hanging, as they had been since the great rainstorm and flood. We were staggered at one-thousand-meter intervals, one *Schwarm* above another, and so on. This was how we liked to fly, in case one element was engaged, another could ambush from height, or attack from below, while the highest element was there as a protective guard, so that no one else joined in.

"On this mission we simply broke out of the clouds, and there they were! We could not have been more than two thousand meters apart, closing so fast that my mind could not even think of firing before they flashed past, then I looked up and saw one pass overhead smoking, and then saw that it was Marseille. Somehow, he had seen them first, or reacted first, and fired. Then I turned to get on their tails, as they were doing the same, but Marseille was on top cover, and his *Schwarm* had already rolled over and dived in on them. The *Schwarm* below me pulled up and then went after the bombers, I think. I managed to get a shot in on a fighter just after I saw Marseille's target, and as we twisted and turned, I shot down another. That was a busy fight, a long one, almost half an hour."[114]

Canadian James "Stocky" Edwards who shot down some of the best German aces (James Edwards)

The next day, December 18, all three *Gruppen* of JG-27 joined the rest of the *Afrika Korps* in a tactical retreat west, as Gazala was abandoned, joining Tmimi falling into in British hands. Derna was also evacuated, along with the hospital and all the wounded. Vehicles and non-flyable aircraft of all types were destroyed, and the convoy fled through the well-mapped out minefields. The last transport aircraft lifted off the field at Derna as British armored vehicles arrived. I./JG-27 managed to relocate temporarily to Got el Bersis, where it would have to wait for the fuel and water transport trucks to arrive.

Just after midday the Germans were in their cockpits, ready to take off to cover the retreat and supply convoys. Marseille sat in Yellow 14, napping with his colorful umbrella over his head, canopy open shielding himself from the sun, enjoying the rare light breeze coming in from the Mediterranean. He had been diagnosed with jaundice again, and the suspicion of malaria was still lingering. He was gaunt, weak, and weighed less than 120 pounds, far below his average of 140–150 pounds, and he was also suffering from amoebic dysentery, in which he was not alone. The water was suspected as the source, and fresh water was ordered while the remaining water was boiled before the relocation.

Franzisket recalled, "I saw him right after the 17 December battle, as I verified one of his victories, and we had a drink. He was exhausted, barely standing without being tired. He was throwing up and sitting in the latrine for long periods of time, and he was going there quite often. His skin and eyes were yellow, and he was running a fever with chills, but then again, we all had aftereffects of the jaundice. No one escaped. I knew he was ill, because I could see blood stains in the back of his shorts, which was the sign of amoebic dysentery. Once you passed blood it was a bad infection. The best and closest full facility was in Rome, so that was where he was to be sent. Ironically, I would be going with him.[115] [Authors' note: The men would be detoured to Athens instead].

"I informed Homuth and he ordered Marseille to the physician, who at that time was just a medic that we had on hand, but he knew enough to report the situation to Neumann. Neumann then wrote the request and passed it on to Woldenga, and that evening Marseille was ordered to a major military hospital for treatment. This illness could kill a man, and we were out of many of the drugs that would normally be given. We had no quinine, almost no antiseptics for wounds, and remember, penicillin was not something we Germans had during the war, so many serious infections that were corrected by the Allies with that drug were unavailable to us. We lost several men who had been wounded due to infections, such as gangrene and staph."[116]

While sitting in their aircraft at Got el Bersis, the call was heard across the flight line that enemy aircraft were approaching, and the pilots jumped out and joined the ground crews diving into ditches as the bombs began to fall. The attack was over as fast as it had begun, and Marseille returned to his fighter, where a bomb fragment had penetrated through the left side of his cockpit, and blown clean through, exiting out the right side. Had he stayed in the cockpit he would have been cut in half at the chest. Emil Clade recalled the event: "I walked up and put my entire fist through the exit hole. Jochen would have indeed been killed had he stayed in the cockpit."[117]

Franzisket recalled that close call where Marseille luckily was not in his cockpit: "I looked that that hole and shook my head. Jochen smiled and pointed to it, 'See I am touched by the gods!' I just laughed and walked away and called him a clown."[118]

Once the new airfield was established, Neumann arrived with his treasured wagon towed by a truck. Soon Woldenga arrived and established his base at Magrun, and the rest of the *Geschwader* converged on what would be their homes for the next few months. Woldenga established his headquarters in the wagon with Neumann, and Homuth now had his own trailer. The ammunition and fuel drums were stored in a dugout cave nearby that doubled as a bomb shelter, itself next to their movie theater called the Marabu, a tent with the floor excavated down about twenty feet with steps at an incline to allow men to walk down, sit and enjoy the rare films that arrived by transport aircraft. This was all courtesy of II *Gruppe*. Gustav Rödel was in charge of the theater project:

"Woldenga wanted us to make a large tent a theater for showing the films, but I thought that a more sheltered location would be best. It took about three days to get it dug and prepared, with a camouflaged tent and netting covering it. After we were done, I recall Schroer saying that, 'Good thing this will be a theater, and that there are no women around. Otherwise, Marseille would make it a brothel.' I laugh liked hell, knowing he was probably right."[119]

Woldenga was impressed by the rapid reorganization. "Our men performed nothing less than small miracles. That storm had done so much damage for us overall. The best thing was that the aircraft were alright, and no one was seriously injured. I also noticed that morale had dropped, as happened on occasion. Then there were the losses of popular pilots. It took some doing to keep their spirits up. Neumann was very good at that."[120]

By Christmas Eve, JG-27 was run-down, worn out and low on parts, ammunition, oil, and fuel. Of the three *Gruppen*, only six Me-109s were available for action, the rest being serviced. That day's combat saw Oberleutnant Erbo *Graf* (Baron) von Kageneck shot down by Clive Caldwell while in a twisting fight with No. 94, 112, and 250 Squadrons RAF over Agedabia, with the Germans fighting twenty Hurricanes and Kittyhawks. Kageneck attacked as they had formed a rapid defensive Lufbery. Although he had been wounded in the stomach, von Kageneck managed to fly the remaining 46 miles to his base at Magrun. Despite his excellent crash landing, medical evacuation to Athens, and then to the main German military hospital at Naples, he died of peritonitis on January 12, 1942, underscoring Franzisket's statement regarding the lack of antibacterial drugs such as penicillin.

Marseille preparing for another mission (Raymond F. Toliver)

From December 25, 1941, through January 2, 1942, the entire *Geschwader* was poised in Cyrenaica around the Arco Philaenorum. On December 25 *Major* Eduard Neumann, the Spanish Civil War veteran and *Kommandeur* of I./JG-27, ordered a meeting with *Oberleutnant* Ludwig Franzisket, who had been *Staffelkapitän* of 1. *Staffel* since December 6.

Franzisket was one of the JG-27 "old men" who, along with Schroer, was one of the originals, and his leadership was well noted. On October 1, 1940, he had been appointed Adjutant of I./JG-27, and by the time the unit arrived in North Africa he had achieved fourteen victories. He was a lethal ace, and among his many victories during the war, he had already shot down South African ace Captain Kenneth Driver on June 14, 1941. He was awarded the Knight's Cross on July 23, 1941, for having scored 22 victories in 204 missions up to that time.

Normally 40 victories were the established rule for receiving the Knight's Cross at that time, but exceptions were made for exemplary leadership as well as success in the air. Neumann explained why he made the recommendation for Franzisket:

"Franzisket was an excellent leader, and not just in battle. He was excellent at organization and ensuring all the aircraft had proper maintenance scheduled, he managed the inventories and kept detailed records of everything in his unit diary. He was also the self appointed morale officer, and he was loved by his subordinates. That was what made him special. He was also to keep Marseille under control. Hell, that would have warranted the medal by itself."[121]

Meanwhile the British were still advancing, and once again the forward German units fell back. That afternoon Marseille was grounded by Neumann and told he was going to Athens, instead of Rome, on the next transport aircraft. As Neumann stated: "I told 'Seille that he was going to get medical treatment, and he must have really felt bad. I know this, because at any other time he would have tried to argue and convince me not to take him off flying duties. He looked terrible, and I was very worried about him."[122]

Neumann wanted to raise troop morale for Christmas, so he asked Franzisket to take a couple of fighters and fly over the coastal region, allowing the soldiers to see some German aircraft for a change. He was aware that his *Gruppe* only had four aircraft in flying condition, taking into account losses in combat, the ones needing parts and servicing, and those that had been destroyed during the evacuation. However, following the numerous Allied strafing and bombing attacks against German supply lines, gun emplacements, convoys and military formations, the ground troops were very nervous of any aircraft they saw. As the two Me-109s passed over an Italian artillery unit they opened fire.

"I was hit in the fuselage and canopy, the glass shattered, and the shrapnel had hit me all over," Franzisket explained. "A piece was in my hand, and I could feel blood running down my face. My oxygen mask was filled with blood, and I had to take it off. My instrument panel was shattered, and I could smell something, probably coolant leaking into the cockpit. I managed to turn back and fly until I landed, but I really could not see very much. I would soon join Jochen on medical leave. My surgeries and recovery took a long time, and I wondered if I would be allowed to fly again."[123]

Franzisket and Marseille both climbed aboard the same Ju-52 transport on their way to Athens. Marseille would not return until February 6; Franzisket was out of the war until March. Their transport landed in Athens on December 27, after refueling in Crete. The patients were carried by ambulance to the main military hospital where most German soldiers would spend several weeks depending upon their condition. Franzisket was taken into surgery to have the remaining steel splinters removed from his face, a piece removed from his right hand and there was some concern that one splinter had entered close to his right eye. Following a few days in recovery, he was sent to Berlin for more in-depth treatment. He would remain in Germany until March 1942, undergoing seven more operations and physical rehabilitation for his right hand, which had some muscles torn and a tendon in need of repair.

Franzisket explained his condition: "I was in bad shape, and I was very worried about losing my right eye which had a small piece of steel in the outside corner. My hand would not work, I could not even hold a pencil. I was pretty sure that I was not ever going to fly again. I was lucky that I had one of the best orthopedic surgeons, as well as a great ophthalmologist. My recovery would take quite a long time. I do not blame those Italians who shot me up. They had been under constant fighter bombing attacks and strafing and their nerves were probably torn to pieces."[124]

Marseille was diagnosed with a series of illnesses, including malaria, jaundice, amoebic dysentery, and gastroenteritis. He also had a serious skin rash. On this third day on his back an officer walked in, sat down next to his bed, handed him a sealed envelope then left. It was a telegram that had been sent to Woldenga in Africa, but then rerouted to Athens where Marseille had been sent, causing a four-day delay since his mother wrote it. Marseille never revealed what he was thinking when he opened that telegram, which was one simple line: "Your sister is dead. Please come to Berlin."[125]

"I received the telegram from his mother that did not provide much information, just that his sister was dead," Woldenga later recalled. "It was not until the following day I again received a telegram, this one providing some details. I called Neumann in, and we had a chat. We both knew that this was a lot different than watching a friend die in battle. How would he [Marseille] react to this? Neumann just said: 'Damn, he does not need this too.' I felt the same way. My heart sank for Marseille."[126]

JG-27 men going to see a film at the Marabu (Eduard Neumann)

Neumann gave his perspective: "I felt so bad for the boy, you know? He was having a tough time with his health, the strain of many missions per week, if not per day, and then to get this news. I was not sure what kind of Marseille we would get back when he returned. It was later that I learned of the circumstances of his sister's death, which made the situation even more tragic. Then I briefed the men on the news, so that they were prepared for his return, whenever that was. Even Homuth seemed deeply touched by the news."[127]

From what could be pieced together, his sister, Ingeborg, had been living in Berlin, until she left for Vienna and had been dating a man when the relationship went sour. The prime suspect in her murder was this same abusive former boyfriend from Berlin who followed her to Vienna and stalked her and in a jealous rage murdered her violently. Marseille was told the details, but these were not relayed to their mother. Her body was apparently brought back to Berlin, and their father, now a general serving on the Eastern Front, managed a short visit during Marseille's medical leave. It is not clear whether or not father and son reunited.

The murder came to the attention of higher authorities, too. In November 1941, Hermann Göring had added Marseille's name to the growing list of pilots who had come to his attention. The *Reichsmarschall* was an intensely vain man, and he used every opportunity to exploit the deeds of his fighter pilots and to illustrate to Hitler and the other command staff the superiority of his *Luftwaffe*, thus enhancing his own prestige. He was always in direct competition with Heinrich Himmler for position as Hitler's favorite, especially following the May 1941 defection of Deputy *Führer* Rudolf Hess. The propaganda value of the fighter pilots' successes could not be underestimated. However, Göring also took a real personal interest in the personal lives of his men, as Hans Baur stated:

"Göring was always reading these reports from the front, or at least being briefed by his aides, such as von Below. If he saw something of particular interest, he would contact Göbbels and discuss what if any propaganda value such information had. I remember that JG-27 had been doing some great things, and a few names came to the forefront, Marseille was just one of many when he was authorized a couple of awards. However, the police report regarding Marseille's sister that came in had gone to the office of [*Obergruppenführer*] Heinrich Müller [head of the *Gestapo* under Himmler] as it came in from the Vienna office under [*Brigadeführer* Franz Josef] Huber. I learned of this from [*Obergruppenführer* Karl] Wolff, as he knew I had an interest in flying and the young pilots. Tragic really.

"However, what is very interesting, is that this was long before [*Obergruppenführer* Reinhard] Heydrich was killed [in June 1942], and since he ran the *Sicherheitsdienst*, he had a file on probably every person in the Reich. I suppose that somewhere in that massive collection there was a file on Marseille, since it was rumored that he had offended a *Gestapo* officer while stationed around Calais. I was not aware of those details."[128]

Marseille was released and sent to the *Krankenhaus* (hospital) in Charlottenburg in the west of Berlin, not far from his mother's home, where he could have home rest while attending his medical appointments. While Franzisket and Marseille were recovering, the war in North Africa raged on. Rommel recaptured Benghazi on January 29, 1942, although the air war to do so was very contained and there were limited engagements.

However, in February, this change in fortune allowed JG-27 to return to the airfields around Martuba. From here they could protect Derna to the northwest and continue their support of the Stuka *Geschwadern*, primarily I./StG-3, as they performed close air support missions and supply route interdiction. These operations were absolute suicide missions unless protective fighter cover was provided. During this time a few of JG-27s high performers maintained their victory count.

Marseille was cleared medically on January 22 for a return to duty. He left Berlin on January 24, reaching Athens on January 27, Sicily the next day, and Benghazi on January 30. While in Benghazi, he contracted to rent an apartment for his leisure time when the men were given a few days off This would become his sanctuary. He arrived by car at the operations shack of I./JG-27 on February 6, and although he still looked ill, his medical certificate stated that he was fit. He wanted to go back into combat. Those who knew him could see that he was different, and the word had spread of course regarding his sister. Schroer recalled the mood of the unit around that time:

> "We were glad to have him back, and even Homuth, who always had an axe to grind with Marseille, took a softer approach, as Neumann had briefed us before he returned as to what had happened. Neumann did not want anyone creating a problem, but to just allow him to ease back into the flow of things, you know. We understood. Everyone in that unit, even those who did not think much of Marseille personally, realized that for him to be his best, his mind must be focused upon flying, and nothing else."[129]

Hauptmann Gerhard Homuth, the rigid and unyielding *Staffelkapitän* of 3 *Staffel* I./JG-27 and his newly, often-assigned, problematic wingman Marseille seemed to be in a personal competition for victories upon his return, with both men reaching forty victories. One thing that renewed the difficult relationship between Homuth and Marseille was the fact that when Marseille returned, he did not follow protocol and report to the *Staffelkapitän*, whom he loathed. Instead, he jumped the chain of command and went to see the one superior he trusted, his *Gruppenkommandeur*, Eduard Neumann, whom he looked up to as the man who had given him another chance and kept the other senior officers off his back. Franzisket explained their relationship:

Marseille spending time with the mechanics and armorers thanking them for their hard work (Ludwig Franzisket)

"Of all the men who needed understanding and a softer touch, it was Marseille. And, also of all the men to be assigned to JG-27, Homuth was just the wrong superior for him. Neumann and Homuth were two very different types of officers. Neumann was happy-go-lucky, and could overlook minor infractions, and even solve the problem with a talk and perhaps grounding a pilot for a couple of days. He did that with Marseille once in a while, and he learned his lesson.

"However, Marseille's attitude, even the casual way he walked and wore his uniform, angered Homuth, who openly praised him for being a great fighter pilot. However, if Homuth had his way, he would have reduced him in rank and shipped him off as well, because he was a challenge to his direct authority, and no professional Prussian-styled German officer will tolerate that. Marseille made a comment that the only way he could beat Homuth was to score more victories, and do it in his face, so to speak. Once Homuth assigned him as his wingman on a few missions, Marseille must have known what he was going to do."[130]

Part of this great animosity between Homuth and Marseille was the fact that Marseille was always pulling pranks and doing these that irritated Homuth. Homuth, like Marseille had a phonograph player. Sometimes they had dueling music as explained by Woldenga:

"One evening, as I was in the wagon with Neumann, we were going over the inventory list. We had to submit our reports on our submissions for resupply, such as fuel, water, glycol, oil, ammunition and type, rations, that kind of thing. Then we heard Homuth turn on his record player. He loved Franz Schubert, Mozart, Bach, Beethoven. He had a nice collection of these classical records. We were both just listening and doing the paperwork, when suddenly, loud as hell, and the whole base could hear it, we heard 'Pennsylvania 6-5000' by Glenn Miller. Neumann and I looked at each other and at the same time said 'Marseille' and we headed out.

"Sure enough, we saw Homuth storming over to Marseille's tent, so we headed him off. I told Homuth I would handle it, and he saluted and said something which I will not repeat, and Neumann and I walked in. There was Marseille, lying on his cot, in his underwear, feet propped up, drinking something which smelled like brandy, smoking a cigar. He did not even get up to stand at attention, but we were used to that. He did slowly rise and get up.

"I told him that the entire camp did not need to hear his music, and that if he ever turned up the volume like that again I would put a bullet in it. He apologized and turned it down to where you could only hear the music within a few feet of the tent. I was satisfied, and left, Neumann followed a few minutes later."[131]

Neumann recalled the event and said: "After he [Woldenga] left, I sat down next to Marseille, and he handed me a brandy. It was good and came from a female admirer. I told him that I was doing my best to help him, but antagonizing Homuth, and angering Woldenga, who was one of his supporters, would not serve him well. After the talk, I left. I never had that problem with Marseille again. But there would be other issues."[132]

The same was true for the leader of 4 *Staffel* II./JG-27 *Oberleutnant* Gustav Rödel and his usual wingman *Feldwebel* Otto Schulz, as they had a rivalry that was fortunately far friendlier than that between Marseille and Homuth. On October 6 and 30, 1941, and November 28, 1941 he scored three victories on each of those days. His October 6 victims were either Lieutenant Miller or Lieutenant Neville McGarr from No. 2 Squadron SAAF as Rödel also downed one of them.

The November 28 victims were a Lieutenant Palm (missing in action), American born Pilot Officer Sidney Nicholas Muhart from Tuscon, Arizona and Flying Officer Vos (also MIA). Muhart was hospitalized with burns when his Hurricane burst into flames from a cannon shot in the gas tank. He managed to land at Tobruk 20 miles away in spite of flames which burned his face and hands. Muhart was released from the hospital but died the next day from heart failure reportedly caused by delayed shock. Otto Schulz would finally surpass his *Staffelkapitän* when he shot down five Tomahawks in only ten minutes on February 15, 1942.

Marseille had an axe to grind of his own, as he had learned that Homuth had once again not recommended him for a promotion. The reasons were "for conduct and appearance unbecoming an officer and lack of proper respect for superior authority."[133] Given the shattered remnants of his personal life following the death of his sister and his estrangement from his father, Marseille was determined to follow his own rules, and he finally had his first chance at beating his own *Staffelkapitän* in the only way he knew how, in the scoring.

He would begin on the second mission after his return. The manner of doing so would also increase the personal tensions between the two men. According to Schroer and Franzisket, Marseille was livid; even Rödel stated that there was a lot of angst between them. Marseille was grounded by Homuth for a couple of days, ostensibly to allow him to gradually ease back into the war. Others thought differently; they believed that Homuth wanted to reach forty victories before Marseille, and Marseille was of the same opinion. Emil Clade has his thoughts on the situation:

"Homuth definitely wanted to beat out Jochen in the victory count. Homuth knew that even with Marseille flying his wing, he would find a way to shoot things down, it was just a natural gift. Marseille had said clearly that he would make it his personal mission to shoot down more enemies than Homuth. I remember he said that 'I do not care if I am not the top expert, as long as I beat Homuth.' Homuth learned of this. I think that was why he did it. Neumann was of the opinion that Marseille should be put back in the air as soon as possible to take his mind off of his personal problems."[134]

Neumann overrode Homuth's decision as he needed every operational fighter and pilot in the air, and he was getting tired of the pedantic personality struggles between those two. Marseille flew that mission, scored a confirmed kill and a damaged, and then landed. Homuth was livid because Marseille had left his position covering Homuth, flew past his flight leader and shot down what Homuth thought should have been his victory. Upon landing Homuth walked over to Marseille and began berating him in front of everyone, not a very professional thing to do with a subordinate, embarrassing Marseille. Many of the men interviewed and mentioned in this book were witnesses. All agreed that it was definitely the wrong thing to do, but Marseille would make the situation even worse.

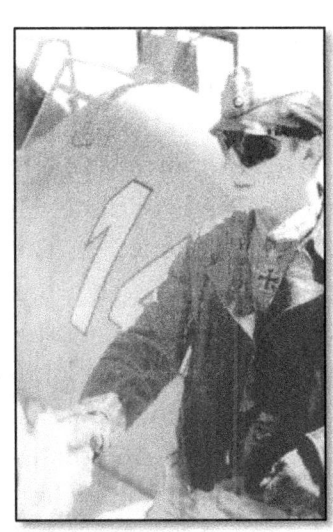

Marseille with "Yellow 14" (Ludwig Franzisket)

Werner Schroer gave his comments on what he saw: "Homuth was all over Marseille. He had a quick temper, and I think that all of the infractions and lack of punishment for Jochen had been too much for him. Also remember that Homuth had tried to limit Marseille's flying. Many of us thought that it was because he wanted to get more victories faster than Jochen. Well, as we all know that was as effective as catching running water in your hands. Homuth was simply frustrated, but I thought that he handled it very badly."[135]

In retaliation, Marseille took off, circled, and strafed the ground in front of Homuth's tent, actually sending a few rounds into the tent while Homuth was sitting at his desk shaving, an action that saw Homuth write him up for a court-martial for attempted murder of a superior officer, conduct unbecoming an officer, dereliction of duty, insubordination, disobeying a direct order in combat, etc. The only unfamiliar charge against Marseille was attempted murder, as all the others had been attempted before and were ignored by Woldenga and Neumann, which further infuriated Homuth.

According to Woldenga: "That was the most stupid thing Marseille could have ever done. My hands were effectively tied, so something had to be done."[136] The end result was that Marseille was again grounded, denied a promotion for the attack against the tent, but the court-martial was averted, thanks to Neumann, at least for the time being. Neumann explained what happened:

"Woldenga knew that this had to be dealt with immediately, but quietly and that Marseille had to be punished for the incident. Hell, the entire *Geschwader* knew about it before dinner. He and I discussed all the charges against Marseille that Homuth had drafted, and we could see dismissing all of the charges with explanations, except for the attempted murder. We both dug into our brains to figure out a way to change that charge to something less detrimental to Marseille. If that allegation made it to *Generalfeldmarschall* Kesselring, let alone Göring, he could have been shot. It was that serious. At that moment I needed a strong drink."[137]

Homuth would never forgive Marseille for that blatant display of disrespect, and Neumann's interference with Woldenga's support.

Homuth would not forget and according to Franzisket: "Homuth vowed that he would have Marseille's ass in jail, or in a grave before the end of the year. He was so angry I just wanted to walk away from him, hoping that he would tell me that I was dismissed."[138]

On February 8, 1942, four Me-109s from 3 *Staffel* I./JG-27 lifted off to take retaliation on a flight of Hurricanes from No. 274 Squadron RAF that had attacked their base just after 08:00, while Marseille was returning to base low on fuel as the last fighter to land following a short escort mission for a reconnaissance aircraft. He knew of the raid and was hoping to refuel after having no contact with the enemy. As he approached the field, the radio came alive, warning him of a second wave of enemy aircraft that were closing in on him for an easy kill. The men on the ground thought that they were going to watch their friend die right there on his own airstrip.

> Ludwig Franzisket had already landed and was out of his fighter, and he described what happened: "Neumann came running out of his circus wagon and told everyone to take cover. The first wave of enemy fighters had dropped one bomb each on our airfield and there was not any real damage. Then someone said Marseille was coming in. I heard his engine and saw him, but he was not alone. He had five enemies coming in behind him without bombs this time to hit our airfield again. Marseille gave one of the greatest shows we ever saw."[139]

As Marseille dropped altitude and lowered his landing gear the five Hurricanes roared in, probably for a strafing run, but obviously the Me-109 in the landing pattern was too tempting a target. They were closing in fast. Marseille was alerted on the radio and quickly retracted his landing gear, gave full throttle, and roared head level over the airfield to pick up speed. Enemy tracers streaked past either side of his canopy some striking the German tents with the lead enemy fighter less than two hundred meters behind him. Most of the men on the ground thought that there would be a collision when Marseille banked left into them his wings vertical, the left wing barely three feet off the ground.

That was when Marseille kicked left and right rudder, then broke hard left and tightened his turn as his pursuer flew past. Once he had enough speed, Marseille began a sharp climb to gain altitude. The remaining Hurricanes coming head on against him flashed underneath his Messerschmitt, just as Neumann came outside to see what was going on. He joined Homuth and the others as they watched a legend in the making. During all of this an amazing thing was happening that shocked a few of the pilots looking up and watching the spectacle:

"Of all the things going on I could not believe what I was also seeing," stated Friedrich Körner. "Some of the men, mostly the ground crews were taking bets on whether or not Jochen would survive this fight. Others were betting on how many he would shoot down before he died, while others were accepted the wagers believing that he would win and survive. I have to say that the entire thing was rather ghoulish to me."[140]

While the men on the ground watched in fascination and betted on his fate, Marseille reached 2,000 feet and then he rolled over, inverted, and dropped the nose down, falling on his back, heading toward earth as he gained speed. He fired. The Hurricane on the far right erupted in smoke and fell away, and before that enemy slowly descended and then hit the ground sliding to a stopped, at 08:22, he had reverse rolled and fired upon another Hurricane, which caught fire and crashed at 08:25. The first enemy he shot down slid into the ground beside the airfield at Martuba, and the pilot, Flight Sergeant P. C. Hargreaves in Hurricane Z4000, was captured uninjured. Neumann recalled what happened:

"The ground gunners could not fire for risk of hitting 'Seille, but he did not need the help, and the Hurricane pilot slid into the desert floor and a large cloud of dust covered the aircraft. He must have been afraid of fire because he was out of that thing, I mean out like a bullet and running away from it. There was no fire luckily. Our sentries recovered him and brought him to me. He was a very polite young man I should say."[141]

Hargreaves would later be the special guest of the rising Star of Africa, as Marseille always enjoyed those moments with enemy fliers.

The second plane crashed and burned with no survivor. It seems that Marseille's third victory, a Hurricane was mistakenly identified as a P-40 in his *Abschuss* (after action report). Marseille climbed again, rolled, and turned to attack the remaining aircraft. The third target he fixed upon required a climb, stall, bank and roll at 500 feet altitude, but it worked. He then gave full throttle and increased his speed after getting on the Hurricane's tail, firing. It was at about this time that Neumann began screaming at the men standing around to get up there and help Marseille, but no one moved.

Just then three fighters from 1 *Staffel* I./JG-27 arrived from the early morning scramble and saw the lone German standing against all those enemies above their own airfield as well as the smoking wrecks on the ground. They roared over the field as Marseille screamed for help. The remaining two Hurricanes, including Marseille's third hit, which was smoking lightly, fled east to safety. The three additional Me-109s, low on fuel, could not pursue.

Marseille pulled straight up, twisting his aircraft in a spiraling chandelle on its seventy-degree nose-up attitude, rolled, lost altitude to gain speed, then flipped on his back, nosed down, and just ten or so feet above the deck, rolled out with full power clearing his tail. He then cut power, extended the flaps, and the landing gear came down and locked a few seconds before he touched down. Schroer recalled the event in detail:

"The fight from start to finish lasted about eight minutes; it was marvelous. The men were cheering with each climb and turn. Some men were wagering on whether or not Marseille would die or survive. I thought it was rather ghoulish. The fight he was in was all over the place. At one time we all had to drop to the ground, as Marseille's fighter was only three meters from the ground. The wind from the propeller blew over us and his wingtip clipped a tent rope, and the Hurricane was right behind him. I could not take my eyes off the event. It was possibly the most spectacular flying I had ever seen, on both sides."[142]

Neumann and all the others cheered, and the ground crew loosened Marseille's parachute harness and restraining straps and helped him out. The ground crews were rarely able to see the results of their hard work put to good use, such as when their pilots' scored victories. On this day they were given a deadly air show. Each kill took an average of 17 rounds each, and the fight lasted less than ten minutes. Marseille filed his report, claiming two victories and a damaged that were uncontested and immediately confirmed, and then he asked the smiling Neumann jokingly if that meant he would get his Knight's Cross now. They were his 37th and 38th victories, and the day was not even over.

Later the same day the *Gruppe* was scrambled again as eleven Blenheim bombers with a full escort of three squadrons from No. 3 Squadron RAAF, Nos. 73 and 112 Squadron RAF were reported heading toward Derna. Four P-40s of No. 3 Squadron broke off early with engine trouble, but soon fell victim to the pilots of I./JG-27, when *Oberleutnant* Keller damaged one fighter that escaped, and then shot down a second for a confirmed victory. The nine remaining P-40s continued.

When the rest of the German fighters attacked, No. 73 Squadron RAF was broken up in the melee, as No. 112 Squadron RAF, having lost four fighters quickly, still tried to protect the bombers. Marseille, still feeling the thrill of his two victories that morning, locked onto a P-40, cutting off Homuth in the process, and fired a quick burst for his third kill of the day, stealing Homuth's victory and sending Flight

Sergeant John Ramsay Tonkin into the ground at 14:20. Tonkin crash landed but he survived and evaded capture. Tonkin would later die on July 7, 1943. Marseille's fourth kill of the day was also his 40th. Homuth did finally score a kill, shooting down Sergeant George Walton Elwell in P-40 (AK593) at 14:32 hours GMT (15:32 Berlin time), bringing his own tally to 39.

Marseille had finally exceeded his superior officer whom he felt had caused him so much anguish. Marseille's last victim of the day (which was misidentified as a P-40 in the *Abschuss*, but was in fact a Hurricane), was New Zealand born Flight Sergeant Alwyn Harold Sands of No. 73 Squadron RAF, who took a full load of 20mm cannon, and then crash-landed at 14:20 and he evaded capture. Sands would later die on May 27, 1942.[143]

Marseille after receiving his Knight's Cross (Ludwig Franzisket)

The ever-resilient Otto Schulz brought his own score to 37 by shooting down a P-40 (AK585) flown by New Zealander Sergeant Brian Patrick Hoare, who died. Friedrich Körner shot down Sergeant Neville Holman's P-40 (AK673) at 14:27 as the battle drifted over Bomba Bay. Holman was listed as missing in action until declared killed in action on February 11, 1942.

Homuth was apparently quite irritated that not only had Marseille again cut him off and stolen his kill, but the young Berliner had bragged before the mission, and even afterward, that he was going to beat his flight leader in getting victories as revenge for not being promoted. According to Körner, "Marseille said that all would soon see who the better man was."[144] Marseille had apparently proven this, and Homuth was not very happy about it. Then Marseille added to the tension. Neuman had listened to the entire event on the radio:

"I knew that as soon as the men landed, I would be in the middle of another Marseille Homuth argument, and it was getting old. Woldenga suggested that we transfer Marseille to another *Staffel,* but I disagreed. My reasoning was that if we did that, it would show the entire *Geschwader* that we could not handle the problem in our own way, and I wanted to establish that regardless of their disagreements with each other, they had to work those problems out."[145]

After the mission the Germans prepared for rather rare meal; someone had purchased a goat and it was being prepared. Their prisoner Flight Sergeant Hargreaves might have been in custody, but he was also honored as a guest of I./JG-27 in typical *Luftwaffe* fashion. Overwhelmed by the friendly atmosphere, Hargreaves was surprised to learn that it was Marseille who shot him down. Many fliers in North Africa on both sides knew who he was to some degree, if only by his Yellow 14 and not by name. Marseille, who spoke English fairly well, had a long discussion with his victim. Schroer heard a few bits and pieces:

"Jochen, who I had known since flight school, the arrogant and unashamed exhibitionist, was truly a humanitarian despite all of his other flaws. He really cared about the men he shot down. Whenever possible, we all wanted to meet those we shot down. Call it a morbid curiosity, but pilots, I suppose like other groups of fighting men, have a fraternity that really goes beyond nationalities. It is a universal brotherhood, one that Neumann fostered, and we all gladly participated in.

"After Marseille landed, Homuth called him in for a real earful, and told him that he was grounded until further notice for disobeying orders, but we all knew that it was also a matter of Homuth not being able to contain Jochen, not by any traditional means. After this Marseille went back to [chat with] the British pilot, and soon [afterward] he took off, by himself, without a wingman, and against the new standing order that he was grounded.

"Homuth came running out and asked, 'Where in the hell does he think he is going?' and he was looking at me. I just shrugged my shoulders as Neumann came out of his tent. 'What is 'Seille doing?' he asked, and again no one knew, until the British prisoner explained that he had inquired as to how he could inform his unit of what had happened to him and his fellow pilots. He did not want to be listed as missing. Marseille told him to write a note, and give him the coordinates to his airfield, and he would let them know. Well, that was what he did. When he came back over an hour later and landed, Homuth wanted him very badly, but Neumann got to him first."[146]

Neumann knew what had happened, and he knew that he could run interference for only so long. If Homuth went over Neumann's head to Woldenga, especially revisiting the tent shooting matter, there would be little that Neumann could do about it. However, even Woldenga knew enough to let certain things lie, and he had to handle a pilot as hot as Marseille carefully, who was shooting down the enemy in batches and making his *Geschwader* look good in the combat reports submitted to *Oberkommando der Wehrmacht* and *Luftwaffe* headquarters.

Woldenga was also aware that he had to balance military discipline with operational necessity, common sense, and pragmatism. Woldenga stated during his interview: "This situation between those two was finally coming to a boiling point. Homuth's ego would not let Marseille's insubordination go, and Marseille would not adjust his attitude to diffuse the situation. I was really almost ready to ship one or the other out, but Neumann asked me to let him handle it. I was happy to."[147]

Rödel was there and witnessed the events: "There was a time to act against a man for doing wrong, and then there was the time to let him know that you may disapprove of his action, even though you completely understood why he did it. Had it been anyone but Marseille, and if it were me, I would have fired him. But then again, only Marseille would continue to violate orders. As I always said, he was a protected species."[148]

Neumann called Marseille into the wagon and told him to have a seat. He asked him how his solo mercy mission went, and Marseille confirmed that it was uneventful. Neumann then reminded him of the standing order from Berlin, given by Göring personally, months earlier, following his missions to notify the Australians of Byers's capture and later the second flight he made to No. 250 Squadron regarding Byers' death two weeks later, that no such flights were to be continued. This was the second such trip Marseille had conducted after the ban. Even Franzisket never repeated his one mercy mission. Neumann mentioned this event:

Marseille with his mother while home in Berlin (Ludwig Franzisket)

> "I reminded Marseille that almost every action he made was a court-martial offense, and that I was personally stunned that he would consciously and flagrantly disregard a direct order from the *Reichsmarschall*. That was insane. And by extension, for not turning him in, he was making Woldenga and I co-conspirators, and I valued my freedom. I also warned him that Homuth was not going to let the day's events go by unnoticed. He had better watch his ass, because we could not cover for him all the time."[149]

On February 12, 1942, Homuth, who thought that grounding Marseille would teach him an important lesson, was overruled by Neumann, as every pilot was needed for operations and Woldenga agreed. Now that his order banning Marseille from flying had been overruled, along with his request for a court-martial for the strafing run on his tent, as well as many episodes of violating his direct orders in combat, and just the simple fact that Marseille annoyed the hell out of him, Homuth probably felt that his position of authority and his respect in the eyes of his men were in jeopardy. He may have been right, according to Schroer:

"Everyone knew that Marseille was getting away with murder, but then again most did not care. He was good, effective, and he raised morale. No matter what he did to anger Homuth, Neumann and even Woldenga knew that nothing was more important than high morale, and Marseille's mercy flights also raised morale. I guess in a strange way it was a type of healing for us. We loved shooting down aircraft, but I do not think there was a single one of us who liked the thought of killing a man. We tried to separate the two. Marseille allowed us that escape, our penance I suppose."[150]

Rödel said, "It was no secret that Homuth had it in for Marseille. He hated his authority being challenged, and he especially hated the fact that Marseille was untouchable as long as he kept shooting down aircraft. No commander in their right mind would ground a man for any length of time for the types of infractions Marseille committed, despite the regulations. This really became problematic after he was awarded the Knight's Cross, and later the Oak Leaves and Swords. The greater the success and awards, the more high-profile he became, hence the more untouchable.

"Marseille did something that had not been done since the Great War. He brought humanity back to the war, in a very personal way, with his flights to inform the enemy of their pilots. He did not think that a man should not be accounted for; that families needed to know, to have closure. I really think that the personal tragedies he suffered, with his sister, as well as losing his good friends in combat spurred him to do this even more. Rather than become hardened by the war and the horrors we experienced, Marseille actually became even more of a humanitarian."[151]

Flying an escort mission on that day of February 12, Homuth gave Marseille strict orders to cover him. Homuth scored a victory, equaling Marseille with his fortieth kill when they engaged No. 274 Squadron RAF. Homuth hoped to take the lead in the scoring on that mission, but his subordinate, resistant wingman, rising star and competitor in chief once again violated Homuth's explicit orders, breaking from his leader's tail when he saw that he faced no immediate threat.

The shouts from Homuth over the radio were heard by everyone in the air, as well as by Neumann and Woldenga in the command post on the ground. Neumann remembered this: "Once we heard Homuth's screams and curses over the radio, I looked at Woldenga, and he looked at me and said, 'Well, you wanted to handle those two. Good luck,' and I knew that there would be another intervention when they landed."[152] But Marseille ignored Homuth and continued hunting. Then he chose a victim. Then he chose another, then another, and then a fourth went down in flames. His victories came at 13:30, 13:32, 13:33, and 13:36, a Hurricane and three P-40s and were verified by several pilots.

Four Hurricanes were shot down from No. 274 Squadron RAF, including Sergeant R. W. Henderson, who crash-landed and was unhurt; Flight Sergeant Parbury, who was forced to bail out of his burning fighter and was uninjured; Pilot Officer S. E. van der Kuhle crashed offshore; and Flight Lieutenant Smith was listed as missing in action. It is believed that Sergeant A. T. Tonkin (no relation to Sergeant Tonkin shot down previously) of No. 112 Squadron RAF was Marseille's last victory, killed while chasing Homuth. Marseille closed in on him, firing into him with a close low angle deflection shot until his aircraft exploded and broke up, saving Homuth's life. Marseille's score now stood at forty-four, and the day's fights were over—at least in the air. Homuth had sustained damage after Marseille had left him alone, and he managed to land at Martuba. The aircraft flew again a few days later.

Upon landing, Homuth walked over to the command post, so furious his heavy boot prints left deep impressions in the hard-packed sand, and he once again demanded a court-martial for Marseille. Neumann and Woldenga had heard everything on the radio, and they knew that Homuth had a valid argument. By regulations he was well within his rights to charge Marseille with several violations, not to mention the earlier strafing attack. There was no statute of limitations in the military. As Schroer, who landed shortly thereafter on the field low on fuel, explained:

"Marseille had really done it this time, but this is where it became very interesting. I jumped out and could hear the shouting coming from the wagon. It was Homuth. Yes, Marseille violated his standing orders. Yes, he violated the rules of *Luftwaffe* combat flying, and of course he also ignored the repeated demands of his leader to return to formation, thereby violating a direct order in the face of the enemy. This is important, because this charge was an offence similar to cowardice or desertion in battle. It could get a man executed by firing squad.

"Marseille was in big trouble, but he had a few things in his favor that Homuth perhaps knew, but in his rage dismissed or simply forgot about. Sure, Marseille had violated the rules and disregarded his orders. However, he had scored four victories, saved Homuth from being shot down, as two of those victories were going after him, and he also managed to bring his own fighter back undamaged."[153]

Woldenga also commented: "I reminded Homuth in front of Neumann that Marseille also saved his life by clearing his tail. He may want to remember that when he wrote his report. It would appear that Homuth followed my advice, as nothing detrimental against Marseille was reflected in the final report."[154]

Neumann spoke about this also: "Homuth was simply frustrated that Marseille outsmarted him at every turn; every violation was overshadowed by a great success. It must have really grated on him, and I could understand that. And I cannot say that Homuth did not have solid ground here. Yet my responsibility was to keep men alive, keep aircraft flying and shoot down enemy aircraft. Marseille helped us complete all of those requirements, and in the end that was all Berlin cared about, results."[155]

February 13, 1942 started as another escort mission for the Stukas led by Kurt Kuhlmey en route to Tobruk. No sooner had the Me-109s taken their high covering position, than enemy fighters from No. 1 Squadron SAAF and the ever-present No. 274 Squadron RAF were spotted, again first seen by Marseille, just as one Hurricane took the initiative and attacked, diving into the German fighters who were at the lower altitude echelon as close protection for the dive bombers. That was a mistake the Allied pilot would never make again.

Marseille saw the Hurricane from his perch as top cover security, rolled over, kicked the left rudder all the way down, and went full throttle into a steep seventy degree dive. He was angled on the Hurricane's tail within seconds, closing the gap with his superior speed. Marseille's wingman was right behind him, sticking as close as he could, when Marseille fired a short burst.

The Hurricane never had the chance to hit the Me-109s, as his aircraft smoked and fell into pieces in the air, with sections of the left elevator striking Marseille's fighter in the radiator, damaging the cooling system, although his wingman was far enough away to avoid any damage. Marseille's 45th victory crashed into the desert east of Tobruk at 09:20 and was witnessed by several pilots after his cry of *"Horrido!"* was heard over the earphones.

Marseille called out that his engine was damaged, and then it died as the coolant ran out, overheating his engine. The engine froze and the propeller stood still, as Marseille reported that he had enough speed and altitude to reach their own lines. Neumann listening in back at the base asked that Marseille confirm his position. Marseille had just given his coordinates when he radioed that he saw an enemy aircraft. Neumann plotted him on the map. Marseille was 5,000 feet higher than the enemy fighter, and without engine power, he began to dive, converting the altitude into airspeed.

The lead enemy fighter apparently saw him and was climbing to engage the lone Me-109, but Marseille was a master of the hard bank and roll, which he did to perfection after completing a perfect split-S even without power, closing the gap as the Hurricane came into gun range. The Hurricane was just leveling out to fire when Marseille pressed the trigger. The Hurricane flipped over and plunged to the ground below. Marseille managed to reach Martuba and glide into a perfect gear-down dead stick landing; the fighter was repaired in two days. He would fly again on the fifteenth. That battle cost I./JG-27 two damaged fighters and no losses to aircraft or pilots.

The Hurricane, piloted by South African Lieutenant Le Roux (not to be confused with Squadron Leader Johannes Jacobus le Roux) became victory number 46 at 09:25, but he survived. Following his dead stick landing, Marseille was introduced to his latest victim, who was fortunately uninjured, and Marseille told him that he was very pleased that he was in fact alive. Marseille took the man into his tent, and they spoke at great length in English and French.

Le Roux told him he had a dead engine, and his Hurricane was on fire as he slid across the desert. His canopy was jammed shut from the bullet strikes that bent in the beveled track, and he managed to finally pry the canopy loose and get out. He had not gone more than 100 meters from the wreckage when it exploded. The plume of smoke indicated to the Germans on the ground where their target was. He was recovered from the crash site and brought to the headquarters of I *Gruppe*, where he was checked out and found medically fit. In usual fashion Marseille took his information and gave Le Roux his contact data, so that after the war they may get together. Marseille assumed that former enemies would have no ill will, and history proved that the great majority of the time, he was correct.

These events from February 8–13, 1942, would see Marseille at last promoted to *Oberleutnant* and finally being recommended for the Knight's Cross for the forty victories, while Schulz received the same distinction for forty-four victories on February 22, 1942. The men of JG-27 had much to celebrate. Their losses-to-victories ratio was one of the best in the entire *Luftwaffe* at that time.

On February 15, 1942, I./JG-27 Neumann sent 1 *Staffel* on an escort mission for a formation of Ju-88 medium bombers as they rendezvoused near their destination, Gambut. Unusually, there was not an enemy fighter patrol over Gambut, which meant that the Germans had the element of surprise. It was Marseille who called out two enemy fighters taking off far below them, which then climbed into a turn to intercept the medium bombers.

The bombers dropped their ordinance on target and Marseille's *Schwarm* ensured that they were safe from interception, when he radioed that he was taking his wingman back to engage the enemy fighters. Homuth called for him to watch out for enemy fighters. Marseille and his wingman Pöttgen turned and climbed to achieve altitude, and as Marseille banked to look over, he saw the two P-40s also climbing for altitude. Once he had over 2,000 feet above the enemy, he made his move.

Marseille rolled over and started to dive headed straight for the P-40 flown by Flight Sergeant Frank B. Reid of No. 3 Squadron RAF, who had almost reach 1,500 feet when Marseille came at him in a dive head on, considered suicidal against a P-40. Marseille had mastered this style of attack; he applied left rudder, right stick, going into a skid leading his target. Then he fired and threw the stick hard left to roll away, avoiding the return fire from the P-40.

Reid's fighter was heavily damaged as the German cannon and machine gun rounds blew out his engine at 13:00. Reid never had a chance to escape his burning machine as the altitude was too low to safely bail out, and he was probably killed by the cannon shells that raked across the fuselage up into the engine. Marseille had scored kill number 47.

Marseille then pulled up as Pöttgen called out the enemy wingman, a P-40 flown by Pilot Officer P. J. Briggs, also of No. 3 Squadron RAF, who made the tragic mistake of turning away from Marseille. While in his climb, Marseille had pulled up, rolled and turned into his second enemy. He had a head-on three-quarter right-side deflection shot as Briggs was passing by and managed a full two-second burst that hit the engine. Briggs rolled over as the fighter tumbled out of control at 13:03, and he managed to bail out at only 300 feet. He survived the jump, although he was injured when he hit the ground and became Marseille's 48th victory.

For the next four days rainstorms choked the airfield. Visibility sometimes dropped to less than one hundred feet on the ground, severely limiting operations. Once the rain stopped a very large sandstorm began, and two days after that subsided, it rained again, turning the sand that invaded everything into a liquefied emulsion.

The weather wreaked havoc on the airstrips as well as the machines, which were still invaded despite being covered with tarpaulins. The water supply was also in jeopardy and had to be strained through filters to remove the sand that entered the water wagons posted near the fuel depots. Fuel contamination was another concern, although after inspection it appeared that the gasoline had not been affected, nor the engine oil, which was in sealed drums and covered.

Marseille was in active combat again on February 21, during a mission that carried I./JG-27 to Gambut/Fort Acroma Libya. Led by Homuth, 1 *Staffel* took off and flew in three *Rotten* for a total of six fighters, with the first *Rotte* led by Homuth, the second by *Leutnant* Hans-Arnold "Fifi" Stahlschmidt, and the third by Marseille. Once they were within sight of the fort, Stahlschmidt called out eleven enemy fighters. These were P-40s from No. 112 Squadron RAF and No. 3 Squadron SAAF, and Homuth took his wingman higher to gain an altitude advantage.

The first activity went against the Germans, when the P-40 flying underneath Stahlschmidt pulled up and struck his engine and radiator. The pilot who shot him down was none other than Clive Caldwell. Streaming glycol and smoke, Stahlschmidt managed to regain control and continued to fly toward the safety of German lines, although he went down in no man's land just a couple of miles short of the sixty-odd miles back to the base at Martuba.

According to Stahlschmidt, in a letter he wrote to his mother: "Homuth and Marseille were of the opinion that it was only the purest chance that the Curtiss hit me at all. Homuth, who normally metes out the strictest measures, didn't hold me guilty for the misadventure."[156] The fighter was a write-off and left where it crashed but Stahlschmidt was not injured badly, just a slightly burned left hand despite escaping the burning wreckage. He was subsequently grounded for three days to recover from the event.[157]

As he fled the scene a British vehicle had arrived, probably drawn by the trailing smoke, and fired upon the already smoking fighter. Stahlschmidt ran into a group of German soldiers, who returned fire at the enemy truck, and then both sides called it a day. The infantrymen gave him a ride back to base. As he arrived, he learned that Marseille had shot down two P-40s of the three victories claimed on that mission, for his 49th and 50th victories scored at 12:10 and 12:18. One of the kills was Caldwell's wingman. Everyone knew Marseille must receive his Knight's Cross very soon.

Marseille with an unknown woman (left) and Hannelies (right) (Raymond F. Toliver)

CHAPTER 7

The Knight's Cross

> *He really wanted that damned medal.*
> *I just wanted to go home alive. To hell with medals*
> Werner Schroer

Unannounced as usual for security purposes, *Generalfeldmarschall* Albert Kesselring landed at the base in his private aircraft on February 22 and was met by the staff officers. Kesselring was their special guest. He had ostensibly arrived to award Otto Schulz his Knight's Cross which was conferred with great ceremony. However, Kesselring did not divulge the complete reason for his visit. The unit was called together again on February 24, before Kesselring departed, and the men formed in ranks wondering what the occasion was, and then the order was again read, almost as an afterthought, stating that the Knight's Cross of the Iron Cross was awarded in the name of the *Führer* Adolf Hitler to Marseille.

Marseille was stunned, still believing that he had been passed over once again, probably because of Homuth. The award was actually dated February 22, the same day as Schulz's medal, and it would appear that perhaps Neumann or even Woldenga had wanted the delay as if to force Marseille into some semblance of humility. Stahlschmidt, who still had his left hand bandaged, was the first to congratulate him followed by Neumann. Schroer recalled the event:

"We were all very excited, especially his ground crew. His success was also their success, and every pilot knew that without your ground crew, you would not have that success, or even be alive probably. Marseille was always good and generous to his 'black men' [named for the coveralls worn by mechanics, although in the desert most wore khakis due to the heat], such as when he received special foods and bottles of good alcohol, he shared them with his crew, and *Staffel* mates. He had earned the distinction long before, but now it was good that he was recognized. I have to admit that for the first time since he returned, he seemed happy for a little while. A part of the old Jochen was back, for a while anyway."[158]

Stahlschmidt (fer left) Marseille (fourth from left) Neumann fifth from left) and Generalfeldmarschall Albert Kesselring (second from right) and Generalmajor Otto Dessloch (far right) during the Knight's Cross presentation. (Eduard Neumann)

The next few days saw bad weather and limited visibility restrict operations, but on February 27, II *Gruppe* was able to take off and begin the war again, and *Hauptmann* Gerlitz scored two P-40s within a five-minute span. III *Gruppe* was also in the air over Tobruk at around 11:00 hours, and they were soon joined by I *Gruppe* led by Homuth, with Marseille looking to add to his laurels. Once they engaged eleven P-40s from No. 3 Squadron RAAF and No. 250 Squadron RAF, Marseille claimed two rapid victories for victories 51 and 52, one being Sergeant Roger Jennings, who died in the subsequent crash, the other, Pilot Officer Richard C. Hart, who successfully bailed out, rejoining his unit.[159]

While Marseille and his men were on their field eating a late lunch that afternoon, his best friend "Fifi" Stahlschmidt and *Feldwebel* Keppler flew a *Rotte* mission as a forward reconnaissance escort, their destination was Bir Hacheim. However, just after reaching Bir el Gubi, Stahlschmidt saw a British column below. He had just started a strafing run when his engine died due to ground fire, and he struck a vehicle, then bounced up, just missing some enemy soldiers as he crash-landed for the second time in a month. Unfortunately for him, the unit was from the Free Polish Brigade. The soldiers ran to his fighter and pulled him out of the cockpit, and they handled him very roughly upon his capture and during the following interrogations.

After a full day of continued rough treatment and several beatings, where he suffered a fractured jaw and a broken nose and his personal decorations were stolen (a strict violation of the Geneva Convention of 1929 then in force, along with the beatings), he managed to escape and cover over 60 kilometers on foot, mostly at night when it was cool enough to travel. Sixteen hours after his escape he came across German soldiers who returned him to his unit. Both Marseille and Stahlschmidt had a very busy month. Stahlschmidt survived being shot down twice, captured, effectively tortured, and escaping. Along the way, Stahlschmidt had become the first German pilot in Africa to fly two-hundred combat sorties. And, Marseille had finally received his long-awaited Knight's Cross. He and the others were visibly shocked at their friend's physical condition upon his return.

Marseille in his tent (Ludwig Franzisket)

Franzisket recalled Stahlschmidt's condition: "When the soldiers delivered him to us three days later, he looked very bad. The Army doctor had examined him and wrote up a medical report which was given to Woldenga. His face was all black and blue, he could not speak clearly and his nose was twice its normal size. Those Poles had beaten the hell out of him until a British officer finally put a stop to it. But according to Fifi, that officer sat by for a while, and only intervened when it looked like the Polish soldiers may beat him to death.

"They dragged him away and began interrogating him, asking him all the usual questions that you would expect. Stahlschmidt feigned being more injured than he was. His eyes were still swollen from the beating, but he could still see, but he feigned blindness. This was why they did not have great security on him. According to him they placed him in a tent with one guard on the outside at the tent entrance. Periodically they would check in on him and he pretended to be sleeping. Finally, that last night, he waited until all was quiet and after sunset he dug out from under the tent and crawled away. He said that he worried about being shot like Espenlaub, so he planned to move only at night. After a few hours he managed to start running until the sun came up. He hid until late afternoon to avoid being seen, then started out west again. The fact that it was rather cold and not hot during the day helped him not to get too dehydrated. Finally, he came across our soldiers, who almost shot him until he identified himself. It was quite remarkable."[160]

Stahlschmidt apparently suffered severe anxiety following his second shoot down and capture, and his severe beatings at the hand of Poles and British. His nerves were shot. His hands shook as he drank or held anything, and sleeping was out of the question. Today he would be diagnosed with posttraumatic stress disorder. According to Schroer, "The medical officer looked him over and suspected a couple of cracked ribs and a fractured eye socket, in addition to the fractured jaw and broken nose, obviously the result of the torture, not the crash landing. He was lucky."[161]

Due to his recent experience and length in the desert on operations, Stahlschmidt was sent on home leave to be medically evaluated, and Marseille, again ill with dysentery, went with him, where he spent two weeks in the *Luftwaffenkrankenhaus* in Munich for medical treatment. Following his release, he visited his mother in Berlin and also became engaged to his fiancée, Hannelies Küpper, a schoolteacher in Berlin, news that shocked those who knew him, given his playboy past. It probably shocked a few women throughout Europe as well. He had never mentioned her before, perhaps to keep up his reputation as a ladies' man.

While he was in Berlin, preparing to return to the front in North Africa, he received a telegram from the *Oberkommando der Wehrmacht* that he was to report to Rome. He was to receive the Italian Silver Medal for Bravery (*Medaglia d'Argento al Valor Militare*), the Italian Pilots Badge, and the German-Italian African Campaign Badge in Silver from of the Italian leader himself, *Il Duce*, Benito Mussolini. Marseille's lack of political correctness knew few, if any, bounds. Upon meeting Mussolini for his decoration, he said to Count Gian Galeazzo Ciano: "That man really thinks a lot of himself, doesn't he?"

This slight against *Il Duce* would have had any Italian officer shot, and perhaps even the average German might not have survived. How Marseille managed to avoid any retribution remains a mystery. Galland mentioned his comment to Neumann, and it was also reported back to Berlin, where Hans Baur recalled Hitler commenting: "It seems that our young Marseille is an excellent judge of character."[162]

On April 18, 1942, Neumann held a large party to celebrate the full *Geschwader's* first anniversary in North Africa. Even without the flamboyant Marseille it was a full carnival event. Germans and Italian units from all over the theater arrived to partake in the downtime and imbibe with the celebrated men of JG-27. III./JG-27 had been relocated to Crete for a refit and reorganization, while I and II./JG-27 remained to bear the brunt of the air war, although some of the men from III *Gruppe* came back early, and even other *Luftwaffe* and ground units were invited. The men needed a break, and Neumann knew it. Then the next day the Germans learned about a bombing raid on Tokyo, Japan, as Franzisket stated:

"We were informed that an American bomber group had attacked Tokyo, and we found that quite interesting. That kind of reinforced some of the concepts that the Americans would be busy with the Japanese, and not bother with us. Marseille was of a different opinion. He said, 'Look at a map, and you will see that there are a lot of countries and islands to take before they can ever take Japan. And they will, I assure you. But America will always save Britain, and we are the greatest enemy."[163]

Marseille returned to combat on April 25. The news had spread that the enemy had strengthened their fighter forces, with new and improved Spitfire Mk IV being part of the program, but in limited numbers starting after March 1942, and these were Photographic Reconnaissance Unit machines later joined by Mk Vs. The Hurricanes and P-40s were manageable opponents: the Me-109F could fly faster and outmaneuver the P-40, although it was dangerous to dogfight at lower speeds with the Hurricane. But the Germans now had information on a new threat emerging.

The newer Spitfire Mk V once deployed with No. 103 Reconnaissance Unit was not a threat, as it was not armed, but the Germans knew that fully armed versions of this fighter could tackle the Messerschmitt on its own terms if it had weapons, and now that they had reports from France that these new combat versions had two 20mm cannon mounted, when it finally arrived it was a fighter to be highly respected in the hands of a good pilot. The Germans knew it was only a matter of time before they arrived in large numbers, but they still had the Mk II through Mk IV Spitfire variants to deal with along with the Hurricane II and P-40 models.

The Spitfire Mk V would be the most produced variant with 6,487 built, featuring four different wing configurations and a variety of weapons. The A style wing used eight .303 caliber machine guns, the B style wing had four .303 caliber machine guns and two 20mm Hispano cannon, and the C style wing could mount either four 20mm cannon or two 20mm and four .303 caliber machine guns. The E wing style housed two 20mm cannon and two .50 caliber (12.7 mm) Browning machine guns giving it great firepower. As the war progressed, the C wing version became most widely used as it was the most versatile. It allowed field crews to install whatever weapons were available. The Mk V could also outturn and out roll the Me-109 in the hands of a good pilot due to the clipped wings replacing the traditional rounded wingtips, but it did sacrifice airspeed as a result of greater maneuverability. Any wing variant could carry two RP-3 rockets for ground attack or carry a small bomb or external fuel tank.

The first mission of the day of April 25 was a Stuka escort mission, where the dive bombers were tasked with attacking and sinking a British oil tanker offshore. 6 *Staffel* II./JG-27 flew as close escort with eight Me-109s supporting I./StG-3, with the balance of the 14 fighters from I *Gruppe* flying as top cover. An Italian squadron was also part of the mission as a support element, as No. 260 Squadron RAF and No. 2 Squadron SAAF, two old nemeses of JG-27, threw up 33 P-40s.

The Germans started their deadly work quickly, just after a Ju-87 was shot down at 09:58 by Squadron Leader Osgood V. "Pedro" Hanbury of No. 260 Squadron RAF. After shooting down the Ju-87 and a Mc.202, he was soon being damaged by the tail gunner of his Stuka victory. He had an engine already dead when he was riddled with fire from Marseille, who dived down and fired at him at 10:06. Hanbury managed to crash land his crippled fighter and survive.

Marseille then climbed into a steep chandelle, twisted, rolled over, dived down, and locked on to the P-40 flown by another No. 260 Squadron pilot, Sergeant John William Wareham in AK808. He closed the distance, firing into the engine and fuselage at 10:08. Wareham died as a result. Marseille would be credited with victories fifty-three and fifty-four. Another No. 250 Squadron loss was Pilot Officer Miller, whose exact victor is unclear.[164]

It is interesting to compare the records of both units. I./JG-27 claimed five victories, while II *Gruppe* claimed three. Rödel and Reuter claimed two each, while *Feldwebel* Fink, *Hauptmann* Karl von Lieres und Wilkau, *Feldwebel* Steinhausen, and *Leutnant* Schiter each claimed one. The Allied units suffered four P-40s missing and presumed lost along with three of their pilots (with Hanbury recovered), four P-40s damaged and crash landed, another P-40 heavily damaged and written off, and the last P-40 lightly damaged and repaired.

On May 1, 1942, Marseille was officially given the citation that promoted him to *Oberleutnant* and five days later assumed temporary command of 3 *Staffel* I./JG-27, a position that became permanent on June 8, when newly promoted *Hauptmann* Gerhard Homuth was assigned as the *Gruppenkommandeur* for I/.JG-27 after Eduard Neumann had been promoted to *Major* replacing Bernhard Woldenga as the new *Geschwaderkommodore*.

With his promotion and new responsibilities as a full squadron leader, and Homuth as his direct commanding officer, and no Neumann constantly present to watch his back, and Woldenga being sent back to Germany, Marseille was walking a fine line. He was never able to take up his new rank and remain aloof from his men, as was the expected standard operating procedure in the German military. A leader should be fair and strict and remain behind a self-imposed barrier, not too friendly with subordinates: the so-called mask of command.

However, as Adolf Galland stated, due to Marseille's unchanging and cavalier ways he was never destined for high rank or great responsibility, despite his gifts as a combat pilot. He could never play the hard-ass commander required by German military protocol, and the example he provided was not exactly what the High Command considered appropriate. Marseille was never known to raise his voice to a man. He saw kindred spirits in the rebels and was able to work with these men in his own unique way. Marseille only grounded two pilots for infractions and never submitted a man for a court-martial. He never saw the need, and given his own history, he would have probably thought such an action would have been the height of hypocrisy. Marseille, as did all good leaders, led from the front and by example.

His superiors knew this, even if some of his examples were considered less than stellar. Many oral and written reports were submitted by visitors about Marseille's unmilitary demeanor, penchant for his banned music, and informal manner of addressing high-ranking officers. Neumann had spent much of his time explaining Marseille and running interference for him. Homuth, the new commanding officer for I./JG-27, was of no such mindset.

May 1942 saw the air war heat up, with II *Gruppe* being led by *Oberleutnant* Gustav Rödel after *Hauptmann* Erich Gerlitz was temporarily reassigned to III./JG 53 at Martuba as that unit recently arrived in total from Sicily in an attempt to supplement the fighter force. The first week was rather quiet, but the air war opened up on May 10, for Marseille in particular.

Squadron Leader Osgood V. "Pedro" Hanbury of No. 260 Squadron RAF (Michael Judd)

Flying with his wingman Pöttgen on a "free hunt," word crackled over the radio that two Hurricanes were en route to his airfield. The two Germans peeled around and headed back. Marseille spotted the two invaders long before they arrived at Martuba, and closing rapidly on the first Hurricane, Marseille began shooting out the engine. The pilot managed to belly land his crippled fighter, but he survived the impact at 09:13. Marseille had already locked onto the second, which took hits in the engine and dove into the ground, exploding at 09:15. His victims were Captain D. Cobbledick in #7780 and Lieutenant N. Flesker in Z4377, both of No. 40 Squadron SAAF, his 55th and 56th victories. Both men were listed as missing in action, presumed dead, but Flesker was in fact captured but injured.

Marseille and Pöttgen again saw action three days later, when on May 13 they were scrambled to intercept a flight of twelve P-40s from No. 3 Squadron RAAF. Marseille immediately attacked head on but made a couple of errant passes, finally scoring a kill at 10:10 using his skid method. The pilot, Sergeant Colin McDiarmid, bailed out wounded, and Marseille then took hits from McDiarmid's wingman, Flying Officer Geoff Chinchen, who later claimed a damaged fighter (Marseille's aircraft). Marseille began leaking oil, yet he continued the fight and completed a turn hard to the right, starting a climbing maneuver and a rollover, getting into a rapid passing firing position as he started the dive. This event was witnessed by several people, including Emil Clade, who recalled this event in great detail:

"I saw Marseille shoot the Kittyhawk and the pilot bailed out. I also heard his wingman call out 'good parachute', which let Marseille know the pilot had survived. That seemed important to him. The second fighter had hit Marseille, and Jochen called out that he was damaged. He then went into a dive, and I rolled to watch, and the enemy fighter was on him. Then Marseille pulled out and went full power into a seventy-degree vertical climb, still followed by this Kittyhawk.

"I called out to him, 'Jochen Indian climbing behind you,' and he called back 'I know, watch this,' and so I did. What I saw was also seen by others, and it was incredible. Marseille was high above, then he suddenly stalled, fell backwards to earth and came head to head with his pursuing enemy. Marseille did his famous skid and shoot then roll away. The enemy tracers flew past his Messerschmitt, but Marseille's shots hit the fighter, the engine started smoking. I called out 'Damn good move!' Then over the radio we all heard someone say 'show off bastard' and I thought it was Homuth but I could not be sure."[165]

Osgood Hanbury's P-40 after being shot down by Marseille (Geoffrey Morley-Mower)

A P-40 flown by Douglas Cecil Golding was smoking and Golding was wounded, and he crash landed. Another P-40 was flown by Flying Officer H. G. "Graham" Pace who was climbing into the two Germans when Marseille, pulling out of his dive on the second P-40 rolled over again and simultaneously skidded away from Pace's projectiles.

Marseille applied left rudder and fired from an inverted diving position, struck Pace's aircraft with cannon and machine gun rounds as he started a climb, continued the dive and then rolled out with Pöttgen right behind him all the way—notable in its own right, since it was not easy for anyone to follow Marseille. This "over the top" firing maneuver allowed Marseille to place a bullet through Pace's canopy and into his head at 10:15, killing him instantly. The fighter simply headed to the ground without any visible damage. His body was later recovered, and he was buried in Knightsbridge Cemetery. Marseille was credited with victories 57 and 58, as he nursed his overheating fighter with an unbalanced propeller back to his field.

Marseille's fighter was down for two days to repair the damage to his engine cooler and to replace the propeller, which had taken several hits. Once these were completed by noon on May 16, he and Pöttgen again took off in the early evening on a free hunt, spotting once again their oldest of nemeses, six P-40s of No. 3 Squadron RAAF just after 18:00 as they encroached toward Gazala. Again, without hesitation, although outnumbered three to one, the Germans jumped into the fight.

Marseille immediately went into his favorite climbing turn maneuver. This allowed him to gain an altitude advantage while looking back to see the location of his enemies, supplementing the observations of a wingman, and plan his diving attack. Like a good chess player, before he even started the attack, he would calculate his escape and work out alternative attack methods against any remaining enemies. Once he achieved the required altitude in the vertical climb, Marseille used full flaps, reduced power threw the stick left or right and applied left or right rudder, then half rolled, diving down into the P-40 of Sergeant T. V. Teede of No. 3 Squadron at 18:05.

Marseille again fired and rolled away before the enemy's rounds could hit him. His rounds immediately silenced the P-40s engine. Without power, Teede was too low to safely bail out, so he went into a gliding descent. Marseille pulled alongside, motioning for Teede to slide into a crash landing while he saluted his enemy, and Teede managed to crash land safely. He later returned to his unit.

Marseille then pulled up again just a couple of hundred feet from the deck, saw the remaining enemy fighters, and rolled his wings ninety degrees perpendicular to the ground in a turn so tight he must have had severe gray out. However, he maintained his composure, pulled back, climbed, rolled, and leveled out, firing at 18:15 into a No. 450 Squadron RAAF fighter flown by Pilot Officer Dudley Parker, who bailed out safely despite his fighter smoking heavily. Then, un-

Marseille enjoying a smoke (Ludwig Franzisket)

seen by the Germans due to the thick black smoke, Parker's abandoned fighter rolled over into the path of his wingman and collided with the P-40 flown by Flight Sergeant W. J. Metherall. Parker survived the crash with a good parachute and returned to his unit, but Metherall was killed. Marseille had destroyed three enemies, but only claimed two upon visual confirmation of Teede's crash landing and seeing Parker bailout. He never saw the collision that killed Metherall, nor did Pöttgen. The latter confirmation was not made, nor was the claim, since neither he nor Pöttgen saw the collision. Technically, although his score now stood at 60 victories, it should have been 61.

On May 19, III./JG-53 again arrived in North Africa from their bases in Sicily and Crete, landing at Martuba as a supplement to JG-27. Rödel officially took over command of II./JG-27 while *Major* Gerlitz was sent to command the new arrivals. That day, Marseille and Pöttgen were once again on their own when they spotted seven P-40s of No. 450 Squadron RAAF from their higher perch at 16,000 feet. Marseille once again winged over and led Pöttgen into the left echelon formation of four fighters. At 07:20 Marseille fired into the aircraft of Flight Sgergeant Ivan Young but did not score decisive hits. Young must have known he was in trouble as the Me-109 gained on him after converting the altitude into dive speed and knew there would be no escape. It was simply a matter of whether he would survive. Young took additional hits and his fighter tumbled toward the desert below but recovered.

Marseille closed to within 100 yards, firing two bursts. One hit the engine, which started to smoke, and the second completed the damage, with a piece flying off the engine cowling. Marseille flew alongside and motioned for Young to crash land, as he was too low to bail out. Young knew that he had to get down quickly, so he waved to Marseille and he leveled out his fighter and slid across the terrain. Marseille waited until the enemy pilot left his fighter and then strafed it in one more pass until it burned. Although slightly wounded Young managed to return to his unit. Marseille had chalked up victory number sixty-two at 07:30. Young's after-action report states that "the other" Me-109 (i.e. Pöttgen) shot his engine.[166]

By this time almost every pilot in every Allied squadron knew Yellow 14, even if they didn't know the name of the German flying it, at least not yet. This was as much due to their access to German newspapers and propaganda as to after-action reports that identified the offending Germans by aircraft numbers. It is best summed up by Geoffrey Morley-Mower:

"I can only say, since we still did not know exactly who Yellow 14 was, everyone had a serious case of paranoia about meeting him in the air. If you were in the air and someone called

'Bandits!' you were immediately alerted to the danger. But if someone called out 'Yellow 14' or "The Bastard' as he was known, that was when every head tuned, and pilots risked whiplash looking to make sure that 'this particular gentleman was not in his vicinity.

"On another note. I will add this; we had a preflight briefing once, and we had some new pilots just assigned. Judd and I both would go over the latest actions, what we learned, and what the new men should be aware of. Then we had our intelligence type give his rendition of wisdom. One of the things he stated, and it brought some laughter from the new men, was when he told them that; 'If you see 'Yellow 14 do not engage him one on one, call for support, do not try and fight him without support. And for God's sake if he goes into a climb do not follow him, wait for him to come back down and scan for his friends who may be coming to get you.

"One of the new men laughed out loud and said, 'Sir, all this bother about one Jerry? Let me meet him, and I will take care of the bugger.' Mike Judd then stood and said, 'Pilot Officer, how many victories do you have?' the man replied that he had four between the Battle of Britain and over Malta. Judd informed him that this particular German had over fifty victories, and a dozen were probably from this very group, and that Yellow 14 had been seen shooting down four victories in just one mission. Well, you could have heard a pin drop after that comment. I think they began to take the situation more seriously. It was not long after this that Marseille became known, just like some of the others."[167]

Marseille had just scored victory number 61 (which would have been a shared kill in the Allied camp and probably should have been Pöttgen's victory), when he again started his signature climbing chandelle as another P-40 tried to follow him. With an extra 2,000 feet of altitude when he reached over 18,000 feet, Marseille cut power to the engine, stalled, kicked right rudder, rolled over, and gave full flaps to increase the tightness of the turn. Once committed to the vertical dive, he retracted flaps, gave full power, and dived, turning into his pursuer, firing as the distance closed between them. The first rounds struck the P-40's wings and cowling without causing major damage, but the wake-up call was enough to force the Australian pilot into a dive and head for the low cloud cover to escape.

Marseille after a successful mission (Ludwig Franzisket)

On May 22 the Germans again scored victories, with Franzisket now back in combat after his medical leave and refamiliarization flights. He tells his story:

"I was cleared for flying duty and looking forward to getting back to the men. I flew a few hours to get back into it, as you may not know, flying is a perishable skill. I was cleared and Jochen came to see me. He jokingly accused me of malingering, and I accused him of idiocy. We had some drinks, and I brought back a couple of bottles of schnapps which made me very popular. It was good to be back, and Neumann congratulated me on beating the doctors and not being grounded."[168]

When enemy aircraft approached Martuba he shot down a P-40 and damaged a second, while Stahlschmidt, Steinhausen, and von Lieres each scored a victory for no losses. Marseille was, unfortunately for him, dealing with new replacement pilots and the never-ending paperwork, the bane of a fighter pilot's existence, but necessary as a leader, and the next day he was back in action.

Leading seven Me-109s into a bomber formation on May 23, Homuth damaged a Baltimore from No. 223 Squadron that eventually crashed. Rödel shot down two Tomahawks of the dozen his II *Gruppe* claimed that day, achieving forty-one victories for himself. He was to be matched by Marseille in the mission scoring; he shot down two aircraft, both Baltimore bombers (all mistakenly reported as Bostons) from No. 223 Squadron RAF near Tobruk for his 63rd and 64th victories within one minute of each other at 11:05 and 11:06. *Oberfeldwebel* Mentnich also downed one. Three bombers had fallen and a fourth limped back to its base as a write-off (Homuth's damaged aircraft). JG-27 claimed four victories for the mission.

Homuth's kill was probably the aircraft (serial number AG 717) flown by Flight Sergeant H. C. Hogsfield (copilot RAF), who was killed in the crash landing near Tobruk. Also killed were Flight Sergeant W. J. Taylor (observer RAAF), Flight Sergeant K. E. Stewart (wireless operator/air gunner RAAF), Sergeant M. D. O'Neill (air gunner RAF), Sergeant D. G. Downing (air gunner RAF). Injured was Pilot Officer D. C. Cummins (observer RAAF). Only Pilot Officer D. M.W. Leake (pilot RAAF) survived the crash without a scratch. The dead were buried at the War Cemetery in Tobruk.[169]

On May 26 *Generaloberst* Erwin Rommel launched his concerted attack that would continue until he reached the Egyptian frontier, starting on a 40-mile front that spanned from Gazala to Bir Hacheim, along with Tobruk—all locations that would prove fertile hunting grounds for Marseille. He was perfecting his personal methods, and his multiple victories per mission and per day were reflecting that.

III./JG-53 was also in the fight during this period, and once again burdened by the responsibility of being a temporary *Staffelkapitän*,

Marseille didn't add to his score until May 30. On this day Marseille and his *Schwarm* found themselves in an early morning melee with No. 250 Squadron RAF and No. 450 Squadron RAAF in the airspace between El Adem and Tobruk. This would be one of those missions that would further define his character.

Ludwig Franzisket was locked onto a P-40, firing, when he was in turn fired upon and his Me-109 hit by the P-40 (AK 704) flown by Australian born Flight Sergeant Graham George Buckland from No. 250 Squadron. Franzisket recalled the event: "I fired at a P-40, but immediately saw tracers fly past me on the left of my cockpit, and then I felt hits in the fuselage behind me. I called out for help and Marseille responded and told me to climb, so I pulled back hard on the stick."[170]

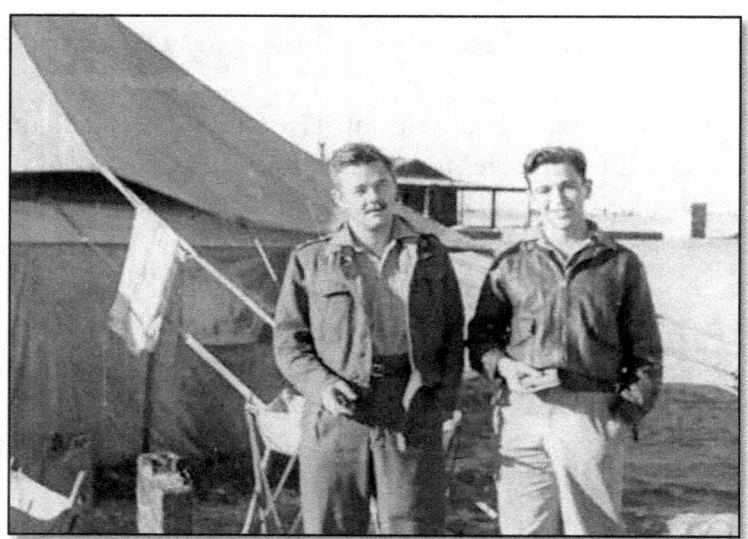

Cecil Golding (right) flew with No.5 Squadron under Maj. Jack Frost in the Western Desert and was shot down and wounded by Marseille at Gazala (Cecil Golding)

Marseille managed to turn into Buckland's fighter that was itself turning into a shallow climb to follow Franzisket, and Marseille climbed higher and then half rolled left and from a slightly higher altitude, he lowered his flaps to slow down, led Buckland and fired just a few rounds from less than a hundred feet. All four German pilots saw the canopy roll back, and Marseille closed in on Buckland's left, a little lower and was able to see the pilot, who seemed to be struggling to exit his burning aircraft, who finally jumped from his damaged fighter at 06:05, and his body tumbled into the horizontal stabilizer of the aircraft as it was spinning out of control. Horrified, they saw Buckland's parachute fail to open after he bounced over the tail. Marseille was heard over the radio to shriek in horror as he saw what had happened to Buckland. "Poor bastard," was heard coming from the young Berliner.

This victory was important for Marseille, and not because it was his 65th, but because Marseille had written down the coordinates, and upon landing he immediately took off in his car with Pöttgen. They found the body of the pilot not a half kilometer from his crashed P-40, which was in fact just behind the Allied lines. After collecting the dead man's papers and some personal items and having his identity confirmed as Buckland, as well as his unit, upon returning to the airfield Marseille then climbed back into his refueled fighter and took off. Neumann recalled this particular event:

"Marseille returned and then climbed into his fighter which had been refueled and rearmed and took off. I asked Pöttgen where he was going, and he told me. I knew that if Homuth found out there would be a stink about it, but I admired Marseille for his chivalrous attitude. He was a true knight, just born in the wrong era, and fighting in the wrong war."[171]

Marseille headed toward the home airfield of No. 250 Squadron RAF, with Buckland's papers and personal effects in a small bag, which contained some photographs, his wristwatch, a religious medallion on a necklace and a very expensive fountain pen along with a note that he had written. Franzisket said that Homuth had seen the effects an took a liking to the fountain pen. Marseille slipped into Homuth's tent and took it back, and it was with Buckland's pen that he wrote the note.

Once again Yellow 14 took off without permission and made a fast pass over No. 250 Squadron's airfield, and after dropping the documents and his note with Buckland's location, he continued just above the deck until he was out of range of the antiaircraft fire that never touched him. Buckland's body was recovered, and he was buried in a place of honor at the Knightsbridge War Cemetery in Acroma, Libya.[172]

Geoffrey Morley-Mower and Michael Judd were in their short command tower when the radio crackled that there was an inbound German fighter. Once identification was made, Judd called for the gun crews to hold their fire. According to Morley-Mower:

"The call went out to not fire on the German flying in. We already suspected he was coming in to say something, had been there before and never shot anything, only notifying us if a mate was dead, wounded, that sort of thing. I suspected it was him, and there he was, Yellow 14, just zooming along close to the floor, and he dropped the bundle. The great irony was that many of the ground crew were standing along in amazement looking at this spectacle, and many dropped to ground so as to not get hit, he was flying so low, and I was told that one of the men had been binged in the noggin by the package. It was retrieved and brought up, and we saw that inside was a note, with a written list itemizing the contents of the package, with Buckland's personal papers and ID.

"The note gave the coordinates of where he was, and that there was safe passage to retrieve him. The note also addressed Buckland's family. As I recall it read said, 'It is with regrets that Sergeant Buckland died today and these personal things are for his mother'. He signed it 'The *Luftwaffe*'. I thought that was rather polite of Marseille to do that, although I am not sure under what authority he could provide such an accommodation. It sort of made me wonder how could we fight such a fine gentleman. Then I remembered how many of our *aeroplanes* [English pronunciation] he had taken out, as well as the pilots. But it was war, and we all did what we had to do."[173]

It was this type of flight more than anything else that gave Marseille his legendary status with his enemies. Many knew his aircraft and unit, and his deadly proficiency. Later they would know him by name. Mike Judd clarified this fact:

Photo taken of Marseille near evening (Ludwig Franzisket)

"We often captured many German or Italian soldiers and pilots, aircrew, that sort. We had many pieces of literature, such as their personal letters which they were allowed to keep under the Geneva Convention, as well as magazines and newspapers. One Italian pilot had a copy of the German *Signal* magazine, in Italian. Well, I did not read Italian or German, so we found a mechanic in the unit who was fluent in Italian. He read the article aloud, named the pilot, and then we knew who The Star of Africa was. We knew the name Hans-Joachim Marseille, as well as others. We already knew all about Galland and pilots like that."[174]

The Allies knew who he was, but they also knew that this was a modern knight, who killed when necessary, but was chivalrous enough to try and ensure that their comrades were accounted for, rather than run the risk of being listed as missing in action whenever possible. To all warriors that means a lot, but to pilots and aircrews, it means more than most. Aviators tend to fall over enemy territory and are sometimes never accounted for, and Marseille felt that this should not be allowed if possible.

"Marseille often spoke about dying," Franzisket stated, "which is a subject that we as pilots avoided even more than desk duty. He was obsessed with the concern that he may be killed and listed as missing. He always wanted his mother to know where he was, and if he was alright. He wrote to her often. He made it very clear that he did these flights out of respect for the families of these men, who he believed perhaps suffered even more than the pilots.

"The uncertainty of never knowing if your man, brother, whoever, was going to come home weighed heavily on them. He knew this, his mother told him this. That was why he did it. He could have been viewed as a contradictory man; killing and then trying save, or inform, and recover the dead. I would say that he was a humanist thrown into a very inhumane environment, and he was just trying to make the best of a terrible situation."[175]

The next day, May 31, I./JG-27 and III./JG-53 were airborne throwing a dozen Me-109s into a Stuka escort, commanded by Kurt Kuhlmey on their mission to Bir Harmat. Twelve P-40s from No. 5 Squadron SAAF were sighted bearing down on the slow-moving aircraft. The South African flight was led by a Major Moodie, and they had altitude advantage, and one screamed in and shot down a Stuka quickly before any German fighters could get to him. Kurt Kuhlmey described the action:

"One of our men screamed over the radio 'Indians!' and we saw the Kittyhawks coming in. I was the lead Stuka and we had I think sixteen Stukas. This Kittyhwak came in fast and shot up one of my crews. I then heard '109s' over the radio, and then I saw them, so I knew that we were not alone."[176] From above Marseille and the others had seen the action.

Pulling around, Moodie caught a Me-109 in a climbing turn and fired, inflicting damage but no confirmed kill. That would be the last advantage the South Africans would enjoy. The men of I,/JG-27 had just arrived and joined Marseille who called that he was going into the fight, and rolled into a dive and fired into a P-40 flown by five and a half victory ace Major Andrew Duncan that started smoking, and headed to the ground. Duncan was killed outright at 07:26. Marseille had just shot down his 66th confirmed kill.

Marseille was still in his dive when the Ju-87 attacked by Moodie started to go down and one parachute was seen. Then Moodie in his climb flashed past Marseille coming in the opposite direction on his right getting hits on his Messerschmitt but no serious damage and then he continued climbing to gain altitude. Marseille sighted another victim.

No sooner had Duncan's plane fallen away than his wingman also erupted in fire and smoke at 07:28, after Marseille slipped the rudder and avoided Moodie's attack to line up a turning deflection shot, accounting for number sixty-seven. Marseille shot down his third for the mission six minutes later, and the two units broke off as Marseille had number 68 confirmed at 07:34. Mentnich and von Lieres each scored a kill while Steinhausen recorded two victories.[177]

Marseille's victories came in such rapid succession he called them out twice each after it was finished, just to see if there were any witnesses. The affirmative came from Pöttgen who called out the confirmations, and others saw the victories as well, such as Ludwig Franzisket:

"You really had to see Jochen in combat to really appreciate his gift. I really have no idea how he managed the impossible angles, stalls and inverted over the top victories, but he always did this, even when greatly outnumbered. However, despite his natural talent, his lack of battle discipline was enough to turn you gray. This clown would dive into a dozen enemies, shoot down or damage a few, and continue twisting, turning, dropping flaps, once he even lowered his landing gear to close in on a Hurricane so that he would not overshoot. He shot him down, raised the gear and flaps, gave full throttle, smoke belching from his exhaust, and then did the same thing three more times. I always wondered when his number would come up doing that. Marseille simply said once that he was 'touched by the gods,' and I told him, 'No, you are just touched in the head.'"¹⁷⁸

Marseille right after his successful defense of his airfield when he shot down three Hurricanes (Ludwig Franzisket)

Kurt Kuhlmey remembered the show and he enjoyed telling the story: "I had lost a Stuka, and three others were smoking but called in that they were still alright. I saw a Kittyhawk fall down on fire, and then saw Marseille still diving, but a Kittyhawk was climbing, I thought they were going to collide. But then Marseille pulled around coming towards us on the tail of another Kittyhawk above on our one o'clock that I was certain was coming for me, so I pushed the stick forward to dive out of the way, but, then he shot down that one. I was breathing much easier afterward. It seemed that our fighters had taken everything in hand. I saw smoking enemies and parachutes. At least neither was mine."¹⁷⁹

June saw a flurry of activity, and there was both celebration and solemnity. Marseille was back in action in the late afternoon of June 1 against No. 112 Squadron RAF, when he shot down the P-40 flown by Pilot Officer Collet over Gadd el Ahmar for number 69 at 19:15. The Germans only scored two victories on this mission, Pöttgen getting the second.

On June 3 Marseille was leading his unit of seven aircraft from 3 *Staffel* to join other JG-27 fighters already airborne to rotate an escort for more of Kuhlmey's Stukas when they once again encountered the

South Africans of No. 5 Squadron SAAF. They had just finished combat against one Ju-87 Stuka formation and their Me-109 escorts from II./JG-27 over Bir Hacheim. They were low on fuel and ammunition, and now out of luck. Marseille's group had radio contact with the Stuka flight leader from I./StG-3, Kurt Kuhlmey, who in turn reported in as they started their dive bombing run. Kuhlmey explained what happened:

"We were on a mission, 3 June and I was leading sixteen Stukas to attack a British ground convoy that was reported by a reconnaissance pilot. The Allies had a lot of fighters over there and they covered their ground convoys and the ships at sea which we also attacked. We were briefed that the third *Gruppe* of JG-53 (III./JG-53) would be our escort, and when we arrived at the rendezvous they were nowhere in sight.

"I called on the radio to find out when they would arrive, then we were hit by P-40s, a lot of them. Twelve came in from the five o'clock position and started firing. One of my Stukas [flown by Hans Deible, shot down by Cecil Golding] erupted in smoke and started going down, and they crash landed. This was at just over 2,000 meters altitude. Then another Stuka was hit, but two P-40s were also smoking and streaming coolant from the tail gunners.

"I was all over the radio, switching channels calling in a mayday, and I am sure those listening heard some very choice words. Then a third Stuka started going down. I ordered the group to drop the bombs and bank away to head northwest back to our base. We were never going to reach that convoy. Then I heard over the radio that my escorts were already engaged, I believe it was Neumann, but he said his pilots were almost there.

"At that moment I heard a familiar voice; 'Albatross 1 we are coming almost there!' It was Marseille and his first *Gruppe* of JG-27 (I./JG-27). I knew his voice. They heard my call and were in the area, returning from a previous mission but were told to rendezvous with me. Two more Stukas were smoking and then I was hit banking left to get away. Then this P-40 climbed and came around behind me. My gunner fired at him, but he was then killed from the P-40s guns, but the P-40 broke away, and five more P-40s took an interest in me then."[180]

2/JG-27 on takeoff in the Me-109F2 ((Ludwig Franzisket)

The Stukas peeled away from the ground fire coming up to greet them when Pöttgen spotted the enemy 3,000 feet above them. The Germans started climbing, and the echo had not even faded in the headsets when Marseille said, "Right going in," gave full throttle and raised his nose, heading straight into the nine P-40s. This would begin the longest single engagement of Marseille's career, and one of his best. It would also be a white-knuckle mission for Kuhlmey.

Again, Kuhlmey explained his situation: "I have to tell you that I was sweating. I had counted five Stukas lost and seven smoking, I was damaged, and the rudder controls were sluggish. Then I saw an explosion, a P-40 passing right by me erupted in a ball of fire and plunged to the desert floor. Then another right behind him caught fire and that pilot bailed out. Then I saw five Messerschmitts fly past us at high speed, and six more diving into the enemy from altitude. I heard one of my men over the radio, "It's Marseille! It's Marseille!" and then I saw the yellow 14 as he flashed past me and climbed."[181]

Marseille wasted no time climbing and entering head-on into the enemy formation and lining up his first kill, still climbing as he completed his left-banking climb. He fired as the aircraft was pulling up to evade him and join the slowly forming Lufbery. Marseille continued to climb, reaching 3,000 feet above the enemy, when he winged over and screamed into the almost formed defensive formation. The quick burst he fired hit the first P-40 that went down at 12:22, and Marseille then locked onto the tail of another P-40 at 12:25, pulling the turn tight, and firing, hitting the P-40, which smoked as it fell away on fire. Marseille had actually entered the Lufbery, which was very loose and probably not an intended defensive formation, as if he were an Allied pilot before it really even properly formed, then it disintegrated.

His Me-109 could pull tighter than a P-40, and he exploited this virtue as he locked onto the next target. Pulling up, rolling over and turning right very tight he closed on another P-40 at 12:27, and after leading the fighter as it turned right, he fired, shooting him down. Marseille then gave another leading shot and flamed his last victim's wingman at 12:28. Pöttgen had called them all out as each went down, but Marseille was not finished.

Marseille then rapidly pulled up and inverted, rolling over to see below and behind him, when he saw another P-40 passing underneath trying to get on Pöttgen's tail. He also caught a glimpse of six more P-40s entering the fray. Marseille called out for his wingman to break left, and when he did, the P-40 behind him continued his climb straight upward. His attention was probably fixed on Marseille, and he was apparently taken by surprise when Pöttgen broke away.

Marseille pulled back on the stick, cut throttle, stalled, hit the left rudder, rolled as he dropped his nose in a dive head on at the P-40 just two thousand feet below him, and fired as they closed with each other. At 12:29 this fifth kill plunged toward the desert floor. Marseille completed the shallow dive and began another climb when a sixth enemy crossed in front of him. He instinctively fired a leading shot, just a quick two-second burst, and at 12:33 his final victim for the day was confirmed. He had used only a dozen rounds of cannon ammunition and less than a third of his machine gun ammunition.

The ratio average was approximately 60 machine gun rounds and 1.7 rounds of 20mm cannon rounds per kill. Marseille later mastered the conservation of ammunition to a degree that would never be matched, at a time when fifteen rounds per kill became the norm. Kuhlmey's after action report as well as that of his surviving crews who witnessed the event left no doubt:

"I must say that was probably the most comfortable moment of my life. I always knew that when Marseille and the first *Gruppe* were with me my men would get home. After about four minutes after Marseille's last victory the P-40s broke away and headed east. Then the radio came to life again, 'Kuhlmey, this is Jochen, you are good now!'

"They escorted us back to the field, landed and refueled at our base. I jumped out and helped lift my dead gunner from his position, and then the fighters landed. He jumped out and I met him personally for the first time, but I had been saved by him and his pilots many times and we had many radio conversations in the air. I went to him and hugged him, which may not have been the most professional thing to do as a superior officer, but I was happy as hell as were my surviving men.

"I was able to confirm two of his victories that I saw and was happy to do so. That was when Marseille informed me that III./JG-53 had been intercepted by a much larger force of P-40s and were engaged, confirming Neumann's radio call. That made them unable to get to us. What really made me angry was they could have at least radioed that fact to me and called for another fighter group to replace them."[182]

Marseille was the master of the precision shot, he wanted the aircraft, not the man. There were only two places to aim for; the cockpit, killing or wounding the pilot, or the engine, which crippled the aircraft most of the time. Hitting the wing tanks was problematic, since fires were the usual result, but a good way to confirm a kill. Marseille did not want to intentionally kill anyone, hence his proclivity for hitting the engines. This would explain why such a high percentage of his victims lived to talk about the experience.

Word of his accomplishment had already spread, and the entire unit gathered to welcome him home. Even Gerhard Homuth, his commanding officer, the man who had berated him and caused him so much grief, congratulated him on the mission. Marseille had managed multiple victories before, but six P-40s within ten minutes and 47 seconds was a *Luftwaffe* record to date. His confirmed six victims and the seven victims of his group in total were as follows:

1: Australian volunteer Flight Sergeant Mortimer, who was killed when his P-40 (AK423) flipped out of control and crashed after taking a cannon round through the cockpit.12

2: 2nd Lieutenant Cecil A. Douglas Golding, who was lightly wounded when his head struck his gun sight. He survived the crash landing.

3: Captain R. L. Morrison, who was badly wounded with shrapnel in his arms and torso from the exploding cannon shell, yet he survived the crash landing.

4: Lieutenant V. S. Muir, who also survived after crash-landing and was shaken up, but uninjured.

5: Lieutenant Robin Pare, who was killed, never getting out of his fighter as it impacted and exploded.

6: 2nd Lieutenant M. Martin, who crash-landed inside the old fortress ruins of Bir Hacheim and returned to his unit unharmed. His fighter came to rest against a stone wall.

7: Lieutenant Louis C. Botha, who crash-landed at Gambut with a dead engine and stationary propeller and was uninjured. He also returned to his unit.

Cecil A. Douglas Golding who was shot down by Marseille had his unique take on the battle.

"We were led by Wing Commander T. B. Beresford and Major Jack Frost, and we took off with twelve of the fourteen Tomahawks as two collided on the ground during takeoff, and another turned back with engine trouble, leaving only eleven fighters. We were supposed to have top cover, but that did not occur, so we went in after the Stukas anyway. They had no air cover when we attacked. That was very lucky for us I can say.

"The Germans later claimed we entered a Lufbery and Marseille shot down six of us, but we did not enter a Lufbery as there was no time. Certainly, we were turning and banking to engage the 109s as they suddenly appeared. The enemy claimed that they shot down ten of us, that would have been all but one of us, but we only lost five. The others made it back to base. These mistaken claims are understandable as when you are in a frantic dogfight more than one pilot may shoot an aircraft and make the claim."[183]

P-40 of Major E.M. Baker of No. 5 Squadron SAAF (Cecil Golding)

Marseille's victories had been scored using only his 7.92mm machine guns after his 20mm cannon jammed after a dozen or so rounds had been fired. Sand fouling was the apparent culprit: despite tarps covering the cowlings, the constant sandstorms, arriving in varying degrees of ferocity, ensured that the sand encroached everywhere, with many mechanical devices becoming inoperable.

These victories also raised his official score to 75, and three days later Marseille received word that he was to return to Germany to receive the Oak Leaves. During the war only 889 men, including foreigners, would be so decorated. However, that order was changed, and the theater commander *Generalfeldmarschall* Albert Kesselring arrived on June 4 to deliver the order for the Oak Leaves in the name of Adolf Hitler to Marseille, although he would have to wait to receive the medal from Hitler personally.

All of the JG-27 staff officers were present as Marseille was informed that he had become the 97th recipient (of 860 Germans to be so honored) of the Oak Leaves to the Knight's Cross of the Iron Cross and the second-youngest recipient in the German military, following *Luftwaffe* ace pilot and fellow Berliner *Oberleutnant* Hans Strelow, who was flying on the Eastern Front with JG-51 and received the award two days before his 20th birthday on March 24, 1942.

Marseille knew Strelow, another Berliner. He had scored 68 victories before he was shot down by a Polikarpov Pe-2 six miles behind Soviet lines on May 22, 1942. His fellow pilots saw him crash land in with a dead engine, and as hordes of Red Army soldiers ran toward him, he committed suicide with his service pistol while sitting in the cockpit rather than be captured.

Marseille would have to wait to receive the medal when he was summoned to meet with Hitler at a later date. In addition, the official orders were handed out by Kesselring: *Major* Eduard Neumann had become the official *Geschwaderkommodore, Hauptmann* Gerhard Homuth was appointed *Gruppenkommandeur* of I./JG-27, and *Oberleutnant* Hans-Joachim Marseille officially took over as *Staffelkapitän* of 3./JG-27, at 22 the youngest officer to hold that position in the *Luftwaffe* up to that time. However, while Marseille may have outpaced his fellow JG-27 pilots in the scoring, another pilot led in the African theater: *Hauptmann* Joachim Müncheberg's score then stood at 80 victories.

On June 7, I *Gruppe* escorted a formation of Kuhlmey's Stukas to Acroma. Marseille was not flying with Pöttgen, who was at that time assigned as *Rottenflieger* [wingman] to their *Gruppenkommandeur* Homuth. Marseille heard the alert as two enemy fighters broke from their loose finger four formation. At first, he probably thought that they were going to initiate another Lufbery, until he saw Homuth's markings, and the Me-109 trailing behind him, his long-serving and faithful wingman, Pöttgen. They were chasing four P-40s and seemed unaware of the danger.

Marseille called out the threats that were banking in tightly to get in behind them. Homuth broke off his pursuit with a hard left turn after Marseille's warning, followed by Pöttgen on Homuth's wing. Marseille gave full power and banked into a falling dive, closing rapidly on the four P-40s. The rear guard must have seen him as the two fighters on the left broke right, up and over, turning to get on his tail. Marseille's impromptu wingman was not yet well versed on his methods and was left far behind. Marseille was alone.

Homuth completed his turn and began to dive followed by Pöttgen, with the two remaining enemies glued behind them less than 300 feet away. Marseille was less than 100 feet away when he fired. The left P-40 broke up, exposing his wingman to the incoming German. Marseille chose the leader and fired a quick burst, shredding the rudder. The second burst created a coolant leak, and the fighter began to go toward the ground. The time was 16:10. This first kill was a Lieutenant Frewen flying P-40 AK 611, who then bailed out after a high climb to jump clear. He was uninjured and landed in Allied territory.

The pilot of the second kill was less fortunate. Marseille pulled into a climb, gained altitude and again rolled into a very tight turn to shoot down P-40 (AK628), flown by Lieutenant Leonard James Peter Berrangé, at 16:13. He was probably killed in the engine fire that erupted into the cockpit. Marseille had scored two P-40 kills over El Adem, both from No. 2 Squadron SAAF, his seventy-sixth and seventy-seventh victories. He had also saved Homuth and possibly Pöttgen from certain death.

Painting the propeller hub of a P-40 (Geoffrey Morley-Mower)

The mission over Mteifel Chebir on June 10 was to be another hallmark day for Marseille, not just for the four victories he scored, but how he scored them. I and II *Gruppen* of JG-27 were on an overlapping mission with a contingent of Italian MC.202 fighters. Great confusion arose as the Germans of I and II *Gruppen* engaged between forty and fifty enemy fighters, while III./JG-53 joined the fray and managed to head off an additional formation of ten Spitfires en route to the brewing battle. This large Allied force was a collection of aircraft from No. 73 and No. 213 Squadrons RAF, which would have been a maximum effort from the squadrons.

By the time I *Gruppe* JG-27 arrived they encountered the first 24 enemy fighters that had just fought through II *Gruppe*, which had damaged four P-40s and confirmed a Hurricane kill over Bir Hacheim. I *Gruppe* alone was to submit seven claims for victories, all P-40s, although Marseille's fourth and final victory would be misidentified as a P-40, which was in fact a Hurricane II flown by Pilot Officer A. J. Hancock of No. 213 Squadron.

The second half of the battle ensued as Marseille's *Schwarm* once again led the *Gruppe* as high cover, his favorite position. Marseille called out the enemies as two P-40s that had broken away early then circled, closing in on Marseille from behind, with a third P-40 joining them. At 500 meters, all three began firing, almost at the extreme effective range of their weapons. The tracers flew by his cockpit, and a couple of holes appeared in the right wing.

Marseille cut the throttle, extended flaps, and skidded to the left to avoid the rounds coming in on the right, but this time he did something different from his tried-and-trusted normal routine. Just in case his pursuers were slowing down to match him, Marseille lowered his landing gear. Two of the P-40s had in fact anticipated his speed reduction and likewise cut their power and extended their flaps, but by dropping his gear Marseille again cut his speed by another 50 percent. He continued to decelerate, outfoxing his enemies.

The first P-40 almost rammed him but pulled up and flew over him, inverting in a rollover as he passed overhead and slowed down matching Marseille's speed. Marseille looked up and the enemy pilot looked down, mirror images of each other as they flew parallel to each other, so that they could see each other clearly less than five feet apart. The image for both pilots must have been surreal, as Marseille stated upon landing. Emil Clade saw the event, as did Werner Schroer.

Schroer stated: "I was watching this, thinking about firing into the enemy, but feared I would hit Jochen. I called over the radio and asked him what he was doing. Then I saw him lift his nose and shoot him down."[184]

The P-40 pilot continued passing Marseille over the top, and according to what the discussion was afterward, Marseille waved to his enemy, and the Allied pilot responded with a rude hand gesture. Marseille then reduced power even more and the enemy pilot passed overhead and pulled the stick in, probably hoping to dive away. All he did was pass down right in front of Marseille's nose mounted weapons. A one-second burst ripped through the engine, canopy, and fuselage, sending it down smoking at 07:35. Emil Clade remembered this event:

"I saw this as did others, and I asked Jochen why he shot him down. I made a joke that I thought he was making a new friend. Marseille responded with; 'Well, he was rude!' so he shot him down. Fascinating."[185]

The second P-40 had also been blindsided by the maneuver and passed overhead just to the top left, banking to pull away. Marseille had retracted his gear and flaps, opening the throttle to full power, then lifted his nose and banked tightly, finally getting into a good five o'clock firing position. The P-40 belched flame and fell away at 07:41. However, there was still another P-40 on Marseille's tail.

The third enemy threatening him had been too far away to be deceived by his maneuver, and he was turning inside Marseille from three hundred feet behind him, a perfect three-quarter deflection shot for a pilot who could pull proper lead. Marseille would have known that. He reversed his bank, threw the stick right, rolled over, inverted, again cut power, pulled the stick into himself to initiate a dive, and then rolled out of it as he pulled up.

Major Andrew Duncan (left) Maj Adrian Montaque "Coly" Colenbrander (center) and Brian Boyle (right) in Egypt (Cecil Golding)

The G-forces would have been brutal, probably about force five or six, enough to make any pilot black out. Marseille managed to pull up, add throttle and greet his final victim almost head on, as the P-40, some 500 feet above him, was pulling up and away, then going into a rolling dive to escape. Marseille also rolled, inverted and pulled incredible lead at 07:45, scoring the kill.

The other P-40 that had flashed past him had fired, the tracers grazing his fuselage, and Marseille banked hard and gave pursuit.

However, by the time he had corrected his aircraft and regained proper trim, the P-40 was almost a mile away. Undaunted he set off in pursuit, and the chase lasted almost twenty miles, with the faster Me-109 managing to creep closer, and closer, until four minutes later Marseille was at maximum firing range.

Marseille knew his ballistics and was the master of every aspect of his machine. He studied the technical manuals of every aircraft he could find, German or Allied, and the weapon systems of every aircraft, including the ballistics of the Me-109F's twin-mounted MG 17 in the cowling above the engine housing. These weapons had a high rate of fire, at approximately 1,100 rounds per minute, providing a muzzle velocity of 2,591 feet per second. The ammunition powder weight per bullet was 10 grams (0.04 ounces). The Me-109F carried either a 15mm or 20mm center mounted cannon that fired through the propeller hub. The 15mm MG 151 fired at a rate of 700 rounds per minute and used a 57-gram (approximately two ounces) projectile that fired at 3,149 feet per second.

The 20mm MG 151 Marseille and the other JG-27 pilots had used two different projectile weights. One was a lighter 92-gram shell that fired at 740 rounds per minute at 2,624 feet per second, and the heavier 115-gram shell likewise fired at 740 rpm, but this round had a muzzle velocity of 2,329 feet per second. Both types were explosive shells, and just one well-placed round in an engine or cockpit was sometimes enough to bring down an enemy fighter. The heavier cannon rounds also had a higher drop rate despite having greater distance.

Still closing in on his quarry, Marseille calculated, and raising his nose slightly, he fired a chance burst, the cannon shells flying through the sky, the tracers marking the arc of the shots, which landed just behind the target. Closing in further, Marseille fired again; this time at over 600 feet he compensated for the elevation, and he saw strikes on the control surfaces as the tracers passed through the elevators. Then he came even closer, as the pilot began to erratically slip and slide out of Marseille's fire. Marseille saw that he was getting low on fuel, radioed his position, then fired a third burst at five hundred feet from a perfect six o'clock position that completed the action at 07:50.

After a 20-mile chase at full throttle in a continuous shallow dive, during which Marseille reached an airspeed of just over four hundred miles per hour, the enemy aircraft fell in flames and smoke. Marseille did not have time to stay around, and he called out the victory on the open frequency in case there were any witnesses in the air or on the ground. As he flew back, he jotted down the time and coordinates on the knee board map that he always carried with him, as he did for every kill he made when he did not have his faithful airborne accountant Pöttgen with him.

Marseille knew that he had shot down four aircraft, believing all were P-40s, but for some reason he claimed this final victory as a P-40 also, even though it was Pilot Officer A. J. Hancock's Hurricane. It is possible that he simply did not get a close enough look and assumed that it was a P-40, since the others were also P-40s. Marseille's score then stood at 81 victories.

No. 2 Squadron SAAF desert camp (Cecil Golding)

The next day, June 11, Marseille would again add to his laurels, as JG-27 flew 182 sorties in total before sundown. No. 112 Squadron

RAF had also taken off at around the same time for the second full force mission, starting late in the day at 16:05 to carry out a sweep of the El Adem/Tobruk/El Daba area as a forward screen. The Germans were again flying escort for another Stuka force led by Kuhlmey, when the Allied pilots spotted six Me-109s to the northwest escorting Stukas. This was Marseille's group; each side saw each other at the same time. Kurt Kuhlmey recalled:

> "I heard someone call out 'Indians!' and I looked over to the right, and there they were. I guess I should have been nervous as they were coming in, but I knew Marseille and the others were above me and they saw them. Three Hurricanes were coming in on us from the two and three o'clock level positions, so I ordered my flight to dive on me and follow me in a turning recovery. We dropped about five hundred meters and then we pulled up and banked right hard, and that was when I saw our fighters get them."[186]

Fighters from No. 33 and No. 274 Squadrons RAF were the first to reach the Stukas, and they launched a ferocious attack, as No. 112 Squadron flew top cover. What the Allied pilots did not know was that there was a total of 38 Me-109s in the air staggered at three altitudes, and Marseille's high cover flying forward was the first to engage.

The Me-109s led by Marseille rolled over to attack the right from astern. The Hurricanes turned to engage the enemy aircraft in a head on attack, when Hurricane BE864 flown by Flight Sergeant Graves was struck by Marseille's accurate fire, forcing him to bail out at 16:25. His wingman was hit but managed to bank away and flee, although Marseille was again pulling for altitude. He then converted that into airspeed then diving and caught up to the remaining enemy aircraft, shooting it down ten minutes later at 16:35.

This last victim was probably Australian-born Pilot Officer Charles William Parry Persse (Serial No. 404184) of No. 274 Squadron RAF, killed while flying Hurricane II BE864. He crashed five miles southeast of El Adem and is buried in Knightsbridge Cemetery at

Acroma.[187] Marseille now had 83 victories, despite again erroneously identifying the Hurricane as a P-40 in his *Abschuss*. On June 12 Marseille flew a ground support mission, attacking vehicles in a British convoy with his wingman Pöttgen, who also emptied his guns in the strafing attacks.

June 13, 1942 would be another four-victory day for Marseille while flying over El Adem and Gazala against No. 450 Squadron RAAF. He chased one P-40 at nearly head level across the ground, closing in until he scored the lethal shots. The left wing of the P-40 (which Marseille misidentified as a Hurricane) touched the ground, sending the fighter into a devastating cartwheel, scattering debris along its path of impact.[188] Marseille managed to shoot down his adversaries at 18:10, 18:11, 18:14, and 18:15, respectively, while *Leutnant* Hans Remmer scored one victory.

Allied pilots shot down by Marseille included Flight Sergeant Bill Halliday flying P-40 (AL127) and Flight Sergeant Roy Stone in his P-40 (AK952), both from No. 450 Squadron RAAF and both were killed in action.[189] One lucky man was Pilot Officer Osborne in P-40 AL106, who crash-landed and was rescued by a British Army ground unit. Marseille's score stood at 87 victories, and the month was not even half over, although Marseille would increasingly find himself being grounded due to fears for his health.

CHAPTER 8

A Growing Threat

Telling Marseille that he was grounded was like telling a small child that it could not go out and play. He sometimes acted like one too.
Werner Schroer

At Neumann's insistence Marseille had a stand down. Neumann knew when a pilot was burning out. Marseille of course argued against it, probably thinking that Homuth wanted him to stand down so that his *Gruppenkommandeur* could catch up in the scoring, which was probably not the case at all.

With just a couple of days off, Marseille was finally in a state of total relaxation, listening to his music as his 3 *Staffel* was having their aircraft fully serviced. While the mechanics and armorers did their work, the pilots took naps, ate, or in Marseille's case just listened to jazz and ragtime music. He also took the time to perfect some of his practical jokes and set them in motion. The following pilots recounted what happened.

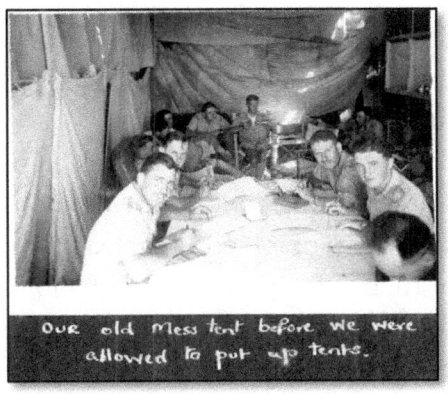

No. 2 Squadron SAAF temporary mess tent (Cecil Golding)

Emil Clade: "I entered my tent, and I tripped a rope that dumped a bucket of water on me. I must have screamed at the surprise of it all. But I was not alone. I heard someone else also shriek right after me. Turned out it was Werner [Schroer]."[190]

Werner Schroer: "I heard Emil, I knew it was him, he had this peculiar voice you know? I laughed, knowing Jochen had done something, and then I had water dumped on me also. I was so angry, but then again, I had been so hot, the cool water actually felt pretty good."[191]

Franzisket also had his experience: "Almost everyone was booby trapped by Marseille this way, either with water overhead or tripping a line that brought their entire tent down around them. Everyone developed a heightened sense of paranoia, checked every doorway, the latrine, anything that could be a potential trap to bring Marseille his great amusements."[192]

Marseille was one of the lucky men who had a mosquito net, which he had fixed to the entrance of his tent, which also helped keep the dreaded black flies away. They were still enjoying this respite from the action when they were given the word to mount up at 17:00 on June 15.

A few minutes after the alert, Marseille led his flight against a squadron of P-40s from No. 204 Group RAF, although which squadrons were involved is unclear. No. 204 Group acknowledged that four of their fighters were in fact shot down and another written off upon return to base. Neumann explained Marseille's victories from the combined after-action reports: Apparently Marseille had seen the enemy first, and he told his second flight to keep flying, as if they had not seen the enemy while he and his wingman remained above, and then climbed. As soon as the enemy pilots attacked from the five o'clock position, that flight scattered, and Marseille's pilots remained above as he rolled over to attack. Those victories were done very quickly. Neumann gave details:

"One of the pilots was smoking badly, still flying yet losing altitude, so Marseille had flown alongside. Knowing that there was still enough altitude he motioned for the pilot to jump. Marseille said that the pilot saluted him, waved and then went over the side. There was a good parachute and since he was over Allied lines Marseille did not feel the need to make a postman's call."[193]

Marseille scored his victories over El Adem rapidly, at 18:01, 18:02, 18:04, and 18:06, finishing the day with ninety-one victories to his credit. I./JG-27 pilots claimed a total of 12 victories in the running fight, despite only five reported Allied losses. This would appear to be an overclaiming due to the melee that ensued, as more than one pilot probably fired into the same enemy aircraft as Cecil Golding stated earlier. Also, several of the aircraft that were shot up by the Germans managed to crash land or even make it back to their base. Despite the collective overclaiming, Marseille's personal victories on this occasion were not in dispute, and he claimed an additional fighter as damaged but had no confirmation of the victory. Werner Schroer also claimed two victories on this mission:

"We were in the middle of this large formation, and suddenly I heard someone shout, 'Here I go!' and it was in fact Marseille.

South African aces (left to right) Major John Frost, Lt. Robin Pare, Capt. Andrew Duncan (Cecil Golding)

I rolled over to attack a fighter when Yellow 14 appeared in front of me. I pulled back and up, and as I did, I saw a Curtiss, so I fired and saw smoke coming from the exhaust. He went down, but I could not follow him. There were more around me, but as I rolled again, I saw Marseille.

"He had entered this Lufbery and shot down one, and when I banked back and rolled again, I saw another P-40 going down. When he pulled up and rolled, I lost sight of him then, and I managed to fire a leading deflection shot at another P-40, got hits, and saw the canopy fly off. I did not see the pilot bail out but assumed that was the man's intention. I could confirm two of Jochen's victories. I think Pöttgen probably confirmed the others."[194]

The next day, June 16, 3 *Staffel* of I./JG-27 took off at 17:50 on a *freie jagd* in *Schwarm* formation led by Marseille, and they engaged Hurricanes from No. 73 Squadron RAF, and P-40s from No. 5 Squadron SAAF, while No. 250 Squadron RAF was also involved over El Adem. Once again Marseille scored four victories in rapid succession at 18:02, 18:10, 18:11, and 18:13. Among Marseille's victims were Lieutenant R. C. Denham, who was killed, and Major John Frost, listed as missing in action. Friedrich Körner of 2. *Staffel* I./JG-27 was also involved and shot down Pilot Officer Cable of No. 250 Squadron RAF at 18:50.

Prime Minister Winston Churchill arriving in Egypt on his 1942 tour of the front where he visited all of the forward operational squadrons from around the Commonwealth (Cecil Golding)

June was a good month overall for Marseille and I./JG-27, with a prime example on June 17. The three *Staffeln* went up from their newly established if somewhat barren air base at Ain-el-Gazala in the late morning, with each *Schwarm* operating in a confined sector. Marseille's four aircraft made visual contact at noon when they spotted 20 P-40s, a collection of fighters from No. 112 and 250 Squadrons RAF, as well as twelve Hurricanes from No. 73 Squadron RAF. Homuth ordered the group to gain more altitude to have the altitude advantage and choose when they would attack, but Marseille had other plans.

With his three-man *Schwarm* covering him, Marseille immediately attacked and engaged a gaggle of a dozen enemy aircraft, and singling one out, shot it down, but had to break hard, climb, roll, and then dive to escape one that was on his tail. He gained distance from his highspeed dive, climbed, went full flaps, cut power in a vertical stall, inverted on his back, gave full power, retracted flaps and then he turned into his enemy head on who was still climbing up into him, while still inverted and shot him down also. All the while Homuth was screaming at him and everyone heard it, even Neumann, who said:

> "Homuth was apparently very upset once again that Marseille disobeyed his order and just decided to attack. I knew that I was going to handle another problem between those two when they came back. It had become a very frequent event for me. I heard the confirmations of each pilot's victories as they were confirmed over the radio, and I wrote those down in a running diary, and then after confirmation I added them to the chalkboard, and then painted a new leaf on my palm tree."[195]

But the Germans were not the only ones listening, according to Geoffrey Morley-Mower: "We later learned that the listening station at Tobruk was monitoring the German channels, and their translators listened in on the communications. They knew that it was Marseille's unit. The Germans just did not seem to care about communications security, amazing really. They acted like excited children, no discipline at all."[196]

Marseille's first two victories came at 12:02 and 12:04, which he misidentified as P-40s. They were in fact Hurricanes from No. 73 Squadron RAF, with Pilot Officer Stone in BN121 and Flight Sergeant Goodwin flying BN157. Both men bailed out uninjured. Marseille had scored numbers 96 and 97, just before these two fighters could join the Lufbery being formed.

Marseille then turned his attention to four fighters entering the Lufbery, flying over the parachutes of Stone and Goodwin; his next two victories were also Hurricanes from No. 73 Squadron RAF. Both pilots, Squadron Leader Derek Harland Ward in BN277 and Pilot Officer Woolley in BN456, were killed. These victories came at 12:05 and 12:08 and brought Marseille's score to 99.

He then fired on another within a few seconds. Marseille's next victory was probably Flight Sergeant Roy Drew (RAAF) of No. 112 Squadron RAF in P-40 AK586, who was listed as missing in action. The kill at 12:09 brought Marseille's 100th victory. This made him the first *Luftwaffe* fighter pilot to score 100 victories against the Western Allies in North Africa and the eleventh pilot to score 100 victories in World War II. By the end of the war another hundred or so pilots would also break the century mark, but none would equal Marseille for Western Allied aircraft destroyed in total.

After a hard day of flying, Marseille and his *Schwarm* were going to head home, but since they still had fuel and ammunition, the young *Staffelkapitän* decided to continue the hunt at his comrades' request, despite Homuth's objections. Having just scored this latest kill, Pöttgen called out enemy fighters above, two reconnaissance Spitfires, one a Spitfire Mk IV number BP916 flown by a Pilot Officer Squires at one o'clock high, and the other flown by Flight Lieutenant Frederick Spicer both from the 2nd PRU (Photographic Reconnaissance Unit).

"Oh, I must have one, "Marseille said over the radio, but Pöttgen was more pragmatic, telling Marseille to look at his fuel. Pöttgen just wanted to follow Homuth's order and break contact and go home, but

Marseille once again had other ideas. "Follow me Reiner!" and he laughed over the radios.

Taking the lead Marseille gave full throttle and pulled the stick back into a high power climb, nearly stalling. He managed to go almost vertical, led the machine that was passing more than 300 feet above him just as he began to lose power, then fired, arcing his 20mm cannon and 7.92 machine gun rounds into the flight path of the fighter. The Spitfire with Squires in it absorbed the impact and belched smoke and then dived out of sight. The second Spitfire, flying much higher, escaped as Marseille was now falling back to earth. There has been some controversy as to which of the two pilots was killed. Some sources claim that it was Squires, while others state that Spicer was killed. From the research done by Christopher Shores, it would appear that Squires was in fact the pilot killed.

Once he gathered his bearings, Marseille was leading the *Schwarm* home when they encountered yet another flight of Hurricanes returning home headed east. Once again, he was able to drift into their formation, unnoticed, from underneath like a phantom, but when he tried to fire, his weapons failed. By that time the enemy knew he was there, and they wanted him. His other three men were already flying ahead and unable to help, so Marseille found himself outnumbered by a dozen fighters. His only option was to dive and gain speed, then outrun his pursuers, although he had to alternate rudder pedals and throw the joystick to slide and roll out of the path of the projectiles as they fired at him.

Just a few feet off the deck most of the enemy broke off the attack, more than likely due to fuel concerns. However, two Hurricanes remained latched onto him. By this time Pöttgen had almost caught up to his leader and had him in sight, hoping to shoot one off his tail. Only by an incredible display of airmanship and mastery of his machine was Marseille able to avoid being caught in the converging fire of both Hurricanes. Finally, after a four-minute chase, they also broke away and headed east, passing Pöttgen who could not get a shot and was worried about his own fuel.

Marseille had scored his 101st victory at 12:12, with six victories achieved in only ten minutes, and survived entering a gaggle of enemy fighters without his weapons operating. He had just become the eleventh *Luftwaffe* pilot to score 100 victories in World War II. As Marseille and the three other pilots were headed back, Homuth and his men landed. Neumann explains the atmosphere:

"As I predicted Homuth came right over to my wagon as soon as he dismounted and did not even knock. He just walked in, and wanted to know how much more insubordination was he expected to endure with Marseille. He wanted to once again file charges against him for disobeying another direct order not to attack, and he disobeyed a second direct order to break contact.

"I told him that Marseille had just scored his one hundred and first victory, and by the time the sun set Berlin would know all about it. Now, if he wished to file his charges, I could not stop him, but he may want to reconsider that option. Well, this time Homuth was not to be dissuaded. He wrote a long, several pages list of charges, going back months, listing dates, times, events where Marseille disobeyed him. He even wrote in detail when Marseille shot up his tent almost killing him.

"I received my copy of the typewritten charges, and my blood ran cold. I had no choice but to forward these to Kesselring. So, I did so with my own recommendations, all short of a court-martial which would have been very bad for 'Seille. The next day the mail plane arrived, and I handed the complete package, along with my recommendation for Marseille to receive a medal for his achievements so far. He was already waiting to receive the Oak Leaves, the next logical step would be to receive the Swords. But these charges could change everything, and the fact that I was the commanding officer made me a conspirator in silence for not bringing these charges sooner. I did not sleep well."[197]

Upon his arrival back at the airfield, Marseille was congratulated by Neumann, who saw the exhaustion in his face, and the bent awkward body of a man completely drained. Neumann shook his hand and told him to file his report. Once finished, Marseille handed it in, and Neumann told him that he was now ordered off flying operations for a while. Then Neumann told him to get a drink, he earned it. He also told him what Homuth was up to.

"Marseille hated downtime," Franzisket recalled. "We all had to take a day or two after a dozen or so missions. People who have not flown in combat, real furious battle, do not understand how much it takes out of you. Every pilot needed a couple of days here and there, and Marseille more than most. An exhausted fighter pilot was a danger to himself and his teammates, so that was the reason, nothing else really."[198]

Werner Schroer (far left) Marseille center) Ernst Börngen (fourth from left) Karl Kugelbaur (fifth from left) Neumann (far right) (Ernst Börngen)

Marseille followed the orders to stand down. He knew that as a leader, if he could not follow orders, then he could not in good conscience expect his men to follow his. Marseille was maturing as an officer. He was coming to realize that he was not a one-man show, despite his success; the losses of his friends as the war continued, as well as his family tragedy, probably forced him to grow up finally.

Tragedy had struck on the day of Marseille's 101st victory. Otto Schulz had scored his 51st victory in a pursuit that took him down to the deck, where he shot down a P-40 flown by a Lieutenant Conrad of No. 274 Squadron RAF. Conrad managed a stellar crash landing, and Schulz waited until the pilot was clear before he strafed the machine, then climbed for another pass to ensure that it was destroyed. However, in turning for the second strafing run, Schulz made the fatal error of not checking behind him, and Conrad was avenged by No. 260 Squadron RAF pilot Canadian born Flight Sergeant James "Stocky" Edwards, who closed in and fired.[199] Schulz's Me-109 did not have far to travel when it slammed into the ground and exploded near Sidi Rezegh.[200]

Neumann saw for himself that Marseille was maturing, beginning to work as a team player. He discovered that by doing so he was bringing back fewer damaged aircraft and gaining more confirmed victories by having his comrades nearby. His wingmen trusted his skills, he was keeping them informed of his intentions, and they were keeping him alive by being there. But even though most of the men who flew with him soon learned his moves, very few would ever say that they really knew him.

Generalfeldmarshall Albert Kesselring received the Homuth/Neumann paperwork that afternoon, and he sent an encrypted telegram to Galland in Berlin. He was after all the General of the Fighters, and Galland received it by dinner time. This was a serious list of charges, and he immediately went to see *Generalfeldmarschall* Erhard Milch, second in command to Göring. Milch stated quite clearly that this was a situation that only Göring could resolve, because the *Reichsmarschall* had already approved the award of the Swords for Marseille. After some deliberation, Göring decided that Marseille's propaganda value for the *Luftwaffe* far exceeded punishing him for his infractions. The telegram was sent to Kesselring with the award approval.

The next day, June 18, Marseille boarded a Ju-52. He had an appointment with Adolf Hitler to receive the Oak Leaves and Swords to his Knight's Cross, the 12th German soldier (out of 159 Swords recipients in total) to be so decorated. He would fly to Berlin then catch the train to Hitler's eastern headquarters in Rastenburg, East Prussia, hopefully followed by a vacation. When Marseille finally arrived at Tempelhof Airport from Benghazi via Naples and Rome, it appeared that the entire city of Berlin had turned out to celebrate their hometown hero.

The newspaper men and photographers were there, along with a film crew led by none other than celebrated chronicler of the Third Reich, Leni Riefenstahl. One man came up to him holding a newspaper and asked him to autograph it. The entire front page was a photo of Marseille in his tropical uniform, with the headline "All Berlin is Proud of Him." Riefenstahl remembered the event:

"He left the aircraft with three other men and the crowd was very animated. Hundreds of people were all cheering and screaming at him. I must say this was the first time that I had ever seen him in person, and he was very handsome, but he looked tired, which was to be expected. I was to take film of him during his short stay, and later I would accompany him and [Artur] Axmann on his tour."[201]

Adolf Hitler with his personal pilot and closest friend General Hans Baur. (Hans Baur)

Then 13-year-old Lothar Löwe, who knew Marseille was there also wanting to see the man he knew and idolized. He remembered the event: "It was completely unbelievable the number of people there. Tens of thousands, it must have been, with so many members of the press and the film crews. It seemed as if the entire city was there to see him. As a young boy I was very impressed."[202]

Despite the great celebratory atmosphere, Marseille could not linger long in Berlin due to a two-day delay in Naples as a result of bad weather. He called his mother and told her that he would be home soon, but that he couldn't stay for long.

Marseille was well known in his neighborhood. Even the taxi driver taking him home recognized him, and he refused Marseille's money for the ride. Instead, Marseille handed him a pack of cigarettes as a gesture of gratitude.[203] Marseille managed to spend a private couple of days with his mother and fiancée.

Marseille carried his travel bag and boarded the train at the main *bahnhof* [train station] where he was seated comfortably in a first-class car, courtesy of the train master. Due to the bombing in various areas the train was delayed on occasion, but he finally arrived at the Wolfschanze and was greeted by several high-ranking men, including *Generalleutnant* Hans Baur, *Fliegerchef* to Adolf Hitler, his personal pilot and a World War I ace with nine victories himself, who drove Marseille to Hitler's headquarters. According to Baur:

"He looked as if he had just crawled out of a laundry bag. He was not even in the dress uniform usually worn by men being received by Hitler. He had his light brown uniform on and his desert boots, which were not polished. I had heard many things about him, he was the subject of a lot of gossip, all of it entertaining, and some of it shocking. *Oberst* von Below[204] greeted us and I had a chat with him as we arrived, and when we stepped out of the auto we were greeted by one of Hitler's bodyguards and telephone operator, [Rochus] Misch who walked us inside. Below reminded Marseille that it was customary for all men meeting Hitler to give the Party salute. Marseille asked why as he was not a Party member. Below just told him, 'Marseille you are already walking on thin ice. Homuth's report came in, do not push your luck. You are lucky to even be here. And try to straighten out that uniform.'

"Marseille then met Göring, and Göbbels was also there. There were a few others receiving medals, and all were chatting when Hitler walked in, and of course everyone went to attention. Marseille gave his impression of attention. He did not seem awestruck like most others. It seemed that he was just as comfortable as if he were at the greengrocers. After receiving the medals, the men had a seat for the customary lunch with Hitler, Göring, Göbbels, Below, myself and others.

"I was near Marseille at lunch, and Göring asked him: 'So, you now have what, over a hundred conquests?' Marseille, perhaps not thinking while eating, responded: '*Herr Reichsmarschall*, do you mean aircraft or women?' Göring laughed so hard, as did all of us, that I thought he [Göring] was going to choke on his meal. Marseille kept a straight face, as if not realizing just how that answer sounded. Then it dawned on him what he had said and how he had said it, and at that moment he turned quite red with embarrassment. Göbbels also laughed uncontrollably and slapped the table, and he told Marseille that this was another reason he was a good model for young German men.

"Later Göring told Marseille that he 'wanted to meet the woman that he finally married, as she would get the Iron Cross for conquering him.' Marseille laughed at the comment, and mentioned that he was in fact finally engaged, and then he leaned over and commented to a *Waffen SS* officer next to him, one of Hitler's bodyguards on the fact that Göring was wearing nail polish, and he continued saying to one of the other medal recipients as well: 'Is there something about him that we should know?' as he lifted his left hand and wiggled his fingers. Göring heard that, he had to. I heard it and I was even farther away, next to Hitler, who lifted his head and turned to look at me and rolled his eyes and shook his head, and I just shrugged it off.

"We all knew that Göring was a strange man. I could say that about all of Hitler's chief lieutenants. All had one strange facet about them or another. I wonder sometimes what they thought of me. However, here was Marseille, who I was supposed to be in charge of until I passed him off to Axmann, and I could only hold my breath and await his next stupid comment. When he made this comment about Göring the entire table fell silent. Göring himself seemed to have never heard a word, he just kept eating."[205]

During the lunch, Galland had arrived as Hitler discussed and inquired of Marseille about the North African Front. They discussed personnel, aircraft, and other matters. Marseille said that they needed more planes and pilots, as the enemy outnumbered them heavily. Hitler simply responded by telling him that the Eastern Front was a great drain on German resources, but that he was planning on bolstering the air contingent in North Africa as soon as possible.

After the meal, Hitler sat privately with Marseille, as he tended to do with the men he decorated, having a private chat. Neumann learned of the aftermath of this chat from Adolf Galland during his later visit to JG-27:

"As they emerged from the room after their private conversation, Galland told me he overheard Hitler say to Marseille that he wanted him to be safe, that Germany would need fine young men like him when the war was over. Marseille responded within Galland's earshot, quite prophetically, that he did not think most of the men he served with, himself included, would outlive the war. Neumann remembered the event as he learned it from Galland:

"Marseille had said some very unflattering things about Hitler and the Nazi Party. Several officers, including Galland and *Oberst* Nicolaus von Below [Hitler's *Luftwaffe* adjutant] overheard it all. One of the staff officers, perhaps von Below himself, asked him if he had considered joining the Party, being a national hero and all. Marseille said something to the effect that,

Adolf Hitler greets Marseille at his headquarters in Rastenburg to award him the Oak Leaves and Swords. The day would become legendary (Raymond F. Toliver)

if he saw a party worth joining, he would consider it, but there would have to be some very attractive ladies present. I can only imagine how well that was taken. Galland was laughing uncontrollably as he told me the story, and I have to admit, I laughed also.

"When he returned from Berlin after receiving the Oak Leaves and Swords, I was informed that Hitler was puzzled, after being initially quite upset with him. After the award ceremony, Hitler began talking about the campaign in Russia, and he said something about future operations using new Italian units. Marseille spoke up and asked him [Hitler] if he thought that was a good idea, given the way things had been going, and that the Italians really had not impressed him a lot."[206]

Following this somewhat contentious meeting with Hitler, Marseille was then ordered to accompany *Reichsmarschall* Göring to Karinhall, the lavish estate and hunting preserve of their commander in chief, where he was awarded the Combined Pilots- Observation Badge in Gold with Diamonds. Göring took him on a short personal tour of the estate, and within an hour he joined Baur and Göbbels for the flight in Hitler's Ju-52 back to Berlin. Hitler was to follow a few days later.

Upon landing he went home where he managed to rest, but the next day he was taken by Göbbels to a café where his wife, Magda, and their children were seated. After a light breakfast and coffee, and an hour or so of light conversation, he was then taken to the Propaganda Ministry, where he was introduced to Hitler Youth Leader Artur Axmann, who was in Berlin for a Hitler Youth rally in conjunction with a large military recruiting program. Despite mandatory conscription into military, this event was just one of many where young men and boys were given the opportunity to determine which branch of the military they might wish to join.

Marseille's arrival along with other *Luftwaffe* men provided the opportunity for recruitment into the air force, as the propaganda machine rolled fast and furious to exploit the success of Germany's air heroes. Marseille was a ready-made poster boy: handsome, successful, charismatic, and already a living legend. Now, Marseille was the responsibility of Hitler Youth Leader Artur Axmann, who discussed the events:

"I finally met Marseille, who had been all over the newspapers and in the press," Axmann remembered. "He was even featured in a few of the *Frontshau* and *Wochenshau* features, films we did highlighting our men on the various fronts. This was a morale boost for the people and helped them keep connected to the war effort. This was all controlled by Göbbels, as were the newspapers, and even *Signal* and *Der Adler* magazines had featured him. Göbbels had said that he wanted Marseille to do a speaking tour, as he had others with high decorations do. Marseille was to travel and speak to various youth groups, cadets and even a few factories making aircraft and parachutes. All of this would be filmed and photographed.

"Marseille was definitely the least military man I ever met. He just seemed so out of place among other military men. He did not carry himself as an officer, more like a schoolboy. He did not always think before he spoke. I had to instruct him on how to present himself, and I accompanied him on these visits, where the newsreel people also filmed his tour. He really liked his drink, but he could handle it.

"Marseille was uniquely qualified to be a role model for the young Germans. The stories about him in the magazines and newspapers naturally made him famous. His good looks and the glamour that was always associated with pilots and heroes in general added to the great interest in him. Yes, Marseille was the ultimate role model for German youth—until he opened his mouth."[207]

One of his admirers during this period was film director Leni Riefenstahl, who worked the camera crew to record the tour events in the *Reichschancellery*. Riefenstahl, a former dancer and actress turned film director, had been appointed by Propaganda Minister Dr. Josef Göbbels to cover the 1934 and 1935 National Socialist Party rallies, especially the great Nuremberg rally. The result was a feature film, *Triumph of the Will*, which is still considered an innovative and influential piece of filmmaking despite it being Nazi propaganda. She also filmed the 1936 Olympics in Berlin and directed several feature films. She became Hitler's favorite propaganda film director, and, as such, she carried a lot of sway when it came to film concepts.

Hitler and Leni Riefenstahl during the 1936 Berlin Olympics (Leni Riefenstahl)

She was rumored to have had a fling with Marseille herself (Baur believed so, as did Axmann), and she never denied this contact when asked, yet she also never openly admitted to it either:

"He was such a handsome man! I only met him once, for a couple of days, but I just could not take my eyes off of him. I know that others could easily see that I was infatuated with him. I always liked men very much, and Marseille was simply irresistible. I had even asked him to be an actor and star in one of my films later.

"He inquired as to what kind of films I may have in mind, and I told him that Hitler and Göbbels liked traditional films, military films. I even said that he would be perfect at playing himself in a great air combat film. Then he asked me if I thought films like that would be popular after we lost the war. I was shocked.

"I had never heard anyone speak like that. It was dangerous talk. I asked him why would he think that we would lose? He said that because America was now in the war, it was only a matter of time. His father was convinced of this, as were many other senior officers. I never spoke of this to anyone, as it was treason to do so, but Hans never really cared what anyone else thought."[208]

Riefenstahl never expanded upon her infatuation with Marseille, or her two days with him, but she winked when she mentioned it in her interview.

Hitler returned to Berlin at the end of June as Marseille was on his public tour. The young pilot attended public schools, flight schools, youth work program camps, and even addressed a Great War veterans' group, as well as military hospitals and convalescent homes containing disabled soldiers. His job was to raise morale, and it seemed that wherever he went, he succeeded. Hundreds of people lined up to have him sign the official Hoffmann postcards depicting German heroes, which were as popular in Germany as baseball cards were in America. Marseille used to get hundreds of these sent to him in Africa.

The highest echelons of the Third Reich felt his charm, and experienced his boyishly innocent humor, as well as his unrepentant lack of military bearing. Hitler joined him and met his mother and fiancée, while Göring escorted him as if he were a prize fighter who had won a world championship. Marseille's stay in Germany was punctuated by visits to his mother and fiancée, and parties with the Nazi elite.

During one of the parties, Magda Göbbels, herself a music lover, chatted with Marseille about his musical talents, and at the request of a large group of very influential people, including Professor Willi Messerschmitt and others, he gave a piano recital. It was almost a disaster.

"One thing that is little known about Marseille was that he loved music," recalled Baur. "He was a truly gifted pianist, as was his mother. We were in the home of one of the big industrialists, I think maybe Professor Messerschmitt. They had this large grand piano, and two violinists, and a cellist. We had no program, we did not know what he would play, but the room was filled with perhaps thirty or so people sitting, others standing.

Leni Riefenstahl and her camera crew filming the arrival of Marseille in Berlin Tempelhof Airport (Leni Riefenstahl)

"I remember that I was sitting next to Hitler, who had just arrived for a meeting, but leaving again later that evening, and down from him was Göring with his young daughter Edda, and then there was Heinrich Himmler, Göbbels and his wife, von Brauchitsch, Koller, Milch, Axmann, Bormann, Wolff and others. Very impressive.

"Marseille started by playing Beethoven's *Für Elise*, and then he played a Brahms tune, and really did a great job playing Chopin, and then other songs that I cannot remember. He played for over an hour, the crowd applauding after each song. He was really good. But then he did something I can only describe as crazy. He gave this little smile, and then started this rapid jazz tune, a jazz song! Jazz was banned music, and I looked over at Hitler and the rest. The look on their face would not have been more surprising than if Winston Churchill walked in waving a pistol. I could not believe it!

"Suddenly Hitler stood, raised his hand, and said: 'I think we have heard enough,' and then he walked from the first row where we sat, followed by Göring and Himmler. The entire time Magda Göbbels was laughing out loud. Milch, who was sitting behind me leaned over and said: 'Well, that overgrown child has really done it now; what the hell was that?' and I just sat there. Someone behind us said 'Scott Joplin,' and I was stunned. I knew of his love of American music, which was considered beneath good Germans, but I would have never thought that he would do something like that, and in that company. Marseille's jazz tune only lasted a couple of minutes, but it cleared the room."[209]

Artur Axmann also recalled the event: "I think my blood froze in my veins. I heard this ragtime music, or whatever it was, and suddenly the entire room went even more silent. When he was finished there was no applause, and half the people had already risen to leave anyway. He was notorious for doing such things."[210]

The events surrounding Marseille's remaining time home are not completely clear, although there was an incident of his speeding in a car with a young lady beside him, perhaps Hanneliese, although it would appear that he was not exclusive in his relationship with his fiancée. After driving through a traffic sign, the car was stopped by a policeman. Baur recalled that "...the violation was suspended due to his status."[211]

Reichsführer-SS Heinrich Himmler, Obergruppenführer Erich von dem Bach-Zelewski (second from left) and Hitler Youth Leader Artur Axmann (third from left) inspecting Hitler Youth Waffen SS candidates (Artur Axmann)

Marseille's legend had expanded far beyond his aerial accomplishments; his sexual escapades were clearly an embarrassment to the powers that be, especially due to the wide variety of women he cavorted with of all classes. Hitler had always touted a "high moral society" where marriage and children were to be encouraged. Outside of combat, Marseille was the antithesis of everything that the National Socialists held dear.

"I do not know if this was true," Baur recalled, "but I was told that when Marseille was in Naples or Rome, after leaving Berlin, he became involved with one of Mussolini's nieces, a married girl or something. This was definitely not a thing that would have been looked upon favorably.

"I do know that Erhard Milch received a phone call from a very distraught Italian officer, wanting to know where he could find this German pilot who had offended the family honor. When I was told this, I was with von Below and a few others. Then we heard that Marseille had gone off, absent without leave. He failed to report for a flight back to Libya and rejoin his unit.

"Upon hearing this, von Below who was nearby during the call simply muttered to himself: 'Jesus Christ, Marseille, have some dignity, man.' At that moment I had to excuse myself, and I went to the lavatory. I allowed myself to laugh until I thought I developed a hernia. My laughing must have been heard in the corridor, because von Brauchitsch walked in, and he asked me what was so funny.

"I told him it was Marseille. You know what he asked me? He said, 'Damn, who has he screwed around with now? I can only imagine.' He immediately assumed that it had something to do with a woman. It was like releasing a starving hound in a butcher's shop, with all the delicacies within easy reach. I know that the [Propaganda] Ministry did all it could to keep news of his stupidity out of the newspapers. They focused upon his exploits in the air, not in the bedroom."[212]

In early August 1942 there was another large gathering of the major players in the Third Reich in Berlin, and despite his less than ideal music show, Marseille was invited. The event was a gala evening and birthday party, and since Göring, Axmann, and Göbbels were going to be there, they liked having the heroes they were exploiting around whenever possible. During the gathering, an event arose that forever altered Marseille's personality as he learned of the Nazi's infamous Final Solution for the first time.

As SS-*Obergruppenführer* Wolff recalled: "[*Obergruppenführer* Odilo Lotario] Globocnik and I were talking about Operation Reinhard, which was in full effect following [Reinhard] Heydrich's murder, and also about the construction of Sobibor and Treblinka. I know I asked him about [SS *Obersturmbannführer* Rudolf Franz Ferdinand] Höss, who was also standing there and had been summoned by Himmler regarding logistics or something regarding the new camp [Auschwitz]. Then Otto [Globocnik's nickname] mentioned to me and [SS-*Obergruppenführer* Ernst] Kaltenbrunner that Lidice had been cleared much earlier, and all the Jews and Czechs had been dealt with. I noticed that this young pilot, who I later learned was Marseille, must have overheard, and I debated as to whether I should go over and say something to him. I decided against it."[213]

The small circle of the men he trusted—Rödel, Neumann, Pöttgen, Clade, Franzisket, and Schroer—all agreed after the war that Marseille definitely overheard something that evening. Things were adding up. When Marseille approached old friends during his awards visit and inquired as to the whereabouts of "so and so" who used to live over there, he found that people he had known since childhood, who now idolized him and greeted him in the street, suddenly changed the subject or turned away.

Upon his return to Africa, he asked a few of his closest friends, people he could trust, about what he had heard. According to Franzisket:

"Jochen asked me if I knew anything about the Jews, what was happening to them, and if there was something that perhaps we did not know. I honestly told him that all I knew was that there had been some deportations to the east, sending many to Poland, relocating them as we had gained more territory. Other than that, I had not really given it much thought.

Marseille entertaining the Hitler Youth on his tour describing air combat (Leni Riefenstahl)

"Then he told me what he heard, and I told him that if he were serious, then what he knew was obviously not meant for the public. He must be very careful. In fact, it disturbed me, and I wondered if he had perhaps misunderstood. We all know now that he was accurate. I saw this great change in him, much like after his sister died, but this was even more serious. Never again after that day did we speak of it, but it was always laying there in the back of my mind."[214]

Werner Schroer was in a small group when Marseille was discussing this issue:

"Jochen came back, and told this crazy story, and we thought he was joking, but he almost cried as he related the story. I knew that he was torn up, and it bothered him. As crazy as the story sounded, I thought that there may be some truth in it. That was because I had a mechanic, who told me something similar, so I called him over. Gustav [Rödel] was there, as was Ludwig [Franzisket] and Emil [Clade].

"I asked my second mechanic to tell them what he had said to me a few months ago. He had been on leave and was home for Christmas, and his older brother was also there. They had not been home in almost two years I think and had not seen each other. My mechanic told me that his brother had nightmares, and he finally asked him what was wrong. His brother, who was in the *Waffen SS*, had been in Russia, and saw many mass shootings of civilians, all rounded up being Jews.

"At first, I did not believe him, it sounded too incredible. But then here was Marseille. He was many things, but he was never a liar and had a deep sense of personal honor. As my man told his story, all of the others looked at each other, and Gustav (Rödel) was the first to speak. He told Marseille that he had be better careful, that if what he said he heard was a misunderstanding and he was spreading rumors like that, it would be prison for him. He also said that if what he heard was true, and they learned that he was exposing this information, he could expect a similar fate. That was a very depressing meeting."[215]

Gustav Rödel remembered this conversation vividly; "He [Marseille] came back and told us this story, and I thought he was joking, and then possibly insane. But the more I listened and knowing how he was I could tell that he believed it. You must understand, that despite the propaganda after the war, not every German knew let alone was involved in this. Sure, we knew about concentration camps, to us they were just prisons. But what the SS was doing that was later exposed was a shocking thing to anyone who had a conscience. That was horrible.

"I knew that there had been killings in Russia, so called anti-partisan operations, and really did not think much of it. But Marseille made me reevaluate those thoughts. I was with him and the others, and I knew that if what he was saying was true, it was not supposed to be known to everyone. I looked at him and told him, 'If what you say is true, and they know you know about it, and it is a secret, then not even that [pointing to his Knight's Cross, Oak Leaves and Swords] will save you Jochen.'

"He was always a sensitive creature, but he was also a person with a good heart who wanted to do the right thing even when it came to the enemy. After we had seen that enemy pilot [Caldwell] kill Förster under parachute, that clicked in all of us, even Marseille. The meeting with Rommel was good, and we all agreed with him and Galland's orders were followed. I felt that this was the best course to follow personally. We were not murderers. Marseille helped us keep things in focus. Every time he saved an enemy's life it made an impact."[216]

Of the many people he met, perhaps the group Marseille enjoyed speaking with the most were aircraft designers and engineers. He always felt most at ease when discussing such subjects as literature, music, history and especially flying. Marseille was invited to the Augsburg factory to meet informally with one of his heroes, Professor Messerschmitt himself. The designer was always eager to speak with the pilots who made his inventions famous. The discussions were probably related to the flight characteristics of each model Marseille had flown, and the fact that the "Gustav" was now available, and soon they were going to Africa, but first Eastern Front units were getting their deliveries. Finally, they took a tour of the assembly plant, where Marseille met the workers, answered questions and thanked them for building such a fine aircraft.

While they were there *Flugkapitän* Fritz Wendel, world-record-setting pilot and chief test pilot for Messerschmitt GmbH—perhaps the best test pilot in the world at that time—came in for a landing in a new prototype of the forthcoming Me-109G-10. Wendel invited Marseille to take it up for a test flight. He climbed in, strapped in, and took off, putting the fighter through every demanding maneuver he would use in combat, including fast rolls, split-S climbs and tight full flap turns, at stalling speed. After a ten-minute flight he set her down gently. Wendel congratulated him on his skill and the air show that entertained everyone on the ground.

Marseille was then asked to write his personal assessment of the fighter, and honest review warts and all so that the fighter could be built as perfectly as possible. Marseille did write his assessment, but what that was exactly is not known. What is known is that he was impressed with the fighter's performance, but not the roll or turn rate. In his world, tight turns and rolls were his life insurance. He flew some of the other models while there, as the new G-4 was being refined. Having the pressurized cockpit was a bonus and that Marseille stated was its best asset.

While Marseille was cavorting in Berlin and traveling around Germany, the war in Africa had been continuing, and the victories for JG-27 were piling up. On June 12, *Unteroffizier* Günther Steinhausen claimed his 19th victory, shooting down Sergeant Jimmy Wrigley in a Kittyhawk returning from an escort mission west of El Adem. On June 16, he shot down four RAF fighters in the El Adem area, bringing his tally to 23. June 27 brought three more victories, and then he scored four additional victories on June 28 over Sidi Haneish, raising his score to thirty victories. *Oberleutnant* Hans-Joachim Heinecke, with eighteen victories to his credit, was the *Staffelkapitän* of 9 *Staffel* III./JG 27. He recorded the first four-engine bomber victory for the

Geschwader, when on June 15 he shot down a Consolidated B-24 Liberator.

Werner Schroer was also steadily scoring in Marseille's absence. "June through the beginning of July was quite busy," Schroer recalled. "I myself managed to shoot down over a dozen fighters, and we were seriously outnumbered. Many of these missions were trying to catch the British planes as they tried to attack the ships bringing supplies into us along the coast. Sometimes we would have alarms where incoming aircraft would try and attack our base.

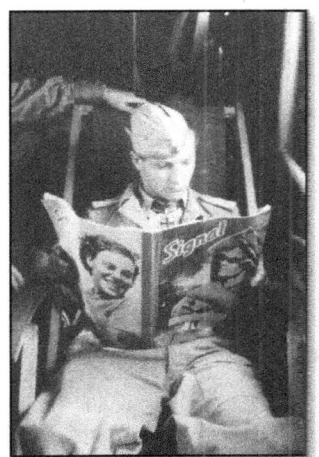

Marseille on a Ju-52 on his way to meet with Benito Mussolini (Raymond F. Toliver)

"Remember that we had no radar, nothing like that. This was very primitive. We had soldiers on the frontline who would radio any sightings of aircraft approaching. We always had a pair of fighters in the air during daylight flying scouting patrols. Sometimes there was a Storch that flew up and down the front, close enough to not get into trouble, but able to see anything approaching. We would receive warnings in the communication tent by radio. This would usually give us enough time to get up in the air and deal with the threat. These were always interesting missions, because we would always be at an altitude disadvantage."[217]

On June 21, Rommel's forces had taken Tobruk, and with a replenished supply line, had crossed into Egypt, reaching the coast near the railway at a small obscure place called El Alamein. JG-27 continued its duties without its brightest star, with III./JG-27 being heavily involved. The front's extension also forced JG-27 to relocate to airfields closer to the front, and between June 24 and 26 all the *Gruppen* had established their fields at Gazala, Tmimi, and Sidi Barrani. These were only temporary transitions, as they relocated as the situation dictated. Between July 7 and October 25 I and II./JG-27 shared the airfield at Quotaifiya, which established a solid *Luftwaffe* fighter presence only 30 miles from the front.

July saw no break in the action, and it also brought losses. On July 4, Friedrich Körner joined in a mission to intercept a formation of enemy twin engine bombers. As he began his diving attack, he was intercepted by a flight of Hurricanes from No. 1 Squadron SAAF. His Me-109F-4Trop (W.Nr. 8696) Red 9 was riddled with holes and smoking after being ambushed by Lieutenant Lawrence Waugh, and at 13:30 Körner was forced to take to his parachute.

"I must admit that it was my fault," Körner recalled. "We were all exhausted, and perhaps I was just not thinking as clearly as I should have. I saw the enemy bombers and called them out, and then I went into a shallow diving attack. I never asked or received any transmission from my flight that my tail was clear, I just assumed that they were with me.

"I was closing in on one bomber, a Boston I think, when suddenly my engine shuddered, the instrument panel started smoking, and I smelled glycol as the fumes were entering the cockpit. There was no way that I could stay in the fighter, so I rolled over, pulled the canopy release and pushed out with my legs. Within seconds I was under a parachute that cracked my back when it opened. As I looked down, I saw British soldiers, and I knew that it was all over for me."[218]

Körner was uninjured, but upon landing he was captured and would remain a prisoner of war in Canada until 1947. He retired in 1979 as a *Generalmajor* in the postwar *Bundesluftwaffe*.

Feldwebel Josef-Emil Clade recorded his tenth victory on July 5, when he shot down a Spitfire near El Daba.

"I had him cold from higher altitude, and I gave full throttle, closed in and began to fire when he suddenly turned and rolled hard left. I could not follow him, so I did the same at hard right. Both of us were trying to pull tight in opposite directions, and we both fired. I saw my strikes hit his engine which began to smoke, and none of his rounds hit me."[219]

Gustav Rödel and Gerhard Homuth led their men into the fray time and again and managed to inflict damage upon the Commonwealth air forces. One of the rising stars was *Leutnant* Stahlschmidt of 2 *Staffel* I./JG-27, who scored a kill on July 7 and then shot down three Hurricanes on July 8, giving him 30 confirmed victories. Stahlschmidt would finally earn the Knight's Cross a month later with 57 victories to his credit. On July 9 *Feldwebel* Steinhausen of 1 *Staffel* I./JG-27 shot down the second four-engine bomber for the *Geschwader*, one of six B-24s on an anti-shipping mission. The bomber, nicknamed *Eager Beaver*, went into the Mediterranean Sea, for Steinhausen's 34th victory.

Lawrence Robertson Stuart Waugh of No. 1 Sqn SAAF who shot down Friedrich Körner. Waugh later served in RCAF 417 and RAF 601 Squadrons in Italy and became a POW in 1943 after scoring 6 victories (Geoffrey Morley-Mower)

All of JG-27 was scoring steadily, and the combat arena became even more congested when the 57th Fighter Group of the United States Army Air Forces began operating its fighters out of Palestine and Egypt. Now the Americans were in the war in the Middle East, no German interviewed believed that the outcome would be positive for Germany. According to Schroer: "Our Japanese allies really did not do us any favors. We had enough to deal with as it was."[220]

On August 3, 1942, between 18:25-19:30 GMT ten Spitfires from No. 145 Squadron took off to patrol over the north at 19,000 feet followed by Hurricane IIcs from No. 33 and No. 213 Squadrons. Eight Me-109s of II./JG 27 took off on a *frei jagd* ten minutes later, joining six more escort 109s already on a raid at that time. The II./*Gruppe's* unit's pilots reported three different engagements with the enemy.

The first encounter was with two Spitfires, one of which was claimed by Emil Clade of 5 *Staffel* II./JG 27 at 19:03 north of El Bahrein and the pilot was seen bailing out. Spitfire Vb (BP865) of No. 145 Squadron was shot down into the sea with Pilot Officer A. E. Mulhall bailing out safely. The second engagement reported was with eight more Spitfires, two of which were claimed. The first engagement was at 19:12 north-west of El Hammam by *Oberfeldwebel* Karl-Heinz Bendert (4 *Staffel* II/JG 27) and the second by *Oberfeldwebel* Erwin Sawallisch also of 4./II/JG 27) north-north-west of El Hammam at 19:15. No. 145 Squadron recorded meeting twelve Messerschmitts, with a Spitfire Vb (BR519) being damaged and crash landing with the pilot Sergeant R. A. Cunningham unharmed. No. 145 Squadron claimed two possible victories over two Bf 109s, these being claimed by Flight Lieutenant Cecil Saunders in Spitfire Vb BR583/Z#-T and Sergeant P.G. C. Thomas in Spitfire Vb BP986/Z#-# over the north end of the battle line.

The third engagement was with a reported 24 Hurricanes, three of which were claimed. *Oberleutnant* Rudolf Sinner (6 *Staffel* II./JG 27) claimed one at 18:55 south-east of El Daba and a second at 19:00 over Bir Ibrahim. The third was claimed by *Oberfeldwebel* Herbert Krenz at 19:20 north-west of Quabr Hanizadr. Again, one of the pilots was seen bailing out. No. 33 Squadron lost two Hurricanes and another one damaged at around 19:00. Pilot Officer W. Friend returned with BP352 slightly damaged while Pilot Officer H. Steward safely bailed out of BP192. Flight Sergeant J. A. Kingdon was wounded, and he crash-landed his badly damaged BE409/G. Another Hurricane (IIc BP331) from No. 213 Squadron was also lost when 23-year-old Pilot Officer Robert Joseph Wallace (RAF No. 49696) was seen to spin out of control and crashed for no apparent reason about 15 miles south-west of Burg el Arab.

At 08:30 on August 4, 1942 twelve Tomahawks of No. 5 Squadron SAAF were provided with top cover by Kittyhawks during a raid, the

South Africans being attacked by two 109s of 4 *Staffel* II./JG 27 which were escorting a reconnaissance Bf 110. *Oberfeldwebel* Karl-Heinz Bendert and *Oberfeldwebel* Sawallisch each claimed one fighter shot down south-east of El Alamein at 08:08 and 08:10 respectively. One Tomahawk IIa was shot down when 2nd Lieutenant E. H. Johnson crash-landing his P-40 (AK429) ten miles west of El Alamein, wounded in his left leg. He remained unconscious in the cockpit for three hours, but he recovered and then walked for another eight hours until he was rescued and taken to a hospital.

At 13:25 No. 213 Squadron patrolled over the El Alamein supporting No. 33 Squadron, as they waited to provide escort for a formation of Baltimore bombers, Kittyhawks and Spitfires from a raid. Eight 109s of II./JG 27 were ordered to take off and Sawallisch and Bendert each man claimed a Spitfire north-west of El Hammam at 13:28 and 13:30. Flight Sergeant S. R. Fry of No. 213 Squadron was shot down, force-landing his Hurricane IIc (BN117) north of El Hammam. Of great interest regarding this after action report, the No. 213 Squadron pilots reported that they had been attacked by *Regia Aeronautica* Macchi MC.202s, but no Italians filed any claims in that area, and in fact none of the Germans ever reported seeing Italians in the area either.

On August 7 at 09:50 eight 109s, four each from I and II *Gruppen* soon encountering twelve Hurricane IIs of No. 274 Squadron, six carrying bombs and six flying as escorts, which were attacking and then turned out over the sea. The I *Gruppe* pilots led by Homuth found them over the Mediterranean Sea near Ras Gibeira, and Homuth claimed two shot down; reported as a Hurricane at 09:21 five kilometers north-west of El Alamein and the second mistakenly claimed as a P-40 at 09:23 south

Franz Stigler, Ferdinand Vögl, Karl-Heinz Bendert, Erwin Sawallisch (Franz Stigler)

of El Hammam. *Leutnant* Hans Remmer called in that he had damaged a third Hurricane.

No. 274 Squadron reported being attacked over the sea by two 109s between 10:05-11:10 (GMT), stating that one of 109 had a blue spinner. Two Hurricanes were lost with 24-year-old Flight Lieutenant Christopher William Wharton Darwin (RAF No. 42050) in BE683/P shot down off Sollum and American born Flight Sergeant Paul Gordon Hemmer (RCAF No. R/83123) in Z5337/O shot down near Burg el Arab. Both pilots bailed out under good parachutes, but neither man was able to be rescued.

The four 109 pilots of 4 *Staffel* II./JG-27 led by *Oberleutnant* Ferdinand Vögl, reported that they had engaged 24 Hurricanes and twelve P-40s also near Hammam, joined by III./JG 53 and then soon afterward later engaging another formation of fighter-bombers. Nine victory claims were submitted by the Germans involved. What appears to have happened was serious overclaiming of damaged enemy fighters without verification of a crash or a bail out by both III./JG 53 and III./JG 27, although many Allied fighters were returning severely damaged and a few were written off. Those pilots filing claims were as follows:

Oberfeldwebel Erwin Sawallisch, who claimed two Hurricanes at 09:12 east of Alam el Kadim and at 09:15 south-east of Alam el Kadim.

Oberleutnant Ferdinand Vögl, who also claimed two Hurricane at 09:12 south-east of Alam el Kadim and 09:16 east of Alam el Kadim.

Oberfeldwebel Karl-Heinz Bendert claimed one Hurricane at 09:13 south-east of Alam el Kadim, a second Hurricane at 09:21 east-north-east of Alam el Kadim and a P-40 Kittyhawk at 09:23 south of El Hammam.

Oberfeldwebel Franz Stigler claimed a Hurricane at 09:14 east of Alam el Kadim and a second at 09:20 east-northeast of Alam el Kadim. Stigler did file damaged possibly destroyed on both.

What appears to have happened is that several pilots hit the same enemy aircraft, saw smoke and then did not follow through due to the heavy air activity. Stigler explained it this way:

> "When we were in some battles, especially this one, once you shot an enemy and he was on fire or smoking, you did not focus upon him. That could get you killed. Fixating on one target was not too smart, so you filed a claim hoping that it would be verified by another pilot or a ground witness. You saw, you shot, you looked around, and if an enemy was near you then you moved to not be a target. It was madness sometimes."[221]

That same day a flight from 5 *Staffel* II./JG-27 made history, when *Oberfeldwebel* (later *Hauptmann*) Josef-Emil Clade led his *Schwarm* of four pilots on a routine long range combat patrol south of Alexandria. The Germans encountered a Bristol Bombay transport assigned to No. 216 Squadron RAF, flown by nineteen year-old Sergeant Pilot H. E. "Jimmy" James, carrying a VIP: the newly appointed commander of the British Eighth Army, Lieutenant General William Gott, who would ironically become the highest-ranking British officer killed in action during the war. As a result of this victory by Clade, Lieutenant General (later Field Marshal) Bernard Law Montgomery was given command of the British Eighth Army just prior to the great Battle of El Alamein in October 20, 1942. Clade had changed history, as he recalled:

> "I saw this aircraft and the others called it out also, so I simply claimed it as mine and dropped the nose and picked up speed while losing altitude. It was a clean pass, a good burst into the aircraft, the left engine blew smoke and started to burn, if I recall. It was going in and made a fast crash landing, and then I flew past and my wingman [Bernd Schneider] then dropped in behind me and fired up the wreckage. It burned and we then pulled away. I had no idea until many years later who was on board that aircraft. Strange how things happen."[222]

Emil Clade portrait (Emile Clade)

During Marseille's absence, controversy surrounded 4 *Staffel* of II *Gruppe*, when an investigation was launched by Neumann into their claims. The men in question were Karl-Heinz Bendert and his *Schwarm*, which sometimes included Erwin Sawallisch, Ferdinand Just, Ferdinand Vögl, and occasionally Franz Stigler. They had claimed 59 victories from August 4–19, while the rest of II *Gruppe* hardly had any victories: 6 *Staffel* of II *Gruppe* only claimed two victories, and very few enemy contacts.

As it concerned his *Gruppe*, Gustav Rödel was ordered to carry out the investigation. The order had come personally from Göring who simply wanted an update on the reported success, passed through Kesselring and down to Neumann, and Rödel was determined to get to the bottom of what had happened. He interviewed all the men and found that Vögl and Bendert were always together and usually separated from the rest of the flight when they made their claims. The rumors were that they were falsifying claims.

"It was quite embarrassing," Rödel recalled. "I did not think then that it was a matter of intentionally lying about their victories, but it was proven to have been gross negligence in claiming victories. Sometimes victories were claimed when the pilots had shot at an aircraft but had not confirmed that the enemy had crashed, or the pilot had bailed out. In those cases, the pilot was to report "damaged" or a "probable" victory in the absence of secondary confirmation.

"We had a reconnaissance aircraft, a Me-109 with a camera, and another unit not assigned to JG-27 stationed nearby, maybe near Derna, with a Fieseler Storch. Also, regular fighter sweeps would fly reconnaissance missions. The coordinates of the crash or engagement were required in the *Abschusse,* but some of the claims made by Bendert and Vögl could not be confirmed outside of their confirming each others' statements. The situation stained all involved in the *Gruppe* and that *Schwarm,* and even Stigler and I were questioned."[223]

Franz Stigler saw it differently: "I do believe that Bendert and Vögl were claiming victories falsely for each other. Erwin Sawallisch was also implicated, but I flew with him a lot, and that was not in his character, and his claims were usually confirmed by ground troops if not by an aerial witness. Erwin had been in Spain with Neumann, Galland, Rödel, and that group. He was a very honest and honorable man, but because he and I were often assigned to that *Staffel,* and often flying in the *Schwarm,* all of us were investigated. It was really embarrassing and annoying."[224]

The greatest tragedy was that although Sawallisch, like Franz Stigler, was cleared of any wrongdoing, there was still guilt by association. Stigler stuck to his guns and maintained his honor, and he was eventually cleared, while Sawallisch who was also cleared, was broken by the accusations. He would later crash into the sea on August 19, 1942. Some of the men believed that he committed suicide, rather than face possible public recrimination for something that he had not done. Gustav Rödel made his comment: "I knew Erwin since Spain, and I knew that he was not a part of this, and I told him so, along with Stigler. But Erwin Sawallisch took his honor seriously, and I think that the stress of the war and the accusations, of which he was cleared, finally broke him. That was sad."[225]

Meanwhile, back in Germany on July 6, Marseille, who was unaware of any of this going on in Africa received a telegram that informed him that while en route back to Libya he was once again to present himself to Benito Mussolini in Rome to receive the highest award for bravery in the field that Italy could bestow, the Golden

Medal for Bravery, or the Medaglia d'Oro. Not even *Generalfeldmarschall* Erwin Rommel, who also held the silver medal, would receive the gold version.

Marseille and his fiancée traveled to the Eternal City, where the couple met *Il Duce* and Marseille received his medal. According to what he told his friends in Africa on his return, apparently Mussolini had liked Marseille from their first meeting. He also told the young pilot that he may want to get a haircut and that he had an excellent barber. (Given Marseille's appearance when he eventually landed in Benghazi, it was unlikely that he took the dictator up on his offer.) Following a sightseeing tour, Hannelies departed for home while Marseille awaited a transport aircraft, and the weather delayed his departure. When the transport finally took off, Marseille was not on board.

Meanwhile, Eduard Neumann was handling all of the headaches that accompanied a combat command. The constant lack of fuel, ammunition, food, and water; overstretched and vulnerable lines of supply; the ever-growing air strength of the Allies; and the looming prospect of a great ground and air battle consumed all of his time, thus limiting his time in the air. And then there was Marseille.

When the Ju-52 landed without Marseille, Neumann immediately inquired as "to where in the hell he was." The German military authority in Rome sent out a missing person's report on Marseille, which landed on the desk of the local *Gestapo* chief in Rome, *Obersturmbannführer* Herbert Kappler.[226] Within hours a manhunt was underway, news of which even reached Berlin. According to Franzisket, the first place they began looking were the brothels, following a tip from an "unknown source."

Marseille was finally located in a village hotel in the Ardeatine area, and he was somehow convinced to return to his unit. Remarkably nothing was ever said about it in the formal reports. He never discussed his absence with even his closest friends, and other than the rumors that were spread among his comrades, the actual details are not known. The most prevalent rumor was that he ran off with an

Italian girl. Others believed that he was suffering from severe depression or lost his courage. Franzisket found the latter reason absurd:

> "Marseille was only human, and he had been through a lot personally, and it would only get worse for him spiritually after he came back and we lost other pilots, and he learned of them men who had died while he was back home. Yes, Marseille was human, and he was many things, but to insinuate that he had lost his nerve in combat or had become a coward was insane at best. It was his bravery or even perhaps his natural aggression that made him successful. There were none braver I can assure you."[227]

That previous accusation regarding the girl of the Italian relative of Mussolini's was probably true, although the belief that he had lost his courage, or his confidence was probably unfounded as stated by Franzisket, although from July 1941 he was known to have kept an apartment in Benghazi for his off time. This was a sort of rest area away from the unit, sometimes only a short drive away from most of their ever-rotating fields, otherwise they took the regular transports flying into the Benghazi airfield. Although no one from his unit ever stayed at the place, rumor had it that this was his private bachelor pad, where women from many places and social strata enjoyed his company. Neumann heard all the stories:

> "By the time Marseille came back from missing his flight in Rome, I had already heard the stories of what happened with Hitler and the others. Even Hitler thought a lot of Marseille. I knew that when he received the Oak Leaves and Swords that Hitler asked him about his thoughts regarding the British pilots and their aircraft, among many other things. I heard all of this secondhand, but I know it to be true. Marseille apparently told Hitler, in his usual nonchalant fashion, that we needed to hire the fellows who were handling the British supply and transport lines. They were better at their jobs than we were."[228]

This collection of women was rumored to have included at least one German general's wife (if not more), a Moroccan belly dancer, a British spy, an Albanian missionary, a niece of Mussolini's, a Hungarian countess, Italian singer Nilla Pizzi, several German and Austrian singers and actresses (including Swedish born Zarah Stina Hedberg Leander, and Olga Knipper), and another Italian woman supposedly related to Count Ciano, hence some of the inquests into his whereabouts. How much of these rumors were true is impossible to say, although Emil Clade saw some corroborating evidence:

"Once Marseille had a few days off, he went to Benghazi, and when he returned he always had good schnapps, wine, or brandy. These were hard to get so you had to be well connected. He once began to open his bag and bring out all sorts of wonderful things, until be pulled out a woman's brassiere. I asked him, 'Who does that belong to? I hope she is not in the bottom of that bag!' He said: 'I have no idea which one this belongs to.' Stahlschmidt spoke up and said, 'Healthy woman from the size.' So, I guess the rumors were true."[229]

Obersturmbannführer Herbert Kappler after his arrest pending the war crimes trials. (Simon Wiesenthal)

Sometimes a few of the men would take their few days off and go to Benghazi on the transport that flew in the mail and supplies and carried outgoing mail and correspondence. One event stood out clearly in the minds of Clade, Schroer and Franzisket, after spending four days in the city on a long and rare four day pass. Schroer recalled:

"We had to catch a J-52 at 0800 to get back to base. We did not have to be back until that afternoon, but we had to leave on the established flight schedule. If we missed that flight there would not be another for two days. We agreed to meet at the front of the hotel where we were staying, but no Marseille, as his apartment was nearby. We had time so we decided to walk the few streets over and see if he was awake, alive, or passed out drunk. We climbed the stairs and when Clade went to knock on his door, this beautiful Arab girl slipped passed us putting her clothes on.

"We just looked at each other and smiled, and Ludwig said, 'I guess he got lucky.' Then the door opened, and another girl came out of the bathroom, putting her clothes on and she smiled at us and ran past, and when we looked another one was getting out of the bed and wrapped herself in a sheet and was picking up her clothes. Marseille was still sleeping.

"I walked over and pushed him and told him to get up, and he jumped up. I could smell the alcohol on him. There were empty bottles on the floor. He asked what the problem was, and I told him that we had a plane to catch. He asked what time it was and I told him it was after 0700, we had to go. He got up and started getting dressed when Ludwig asked him about the three girls. You will not believe what he said. 'What do you mean three? Where are the other two?' We just looked at each other in stunned silence."[230]

Ludwig Franzisket added to the story: "Marseille asked us to look under the bed, I did, but no one was there. Emil checked out the bathroom, and it was clear. Marseille then realized that his wristwatch and wallet were missing. 'I guess I was robbed' he said. Little loss I did not have any money in it. Oh, look I still have my *soldbuch* [identification paybook] and medals!"[231]

Marseille also received many letters from Nilla Pizzi, the most famous Italian singer, musician, and actress of her day, and there is no doubt that they had an affair. She sent him love letters and gifts, including expensive champagne and wines, as well as very provocative photographs of herself. The same can be said of Swedish born actress Zarah Leander. Other actresses also sent letters and signed cards. This probably created envy more than anything else among his squadron mates. Clade saw the letters, and Marseille even once mentioned that Pizzi "was devilish."[232] Perhaps the one giveaway to the affair, besides letters, was the record he brought back, the "Rumba Azul" which was his favorite song. It was signed by Pizzi, with "Dearest Lover" written on the back, apparently a gift from her to Marseille.

Marseille had been missing out on a lot of action, but when he returned the unit was back full force, such as on August 10 when twelve Kittyhawks of No. 4 Squadron SAAF took off on a patrol at 08:30, when they encountered four II./JG 27 109Fs which had taken off at 09:09. The Germans radioed that they had 16 British fighters southeast of El Alamein and when it was over they claimed four shot down, two each by Sawallisch at 08:31 north of El Muhafid and 08:30 northwest of El Muhafid, with Franz Stigler calling in a victory at 08:32 north of El Muhafid and a second at 08:33 north-north-west of El Muhafid.

On the Allied side, No. 4 Squadron reported that two 109s hit them from out of the sun, one being claimed damaged by Lieutenant J. W. Wheeler in Kittyhawk Ia (ET901/KJ-U) over El Alamein at 09:25. His Kittyhawk was damaged, but he managed to return safely to base. One Kittyhawk was shot down killing 28-year-old Canadian Pilot Officer John Kitson McIvor (RAF No. 107257) in Kittyhawk I (AK623) and another flown by Lieutenant T. B. Milne (ET512) crash-landed upon his return to base.

The morning of August 11, 4 *Staffel* II./JG 27 sent four Me-109s on a patrol and the German pilots reported encountering ten Hurricanes of No. 1 Squadron SAAF which left their base at 11:20 GMT, claiming five victories in the El Hammam area. Sawallisch called out one Hurricane at 10:10 north-west of El Hammam and another Hurricane at 10:13 east of El Hammam. Ferdinand Vögl also claimed two Hurricanes at 10:11 west-northwest of El Hammam and another Hurricane 10:17 east-northeast of El Hammam. Franz Stigler also claimed a Hurricane damaged possibly destroyed at 10:13 south of El Hammam. Stigler remembered this mission:

> "I came across this one Hurricane who fired on me and he hit my Messerschmitt, then I pulled up, rolled and got behind him as he passed by me and I fired on him, I saw great strikes on him, and he was smoking badly, but then I heard on my headphones that I had another coming for me so I broke off contact and pulled a hard right turn. I did not see the enemy aircraft, so I was unsure if that warning was for me, I did not see the crash and a parachute, as I was low of fuel, I had a sluggish rudder and right aileron, and decided to head home. So, I only claimed a damaged, but the way he was smoking he was not going to go very far."[233]

The Hurricanes of No. 1 Squadron SAAF were in fact under constant 'hit and run' attacks by the six 109s and Captain L. R. S. Waugh flying Hurricane IIb (698/A#-P) returned to base claiming one of the Me-109s damaged fifteen miles west of Burg el Arab, which may have been Franz Stigler who brought back a damaged fighter after taking hits in the fuselage and right wing. Several Hurricanes returned with varying degrees of damage but despite the claims no aircraft German or South African were shot down

On the morning of August 12, three 109s from 4 *Staffel* II./JG-27 took off, with the exception of *Oberleutnant* Ferdinand Vögl who could not start his engine. Simultaneously twelve No. 2 Squadron SAAF P-40 Kittyhawks flew a reconnaissance and attack mission, some carrying bombs. After the bomb run, the three aircraft flying top cover were attacked by two 109s, and Lieutenant W. L. O. Moon's Kittyhawk I (AL174/U) was badly damaged requiring a gear up crash landing. Likewise, Lieutenant T. M. McLeod in AK906/O was also damaged and wounded, and he crash landed back at his base at 07:30. Lieutenant A. Morrison was hit by anti-aircraft fire and he crash landed at El Hammam station with ET874/D on fire. He managed to get out just before it blew up. Lieutenant J. R. Burls in Kittyhawk (AK760/K) claimed a damaged 109 at El Imayid at 07:35.

Franz Stigler claimed a Hurricane at 06:44 south-south-east of El Alamein, another Hurricane at 06:53 south of Alam el Kadim and one P-40 at 07:03 south-west of Alam el Halfa. The P-40 was probably the aircraft flown by Moon as he saw it crash land. What is not understood are the claims filed by Bendert who reported that they had encountered around 40 Kittyhawks carrying bombs and another 16 escort fighters, when there were not that many enemy aircraft. It would also appear that misidentification was rampant, which sometimes happened.

Sawallisch claimed a Hurricane at 06:42 south-east of El Alamein, another Hurricane at 06:48 west of Alam el Kadim, and a third Hurricane at 06:51 north of Alam el Kadim and an additional P-40 at 07:00 south-west of Alam el Halfa. Karl-Heinz Bendert claimed a Hurricane at 06:43 south-east of El Alamein, another Hurricane at 06:50 west of Alam el Kadim, another Hurricane at 06:52 east of Alam el Kadim, and two P-40s at 07:02 and 07:04 both south-west of Alam el Halfa.

Photo taken of Marseille after his first mission on September 1, 1942 (Ludwig Franzisket)

The 4 *Staffel* II./JG-27 was once again active on August 14 when they crossed paths with eleven Kittyhawks of No. 2 Squadron SAAF and eleven more from No. 4 Squadron SAAF as they escorted twelve Baltimore bombers on their mission to bomb LG 18 in the Daba-Fuka area. These aircraft were followed by twelve more Kittyhawks of No.

260 Squadron with six attached US P-40Fs of the 57th Fighter Group, to provide top cover for 12 Boston bombers on their mission to hit Fuka Station. Following 20 minutes behind were eight Spitfires of No. 92 Squadron on their first patrol since re-equipment, their task being to cover the returning formations against any pursuing Axis fighters.

At 06:57, four Me-109F-4s of II./JG 27 took off, followed seven minutes later by six more. The 109s focused their attacks on the Baltimores and their fighter escorts, with one Kittyhawk being claimed by *Oberleutnant* Rudolf Sinner of 6 *Staffel* II./JG 27) north-west of El Alamein at approximately 06:25, but this victory was not confirmed due to the lack of either air or ground witnesses.

The Italians were also involved on this mission when MC.202s of the 9o *Gruppo* were vectored into the battle. At 05:58 *Tenente* Antonio Canfora led six MC.202s of the 97a *Squadriglia* that took off at Fuka to face incoming bombers. Near El Daba at 06:20 they intercepted twelve of the bombers, which they identified as Marylands and their escort of eighteen P-40s. *Tenente* Canfora claimed a P-40 as a probable with another unknown pilot claiming a "Maryland" (actually a Baltimore) as a probable and several other bombers reported as damaged.

No. 4 Squadron SAAF was engaged by at least seven Me-109s and MC.202s while operating as top cover for the bombers over Fuka at 06:20. No. 4 Squadron lost one fighter shot down killing Lieutenant Neil Washington Hancock flying Kittyhawk I (ET978, SAAF No. 104008V), and two more fighters were badly damaged. One of the damaged aircraft belonged to Lieutenant David Woodliffe in Kittyhawk AK720 which was damaged by a 109. His undercarriage was not functional, so he slid into a controlled crash landing back at his base and was uninjured. The third P-40 (AK788) was damaged, but the unidentified pilot did not sustain any injuries.

The fighters of II./JG-27 then attacked a formation which was identified as ten Boston bombers and twenty Kittyhawk escorts but no victories were called out. Other bombers entered the area and were escorted by No. 260 Squadron. Here Sawallisch claimed a P-40 at 06:15 north of Fuka and a second at 06:30 south of Ras el Maquiran,

Oberleutnant Rudolf "Rudi" Sinner[234] called out a kill at 06:30 northwest of El Alamein and *Oberfeldwebel* Herbert Krenz claimed a fourth at 06:25 north of El Hammam. The 6 *Staffel* was quite active, but the fight was not over.

No. 260 Squadron's top cover was attacked out of the sun with two Kittyhawks being shot down immediately, almost simultaneously another flight of four P-40s was attacked over Daba by two more 109s, as they patrolled the area until they spotted the Baltimores which had just bombed LG 18. The bombers were under attack by II./*Gruppe* and the Kittyhawk pilots jumped right into the fight. The third flight of four P-40s pushed on with the bombers and were the only fighters from No. 260 to even reach the target and as soon as they did they were also attacked by the Germans forcing one Kittyhawk into a crash landing. Two P-40s returned to base, the fourth fighting a lone combat with Sergeant William Ronald Cundy flying Kittyhawk I (ET1016/V) claiming a 109 as a probable.

Not to be left out No. 92 Squadron Spitfires joined the action, with Squadron Leader 'Jeff' Wedgwood in a Spitfire Vc (BP476/QJ-B) being the first to score a kill by shooting down *Leutnant* Gert Mix's Me-109F-4 "Yellow 5" of 6 *Staffel* II./JG 27 who was hit in the cooling system and crash-landed uninjured but was captured.

The result of this day's activities saw No. 260 Squadron lose two aircraft, but both pilots Squadron Leader P. P. Devenish and Warrant Officer O. Bowerman were uninjured, while a third Kittyhawk (AL149) was attacked by a diving Me-109 while less than only 100 feet above the desert floor as it approached its home base and crash landed ten miles away with Pilot Officer E. G. Aitchison uninjured. Lieutenant William O'Neill of the USAAF called out that he was involved with five Me-109s claiming two shot down, before he was shot down himself and ditching into the sea where he was rescued uninjured.[235]

On August 16, 1942 at 07:27, Neumann sent a *Rotte* (two Me-109s) from I. *Gruppe,* one flown by *Leutnant* Hans-Arnold Stahlschmidt on a forward reconnaissance. This pair was involved in two separate actions. At 09:15 Stahlschmidt claimed one P-40 out of six engaged north-west of El Hammam. He then claimed a second P-40 ten minutes later from a different formation of 20 enemy fighters west-south-west of El Alamein. Neumann then ordered more of his fighters into the air and five more Me-109s from 4 *Staffel* II/JG 27 took off at 0912, and they encountered the second Allied group Stahlschmidt had just fought.

As this was going on, eleven P-40 Tomahawks of No. 5 Squadron SAAF joined the formation of Boston bombers on a photo-reconnaissance mission when they were attacked. One P-40 flown by Lieutenant Clifford Trenchard (SAAF No. 205455) was shot down at 09:15 and the 21-year-old pilot was badly wounded when he jumped from his fighter (ET522/W) as it was engulfed in flames seven miles southwest of El Alamein and he was captured, but he died next day. Three more P-40s were damaged including Captain R. F. Armstrong in AN427/D who landed uninjured. Three 109s were claimed as damaged, at 09:35 about 14 miles southwest of El Alamein. The three pilots who filed the reports were Captain D. C. Dove flying AN366/GL-N, Lieutenant Robert Hirst in AN238/GL-O and 2nd Lieutenant Hendrik Smith in AN461/GL-K.

No. 2 Squadron SAAF had eight Kittyhawks deployed on a fighter reconnaissance attacked by 109s, with Captain R. Clifton in ET522/W bailing out wounded and landing in the sea offshore of El Alamein. Another P-40 (reported as AL160) was hit and damaged. Logic would dictate that these two South African aircraft shot down were Stahlschmidt's victories when matching the records. It also makes sense that the other P-40s that returned to base and reported as damaged were due to Stahlschmidt and/or his wingman. This is merely supposition since several 4. *Staffel* II./JG-27 pilots were involved in one of these contacts with No. 5 Squadron SAAF.

Five pilots from 4 *Staffel* II./JG 27 reported their actions deep into enemy territory starting at about 09:30 with five P-40s and ten Hurricanes. During the 15-minute fight they claimed to have shot down all five P-40s and seven of the Hurricanes. The following pilots filed the claims:

Oberfeldwebel Sawallisch claimed one Hurricane at 08:26 west of Alam el Halfa and another at 08:32 south-west of El Hammam and his third victory at 08:39 south-south-west of El Hammam.

Oberleutnant Ferdinand Vögl claimed one Hurricane at 08:27 over Alam el Kadim, his second Hurricane east of El Hammam and a P-40 at 08:38 east of El Hammam.

Oberfeldwebel Karl-Heinz Bendert claimed a P-40 08:28 south of Alam el Kadim, a second P-40 at 08:35 east of Alam el Kadim and a third P-40 at 08:40 south of El Hammam.

Oberfeldwebel Franz Stigler claimed a P-40 at 08:28 south of Alam el Kadim and a Hurricane at 08:38 south-south-west of El Hammam.

Unteroffizier Ferdinand Just claimed one Hurricane at 08:40 south-west of El Hammam.

Marseille and his mother Charlotte having tea in their home (Robert Tate)

However, this was where the "claiming" controversy came into being, because when Stahlschmidt landed and heard the claims of the II *Gruppe*, his rendition was not the same story. He and his wingman had completed their mission and joined the remaining 4. *Staffel* pilots. He knew who they were by their markings, and he mentioned Bendert and Vögl who he saw shooting off their ammunition into their shadows on the desert sand. Stigler, Just and Sawallisch had already departed for base low on fuel.

The prevailing thought was that Vögl and Bendert were practicing "shadow-shooting" to improve their marksmanship. Stahlschmidt found it curious as to how they had any ammunition remaining if they had in fact scored those victories. Neumann took an interest, and the Allied records did not reflect all those losses as claimed. Others began to question their claims also.

Given the confusion of air combat and all the variables, the claims by JG-27 up to this period had been remarkably accurate. This situation was a far different matter, and for the first three weeks of August JG-27 had been pulling daily escort missions for German supply convoys at sea between Tobruk and Mersa Matruh and there had been few combat opportunities. These facts forced an even harder look at the 4 *Staffel* pilots. It should be noted that several II *Gruppe* aces such as Sinner, Stigler, and Börngen did not believe them. Stigler found it interesting that every time he was separated from Bendert and Vögl was when they claimed their encounters. He was questioned by Rödel and Neumann as he was in their *Staffel*, and often flew with them and these are Stigler's words:

"We did become involved many times with the occasional enemy formation, and we tried our best to get an accurate report on claimed victories and damaged aircraft. The rule was that once we reached a certain low fuel level we returned to the base, do not risk your aircraft. I never ran out of fuel as a result and always came straight back. But on many missions Vögl and Bendert would be several minutes behind us. They would dismount and state that they encountered a few Kittyhawks or Hurricanes or something like that, and they verified each other's victories.

"Their ammunition had been used, that was proven. But without gun cameras we could not confirm many of our claims, just hoping that someone in the air or on the ground could confirm the crash. When I heard what Stahlschmidt had reported, it really started to make sense to me. Sinner came to me and questioned these claims, and I told him I was not with them during most of these encounters. When I was with them in combat, sometimes Vögl and Bendert would call out the enemies they had hit, sometimes I saw this also, and then claim the victories, whether I saw anything or not, such as a crash or parachute. But you must remember that was not unusual in combat. You do not waste time watching for a crash or a pilot to leave his fighter to confirm a victory. That will get you killed."[236]

However, when they were questioned by Rödel, Vögl and Bendert denied falsifying their claims, and that suspicion also fell upon Stigler, Sawallisch and Just. Neumann ran the investigation with Rödel. Neumann stated:

"I made the decision to separate the pilots after the investigation concluded. We managed to figure out that only Vögl and Bendert were the true offenders, but we could not prove it. This was the result of going back and looking at the return logs. Stigler, Sawallisch, whom I had known in Spain, Just and the others were not with those two when most of the claims were made. This made perfect sense to me, and I decided to separate them and spread them out throughout the unit. They were to be watched and any claims had to be witnessed by others, not just their wingman. Rödel believed that it was more of a case of them being careless in not properly confirming, just making their claims. I was not so sure. I know that later when Bendert returned home would receive his Knight's Cross [awarded on December 30, 1942.]"[237]

Photo of Marseille showing the strain of combat (Ludwig Franzisket)

CHAPTER 9

Back in the Sky

When Marseille returned, he was a very different man in many ways.
                                                    Werner Schroer

The day after Marseille returned to the unit, his official paperwork did not reflect any unauthorized absence, and he was introduced to a black South African everyone called Mathias, and the two formed a solid friendship. Marseille wanted to read all the combat reports from all of the *Gruppen*, and he was well aware of the 6. *Staffel* II. *Gruppe* controversy. He asked about it as he knew the pilots. According to Franzisket, Marseille was pretty upset about it:

South African Corporal Matthew Letuku in uniform whom the pilots called "Mathias." (Raymond F. Toliver)

"When he arrived, he looked good, and he really needed the rest. He told us about his meeting with Hitler and all the other members of the leadership. He made some jokes about them, and he was apparently not very impressed with them. He then asked about the situation with Bendert, Stigler, Just and the others. I told him what I knew, and he read the paperwork on the investigation. He came to his own conclusion, and it was not a good one. After he reviewed the material, he believed that only Bendert and Vögl were the truly guilty parties. He based this upon the fact that they were always alone together when they made their claims; and no other pilot was there to verify. This was because when those two flew with different pilots, and not each other, those questionable claims never arose. That was enough for him, and I agreed. He was actually disgusted about the entire affair."[238]

Marseille made the rounds and was greeted by his fellow pilots, and he learned of the losses they had sustained in his absence. This was when he was introduced with Corporal Mathew Letuku, a black prisoner of war captured at Tobruk, who was a South African conscript who had been working as a driver, barber, and general handyman for the *Staffel*. Franzisket was the man who made the introduction:

"I introduced Jochen to our prisoner, Mathias. They immediately hit it off and became friends. Kugelbaur was gone, so he moved Mathias into his tent. Marseille paid him to do his laundry, and other things that would give him more free time, and when he became the official leader, he had little time for anything else due to the paperwork."[239]

Schroer had his opinion of Letuku: "He was just a very happy kind of man and did not take anything too seriously. Those who spoke English had great conversations with him, and I did not speak very much English at all, but I was learning. But once he and Marseille met it was an immediate friendship, and they both listened to Jochen's record collection, most of the songs Mathias had never heard before. They were like school friends."[240]

Neumann always had visits from high-ranking officers, whether doing inspection tours or just passing through out of curiosity. It was during one of these visits by several Army and *Luftwaffe* generals that Marseille added to his list of politically incorrect statements, as Neumann recalled: "I recall after his first visit with Hitler, Marseille returned and said that he 'thought the *Führer* was a rather odd sort.' The bad thing was that he said this in front of three generals, and with his Negro aide Mathias laughing with him."[241]

When Marseille learned what had happened in his absence, his depression increased. Despite the great numbers of victories scored while he was away, the list of comrades killed was staggering. His occasional wingman and tent mate Karl Kugelbaur, pilots Berben, Pfeffer, Sawallisch, and others were gone. The men had rearranged his living quarters in his absence, since they had been using the tent, and had not cleared out their new bar stocked with wonderful beverages. Marseille helped himself upon his return. He was drinking again. He was clearly not the same man who had left.

Stuka pilot Heinz-Georg Wilhlem Migeod (Dr. Heinz Migeod)

When Marseille later threw his lavish parties, especially when they had honored guests, Mathias served drinks as the bartender. He was also a great cook, taking the meager German rations and creating quite palatable meals out of them. Former Stuka pilot Dr. Heinz-Georg Wilhlem Migeod who flew with Kurt Kuhlmey shared his opinions on Marseille, Letuku and the parties, as they were sometimes special guests:

"Marseille was not a very military type of man. He did not seem to take things very seriously, but he had a great bar and good drinks which we did not have. His negro the black South African was his helper and also his friend. We all knew that this was not a relationship that Berlin would have smiled upon, but Marseille did not care. We did not care. None of us were dedicated believers in the racial nonsense, and it was nonsense, you know? But Marseille and Mathias were very close."[242]

Marseille paid Mathias a standard wage, and for this, he also had his tent cleaned and laundry washed and dried. The two men formed a bond that appeared as if they had known each other for years. Still, this friendship was considered illegal by many ranking visitors, since not only did the Nazis believe that blacks and Jews were inferior to Aryans, but there was an idiotic assessment that the two "degenerate" groups were racially related. "Jochen thought that this was the most ridiculous thing he had ever heard, and he said so, no matter who was within hearing," Clade stated.[243]

When asked by *Generalfeldmarschall* Albert Kesselring during his visit with Adolf Galland to the unit that month: "Why do you have a negro in your tent?" Marseille answered: "He is a good man, and my best friend, *Herr Feldmarschall*! He goes where I go." According to Neumann, "Marseille would allow no one to harm his friend, racial rules be damned."[244]

Likewise, the jazz and swing music Marseille loved was also labeled "degenerate" and he couldn't have cared less. He just lived his life to the best of his abilities, not caring what anyone thought. Marseille, Schroer, Franzisket, Clade, Mathias, Stahlschmidt and Steinhausen became a very tight group.

"Marseille left his living quarters a mess," Franzisket recalled. "Once Mathias began working for him, it was a different world. We all liked Mathias; he was a good man who just wanted to leave the war and go home. In his opinion, this was not his war, it was a white man's war, and I guess he had a point."[245] Gustav Rödel made a very interesting assessment regarding his discussions with Letuku:

"We had many conversations with him, and the men who spoke better English translated for all of us. He was very entertaining, but what was the most interesting thing he said was that he wanted to stay with us, rather than be sent back to his unit. He said that we Germans treated him better than even the white men in South Africa did, and he had reservations about going home."[246]

Mathias also loved Marseille's record collection, which Marseille inspected upon his return in case anyone had stolen anything from it. While he was in Germany the men had helped themselves to his music, and even his alcohol, but Marseille had no problem with that. He always shared what he had with his comrades, and his chief mechanic always received the first portion of any gifts he received as a sign of respect.

However, it did not take long for Marseille to once again run afoul of Gerhard Homuth. The men interviewed all agreed that Homuth was out to get Marseille on something, but as Marseille became more successful, scored more victories, received more decorations and became even more famous as a hero, it was much harder to charge him with infractions and make the charges stick. In effect Homuth was despondent that his authority was always being undermined.

Marseille had returned just in time, as the Allied air power was increasing. With the Americans now operating with the Commonwealth forces, and the additional threat of a western landing pending dividing the German forces, the noose was tightening around Rommel

The last known photo taken of Marseille while with his mother in Berlin and fiancé Hannelies Kupper, July 1942 (Raymond F. Toliver)

and his *Afrika Korps*. Germany would suffer defeat after defeat on the ground, but the *Luftwaffe*, in particular JG-27, would only achieve success.

"When he returned that August, Marseille was eager to get back into the scoring," Neumann recalled. "He had a new Me-109G-2 that was waiting for him, and even the rudder had been painted by Mathias displaying his victories. The Knight's Cross with Oak Leaves and Swords was also painted at the top of the rudder, just above the victory bars."[247]

Marseille's first mission after returning from two months of rest and parties was on August 31. This was a big battle, and the men of the I *Gruppe* heard the calls from II *Gruppe*, and Rudi Sinner's call of "*Horrido!*" signaled his victory over a Hurricane near Alam el Haifa flown by South African Ace, John "Harry" Gaynor of No. 1 Squadron SAAF who crash-landed unhurt. [Sinner claimed his 30th victory on September 3, 1942, and his last and 32nd in Africa was on September 6, a U.S. fighter downed South of El Imayid.]

Marseille felt compelled to get back into the action after a few days back in Libya with no air activity at all. He had lost a lot of opportunities for victories and with others catching up to him, according to Franzisket: "This fact made Marseille insane to get back into the war. You could see that every day without a mission after he returned, he was pacing the ground, like a caged lion."[248]

Marseille led his *Schwarm* as part of a larger effort on another Stuka escort mission. Marseille called out "*Indianer!*" and then jumped into a group of Hurricanes, flying their Lufbery formation. His first uncontested victory was a Hurricane flown by Pilot Officer L. E. Barnes, who bailed out at 10:03, but was so badly wounded he died in hospital on September 12. His wingman did not fare much better, and with a slight adjustment of the rudder Marseille brought him down in flames at 10:04, with both Hurricanes crashing close to each other. Marseille's score now stood at 103 victories.

The second mission late in the afternoon was also standard fare for Marseille, when he managed to engage a new Spitfire V, one on one, testing his plane and his skill against the ultimate enemy fighter in the theater. This was only his second engagement against this type of fighter, although in his absence his comrades had seen plenty of them. The duel between the two men lasted less than three minutes, although the enemy pilot was apparently no rookie. It took Marseille quite a bit of turning and negative and high-G maneuvering to finally slip in behind the Spitfire, which went down after a slow turning deflection shot. Marseille had his 104th kill at 18:25. He was back, and he was making his presence felt once more.

Also back was his undisciplined behavior. Once in August he was walking around with a rainbow-colored sun umbrella, obviously a gift from a female admirer, when a high-ranking officer from the Army arrived to inspect the unit, joining none other than *Luftwaffe Generalmajor* Otto Dessloch. Marseille stood there in shorts, sandals made from an old tire, and his blue, yellow, white, and red umbrella over his shoulder, wearing his non-regulation sunglasses holding a brandy glass, and joking with Mathias. Schroer recalled the event:

"The entire *Gruppe* was in formation, except Marseille and Clade. They were on bed rest, but Marseille decided it was a good time to step outside. He had really bad timing. Every man in formation was locked at rigid attention, but all were trying to look to their left and see the spectacle. Some were laughing, Neumann just shook his head, but the Army general was talking to Neumann, when Dessloch asked; 'What in the hell is that?' pointing to Marseille. At that point everyone laughed."[249]

Neumann explained this rather embarrassing situation: "I told the generals that Marseille and another pilot were on bed rest from exhaustion, my orders, and their aircraft were being serviced. Dessloch asked about the lack of proper uniform for Marseille. I just told him that he was off duty, hoping that would be enough. Dessloch knew all about Marseille, so he was a very lenient type of officer, and he said something to

Marseille, which I do not remember, they spoke with each other and Dessloch laughed. But the Army general was less amused, I should say.

Pilot Officer Richard C. Hart of No. 250 Sqn who was shot down by Marseille February 27, 1942, and bailed out uninjured (Michael Judd)

"I cannot remember who this general was right now, but he said that Marseille was an embarrassment to the military, and he should learn some discipline. I knew something was coming from Marseille, I just did not expect what I heard. Marseille looked right at him, did not salute him, but he did salute Dessloch previously and he said, '*Herr Generalmajor*, I do not think the British really care what I am wearing when I am shooting them down.'

"Well, the Army general was not as amused as Dessloch who tried to hide the fact that he was laughing, and he looked at me, and I was too shocked to even think about laughing although I wanted to. You just had to see him in his natural habitat, and that was either flying combat or making superiors go mad at his demeanor and lack of military bearing."[250]

The morning of September 1, 1942, started like most others. The rising sun warmed up the chill night air as the mechanics went through the final checks on the fighters. The pilots received their preflight briefing, radios were checked to ensure they worked, weapons were armed, and ammunition loaded and double checked. There was nothing to indicate that on this day history would be made.

At 07:56, fifteen Me-109s from I./JG-27 started their engines for their first mission of the day, another Stuka escort assignment to El Taqua, while ten Me-109s from III./JG-53 provided additional covering support at a higher altitude, protecting the JG-27 men as they protected the Stukas. III./JG-27 also threw another ten fighters up, making this mission a maximum effort by the Germans.

Marseille sighted the enemy fighters first, and he called out 16 "*Indianer*" as he prepared his attack plan. His new wingman was *Oberleutnant* Schlang, who was assigned to replace the lost Kugelbaur, who had served Marseille so well when Pöttgen was unavailable. Schlang was jokingly referred to as "the new mathematician" since Marseille's wingmen had the responsibility of counting his victories while he focused on the job at hand.

Marseille saw that the enemy fighters were about 4,000 feet below headed west, so he continued on his easterly course until he passed them by, then led his *Schwarm* into a rollover diving attack. They picked up airspeed and Marseille dropped to 1,000 feet below the enemy fighters, which were identified as Hurricanes. At 08:26 he closed the distance and climbed into the blind spot rising underneath his first kill, which he picked out of the group of twelve fighters from No. 1 Squadron SAAF, as the other JG-27 men engaged the twelve fighters belonging to No. 238 Squadron RAF. Marseille closed rapidly and fired a short burst. Less than three cannon and a dozen machine gun rounds hit the Hurricane, which belched smoke and started to burn as it dropped from the sky.

At 08:28 Marseille was already on his second victim, another Hurricane that exploded in a brilliant flash when his rounds struck the wing tanks. Large pieces of the fighter spread out and Marseille and Schlang had to break left and right, respectively, and pull up to avoid the debris. Marseille lost sight of the enemy aircraft below him, as they were in his blind spot, until Schlang called out a threat at six o'clock low. Marseille extended his flaps and kicked the left rudder, throwing the stick left, pulling back, and then applying right rudder and pulling up as a Spitfire V passed by. A short burst at 08:35 sent this fighter, his 107th kill, dropping to the ground.

Marseille and Schlang were pulling out of the attack when a dozen additional Spitfires from No. 92 Squadron RAF dropped upon them from altitude. As they came closer, converting their altitude into airspeed, Marseille waited. When the enemy fighters were perhaps three hundred yards away, he told Schlang to break right, and he broke left. Reducing power, using flaps, he reduced his airspeed, then turned right sharply allowing the Spitfires to pass him by. Then he reversed the previous actions, increased throttle, retracted the flaps and again became the hunter. At 08:39 he caught one of the last Spitfires that had flown by and led him, firing until he left the aircraft smoking and burning for his 108th kill.

Marseille's victims could have been any of the following pilots: Flying Officer Ian Matthews of No. 238 Squadron, who was killed in the explosion; Pilot Officer Bradley Smith of No. 92 Squadron, who bailed out of his Spitfire and returned to duty; or Maj. P. R. C. Metelerkamp, who was able to fly his fighter back to his base despite severe engine and structural damage. The smoke pouring from his Hurricane probably explains the Germans' erroneous claim, although they were far too busy to watch their victories fall to earth as two dozen enemy fighters were in the area. However, the enemy did not inflict much damage. The Germans saw them peel away and they did likewise.

Marseille had scored four victories in 13 minutes and brought his *Schwarm* home safely, despite the numbers they faced. Upon his return it was determined that Marseille had only used 240 machine gun and 18 cannon rounds. This was not his best rounds per kill ratio, but the day was not yet over. The fighters were refueled and rearmed, preparing for another escort mission, this time to the fortified positions at Alam Halfa.

Following the upcoming mission briefing Marseille managed a quick latrine call and filed his first mission report before jumping back into his fighter. During the break Mathias had painted four additional bars on his friend's rudder, which was considered a great privilege. Marseille had been on the ground for just over an hour when the signal was given to take off again. The Me-109s rolled down the hard-packed sand airstrip once more and lifted off, heading east northeast to rendezvous with the Stukas once again led by Kurt Kuhlmey.

Marseille's group then encountered enemies unexpectedly. I./JG-27s opponents this time were once again P-40s of No. 2 and 5 Squadrons SAAF. Several American pilots from the 57th Fighter Group were assigned to fly with the South Africans of No. 2 Squadron on this mission to gain experience. They had no idea what they were getting involved with, as Marseille alerted his men and radioed Neumann to the thirty enemy fighters escorting Allied twin engine bombers. However, unlike previous engagements where the Germans initiated contact, this time eight P-40s in the lead formation took the initiative and climbed upward to attack the Germans first without any hesitation.

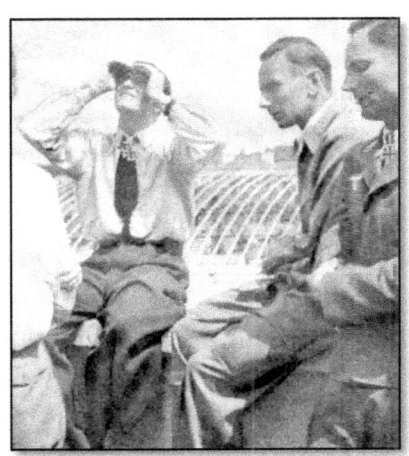

Marseille while at Augsburg during the test flight with Prof. Willi Messerschmit. Left to right: Marseille, Fritz Wendel, and Josef Pöhs (Raymond F. Toliver)

In fencing, the first thrust can be parried away, leaving the attacker exposed to a fatal counter thrust if one's opponent overextends his reach and is caught off balance. Similarly, on this occasion, the eight P-40s were at an altitude disadvantage, unsupported by a higher-flying echelon. Marseille would have planned his attack accordingly. He knew that going head-to-head with a P-40 was dangerous: the six .50-caliber machine guns were more effective than a 109's 7.92mm guns, and almost as effective as a 20mm cannon, but with a faster rate of fire, and there were a lot of them on a P-40. But he had done this many times before.

Despite taking the initiative, the eight P-40s were unable to reach the Germans flying three thousand feet above them at their eleven o'clock high position in time to press home an effective attack. Marseille led his *Schwarm* in a peeling roll over as the enemy passed underneath, with the Germans going over the top and flying in behind them, while the rest of the 1 *Staffel* covered their rear, creating a barrier against other P-40s from coming to their rescue, and preventing any escape for the eight P-40s already committed to the fight. Upon seeing that they could not reach the Germans, who now had the tactical advantage, the P-40s began to form the traditional Lufbery. Marseille was, as usual, unimpressed. He climbed to obtain a perch from which to begin his deadly work.

With his altitude advantage converted into airspeed he began a dive on the loose formation, cutting down his airspeed as he entered the still forming Lufbery, and at 10:55 the first P-40 received a deflection shot from less than 200 feet away, leaving a gap in the circle as it fell in flames. Marseille then locked onto the fighter in front of his first kill, pulled his nose up giving lead and 20 seconds later he fired. At 10:56 another P-40 fell away trailing smoke. Turning tightly inside the right turning Lufbery, Marseille fired another deflection shot, leading the third kill into the cone of fire. The aircraft fell away burning at 10:58.

Marseille was still inside the enemy formation. His three victories had left a large gap in the circle, but Marseille knew that another enemy fighter would close that gap and be on his tail. Marseille would have also known when not to press his luck, and his Parthian shot damaged another P-40, but not sufficiently to claim a kill. Then, rather than tightening up, the formation broke apart, the P-40s scattering as they abandoned the Lufbery. Every German pilot heard Marseille call out "Get them now!"

The enemy were now flying in pairs and trying to turn inside the Germans. When they realized that was not a great idea, they began heading north at full throttle. Marseille called out that he was in pursuit, and he firewalled the engine, slowly gaining on the last P-40 in the formation. He closed within three hundred feet and fired dead ahead at the enemy's six o'clock. Kill number four for the mission fell away burning at 10:59, and before it disappeared, Marseille fired at another fighter, number five, which also peeled away smoking and heading straight down at 11:01.

Marseille then called out a P-40 closing in from the six o'clock position onto the tail of another Me-109, so he applied hard left rudder and cut inside the enemy fighter, leading the P-40 when he fired. The P-40 flew into a storm of cannon and machine gun rounds, then burned as it headed toward the desert floor at 11:02. The man Marseille had saved was Franzisket, who was "very happy to confirm that victory."[251]

Franzisket stated, "I heard that I had an Indian on my tail, and when I looked, I saw that I was in a very bad position. I heard someone say, 'break left' and I hoped they were talking to me, so I did. That was when I saw the P-40 start to smoke, and then Jochen flashed right by me and slowed down. I looked over at him and he was smiling, having pulled off his [oxygen] mask and I waved back at him. 'You owe me drink' he said over the radio, and I said, 'Yes I do, thank you.' He was still smiling."[252]

Number six for the mission was counted, which was number ten for the day, but Marseille ordered his men to climb again to get altitude, which was life insurance for a fighter pilot. Within a minute of giving the order Marseille saw another group of enemy fighters heading home. Without hesitation Marseille dropped altitude and gained airspeed, closed quickly and shot down number seven at 11:03, as Schlang followed him and fired at a P-40, which did not sustain any appreciable damage. Marseille then performed a rolling split-S, getting onto the tail of a pilot

Marseille at the train station on his way to see Hitler (Raymond F. Toliver)

who probably thought he was lucky to have just survived one Me-109 attack from Schlang, only to be flamed at 11:05 as Marseille's eighth kill for the mission, and his twelfth for the day so far. His score now stood at 116 victories. Cheers went up on his airstrip as they heard the transmission over the loudspeaker, as stated by Neumann:

> "The uproar from all of the pilots was deafening. They were all screaming into their throat microphones at the same time talking about Marseille, while also calling out their own actions and warning about enemy aircraft. I just broke in and told them to calm down and get back home."[253]

To make the mission even more memorable, none of Marseille's men were shot down, and none of the aircraft sustained any appreciable damage. Marseille's Yellow 14 was never touched by an enemy projectile. However, even Marseille admitted that, if not for the protection of his fellow pilots, his scores would not be as high as they were, and his life would probably have been over some time ago. Marseille certainly had a healthy ego, as do all fighter pilots, but his was well earned, yet he was also humble enough to pay due respect to others and mean it.

Marseille's victories on this mission may have included the following pilots: one being a Lieutenant Stearns who was wounded and crash-landed but survived, while Lt. W. L. O. Moon bailed out of his P-40 (EV366) and was luckily unscathed as a result. Less fortunate were Lieutenants Morrison and G. B. Jack, who were both reported as missing in action.

When the flight returned to their airfield Marseille made two passes and waggled his wings four times each time, which was not really telling those on the ground anything they didn't already know. Neumann had the battle on loudspeaker so the ground crews could hear the action. He normally did not do this in case there was grim news coming over the radio. However, on this day, he made an exception.

Marseille landed and held up eight fingers to the ground crew, and Mathias smiled and collected his paint can. "Not yet," one of the mechanics told him. "Wait until we get the confirmation." Then Neumann walked out of his wagon and yelled across the flight line: "Eight for 'Seille! Eight for 'Seille!" The crew chief then turned to Mathias and said: "OK," and Mathias stood back as the dust was settling when Yellow 14 came to a stop.

Mathias was walking to the rudder as three of the other pilots walked over having just landed, and congratulated Marseille, who in turn looked at Franzisket smiling. "He was beaming, but he was tired, we all were, but he was already exhausted," Franzisket recalled.

"He touched Mathias on the shoulder and told him, 'Eight my friend, and I need a drink after.' Mathias handed the bucket to the unit artist in residence, who painted the eight additional vertical bars, and then Mathias went to get a glass with a small amount of something in it. Jochen lit a cigarette, and I said something about, 'Those will kill you.' He just laughed and said: 'Well, since the British cannot do it, I suppose something must. You know that we will never live forever, Ludwig.'"[254]

Neumann congratulated him, and as the fighters were getting ready to take off again within an hour, the commanding officer told him to sit the next one out. Marseille uncharacteristically did not argue the point. Instead, he took his glass of liquor and cigarette and walked to the command bunker. He wrote his *Abschuss* detailing the mission, and then fell asleep in the worn leather chair.

About an hour later the midday meal was served, and Marseille joined those not on the current mission, includ-

Marseille in the driver's seat, Werner Schroer on his left, Kugelbaur behind Marseille smoking, and possibly Pöttgen on Kuçelbaur's left behind Schroer wearing officer's cap.

ing the ground crews. Once finished he returned to his tent, closed the mosquito netting and fell fast asleep. Franzisket was also not on this mission, and he remarked that Mathias stood guard keeping anyone from waking Marseille. It was during this period some Italians "borrowed" his Kubelwagen (a jeeplike vehicle built by Volkswagen) and painted "Otto" on it, the Italian word for "eight."

Kurt Kuhlmey gave his assessment of the fact that Marseille and his unit did not arrive on station for his protection:

> "I heard the transmission that the *Staffel* were involved with the enemy, and Neumann confirmed, and redirected JG-53 who was supposed to pick me up on the way back from the mission. That worked out well. At least the JG-27 men informed me of a problem. Sometimes I would just be wondering where in the hell my escorts were, knowing nothing until I was being attacked. Luckily, we were not attacked that time."[255]

Marseille was awake and alert as the *Staffel* returned from the third mission of the day, followed by ten fighters from II *Gruppe*. There would be a fourth mission and he would lead 3 *Staffel* yet again. With his faithful Me-109F Yellow 14 serviced and ready, Marseille climbed in, strapped in, and moved his thumbs to the outside, indicating to remove the wheel chocks as he waited for the crew chief to crank the engine to life. Eleven fighters from I *Gruppe* and ten from II *Gruppe* (who were operating there also) lifted off at 17:06 on another of the "magnet" missions, a phrase Marseille coined due to the enemy fighters being drawn by the lure of an easy kill when Stukas or medium bombers were present. The mission now was to escort a flight of Ju-88s from KG-1 to El Imayid. To Marseille they were live bait, which, as every hunter knows, is the best kind.

The Germans in both *Gruppen* encountered a stiff enemy force over Deir el Raghat. With I *Gruppe's* eleven fighters engaging fifteen Hurricanes from No. 213 Squadron, II *Gruppe* also encountered many enemy fighters themselves. Marseille called out the enemy, again the first to spot them in the distance. The German and Allied squadrons approached each other head on at less than 8,000 feet altitude.

THE STAR OF AFRICA

Marseille led his *Schwarm* straight into the enemy, each pilot selecting a target, although Marseille knew how to defeat an enemy attacking head on when the opposition had superior firepower.

Marseille closed in, the gap minimizing rapidly, and he waited until he saw the flash from the guns. He then hit the left rudder hard, right stick, performing a wide skid left. The enemy rounds passed by him and just underneath his wingman Schlang. Marseille then fired and saw strikes on the one Hurricane he chose, which flamed and trailed smoke as it plummeted earthward at 17:47. This maneuver gave him the required angle to lead his target, yet once he threw the stick over he could roll away, and this allowed him to slide out of the path of the bullets.

Marseille then pulled lead on another that was passing by his three o'clock when he fired, and kill number two for the mission fell at 17:48. Marseille continued his turn, latching onto a third victim, which also caught fire and dropped from the sky at 17:49. Now, Marseille was behind the enemy formation, which had started to split up and break left and right, with each echelon trying to turn to get around and behind their tormentor. Marseille simply used his flaps and tightened his right turn to lead another Hurricane that blew up at 17:50.

With four cries of "*Horrido!*" coming from Marseille, the radio traffic was incredible. Then Marseille saw several additional targets trying to head east. He gave full power and proper trim and sped toward these enemy fighters. He closed in and at less than 200 yards he fired. Smoke belched from the fighter, but there was no great damage. He fired a second time; the fighter rolled over and the canopy flew off. Marseille's fifth and final victory on that sortie was his seventeenth for the day, a Hurricane (BN273)

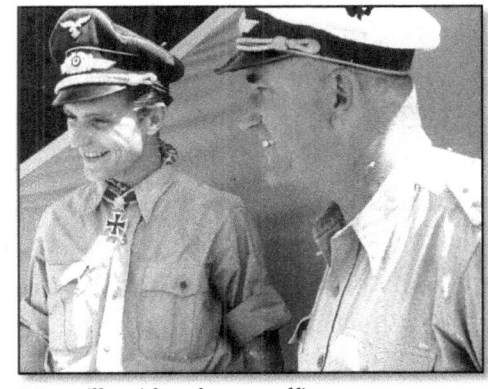
Marseille with unknown officer

flown by Sergeant A. Garrod, who bailed out uninjured at 17:53. Marseille and his men saw the parachute, and the victory was confirmed.

The men back on the ground listened to the air battle, with wagers often made on how many victories Marseille would get every time he took off. Neumann joined the men at the radio, mentally adding up the score for Marseille that day. Within 30 minutes of the last transmission indicating that contact had been broken the Messerschmitts returned, and Marseille performed his wing waggles to show his victories. The entire unit had claimed a total of 26 aircraft shot down in four missions; 17 were Marseille's alone in three of those missions. His score stood at 121 victories.

Neumann was the first to push his way to the front of the throng of men waiting to congratulate their leading ace. The crew chief unhooked the restraining straps and parachute harness, and they lifted Marseille out of the cockpit. His feet did not even touch the ground for a few minutes as they carried him in the air like a victorious gladiator, as he was handed a desert rose flower by Mathias in tribute, like garland for a victorious gladiator. Given his appearance, it was probably for the best that he did not try to walk.

Neumann could see that Marseille was exhausted, visibly haggard, his face drawn and pale, but he was still smiling as he lit a cigarette and took a long drink of water. He drank five cups, replacing the sweat he had lost during the mission. His clothes were soaked. Neumann had ordered that every man was to drink at least two liters of water every day to remain hydrated. Schroer stated: "Marseille drank a total of five liters that day [about a gallon and a quarter of water.]"[256]

The victories claimed by JG-27 that day were impressive. Allied loss records do not really challenge these figures, as every claim was confirmed by at least one eyewitness, if not several, in the case of many of Marseille's victories. Marseille retired to file his *Abschuss*, and he had just finished when the men told him there was a film on in the Marabu Theater, the nickname for the subterranean movie theater that was placed next to the bomb shelter. The film, *Dance with the Kaiser*, had just started when he was told that Neumann wanted him in the command post. He grudgingly stood and walked out into the fading daylight. A light breeze had started. The welcome wind coming off the sea was always nice in the evening as the heat gave way to cooler evening temperatures. Ushered in to see Neumann, he was told that he had a telephone call; it was from *Generalfeldmarschall* Albert Kesselring, who congratulated him on his successful day. Neumann recalled the incident:

"I had just finished painting the leaves on the large palm tree on the wall of my wagon. I added a leaf for every victory the unit scored, and I had a lot of them. I also had a chalkboard listing each *Gruppe* and *Staffel* with every pilot. The first line was the pilot's name, next was his rank, then his assigned flight, and the last on the lines were the victories for each pilot. Then my telephone rang, and my assistant answered, and told me it was Kesselring. I was always somewhat nervous when he called. I never knew if Marseille was trouble, or if one of the other pilots had done something stupid.

"But this was a very good call, and Kesselring was very excited after he heard of the day's actions, especially Marseille. Kesselring said that he wanted to speak with 'Seille personally, that he had been recommended for the Diamonds by the field marshal himself. I had already sent this recommendation to Galland before that day as he was of course General of the Fighters. [That meant that *General der Jagdflieger* Adolf Galland would get the official report as a courtesy, and if he supported the recommendation, it then went to the *Reichsmarschall*, and if he approved it, then onto Hitler for signing.] Within an hour the response came back from Berlin, apparently Galland submitted the request to Göring some time before and that the additional recommendation from

Kesselring would also go to Hitler. That was all I knew at the time until this call from Kesselring."[257]

Marseille took the call and was congratulated by Kesselring and informed that he had been recommended for the Diamonds by Kesselring personally. Marseille replaced the phone after concluding the call

A P-40 Kittyhawk of No. 112 Squadron prior to take off (Geoffrey Morley-Mower)

and was congratulated by Neumann. Kesselring approved Neumann's recommendation, Rommel was supportive, but it still had to be approved by Berlin. Late that night a teletype was received. Marseille was requested to return to Berlin to be invested with the Knight's Cross, Oak leaves, Swords and Diamonds. There was no higher honor at that time.

Marseille then returned to the film, and when it finished, he joined Mathias, Stahlschmidt, Steinhausen, Schlang, Pöttgen, Franzisket, Schroer and others in his tent. The music played, cigarettes were smoked, and drinks consumed as they relived the greatest day of their lives as a unit. All congratulated Marseille after hearing the news.

However, Marseille was still troubled by the day's events, according to Franzisket:

> "Jochen was very happy to receive the Diamonds, but he was also worried. He reminded us that every pilot who received the Diamonds, especially Galland, had been taken off flying duties for extended period, some not going back at all as they were propaganda heroes. That meant that if Marseille went and received the medals he may not be back, and that meant that Mathias would not have his protection. This was a major concern for him, and he reminded us of what he learned in Berlin about the Jews. All of us thought very hard about that, and we all assured him that we would take care of Mathias should he not return."[258]

Finally, the lights out order was given, and at 23:00 the camp fell silent, with only the occasional footsteps of the perimeter guards walking the lines barely audible in the still of the desert night. Marseille slept like a dead man, with Mathias on a cot nearby. Marseille's loyalty to his friend was unwavering, and vice versa. Upon being informed about the Diamonds, he told Neumann that Hitler could keep his medals, if it meant that he had to leave Mathias to fend for himself. Marseille knew that he might be transferred to Russia or even be relieved from flying duty altogether to work in the Propaganda Ministry, and he didn't trust his government to treat Mathias properly. Neumann mentioned the conversation:

> "I had heard about Marseille discussing his information as he claimed to have heard about the Jews back home, and I thought a lot about that also. I knew that he was very concerned about the fate of Mathias should he be taken off flight duty, which was very possible. Or he could be sent to another unit on another front. There would be no way that he could take Mathias with him, and he knew it. I understood his concerns, as we all liked Mathias, and he was his friend after all. I know that he spoke to all of the other men at some point."[259]

Franzisket recalled, "He asked that if anything happened to him, would I look after Mathias. He had great concerns that he would be taken away, and not to a prison camp. I knew enough from him to believe that he was on to something. I felt very uneasy about the rumors, and Marseille had told me about the Berlin situation. He even said that we were not a moral nation anymore. We had changed, or that the Nazis had changed Germany. 'Franzi, we will pay for this at some point, I know it.' He would never know just how correct he was."[260]

The next morning, September 2, 1941, dawned and Marseille awoke to the mission briefing. II *Gruppe* was scheduled to fly a close escort for the Stukas under Kurt Kuhlmey yet again with the target being El Imayid, while III *Gruppe* would perform a forward *freie jagd* as a forward fighter screen that would detect and hopefully intercept any fighters first, allowing the dive bombers the chance to accomplish their mission. After that, all the fighters could then function as a staggered defensive layer. Should some enemy fighters get through the first screen, the next *Gruppe* would greet them, and so on.

Taking off just before 08:45 the fighters from Marseille's two *Schwarme* from 3 *Staffel* were the second group to take off. They were specifically tasked to rendezvous with Kuhlmey's Stukas and escort them back home after their mission as close cover, with II *Gruppe* led by Rödel flying high cover. III *Gruppe* flying ahead would radio any contacts. III *Gruppe* had not yet radioed any contacts when Marseille and his eight Me-109s caught sight of 18 British bombers and their escort of fighters at 09:15. Marseille radioed the contact to Neumann and Kuhlmey, and then started his attack and at 09:16 he fired into a P-40 of No. 2 Squadron SAAF for his first kill of the day. This aircraft was actually flown by an American, 1st Lieutenant M. "Mac" McMarrell, who survived the crash landing after being wounded.

He then scored hits on the first victim's wingman, Pilot Officer G. R. Dibbs (who was declared missing in action), who had fired into

Marseille, but the German won at 09:18, although Marseille would misidentify the fighter as a P-40, when in fact it was a Hurricane Mk II. He then turned into a tight maneuver to gain aim on his third target, another P-40, flown by a Lieutenant Stuart (probably of No. 260 Squadron RAF), who safely bailed out at 09:24 and was uninjured. The mission was another success: Marseille once again brought all of his men home, and three more bars were painted on his rudder. He now had 124 victories.

Stahlschmidt recorded the mission: "Today I have experienced my hardest combat. But at the same time, it has been my most wonderful experience of comradeship in the air. We had a combat in the morning, at first with forty Hurricanes and Curtisses, later some twenty Spitfires appearing from above. We were eight Messerschmitts in the midst of an incredible whirling mass of enemy fighters. I flew my 109 for my life, but although the superior strength of the enemy was overwhelming, not one of us shirked our duty, all turning like madmen.

"I worked with every gram of my energy, and by the time we finished I was foaming at the mouth and utterly exhausted. Again and again, we had enemy fighters on our tails. I was forced to dive three or four times, but I pulled up again and rushed into the turmoil. Once I seemed to have no escape; I had flown my 109 to the limit of its performance, but a Spitfire still sat behind me.

"At the last moment Marseille shot it down, fifty meters from my 109. I dived and pulled up. Seconds later I saw a Spitfire behind Marseille. I took careful aim at the Spitfire, I have never aimed so carefully, and the enemy dived down burning. At the end of the combat only Marseille and I were left in the dogfight. Each of us had three victories. At home we climbed out of our planes and were thoroughly exhausted. Marseille had bullet holes in his 109, and I had eleven machine gun hits in mine. We embraced each other but were unable to speak. It was an unforgettable event."[261]

The second mission late that afternoon was a reconnaissance escort and Marseille led his *Schwarm* of four aircraft into a hornets' nest of forty enemy aircraft, from primarily No. 5 Squadron SAAF and No. 33 Squadron RAF. Marseille was the first to attack, and, without any fanfare, shot down a P-40 flown by Lieutenant E. H. O. Carman in aircraft AM390 in a high-speed pass as his wingmen covered him at 15:18.

Once he pulled up, followed by his entourage, two P-40s tried to catch him, only to be intercepted and shot down by the Me-109s covering him in the trail formation. Marseille continued his climb for altitude, chandelled, and then entered a dive just as another enemy fighter passed before his guns. The P-40 he then shot down at 16:21 (15:21 GMT) was in fact flown by Flight Lieutenant J. Lindbergh (AM349) who was declared missing in action. Both pilots were from No. 5 Squadron SAAF. Marseille's score stood at 126.

When Marseille started to fill out his *Abschuss* he received another telephone call, this time from Rommel; he was informed once again that he had been recommended for the Diamonds to the Knight's Cross, and the Field Marshal congratulated him. It would appear that Rommel and Kesselring did not know that the other was going to make a telephone call.

Marseille had little time to relax, because the next day, September 3, the British Eighth Army started a massive ground offensive striking west from Alam Halfa and taking the German units they encountered by surprise. The Germans withdrew quickly and in good order, only to prepare a counterattack with a double envelopment maneuver. This could only be accomplished if the airspace over the airfield was in German hands. Whoever controlled the sky controlled the battle.

The British sent every available bomber to attack German ground forces, especially their convoys, and known fuel and munitions depots. JG-27 was on full alert and the orders came down at 08:00, just about the time that the first 18 bombers and 22 P-40 escorts were sighted and reported. They were supported by 24 Hurricanes flying in a forward reconnaissance in force, hoping to stall any German aerial interdiction. That interdiction came in the form of 14 Me-109s from I./JG-27 led by 3 *Staffel* and Marseille.

The Allied forces in the air at that time were 24 Hurricanes of No. 127 and No. 274 Squadrons RAF, joined by fifteen P-40s of No. 260 Squadron RAF, No. 2 and No. 4 Squadrons SAAF and eight Mk V Spitfires of No. 145 Squadron RAF. Pilots of the U.S. 57th Fighter Group flying P-40s were again attached to some of the above units.

Spitfire V brought down in combat (Geoffrey Morley-Mower)

The first radio call that enemy fighters were present came from Stahlschmidt leading his *Schwarm*. He started his attack, as did Marseille with his *Schwarm*. Stahlschmidt scored three rapid victories; Marseille's first victim fell at 07:20, a Spitfire V (AB349) flown by Sgt. M. Powers of No. 145 Squadron RAF, who was wounded in the engagement but managed to bail out. Marseille then shot down Flight Lieutenant Canham in his Spitfire V at 07:23 followed by Pilot Officer Bicksler at 07:28; both men from No. 145 Squadron RAF successfully bailed out uninjured. Marseille's score then stood at 129 victories. The men landed to the cheers of the ground crews and Marseille was again congratulated.

The second mission also brought Marseille success, when he took eight fighters into the air a few hours later. At 15:08, 15:10, and 15:42 hours he shot down two P-40s piloted by Warrant Officer Stan Bernier of No. 260 Squadron RAF, who was killed, and a Lieutenant Ryneke of No. 2 Squadron SAAF; and another Spitfire V, probably from No. 145 Squadron RAF. These victories brought Marseille's score to 132 total victories. Remmer and Steinhausen also added to their tallies, as did Stahlschmidt.

On September 4, Marseille and his group stood down, the fighters needed servicing, but the following day would prove interesting. I./JG-27 got off to a late start, waiting to rendezvous with Kuhlmey's Stukas and not taking off until 10:00 hours (09:00 GMT) with 14 fighters, while II *Gruppe* had already been airborne and was on a fighter sweep with 19 fighters led by Rödel.

Marseille's group soon spotted and then engaged a mixed bag of Spitfires and Hurricanes from No. 112 Squadron RAF and No. 450 Squadron RAAF. The battle raged from Ruweisat to El Taqua. Marseille managed to shoot down a Hurricane at 10:48, but his centrally mounted cannon jammed after three rounds. The machine guns completed the task, and his first victim had not even hit the ground before he managed to shoot down another Hurricane at 10:49.

The second kill was still headed toward earth when Marseille completed a climb and rolled over the top and fired his still functioning weapons in a head on pass at kill number three, a Spitfire V possibly flown once again by the very lucky Flight Lieutenant Canham of No. 145 Squadron RAF, which was recorded at 10:51. If he was indeed the pilot who bailed out of the crippled aircraft, it would make Canham the luckiest man in North Africa after surviving a similar mishap a few days earlier at the hands of Marseille. The remaining fighters scattered, some fleeing east, but Marseille gave pursuit, catching up to a second Spitfire V at 11:00, also from No. 145 Squadron, sending it to the desert below. Marseille's score at that time was 136.

September 6 would be another successful day for Marseille and JG-27, but it would also bring more heartbreak. The first mission of the day was conducted without Marseille's 3 *Staffel* in action, so Karl von Lieres und Wilkau took control and led the scoring, with four victories added to his victories. *Unteroffiziere* Winkler and Becker and *Feldwebel* Keppler each scored a kill apiece. Steinhausen also shot down an opponent for his 40th victory. Marseille listened to the action as his friends were racking up victories.

The second mission of the day was another Stuka escort for I and II./JG-27. Twenty-eight Me-109s in total flew east, with II *Gruppe* taking off early as a forward fighter screen, using eight aircraft led by Rödel. They would be the alert force to engage and report back to the main force following five miles behind them. Ahead of Rödel's II *Gruppe* was a flight of eight fighters from III./JG-53. They were the tip of the spear. The Stukas were well protected, and the mission was not that eventful.

However, the last mission of the day would be more exciting. The Allies threw up a large fighter force to support the ground offensive. Involved in this engagement were No. 5 and No. 7 Squadrons SAAF and No. 260 Squadron RAF, with American pilots from the 64th Fighter Squadron, 57th Fighter Group, again flying their P-40s to gain combat experience.

Marseille finally took off and led his 3 *Staffel* on another escort, but this time they took the forward echelon position. Marseille called out the 20-odd enemy fighters over El Alamein flying toward them at one o'clock low only 2,000 feet below, and he led his other seven pilots into the fight immediately. Marseille quickly scored a P-40 kill in his dive at 17:03. His 137th victory was Pilot Officer Richard "Dick" Dunbar, who would be reported as missing in action. This action is remembered by a survivor of that battle, Ron Cundy, who managed to outfly an "outstanding German." Cundy wondered if Marseille was the man who nearly shot him down, and the evidence would suggest that it was. Ron Cundy stated:

"I saw one of our chaps go down, and the Germans were all over us. I looked over and saw Yellow 14, and I knew who that was. In fact, once we were engaged someone called out 'It's the bastard,' and that meant Marseille. Once you heard that in your headset all of your senses went into full alert, I can tell you. I then had a 109 on me, and I was trying to shake him off while calling for assistance. I pulled every trick I knew; I cut power and stalled, full flaps, hard banks left and right, back on full power for a dive, and then another stall and skid left or right while rolling then pulling an inverted climb coming out of my dive. He was on me for every maneuver until I dropped to the floor and made a hard turn right. I looked and he was no longer there but three of my own mates were. They had pushed him off. That German was the best pilot I ever fought, and I could not believe that he matched my maneuvers so precisely."[262]

The twisting and turning fight saw fighters from both sides almost collide with each other in the confusion, some trying to get into shooting positions, others trying to evade enemy fire. Several P-40s attempted to form the standard Lufbery, but this was interrupted as Marseille began to climb for altitude and remove himself and his flight from the melee below.

Taking advantage of the confusion, before the Lufbery could be formed, Marseille rolled over into his diving attack, entered a collective group of eight P-40s from No. 260 and No. 5 Squadrons, and shot down his second victory at 17:14. He pulled hard in a left banking turn and quickly shot down another P-40 at 17:16, pulled into another climb, then called out the second and third victories. His final victory was a Spitfire at 17:20, and his score stood at 140 victories. Allied losses were heavier than the *Luftwaffe* claimed. The leader of I./JG-27 *Hauptmann* Homuth was heard calling out his victory as well, a P-40, which was confirmed.

No. 7 Squadron SAAF lost five Hurricanes; No. 260 Squadron RAF one P-40 with another badly damaged and written off; No. 5 Squadron SAAF lost five aircraft. German claims were: I./ JG-27 five P-40s and one Spitfire; II./JG-27 one Hurricane; III./ JG-53 a P-40, a total of eight claims. The underclaiming for victories by the Germans is surprising, although several pilots filed "damaged" or "probable" in their respective *Abschusse*. However, the Germans did suffer a great loss.

One of Marseille's good friends, Günther Steinhausen, was flying his Me-109 F-4 Trop (W.Nr. 13 272) White 5 when he shot down a Hurricane at 17:25 in a diving turn southeast of El Alamein. However, he was then shot down in turn by an unknown pilot under uncertain circumstances, and he was listed as missing in action as his fighter fell over enemy territory. It is quite possible that Steinhausen, separated from his group, was shot down by Canadian James "Stocky" Edwards, the same pilot who killed Otto Schulz.[263] When asked about this encounter, Edwards recalled the following:

"I remember that we had just been in a great row with a lot of Germans, and I had made some great hits on a 109, and I saw glycol coming from it, but being so low on petrol I had to break contact. I claimed a damaged or probable victory, but I did not have anyone with me who could confirm I saw the 109 going down smoking, but there was a thin low cloud cover, and I could not see a crash or a parachute. Since I did not have a camera, and being alone, it was impossible to confirm that victory."[264]

Edwards's action matches the events as known exactly with time and location, although Edwards never claimed the kill, just a "damaged." None of the other JG-27 pilots could account for him due to the mass confusion in the air, where several pilots fired at the same fighters, and others on the Allied side were probably shot down by their own men. This would explain the loss to claim discrepancy from the Allied and German sides.

Everyone saw that Marseille was greatly disturbed upon hearing the news, although he never stopped his efficient practice of shooting down aircraft, despite his personal demons. His pantheon of troubles would only grow on September 7, when I./JG-27 flew several missions. Prior to Marseille taking off, Stahlschmidt and von Lieres und

Wilkau had taken off on a free hunt reconnaissance as a *Rotte* in a *Schwarm* of four fighters. Given the lack of any ground reporting or radar warning networks, Neumann liked sending a *Rotte* or *Schwarm* up, flying up to 100 miles east in an intelligence gathering mission. If they saw anything, their radio warning would provide ample time to scramble the remaining fighters for an interception.

When Marseille heard that there was to be a *freie jagd* he immediately volunteered to lead it, but Neumann told him to wait. He would be leading the main formation with his 3 *Staffel* later. Marseille had wanted to fly with Stahlschmidt, who was one of his best friends and only real confidant (although Mathias was rapidly earning that trust). What exactly happened next is uncertain, but the first *Rotte* of Stahlschmidt and von Lieres encountered the Spitfires first, and they engaged as the second *Rotte* provided cover. When more enemy fighters appeared, the Germans were overwhelmed.

The command post heard the radio calls, and it was clear the Germans were on the losing side. Von Lieres was shot up and crash-landed unharmed, losing contact with Stahlschmidt over enemy territory, as did another pilot who landed damaged at Quotaifiya. The Me-109s were downed at around 14:39 and 14:40, respectively. The third pilot was also down, and all three managed to land in German territory. The last anyone saw of Stahlschmidt he was smoking, with three Spitfires on him, and he was going down. He was not observed to have impacted, and no parachute was seen.

By this time, Marseille was in the air, unaware of these events. The sortie that he was on was not a great success, with I./JG-27 only claiming four victories, two to Marseille and one to Homuth; two of Marseille's P-40s went down quickly, with the first from No. 4 Squadron RAF at 17:43, the second from No. 5 Squadron SAAF at 17:45 southeast of El Alamein. His score then stood at 142 victories.

Upon landing, Marseille reported to the 3 *Staffel* command post to file his *Abschuss*, when his telephone rang. It was Neumann informing him that "Fifi" Stahlschmidt was missing. Marseille, perhaps in a state of panic, dropped the receiver and ordered his fighter immediately refueled and armed. He was taking off immediately, once he had the coordinates from von Lieres who had been picked up with a second pilot. The word spread rapidly that Fifi was missing, and that Marseille was going to look for him. Von Lieres confirmed that their action took place almost thirty miles behind the lines, and he showed Marseille the location on the map.

Marseille was already out of the door and headed to his fighter when Neumann the *Geschwaderkommodore* came out to meet him. He knew what Marseille was planning, and he told him he was grounded for the time being. The exhaustion in his face was not the only reason Neumann put his foot down. He knew that an emotionally charged pilot was not a clear-thinking pilot, and as such he was a danger to himself if not others. Neumann knew the strong friendship between Stahlschmidt and Marseille, but he also knew that an exhausted, angered, and emotionally involved pilot had no business being in the air.

Stahlschmidt, who had over 400 missions and 59 victories in his Red 1, went into the official record as missing in action. It is most probable that his victor was an American flying with the Canadians, Flight Lieutenant John H. Curry (RCAF with 7.5 claims), of No. 601 Squadron RAF. In addition, the same mission cost JG-27 *Oberleutnant* Karl von Lieres und Wilkau his aircraft; at that time he had 24 victories. Von Lieres would not live much longer, and at the time of his death he would have 31 victories. Although grounding Marseille's 3 *Staffel*, Neumann sent 1 and 2 *Staffeln* on a search, which produced nothing.

Steinhausen's and Stahlschmidt's losses were taken hard by Marseille since he was supposed to fly the mission with Stahlschmidt but had not been allowed. This hit him almost as hard as the loss of his sister, according to those who served with him, as they were the best of friends. For his 40 victories Steinhausen was posthumously promoted to *Leutnant* and awarded the Knight's Cross on November 3. The loss of Stahlschmidt really created a stir that evening among the pilots, after already losing Steinhausen. Neumann, as was customary upon losing a pilot in action, held a simple memorial service. The men gathered as Neumann spoke a few words.

Upon learning of Stahlschmidt's fate, Marseille spoke to no one for the rest of the day. He ate alone in silence, did not drink any alcohol, smoked like a fiend and avoided all companions but the ever-loyal Mathias. Before the night was over Neumann had received telegrams congratulating Marseille on his being awarded the Diamonds from dozens of people, including Kesselring, Rommel, Göring, Göbbels, Foreign Minister Joachim von Ribbentrop, *Luftwaffe* Chief of Staff *Generalfeldmarschall* Erhard Milch, Benito Mussolini, and even General of the Fighters *Generalleutnant* Adolf Galland. The congratulations were hollow.

"Neumann as usual always had the right words to say," Rödel recalled. "We did not know where he was and will probably never know. It was not so bad being killed fighting for our country, although almost all of us hated the Nazis, and this was no secret. Neumann not only tolerated that position, he even told his pilots that we should never consider ourselves as fighting for Hitler and the National Socialists, but fighting for Germany, our homes and families. Parties, he said, come and go, as do leaders. Nations and their people will always remain if there are brave men willing to protect them.

"Steinhausen, he said, was one of those men, as was Stahlschmidt, and as were all of us. Remember their friendship and service, and they will always be immortal. I thought that was a good speech. Neumann thought a lot of Steinhausen in fact. He was more settled, more mature than Marseille, and he also saw that Stahlschmidt was a good influence on Jochen."[265]

Werner Schroer noted: "Losing our pilots, our comrades was always tough, but you knew that in war this was a possibility. It is how you handle these losses that determines your mental health. Some men became more determined to avenge these dead men, sometimes becoming reckless, while others simply lost heart for the fight and failed to engage sometimes. These last men were the minority, to be sure, and Marseille could have gone either way. I think that he became more determined. His sense of competition was strong, although to his credit he never lost his sense of chivalry. I admired him for that. He had really grown as a man and developed as a pilot and leader since our days in flight school."266

Ludwig Franzisket was there and remembered the climate: "Losing Steinhausen and Stahlschmidt hit the entire unit very hard, but no one was more impacted than Marseille. His grief was evident."267

For months Marseille had been deeply troubled. Ever since he arrived in Africa, he had suffered from insomnia, but this had transformed into occasional instances of sleepwalking. These became even more prevalent following his return after the death of his sister. As the deaths of his friends mounted, and his victories rose, so did his episodes of wandering around at night. It was a combination of guilt, loss, and pure emotional exhaustion.

Neumann recalled: "On more than one occasion I saw Mathias actually help Marseille out of the cockpit, as he was sometimes completely exhausted from flying multiple missions. This was especially true after we received the newer G model of the Messerschmitt. Marseille would fly his Friedrich as much as possible, not only in combat but in practice. Mathias would help him keep his gear sorted out, prepare him a meal, set up his wash basin, and put him to bed just as one would a child."268

Franzisket alliterated further: "I would have to say that Mathias really took care of Jochen. I know that he was greatly disturbed after his return from two months back home, and losing our friends weighed heavier upon him than most I would say, because he had been away from the war for so long. I also saw him sleepwalking a few times, as did the others. That would have been grounds for a medical discharge, or at least removing him from flying status, but Neumann just told us all to keep it quiet, that it would all work out. To be honest I felt sorry for him. He had a lot of pressure being a squadron leader, great war hero, and he had to change his ways once he became a leader and lead by example."[269]

Werner Schroer had his views: "Marseille was shot to hell. He needed a long rest, perhaps taken out of flying altogether. There is no doubt in my mind that Marseille was losing his. We all discussed his condition privately together, away from Jochen, and all decided that we would try and interact with him, discuss things not related to flying, the war, and get his mind off the losses which seemed to hit him the hardest. Ever since flight school he had been an ass, playing his damned jokes on me, and at first, I hated him, but I grew to accept him and then like him. I could not say that we were great friends but were comrades and he was one of our best pilots. But when I saw the condition that he was in I felt damned sorry for him."[270]

Mathias also quietly followed Marseille on the occasions that his sleepwalking took him out of his tent. He made sure that his "boss" always found his way back. Marseille never remembered any of the events. This was important since Marseille had left for Germany in June there had been a standing order to emplace minefields around all airfields. The British Special Air Service and Long-Range Desert Group units had been driving to German airfields and destroying aircraft.

Neumann speculated that Marseille had behaved as he did because he believed his father's status as a general, or his own reputation as a near-mythic hero, made him untouchable, perhaps immortal; but he also speculated that Marseille, previously always reckless, may have become so disillusioned with the war after his return to the unit in

August 1942 that he simply ceased to care about almost everything. Only the flying kept his head clear. The downtime gave him too much time to think about the phantoms in his mind.

The fan mail kept coming also. A large full bag, usually reserved as mail for an entire *Geschwader* often contained letters and postcards for Marseille alone. One of those letters that meant a lot to him came from the *Geschwaderkommodore* of *Stukageschwader* 3, *Oberstleutnant* Walter Sigel, who had just returned from visiting Hitler himself to receive the Oak Leaves. Similar congratulations came from *Hauptmann* Kurt Kuhlmey, now *Kommandeur* of II./StG-3. Sigel's complimentary and congratulatory letter, along with Göring's telegram, provided in full by Kurowski, are testaments to how highly these men regarded Marseille.

After being grounded by Neumann on September 7, Marseille was out of the action for the next three days. He had been behind in his paperwork as a *Staffelkapitän*, a duty he hated but knew was necessary. Marseille, with his position and promotion to *Hauptmann* was also now responsible for recommending awards for his pilots whom he saw deserved such recognition, and those documents had to be written, signed, and sent to Neumann for approval.

Marseille often grumbled that the ground crews never received medals, because they did not engage in battle, but that there should be a special award for those men who worked day and night around the clock keeping the fighters in the air. They were the men who usually suffered the most during enemy attacks against the airfields. However, with Stahlschmidt missing, Marseille could focus on nothing but that. He would never know what had happened to his best friend. Within a week, with no word on Fifi, Marseille wrote a personal letter to Stahlschmidt's family, as did Neumann, although the contents of both correspondences are unknown. Neumann politely declined to discuss his letter, saying that it was forever a private matter. He said the same when asked about the letter he wrote to Marseille's mother after his death. "Those should remain my private thoughts," Neumann said.[271] [Author's note: I personally respected that position and over the many years of meeting with Neumann I never again pressed the issue].

With the last of his close friends gone, with exception to Schroer, Clade and Franzisket Marseille grew ever closer to Mathias. The fact that his friend from the Transvaal was not a pilot and did not risk death daily must have been a great comfort for Marseille, who had lost so many people in his life. Marseille would never be the same. The fire had burned out. Everyone saw it. On a later occasion (recounted in Chapter 1), Marseille attacked eight enemy aircraft, shooting down four, damaging two others, and was going in for the kill when he saw the British Hurricane pilot was badly wounded. Marseille flew alongside the stricken aircraft, which was belching flame and smoke, and indicated to the RAF pilot, who was covered in blood, that he was too low to bail out and should land. Schroer witnessed the event. He called it "a most amazing spectacle."[272]

Cecil Golding (center standing in cap) with his mates of No. 5 Squadron SAAF (Cecil Golding)

Marseille, knowing he was close to British lines, followed the man down while his other three Me-109s flew top cover. The young German guided the RAF pilot, who was apparently unable to see in front of him, until he landed safely in Allied territory. Marseille passed on scoring an easy kill (he still received credit for the victory), believing that a man who fought an honorable fight should be allowed to live since the aircraft was destroyed. He lived by a code that most of his fellow pilots understood, and even his enemies respected him for it.

What disturbed him the most was that he knew that his national leadership in their majority had no such honor.

In this belief in chivalry, he was not unique among German pilots, since men like Georg-Peter Eder and Marseille's squadron mates Ludwig Franzisket and Franz Stigler in JG-27 were also noted for their chivalry towards their enemies, despite postwar propaganda to the contrary. In contrast, such gallantry was rarely displayed on the Eastern Front, and this was admitted by the Germans, but it did exist, where men like Johannes Steinhoff (see Krupinski's interview in *The German Aces Speak*) were the prime examples of chivalry on the German side.

I./JG-27 in total stood down for a couple of days. The aircraft needed maintenance, and they were awaiting fuel, water, food, and ammunition resupply. However, II and III *Gruppen* were flying in full strength, with 24 fighters escorting StG-3. Schroer managed to score two Spitfire victories. But September's losses had only just started.

CHAPTER 10

His loss was a bitter blow to his compatriots in JG-27 but a blessing to those of us on the other side.
Ron Cundy

On September 11, 1942, Marseille again led an escort mission toward El Imayid, taking his 14 men into a fight against 20 enemy fighters. Marseille called out his intentions and peeled off with his wingman to attack. Marseille scored two quick victories at 07:40 and 07:42, hitting both aircraft in a single pass, flaming one, and then circling back to finish off the second smoking enemy fighter. Both Hurricanes were misidentified as P-40s, probably due to Marseille attacking from behind and pulling up from underneath immediately after hitting both aircraft. One Hurricane was from No. 33 Squadron RAF, the other from No. 213 Squadron RAF. One of these victims was Flight Sergeant R. R. Fry, who died in the cockpit. Marseille's score now stood at 144.

For the next three days, Marseille was on the ground performing administrative duties to all 3. *Staffel* fighters. His Me-109F also needed parts, although he had the G-2 sitting there waiting to be flown, but he avoided it, so the mechanics worked on his favorite Me-109F while he handled requisitions, leave requests, promotions, and inventories of fuel, food, ammunition, and water, and took the time to read and respond to hundreds of pieces of fan mail. The many conflicting odors from the perfumed envelopes reeked throughout the tent. While Marseille was not flying, II and III *Gruppen* were still active. Schroer added three more victories to his score during the first mission on September 15.

Later that afternoon, 18 fighters from I *Gruppe*, 15 from II *Gruppe*, and ten from III *Gruppe* lifted off just after 18:00. They faced Allied units from No. 112 Squadron RNZAF, No. 250 and No. 450 Squadrons RAF and RAAF respectively, and No. 3 Squadron RAAF. The 36 Allied aircraft may have provided comfort to the men based in Egypt, but to Marseille they simply offered more targets. Marseille radioed his executive officer *Leutnant* Friedrich Hoffmann that he was leading his section into the attack. Somehow, Hoffmann collided with *Unteroffizier* Prien, who could not get out of his damaged fighter and fell to his death. Hoffmann, who at that time had 11 victories, managed to get out of his cockpit despite losing a wing, yet he was struck by the rudder of his own fighter, breaking both his legs and sustaining internal injuries. His parachute saved his life, at least temporarily.

Marseille after his official promotion to Hauptmann (Captain) and the new 3. Staffel squadron leader (Raymond F. Toliver)

Marseille and the other pilots saw the collision, but he then focused upon their job. The lost comrades would wait. He closed in on a Lufbery that had formed, selecting a P-40, and shooting it down at 16:51, but he then tightened his turn and gave lead on the next P-40, fired, and as it fell away at 16:53 Marseille, still turning inside the Lufbery, fired again. Number three also fell away burning at 16:54. Marseille uncharacteristically did not break off his attack and climb for altitude after making the first three victories, waiting for the formation to break up and scatter, as was his usual method. Instead, he stayed inside the circle and chose another target, which streamed smoke and burned at 16:57.

With the enemy pilots well aware of the wolf within the flock, Marseille broke out of the now panicked Lufbery. As he pulled up a Hurricane flashed above him, and he fired at 16:59, scoring his fifth kill. Reaching a higher altitude, he then rolled over, looked down and selected the next victim. Pulling the stick into his stomach he started his inverted dive and closed on a group of Hurricanes. He fired again at 17:01, sending a sixth aircraft hurtling toward earth leaving a long stream of black oily smoke, although no crash or parachute was reported. Marseille simply slid into another Hurricane and fired yet again, with the seventh victim (and the sixth confirmed victory) following his predecessors, and before the echo faded, he fired once more into his latest victim's wingman, who followed his leader to the desert below at 17:02. Marseille had shot into eight fighters and scored seven confirmed victories in eleven minutes; not a single enemy round had touched his aircraft.[273]

> Franziskett recalled the action: "Jochen had immediately eliminated a large part of the enemy aircraft, but what he did in the idiot snake (Lufbery) was just insanity. I had seen him inside that type of formation many times, and he always scored the victories, but he also took damage most of the time. I called to him to get out of it, Emil (Clade) did the same, but he stayed inside, and more airplanes fell to earth. I was afraid to jump in because all of the enemy fighters were trying to turn into Jochen and shoot him, you could see red tracers all over the sky and our fighters were also chasing the enemy. It was really crazy. I would not be surprised if they hit some of their own men. How he did not take a single enemy bullet is something that I cannot understand."[274]

Squadron Leader Michael Judd of No. 250 Squadron RAF was also involved in the melee, and he saw what was happening, but he was also heavily involved with the other Germans to do much about it as he stated:

> "No sooner had we spotted the enemy, someone called out 'Yellow 14' and someone said 'Marseille' over the radio. Well, let me tell you that garnered the attention of every man in the air. I had pulled up after firing on one Messerschmitt and looked over to see three of our aeroplanes smoking and going down, and there he was, Marseille. We called him 'The Bastard', but we also had great admiration for his chivalry, but we still wanted to shoot him down."[275]

Marseille's victims and claims were probably among the following losses reported: No. 3 Squadron RAAF lost Jack Donald in P-40 (EV345) who bailed out, landing on top of an Italian mess tent and was taken prisoner; Pilot Officer Keith Kildey managed to make it back to his airfield, minus half of his rudder and much of the elevators shredded; Sergeant Gordon Scribner in P-40 (EV322 CV-I) was killed. Sergeant Ken Bee also made it back with a badly damaged aircraft and was wounded himself. No. 112 Squadron RAF lost Sergeant Cedric Young, who may have been damaged further if not brought down by antiaircraft fire. No. 250 Squadron lost a pilot named Thorpe who was captured.

Marseille as the new Staffelkapitän giving a briefing in his tent (Robert Tate)

No. 450 Squadron RAAF lost Sergeant Peter Ewing, who bailed out of his P-40 that was flamed inside the Lufbery, and was probably Marseille's first or second victory, and became a prisoner of war. Before he was sent to the transition camp, he was the personal guest of Marseille and I *Gruppe* and treated as a VIP. Marseille had a photo taken with him, as he did with all of the Allied pilots who survived his attacks and fell into German hands. Another No. 450 Squadron pilot named Strong also became a prisoner and a guest. Franzisket discussed the evening:

"Marseille was the most gracious of hosts, and we treated our prisoners as special guests. That was just a tradition. I remember both men, and it was perhaps Ewing who spoke with Marseille the most, as Jochen's English was very good if not fluent. I took the photographs as I had Jochen's camera. We even had a photo taken with Mathias in the group as well. Neumann liked these events very much.

"We learned from them that the enemy knew exactly who Marseille was, and they respected him as a great and lethal pilot, but his chivalry in notifying the units about the wounded men he shot down was what gained him their respect. We also learned that when one of the enemy pilots called out Yellow 14 each man was on the alert, and also because there was a one thousand pound bounty from the squadron fund of whichever pilot could shoot him down. This Marseille found interesting. I had never heard that before and it shocked Jochen.

"Schroer then asked the two Allied pilots if that bounty was limited only to their men collecting the money, as he could use that money himself. Everyone laughed except Jochen. 'Not funny Werner,' he said. We all had a good time, especially since we managed to buy a goat from the Bedouin and Mathias was an expert with preparing and cooking the meat. That was a rare treat indeed."[275]

The Allied losses reported from all the squadrons are quite interesting: only five P-40s were listed as lost, with the Hurricane losses being undisputed. It is possible that several Germans fired at the same aircraft in the swirling melee, thus each claiming the kill, and each cry of *"Horrido!"* brought the eyes of their fellow pilots to see an enemy going down. Two of Marseilles "victories" actually made it back, but the fighters were written off, so those victories should not be disputed.

I *Gruppe* claimed eleven (credited with ten) victories with Homuth and *Oberleutnant* Ernst Börngen claiming one kill each; II *Gruppe* confirmed one, and III *Group* claimed seven aircraft, with four being shot down by *Unteroffizier* Krainik, and Schroer claiming three, which were confirmed. Marseille had once again been the star of the show with his seven, bringing his score to 151 victories. Only Gordon Gollob of JG-77 and Hermann Graf of JG-52 on the Eastern Front had more victories at that time, and they had both been nominated for the Diamonds also, although unlike Marseille, they would live to receive them.

> Ernst Börngen recalled the battle and a horror he witnessed: "Homuth was chasing this Kittyhawk I think, and I was his wingman. Homuth's target tried pulling high and left and Homuth pulled lead, just as the other pilot brought his fighter hard right, Homuth missed, but I had a clean straight shot as he crossed my path. I fired, the fighter pulled up smoking, then a fire erupted. The wingman was below and climbing, and the pilot I shot left his fighter, and I rolled over to see where his wingman was. Then I saw my victim's body bounce off his wingman's right wing. I thought for sure he was dead, then Homuth called out the wingman and I confirmed the victory for him as did others. Then I saw that my unfortunate victim had a good parachute, so he must have been in good enough condition to open it."[277]

Upon landing, Marseille immediately headed for the field hospital where Hoffman had been brought. He must have known, even before the attending physician informed him, that the young pilot was not going to make it. Hoffman died shortly afterward, joining all the other friends as phantoms in Marseille's mind. Marseille had Mathias prepare the bar and food to be served, while he did his paperwork and filed his *Abschuss*. When finished he entered his tent where the others had gathered. Outlawed music blaring from the record player, and for the first time since Stahlschmidt's death, Marseille smiled, laughed, and enjoyed drinks and light conversation with the men he had shot down. Franzisket also enjoyed these moments with enemy pilots:

"We all enjoyed meeting our enemies, I suppose it is a curiosity that all pilots have, perhaps all soldiers really. It was like the old days when the Great War pilots entertained their captured enemies. Some of the enemy pilots spoke German or French besides English, and some of us spoke French and English, so there was hardly a language barrier. We always had someone who could translate. Marseille really did enjoy these meetings, and we never tried to collect intelligence information. That was not our job."[278]

Marseille performed another of his chivalrous missions. He shot a Hurricane to pieces, but rather than administer the *coup de grace* he once again flew alongside the enemy pilot and motioned that he should set down. The enemy pilot, given the choice of death or capture, chose the latter, and eased into a controlled crash landing. Marseille dropped another unsigned note (trying not to advertise he was breaking the rules again) alerting the downed pilot's airfield that he was safe and a guest of JG-27.

Upon returning he was chastised once again by Neumann. He reminded Marseille of Göring's ban upon not only Marseille, but any German pilot. It never seemed to sink in. Marseille continued to fly these sorties in direct violation of the standing order. Neumann knew it and turned a blind eye, as did the usually rigid Gerhard Homuth, who routinely wrote up pilots for being late to morning formation. They all saw that Marseille displayed the best in men. In his own way he kept the war humane and the morale up. Even Homuth acquiesced on this issue.

Franzisket explained why Homuth relaxed on Marseille regarding these mercy flights: "I spoke with Gerhard (Homuth) a few times about Marseille, always at his insistence. The subject of Marseille flying to the enemy airbases came up on occasion. Strangely, this was the only violation of standing orders that Homuth did not really complain about after a while. We all remembered when Stahlschmidt had been shot down, captured, beaten and then escaped. His story was horrific. Then there was Espenlaub who was killed after being captured. I think Homuth realized that Marseille's flights and the ones I did probably gave the enemy a better impression of us, should anyone else become a prisoner."[279]

Ernst Börngen also had a few discussions about Marseille's flights: "He was admired by the others for his sense of compassion, especially if a man was wounded, or captured. We all knew that we would want our families to know how we were should the same thing happen to any one of us. I personally thought it was a polite thing to do but foolish as hell."[280]

Franzisket also recalled, "I told him, ''Seille, you should perhaps radio the British in advance that you are coming with another one of your letters. That way they can save their flak ammunition.' He just smiled and said that it was a thought, but then again, they would probably shoot him down anyway, and still get the note. We laughed about that over a drink."[281]

Marseille and his 3. *Staffel* were on the ground on September 16, when he was informed by Neumann that he was no longer an acting captain, he was being officially promoted to *Hauptmann*, which was followed by a telegram from *Generalfeldmarschall* Erwin Rommel congratulating him for being the youngest man in the *Luftwaffe* at age 22 to hold that rank. Marseille, at first passed by for promotions, had later caught up to his flight school contemporaries and then rapidly surpassed them.

Later in the war such ranks would be held by even younger men as attrition necessitated promotions. The telegram from Rommel was followed by a telephone call from the *Afrika Korps* commander. Marseille received another invitation to be the honored dinner guest of the *Generalfeldmarschall* at his headquarters. He decided to take some of his *Staffel* and other successful pilots with him, including Franzisket, Clade, Rödel, Pöttgen, Schlang, Schroer, and a couple of others.

It was around this time that Marseille managed to wrangle a test flight in the Macchi 202 of Italian nine victory ace Lt. Emanuele Annoni. Marseille did fine until landing, when he either misjudged the height of the landing gear or realized that he made an error as the landing gear lever was the opposite of a Messerschmitt and set down too hard, and collapsed the gear, fracturing his left arm in the process. With an apology and a wave, he then joined the others for the visit to see Rommel. He had his arm wrapped, since it was not a clean break, but badly bruised and he was still able to fly.

Franzisket recalled the vent with humor: 'Well Marseille decided that he wanted to test fly the Italian fighter, and he took it up and did a lot of really hard maneuvers, very impressive. Then he decided to land, or something resembling a landing anyway. It was a disaster. He climbed out and looked at the damage, which was minimal and the Macchi was repaired in two days by our ground crew. I asked Jochen how he was going to pay for the damage, and he said that if necessary, he would give them the Kubelwagen."[282]

The men of JG-27 sat with the supreme commander of the *Afrika Korps* and discussed almost everything except the war, as if the chat with the pilots was a treatment for his obvious weariness of constant battles. The wine, brandy, and schnapps flowed, although Rommel like Montgomery, was not himself a drinker, nor did he smoke, and the atmosphere was relaxed and inviting. Rommel was very much like American General Omar Bradley; a soldier's general. He did not hold himself aloof from the lower ranks. He led from the front and shared the dangers leading by example.

Rommel lived by the simple phrases: "Always be professional in your public and private life, because others will see you and learn." He also said: "When your men see the back of your head, they will follow you anywhere. If you can see the back of theirs, then you are in the wrong job," Rommel told his officers. He expected all officers to do the same, and in Marseille he had probably seen a younger, less mature version of himself.

Marseille was unusually professional and not his usual cavalier self while with Rommel. He had met the field marshal before several times, they had both been to visit Mussolini and they had a healthy respect for each other. Rommel also mentioned the fact that Marseille was in line to receive the Diamonds (Rommel would also receive this award), and he commented on Marseille's Italian Medals for Bravery in Silver and Gold, as Rommel only had the silver medal. Rommel, obviously very curious and knowing Marseille's penchant for being brutally, if not undiplomatically, direct, asked his honest opinions of both Hitler and Mussolini.

Marseille mentioned his uneasiness with the political aspect of being a soldier. He also called the Nazis a "ridiculous group" and stated he would not "join any party that did not have a lot of pretty girls," echoing his comments while in Berlin to receive the Swords.

Franzisket recalled that meeting: "Marseille said that he was very impressed with Hitler's knowledge of the war, his ability to retain even the smallest details of a situation, but that he seemed to be uncertain in some areas. He also said that he thought Hitler was probably a brave soldier in the First World War, having both Iron Crosses, but that he just did not seem to be the kind of man one would expect to have been the conqueror of Europe.

"Then the conversation changed to the Americans being in the war. Rommel asked what we thought about that. Marseille said that it was not good for us in the long term, as we could never outproduce American war machinery. We could not bomb their factories. The best we could do was to sink their ships as they came over, whenever that was. Rommel agreed, and Marseille even admitted that adding America into the

Allied camp simply meant that we would probably lose eventually.

"Now, this was dangerous talk in our military community, you know? Men were shot for saying similar things, or at least I had heard. Rommel, who was obviously not a Nazi sympathizer, and laughed at Marseille's jokes and comments about the big chiefs he met. Rommel already knew about some of Marseille's less than tactful comments in the past. Marseille then said that Mussolini seemed to be a kind of clown, very self-important, and someone who seemed like a bully. Of interest, Rommel agreed with every assessment Marseille made. I was shocked that they were openly discussing this in front of us."[283]

Schroer felt that Rommel wanted to know more about the men who flew air cover for his ground forces: "I was very flattered when he said that he would not be able to achieve success without JG-27. He also asked about our lives back home, and what we thought about the enemy's strengths, that sort of thing. Marseille had stated that he had great respect for the British and other Allied pilots, due to their skill in general. I agreed with him, and Rommel said that we should respect our enemies, and not forget that we are all human beings. Honor was a code that kept us together, and that was the one thing he demanded from his men along with courage.

"I spoke with Rommel, and we discussed how we treated our captured enemy pilots. He nodded his head in approval and agreed that once a man was out of the fight, he should be an honored guest, and treated as such. Rommel was very critical of other organizations, that he did not name as such, that were less than gentle with their captured prisoners. Then Rommel also brought up the old issue of one of our pilots (Förster) and others (including Kulmey's men) being strafed in their parachutes, which had become well known.

"At that point Marseille jumped into the talk, cutting me off, and he told Rommel what Gustav Rödel had told us. Regardless of what one of our enemies may do, we must remain above retribution. We have to be the greater man, and the British in general were very honorable on the battlefield. It may have been an accident, or just a one-time situation where a pilot lost his cool, lost his mind. Who knows, but Rommel agreed that we must follow the Geneva Convention. There were rules, even in war he said. We all agreed and made a toast to all of the fallen soldiers, German, Italian and Allied. But Schroer reminded Marseille that we had seen several pilots killed that way, and that Kuhlmey even made such a report.

"Then the conversation turned to our impressions of our Italian allies. Rommel was very interested in seeing what our opinions were, since we had flown many missions with the *Regia* fellows. I simply stated that it may be better to give them Messerschmitts, which were better fighters than their Macchis. It would give them a better chance in combat. Rommel said that my opinion was interesting, and that he would have a chat with Kesselring about that. It was feasible that it could be done, since we gave the fighters to the Romanians, Hungarians, Bulgarians, Croatians, and I even heard that some Ukrainians were flying with our units there. It just made sense.

"Marseille then stated that the Italians suffered from a lack of advanced flying skills, from what he saw. Certainly, they would benefit from having German fighters, which were more reliable, better armored and faster. However, the Italians just did not display the same tenacity in the fight as we, or even the British, did. We were usually somewhat nervous knowing that they had our backs. I know what Marseille was saying. The Italians did not seem really that enthusiastic in being our allies, so their dedication to working with us was often called into question. Rommel stated that he had seen the same thing in their ground forces."[284]

Early photo of the I Gruppe taken by Ludwig Franzisket: Identified are Schroer (fer left with foot on Steinhausen bottom left on ground) Kugelbaur (fifth from left with cigarette), Pöttgen (sixth from left with cigarette) Marseille (seventh from left with cigarette foot on Espenlaub on ground next to Steinhausen on left) von Kageneck (second from right) Neumann (far right) (Robert Tate/Ludwig Franzisket)

Rommel was obviously very much at ease with the *Luftwaffe* men. He saw them as comrades, not junior officers to be read political or inflated rhetoric. He was far beyond that. He was just a soldier, nothing more, and he acted like it. There was no pretense when Rommel met the men he called "real heroes," as he never considered himself one, despite having the *Pour le Mérite* from World War I, and the Knight's Cross, Oak Leaves, Swords, and later the Diamonds for his personal bravery and leadership in World War II. Rommel was fascinated to hear Marseille discuss the three missions of September 1, where he confirmed 17 victories. Rommel apparently commented to Marseille that that day alone was enough to warrant the Diamonds, in his opinion.

It was also during this time that British propaganda, which seemed to be less dehumanizing than the German version, made mention of Marseille in their reports: "Marseille is the best the Germans have here. Like the others, he flies the Bf 109, but he flies it better than all the rest. He can only be attacked by several planes at the same time. You must make sure to attack him from the front or flanks before he is in a position to maneuver."[285]

> Geoffrey Morley-Mower reiterated this fact: "I know that we have been focused upon talking about Marseille, but there were other Germans we kept an eye on, and who we knew from our intelligence sources. We knew all about blokes like

[Joachim] Müncheberg, Homuth, Schulz whom we know was killed, that sort of thing, because the German propaganda was always on about them and we had access to their newspapers and magazines, even some of their radio broadcasts.

"But what set Marseille apart was his flying skill. I saw that firsthand three times when he flew to our group airfield. That was what made him so dangerous. When all we knew was Yellow 14 and had no name attached at that time, but that was enough. I cannot tell you how many times we received these new pilots and gave them briefings, rather warnings, about how to fight in theater and they would laugh. I told (Michael) Judd that to come to a point to where he should stop wasting his time talking to them, just bring in the men who had fought against Marseille and were lucky enough to live after being shot down and let them tell their tales."[286]

On September 26, Marseille took off with his arm still in a soft cast and led a flight of five fighters from his 3 *Staffel* toward El Daba. When Marseille called out *"Indianer!"* the men at first saw ten enemy fighters, Hurricanes from No. 33 and No. 213 Squadrons RAF, plus an additional eight Spitfire Vs of No. 92 Squadron RAF that were late to the party. Also in the area were 11 additional Spitfires from No. 145 and No. 601 Squadrons RAF. The melee was spectacular.

The Hurricanes and Spitfires, who must have seen them also, began to form the very familiar Lufbery circle. Marseille gained altitude and then rolled over into his signature attack, as his wingman Schlang found himself flying above Marseille and all the enemy fighters. Marseille closed in on a Hurricane, BN186 (which Marseille misidentified as a Spitfire, since so many were around him), and fired at 09:10, sending Pilot Officer Eric Lawrence Luxton's aircraft down smoking heavily, then called it out. Schlang confirmed the victory. Luxton survived the crash landing.

By this time Marseille was firmly embedded into the Lufbery, closing the distance on his next target, a Spitfire, which also smoked and rolled over at 09:13. Marseille then gave more throttle and closed on the other Spitfire in front of him. He fired at 09:15 and sent his third victim earthward. With enemies on his six o'clock, Marseille then reduced throttle, went full flaps to slow down to stall speed, pushed the stick forward and his two pursuers passed by on his right as they completed their turn, taken by surprise. Marseille then retracted flaps and gave throttle, and fired, but missed as they abruptly broke left. Marseille told Schlang to take over and get them. Schlang closed in on one of the runaways, banked left, and fired. Marseille saw the right wing break away from the Spitfire, and the fighter spiraled in at 09:15.

The other Spitfire apparently realized that he was in a bad situation now that Yellow 14 was behind him, and he went to full throttle to get away. Marseille also went full throttle, closed in quickly, and fired again at Pilot Officer Turvey, who had been turning to get on Schlang's tail. As he was hit Turvey rolled over and lost altitude, then slid the canopy back and bailed out of his Spitfire V (BR494) at 09:16. As soon as he parted company with his aircraft it erupted in fire and smoke and then blew up. Number four for Marseille fell away in large pieces and was removed from the formation. Turvey's parachute was observed, and Marseille pulled for altitude and wrote down the coordinates, followed by Schlang and the remainder of his flight.[287]

The Me-109s returned to their airfield in glory once again. Marseille and Schlang filed their individual *Abschusse*. Marseille praised his wingman on a nice victory, and Schlang thanked Marseille for clearing his tail, as Neumann walked up to congratulate them. "I remember what flying as a wingman was like," Marseille said laughing, as the painter went to work adding four more bars to his rudder. Marseille had 155 victories, and they had another mission to look forward to.

At 14:30 Neumann gave a mission briefing. I *Gruppe* would send nine fighters (Marseille's 3 *Staffel*) to join a total of thirty-three Me-109s on another Stuka escort mission for Kuhlmey. At 16:00 3 *Staffel* of I./JG-27 lifted off for this mission toward El Hammam. It did not take long for the enemy to appear. Marseille's men were not flying close escort, as he preferred to fly higher and have greater visibility, which gave him an altitude advantage and a better chance of making the initial contact. Kuhlmey recalled this mission:

"We were getting close to the target, some British gun positions, when I heard 'Hello Albatross, this is Jochen!' I felt my world get brighter, and I called back 'thank you', then we had to get to doing our job."[288]

At 16:52 the Stukas had made their dive-bombing run and were heading back when Marseille called out the *"Indianer!"* Six Spitfires began to climb up into the Me-109s rather than try and attack the fleeing Stukas, a departure from their normal routine, but they were at least 4,000 feet below the Germans. Marseille took only a few seconds to determine his attack, and as the Germans flew directly over their enemies, he violently rolled over into an almost 90-degree vertical dive, leaving his other fighters above him, confused. Schlang followed him as fast as he could.

Marseille met his first Spitfire climbing at him almost head on at 16:56 and fired, breaking the aircraft apart. His victim's wingman then passed him in his climb as Marseille pulled back on the stick to pull out of his dive and steepen his climb, then he half rolled left and hit the left rudder, pulling more Gs than he probably wanted, as the Spitfire tried to reverse its course and rolled into a dive. Halfway through his maneuver Marseille had extended his flaps, cut his speed by increasing drag, and pulled harder into his left turn. This allowed Marseille to cut inside the Spitfire's turn, and, with a quick leading burst, the aircraft caught fire and fell away, streaming thick smoke that blinded both him and Schlang who recorded the time and coordinates, although the crash or the pilot bailing out was not observed.

Marseille climbed to be clear of the smoke then banked right to see what was below him at his three o'clock, when Schlang called out a threat at nine o'clock low. Completing his roll over Marseille saw another Spitfire climbing. He then gave hard right rudder and threw a hard right stick as he pulled back into a dive. The Spitfire then banked away to Marseille's left, continuing its climb, but in doing so exposed its fuselage. Not requiring any deflection, Marseille fired, sending the fighter hurtling down belching smoke at 16:59.

No sooner had the third kill fallen than his wingman, who was not observed during the process but must have been right behind him, emerged from the smoke, and fired at the Me-109. Marseille, still in a shallow dive, began to pull up, but had to skid and roll away from the enemy rounds, and a possible collision, as the tracers began streaking past him. The Spitfire never broke left or right but continued straight at him. As Marseille rolled out of the line of fire the Spitfire pilot managed to turn and get on his tail. Marseille must have known that this enemy pilot was not a rookie. He rolled again and started to dive, knowing that he was faster in that maneuver as well as in the climb, although not as maneuverable as his opponent.

Me-109F4 with a Ju-88 that landed for refueling (Ludwig Franzisket)

Schlang peeled over to try to clear Marseille's tail, but he immediately found himself with a Spitfire on his own six o'clock. Schlang pulled up, rolled and used some of the Marseille magic by cutting power, hit rudder, skidding away to allow his enemy to fly past. Schlang abandoned pursuit of a possible kill to try and get back to help his leader. On the ground Neumann was listening to everything as the battle raged.

Marseille pulled up to perform a loop, and as he did so, he went vertical right in front of Schlang, who pushed his stick forward to avoid colliding with the Spitfire following Marseille. This fight would last for almost 11 minutes, with both the Me-109 and Spitfire flown by exceptional airmen, dueling over the desert. Marseille then cut all power, gave full flaps, right rudder and dropped his landing gear, and hit zero airspeed. The Spitfire pilot rocketed upward and past Marseille's Yellow 14.

With no power, Marseille was unable to follow his enemy, so retracted his landing gear and flaps, gave hard left rudder, full left stick, then gave full throttle and headed toward the deck at full speed. Schlang was involved with a Spitfire of his own and unable to assist but managed to fire a warning shot that forced Marseille's tormentor to break off for a moment. That was all Marseille needed. At full power he flew away, putting great distance between himself and the Spitfire. He then pulled up, getting altitude and rolled level, then turned into his pursuer. They came at each other head on again at the same altitude, less than 300 feet from the ground.

Both fighters fired and both pilots skidded to avoid being hit by his opponent's rounds. Neumann and the others at the airfield, listening on the loudspeakers were white knuckled as they heard Schlang's calls and Marseille's responses, knowing that he was probably in the toughest dogfight of his life. Pilots landing sat in their cockpits listening on their own radios at what was transpiring. Marseille then radioed that his fuel light had come on. On a good day at cruising speed, he would have about 15 minutes of flight time left. In a fuel-burning dogfight, he would have a lot less.

Marseille pulled up into the afternoon setting sun, burning brightly in the west as he headed toward home, having lost contact with his comrades who were already headed back on fumes. Once the Spitfire pilot turned to follow him, possibly thinking that the German was trying to get home, he would have been blinded by the glare. The Spitfire pilot gave full throttle, hoping to close the distance and get sight of his enemy, when suddenly his own aircraft erupted in flames.

Marseille had flown vertical into the sun then cut power to his engine and rolled over into a dive. He then pulled up, completing a full vertical climbing roll, ending up on the tail of his enemy. At less than 400 feet from the Spitfire, which was already smoking, a thick black trail obscuring Marseille's visibility, but he fired anyway, and as Marseille reported, "It seemed that its wing separated from the fuselage," he radioed his kill at 17:10. The enemy pilot, a truly gifted airman in Marseille's opinion, probably did not survive.

Schlang could not see the aircraft impact, did not see a parachute and did not see the wing come off, and in fact he thought that it was the canopy that flew by, because it all happened so fast, and the smoke obscured his vision of the Spitfire. Marseille had just scored his 158th and final victory, and his 151st in the 17 months he had been in North Africa. When he finally approached his field, he did not do any victory rolls, but quietly landed, out of fuel, at Quotaifiya. The Marseille who took off on this sortie was not the same man who just reached *terra firma*. He was exhausted.

The first to reach his fighter was Mathias, with his crew chief Meyer right behind him. Marseille was so exhausted he was almost falling asleep as the engine stopped. He was haggard, white as a sheet, soaked in sweat, hands trembling. This had been the longest, most draining fight of his life. Mathias reached in to help the crew chief unstrap and lift Marseille, who was dead weight. Marseille's comments on the event are recorded by Robert Tate: "I almost thought it would be my last fight; but it seems that time has not yet come for me. That was the toughest adversary I've ever had. His turns were fabulous."[289]

Schroer recalled: "Marseille was carried like a dead man, until his feet finally touched the ground, but he could hardly stand. His uniform was dripping, as if he had just come out of a bath fully clothed. His face was white as snow. Neumann came over quickly and asked if he was wounded, Jochen shook his head. Just listening to that fight on my radio made me tired."[290]

The enemy pilot was good, knew his business, and was perhaps better than he was. It was all a matter of luck as to who would get into the best position first. Marseille's hands trembled as he lit a cigarette. Both Franzisket and Neumann confirmed that his hands did not stop trembling up until the time he climbed into the cockpit on his final mission four days later. Neumann knew that he needed time off, and he grounded him for a few days. Marseille even had trouble typing out his *Abschuss*, and he asked Mathias to bring him a drink. This was the first alcoholic drink for him in some time, and they kept coming.

Werner Schroer was there: "He was really more dead than alive. After he went into his tent, I saw Neumann coming out, they must have had a discussion. I walked in and asked how he was. He looked like he needed three days of sleep. Mathias poured him another brandy, and then he poured me one, and I sat down. Marseille's hands were still shaking. That was when he reminded me of the story of the Gypsy fortune teller at the carnival. He said he saw her in his mind thinking that he was going to die. I had never seen him like this, and despite our tortured history together, I felt sorry for him for everything that he had to go through since I first met him."[291]

All three *Staffeln* of I *Gruppe* were on total stand-down until the fighters could be serviced. The last few days and missions had been grueling by any standard. Besides, Marseille had two more 20-kilogram bags of fan mail to answer. He filed his reports, completed his paperwork, and addressed the fan mail, while taking time to play chess with Mathias and listen to his banned music. Franzisket described Marseille's appearance:

"Jochen looked twenty years older after that last fight. It had been the one battle that all pilots anticipate, yet we all feared. The fact was we could come up against the one pilot who was perhaps better, or luckier, quicker, or maybe the gods would not smile upon you that day. The images of your friends and even your enemies burning in their falling airplanes was always in your mind. How could it not be? That could be any of us at any time. I think Marseille saw that his mortality was just that. He had faced the best enemy in his life, and he had won. But rather than becoming arrogant, he became deeply introspective. I believe at that moment he knew that he was nothing special, he was mortal also. The reality really shook him up."[292]

Marseille finally relaxed and was smiling upon hearing that he was scheduled to go back home to receive the Diamonds and an extended home leave. Usually when he was told that he was leaving the front to return to Germany, he objected due to his fear of losing out in the scoring. He also typically objected because he did not want to leave the unit, as he felt responsible for his squadron mates. In his absences many of his friends had been lost, and he had not been there to help them. Fifi Stahlschmidt was also gone, and Marseille felt guilty since he did not fly that mission with him. Steinhausen was also dead as was Kugelbauer. Survivor's guilt seemed to plague him, along with an understandable condition that would today be called posttraumatic stress disorder. He was also very concerned about the fate of Mathias should he not be there. But he was assured Mathias would be well looked after until he returned.

It should be noted that in the first week of September Prof. Willi Messerschmitt had a factory fresh Me-109G2 delivered specially for Marseille. The unit was getting them in to replace the F models. There had been a *Kriegsberichter* (War Correspondent) on location since August 28 and joining a film crew sent by Propaganda Minister Dr. Josef Göbbels for the news programs *Die Frontschau* (The Front Show) and *Die Deutsche Wochenshau* (The German Weekly Show) to cover Marseille flying the new G model Yellow 14. But Marseille had flown it, did not like it and stayed with his worn-out F model. They were there for a few weeks and were still waiting to film him in his new fighter.

Neumann saw Marseille's combat fatigue, hence his grounding him for a while. The commanding officer even prepared the transportation paperwork to send him on official leave. Besides, Hitler wanted to see him and hand him his Diamonds, which had been specially made for him per Hitler's personal design specifications. Every set of Diamonds was unique, unlike the silver cast Oak Leaves and Oak Leaves and Swords, stamped with the maker's mark of the official jeweler responsible for making them, along with the Iron Crosses and Knight's Crosses.

Gustav Rödel during the investigation into the pilot scandal (Gustav Rödel)

Marseille even resisted taking the time off when Rommel called him, telling him that they would fly back on the same transport together. Marseille also knew that if he left on a vacation at this time, he would not be eligible for a vacation around Christmas, when he was planning to get married. Marseille also had another reason for not wanting to go so soon, if at all: his friend Mathias. Marseille was quite concerned, but Neumann and Franzisket assured him that nothing would happen to his friend while he was gone. They both gave their word.

Franzisket added to this issue: "Jochen asked me, in front of Schroer, Clade and others to look after Mathias should something happen to him. He was worried that he may be ordered home and removed from combat as a propaganda tool. He reminded us of what he had overheard in Berlin. He did not trust those people. I promised him that I would take care of Mathias. In fact, all of us did because we liked him so much. I know that put his mind at ease especially after that last incredible fight with the Spitfire."[293]

During this downtime the rest of JG-27 had been receiving the newer Me-109G-2 models, just like one of the models Marseille had flown when at the Messerschmitt factory when Fritz Wendel invited him to try one out, only not with the more powerful engine as found in the later *Gustav* variants. Marseille's comments about the new plane to his squadron mates upon his return had been mixed. He liked the extra horsepower, especially the climb rate, and the redesigned forward leading edge of the wing as well as a better trim tab configuration. He also liked the extra firepower the G series provided and the extra control surface on the elevators, rudder, and wings.

The only downside he reported was the fact that it was a far heavier machine and not as nimble in turns and rolls as the F model due to the wing-mounted weapons and additional armor. He also commented that in extending the flaps and reducing power in the practice flight, as he did in combat, the engine was more responsive, and the flaps were better at reducing speed faster when power was also reduced. One positive comment that he did make was that the extra armor plating around the cockpit and behind the pilot's head gave some comfort. Many pilots had been decapitated by an enemy cannon shell that struck from behind or died when an armor piercing round entered through the fuselage or canopy.

Of great interest, which Galland discussed with the pilots during his last visit to the unit, was the actual evolution of the armor-plated head protection behind the pilot. Galland told them of the time when his chief mechanic had a steel plate welded into the coffin lid canopy frame as an extra precaution for his boss, when Galland was flying the Me-109E series in 1940, when he was *Kommodore* of JG-26 during the Battle of Britain.

Upon climbing into his cockpit and closing the canopy, the steel plate had cracked him in the head, giving him a mild concussion and a massive bump on the top rear of his head, despite his leather flight helmet absorbing much of the impact. Still cursing the man who had altered his canopy Galland took off. Even the future General of the Fighters was considering the various ways he could punish his chief when he returned. Galland's attitude had not changed, and his temper had not abated when he landed, and upon exiting he screamed for his chief.

Yellow 5 of I./JG-27 cannibalized for parts (Gustav Rödel)

Galland then related to the men of JG-27 how, as he was creatively cursing his chief mechanic for the injury and unauthorized alteration, one of the other mechanics politely requested Galland's attention. *Major* Galland then went to the man, who asked him to please take a look. Galland climbed up and inspected the back of the steel plate that was added the evening before. A nearly two-inch indentation from a 20mm cannon shell from a Hurricane (the aircraft types Galland was involved against and scored a victory) was clearly visible. Had that plate not been added, Galland would have lost his head, literally. "Better a headache than no head," he said to the desert pilots.

After that, Galland wrote a report that went all the way up to Göring. Upon review all German fighter production firms, including Kurt Tank, who designed the fabulous Focke-Wulf series of fighters, and of course Willi Messerschmitt, introduced the head plate armor behind the pilot made of heavy gauge steel that was between two and three inches thick on average. The F series had them as part of the production series, and this was carried over into the new G series of the legendary fighter.

Marseille's new fighter, factory fresh with less than 100 hours on the engine, received its paint job. The dark green of the standard *Reichsluftfahrtministerium* color-coded paint that replaced the old graduated mottled green on sand brown that blended into the sky blue already present underneath the fuselage had long been abandoned and replaced with the mustard brown/khaki tan paint so familiar to the desert camouflage used since the F models had been introduced a year and a half before. Most of the F models were gone, shipped back to Europe. But Marseille still had his.

Neumann told the story: "We had just received the new G model of the 109s, which Marseille test flew, and despite the heavier weapons, he did not like it as much as the F model. He liked the fact that the F was a more agile and streamlined machine, and he even wrote a report with his observations, stating that in his opinion we should simply place the newer G engines into the F model airframes. However, the loss of agility and slightly slower rate of climb when fully loaded did not impress him. He did like the additional armored cockpit and new canopy as I did."[294]

Then the most fateful event in Marseille's life occurred; Kesselring arrived unannounced as usual and exited his Fieseler Storch to be greeted by Neumann. He then met the other pilots, and the usual small talk erupted with "Smiling Albert." Franzisket and others were there when Kesselring looked around, and saw two Yellow 14s, a G and F model. Franzisket remembered what happened:

"OK, this is what I remember: 'Is that not Marseille's fighter, Yellow 14?' Kesselring asked Neumann.

"'Yes, *Herr Feldmarschall*,' Neumann answered.

"'Well, which one? I see two of them?' Kesselring asked.

"'He still flies the older F, he prefers it,' and then Marseille walked up and saluted.

"'Marseille, why are you still holding on to that old fighter, and not flying the new one?' Kesselring asked him.

"'Well, *Herr Feldmarschall*, because it is better adapted to my flying style, it is just a better close battle fighter. I prefer to keep it.' Marseille answered.

"'Well, Professor Messerschmitt sent that new one that to you as a gift at Göbbels request, that was why he sent the film crews. The German people need to see you in that machine, so does the *Führer*. Am I clear?'

"'*Herr Feldmarschall*, I think that our masters in Berlin would prefer I keep getting victories regardless of which aircraft I am flying, so I would like to stay with my old bird,' Marseille said, and Neumann must have been feeling very uncomfortable considering where this conversation was going.

"'Marseille, what I am saying to you is not a suggestion, it is an order, do I make myself clear?' Kesselring said, and he was smiling as if he was having a good time. 'Neumann, do you understand me?'

"'Both Marseille and Neumann were quite clear on what Kesselring was telling them. Old Yellow 14 was put into retirement.'"[295]

On Neumann's order the unit artist then painted Marseille's rudder with the Knight's Cross, Oak Leaves and Swords suspended by the jump ring, with a wreath encircling the number "100" with 58 vertical bars underneath for the additional victories. The stencil went against the sides of the fuselage as his Me-109G-2 Yellow 14 was painted, labeling the fighter as his by designating him as the pilot, followed by the unit insignia. His rudder was painted red to identify him as the leader at Marseille's request. As he was the squadron leader, he could have had his markings changed, but he preferred to keep Yellow 14.

Two days later Marseille had a meeting with Neumann and the other squadron leaders. They were having to combine their logistical requirements on all items, such as fuel, ammunition, glycol coolant, water, food rations, etc. The combined report went to Kesselring who then sent that request to Berlin. In addition, on the evening of September 29 Marseille had to complete all of his reports. He made the joke that he heeded a secretary. The photographs of Marseille at his typewriter were taken by Franzisket with his ever-present camera, the last photos of Hans-Joachim Marseille taken while he was alive.

Franzisket remembered that evening: "I had a few shots left on the roll of film so I thought that I would take the last few photos and insert a new roll. I went into Marseille's tent where he was typing, and I called to him. I said, 'Hey bastard!' and he looked up and smiled, so I snapped the photo I had no idea that those would be the last two pictures of my friend while he was alive."[296]

Franzisket also recalled Marseille's demeanor the day of his death: "Marseille seemed to be in good spirits. The four days off had served him well. He had rested and ate and hydrated after a grueling week. Soon he would be leaving to receive his Diamonds, and I think that he had managed to work out a plan that he would not take his vacation until December, just a quick trip to Berlin and back, if not in fact delayed entirely until his December trip. I would say that his mental state was very good given what he had been through."[297]

The last photo taken of Marseille by Ludwig Franzisket on the evening of Sept. 29, 1942. He would die the next day (Ludwig Franzisket)

On September 30, 1942, StG-3 in total launched their ground attack mission early in the morning, with III./JG-53 providing air cover, who would depart once relieved by elements from JG-27. 3 *Staffel* of I./JG-

27 led by Marseille lifted off just before 11:00 to cover the return flight of the Stukas and relieve III./JG-53. Kurt Kuhlmey recalled the mission:

> "This was one of the rare days when we did not get hit by the enemy, and as soon as Marseille's men arrived JG-53 left due to fuel concerns. I was feeling better about that. Joachim Müncheberg's boys were good, but I just always felt much safer with Marseille overhead. He was like a life insurance policy, and every time one of our crews saw him, they would call him out. Sort of like putting everyone at ease."[298]

Fifteen minutes after Marseille's group took to the air III *Gruppe* JG-27 also lifted off, as ten more Me-109s from III./JG-53 also took off to relieve their brethren who would be low on fuel. The first group from III./JG-53 radioed that there were enemy fighters in the area and provided the coordinates, just east southeast of El Imayid and they were obviously looking for the Stuka formation. When Marseille's *Staffel* arrived, the enemy fighters did not want to engage the Germans, and in fact they flew in the opposite direction. They may have been under orders to hit the dive bombers at all costs and avoid fighter contact, or perhaps low on fuel.

However, as the enemy fighter formation of perhaps a dozen machines turned away to the north they ran into III./JG-27, who were flying a parallel course to I *Gruppe*. As Marseille radioed the enemy position and their direction of travel and altitude back to Neumann, working as the ground controller, he directed III *Gruppe* to intercept the fleeing enemies. Over the radio "*Horrido!*" was heard as Werner Schroer, leading 8. III./JG 27, called out a Spitfire victory over Abu Dweis. Schoer explained the situation:

> "I had several targets, but I had to attack one that would not leave me vulnerable to his comrades, so I chose a Spitfire that was a few hundred meters below to my right, and I rolled over. It was a quick pass, I fired, and he smoked and fell away. I called it out and I heard confirmations in the headset."[299]

After a rather uneventful Stuka escort mission for Marseille's *Staffel*, Neumann and the entire *Geschwader* heard a radio call at 11:30 hours that concerned them. Marseille radioed without using his call sign of "Elbe 1" that he had smoke pouring into the cockpit and had developed engine trouble. His Me-109G-2 (W.Nr.14256) could be seen streaming white vapor at first, followed by gray smoke. The command post was confused as to who the pilot in trouble actually was. Marseille's wingman Schlang called out his leader's call sign and problem to the command center.

"What is his altitude?" Neumann asked over the radio.

"Four thousand meters," replied Pöttgen.

Then Schlang told Marseille that they had four minutes to German lines. The men back at the airbase heard the transmissions. "I am blinded, can't see a thing," Marseille told his comrades. Pöttgen and Schlang both called back to Marseille. "Almost there, Jochen," Schlang said calmly as he and Pöttgen flanked him on either side, keeping vigil in case any opportunistic Allied fighters made an appearance, drawn by the long smoke trail behind the Messerschmitt. Marseille was on oxygen, but that was also a danger if the heat became intense enough to explode the cylinder in the cockpit. Marseille asked how long before he was safely over German lines. Pöttgen told him three more minutes. Meanwhile back at the base Neumann and the others were listening over the headsets.

Pöttgen and Schlang were flying on either side of Marseille, who was gasping, even with the oxygen mask on. Schlang reported that he flew alongside and looked over. Marseille's face when he could see it was ghostly pale. At 11:35 the words "two more minutes" were heard. Neumann had his wall map, and he knew exactly where they were. At this time Schroer was converging to provide support with his *Schwarm* and he radioed his intentions. At 11:36 Neumann radioed to Marseille to bail out right then; he could be recovered if he took to his parachute. Neumann then ordered a vehicle to take off and head in that direction.

Once Marseille was told that they had reached German lines as they passed over the Sidi Abd el Rhaman Mosque, the critical landmark used in visual flight reference navigation, he decided to leave his fighter. "I have to get out now... can't stand it anymore..." were the last words Marseille spoke, as the heat and smoke apparently became unbearable.

Yellow 14 had been slowly yet steadily losing altitude and airspeed, and there was concern that he may not have enough altitude to safely bail out. Pöttgen maintained an altitude check over the radio; he was still all right. At 11:40 and at 15,000 feet altitude Marseille opened the coffin lid canopy and hit the release, which flew away in the slipstream. The two escorts saw Marseille pull the nose up slightly as thick smoke poured from the fighter, and then he rolled over, inverting the fighter for a rapid exit.

Oberleutnant (later Major) Rudolf Sinner was appointed Staffelkapitaen of 6 Staffel III./JG27 and served in Gustav Rödel's Gruppe. He was credited with 39 victories in 305 missions. 36 of his victories were achieved over the Western Front, 32 being in North Africa including three four-engine bombers and three flying the Me 262 jet fighter. Three were scored over the Eastern Front. He was shot down 12 times, baling out three times, and was wounded five times, the last time on April 4, 1945 when his Me-252 jet was shot down and he baled out, and strafed on the ground by P-51 Mustangs. He was out wounded for the rest of the war. (Raymond F. Toliver)

Pöttgen and Schlang reported to Neumann the events as they unfolded, and Schroer also heard over his radio as he gave full throttle heading back. Franzisket also called in that he was also on the way back, low on fuel. Every man on the ground was listening over the speaker before Neumann shut it off, and every German in the air listening held their breath. Schlang was closer on Marseille's right wing, a little lower, watching his progress. Pöttgen, flying on Marseille's left wing, pressed the microphone button and said "Jochen is out!" It was 11:41.

Both pilots saw Marseille drop out, his body partially obscured by the thickening gray smoke, but clearly visible. In pushing out of the fighter, and probably blinded by the smoke pouring out of the cockpit from behind the firewall, he failed to notice the aircraft change its horizontal attitude, and being inverted as the nose went forward and down. The horizontal stabilizer struck him across the chest and groin, flipping him over on his back before he could open his parachute. According to both Schroer and Franzisket, after a few seconds of silence, a voice quietly broke over the radio; "Jochen is dead, no parachute."

Schroer arrived on the scene to see the fighter impact into the ground, although he saw no parachute. Pöttgen and Schlang had seen what had happened. It is unclear which pilot sent that radio call, which hit Neumann hard. The headset and microphone hit the desk as he stepped away from the radio. Those outside of the command post had not heard everything; they only knew that someone was in trouble, and the rumor had spread that it was Marseille. Neumann looked at the men gathered wanting to know, and never said a word. He did not have to. Franzisket had just landed as Neumann stepped outside.

Neumann stated: "When I heard this, I felt very sad. I was used to losing men; that was war. But Marseille was special, like a small boy playing war. He never took it too seriously, and his smile, which was less evident as time progressed, was infectious when present. His loss was a very serious morale issue for the unit, and we held a ceremony for him in Derna. Marseille had this mythical quality about him. He could not be killed, despite crashed fighters or returning with dozens of holes in in his fighter. It was as if a plug had been pulled and the lights went out. The person who took it the hardest was Mathias. I felt very sorry for him, as his friend was now dead. He above all others was completely alone."[300]

Franzisket landed and had heard everything: "I knew that Jochen was dead. I felt like crying right there as I rolled to a stop. I just sat there for a few minutes, and then it occurred to me that I was now responsible for Mathias. I also thought of his mother, now losing two children. I did not meet her until many years later, but when I did, it was very hard. She asked many questions about his friends, and other subjects. I answered her with what I knew. I did tell her that he was a special man in many ways, and very special to many people. I think that gave her some comfort."[301]

The men who witnessed this event believed that he was killed instantly, as they reported this upon landing. Marseille fell to his death, probably already dead from the impact or at the very least knocked unconscious. Regardless of his condition, he could not open his parachute. The final investigation of the crash site concluded that the hydraulic fluid line had been ruptured in the reduction gear by broken interconnecting teeth in the large gear wheel, severing the line and allowing the fluid to spray. This hit the hot engine surfaces, creating the light gray smoke, increasing the heat, thus forcing Marseille to bail out.

According to Franz Kurowski, the action above was also witnessed by German ground forces, in particular the chief physician for the 115th *Panzergrenadier* Regiment, Dr. Bick, who was close enough to take his staff car and drive to the point of impact. Marseille's body was later recovered by the doctor from the desert floor, where he had landed face first into the ground. "The pilot lay on his stomach as if asleep," Dr. Bick's report stated. "His arms were hidden beneath his body. As I came closer, I saw a pool of blood which had issued from the side of his crushed skull; brain matter was exposed. I then noticed an awful wound above the hip. The pilot must have slammed into the airplane upon bailing out.

"The parachute rested a few meters next to the dead man. The pack which still contained it was torn about forty centimeters along its side. White parachute silk spilled out like intestines. The release handle for the parachute had buried itself deep into the sand right next to the dead man. It was still on 'safe.' I carefully turned the young pilot over onto his back. The finely cut features of his face below a high forehead were nearly undisturbed. It was the countenance of a tired child.

"I opened the zipper of the flight jacket, saw the Knight's Cross with Oak Leaves and Swords and immediately knew who this was. The pay book told me: in front of me lay *Hauptmann* Marseille. I glanced at the dead man's watch. It had stopped at 11:42 hrs. I left to get help in order to recover the body. When I returned with some Italian engineers, two of the dead pilot's comrades were already on the scene."[302] The two men who arrived were Ludwig Franzisket and the *Gruppe* surgeon, Dr. Winkelmann.

"We collected his body, and placed him on a stretcher," Franzisket described. "I took his medals and placed them in my pocket, and we lifted him carefully and placed him in the back of the auto. I sat with him, and all I could think about was the last conversation we had together. I also thought immediately of Mathias. What was I going to do? I had given Jochen my word, as had Neumann. I felt very depressed. I looked at his face, slightly disfigured, but at peace. The age that had etched into his face was gone. He once again looked like the young man who celebrated life. The ride back to the airfield was in complete silence.

"When we arrived, the first person we saw was Mathias. He came to me and looked at his friend. Our friend. He was crying. I think we all were, we brave German pilots, acting like women. But we did not care. Neumann was even affected. He looked into the back seat and quietly told us to take him into the medical tent. The entire *Geschwader* arrived throughout the day, everyone saying goodbye in their own way.

"I remember Mathias had come in several times. He sat next to the body. He was there when Neumann came in and I handed over Jochen's medals. I said something like, 'for his mother,' but I do not remember. Neumann patted my shoulder, as Schlang walked in. Then Neumann touched Jochen's hair and said '*Auf wiedersehen* 'Seille,' and he walked out. I was numb, and Mathias was devastated. I placed my hand on his shoulder and told him that he should come to my tent later for a talk."[303]

Werner Schroer and Ludwig Franzisket (kneeling in foreground) collected Marseille's body. Franzisket removed Marseille's medals and gave them to Neumann. (Eduard Neumann)

Kurt Kuhlmey heard the report, and he stated the following: "Once I had confirmation that Marseille was dead, I assembled my men, and I told them what I knew. I could see the look of astonishment on their faces. It was as if they did not believe what I had said. Just as the pilots in JG-27 must have felt, we had a feeling of great loss, because many of those men gathered around me had been saved by Marseille and his third *Staffel* many times. We owed him and his friends our lives. Yes, I would say that we were quite depressed at the news."

As Marseille laid still and the men arrived and paid their silent respects, the sounds of a song echoed over the base. Marseille's favorite, the "Rumba Azul," came from Marseille's tent. Jost Schlang had put the record on as he sat on Marseille's vacant cot. Soon he was joined by others, as Reiner Pöttgen and the rest of the men entered. They all had a drink and began to sing as Mathias walked up and entered the tent. He had just finished burning Marseille's clothes, that were meant to be washed and dried, in an empty fuel drum.

Gustav Rödel commented as well: "Everyone was coming in to see Marseille one last time, even Homuth came in, and I know he had been crying. I would have never thought that he, Marseille's greatest enemy, would have ever felt compassion for him. But I think Homuth realized after his death, just how important Marseille was to the morale of the unit."[304]

Marseille's body after recovery and placed in an ammunition box as his makeshift coffin (Ludwig Franzisket)

According to Franzisket, "Mathias was a wreck, totally destroyed, and I worried about him. He was caught between two violent worlds. He was officially our prisoner, and subject to whatever higher authority determined would be his fate, and Marseille had already voiced his suspicions and knowledge of the Jewish issue, and the racial laws also pertained to blacks as well. He also ran the risk of being labeled a collaborator by the British unless he went to a prison camp, and Marseille worried about his safety if that happened. It was hard, I tell you. That was when I knew what I had to do, and to keep Neumann out of trouble, I did not say a word to him. I think he knew, but he never asked."[305]

The pilots of JG-27 did a great job of protecting Neumann, should it have been known that they were harboring an enemy prisoner. Neumann even said:

> "As I remember, after the funeral service that we held [October 2] which was where his grave was located, that was perhaps the last time I saw Mathias. He just wandered away and disappeared. I do not recall whatever happened to him. That was until we located him in South Africa and brought him to Egypt."[306]

Franzisket kept his word to Marseille and took Mathias in as his servant, providing him safety, keeping him with the unit even after they left North Africa the following year. As cited by Kurowski, Franzisket said after the initial shock wore off, the men were "... so unbelievably hardened that they accepted the death of Marseille without any external signs of mourning. Nevertheless, all of us had the feeling that our lives were over."[307]

On October 1, 1942, Marseille's body was taken to the German cemetery at Derna, not far from the largest German/ Italian hospital in Libya. They waited for the arrival of *Generalfeldmarschall* Albert Kesselring at his request. The next day his *Staffel* were going to fly in tribute over the ceremony. *Generalfeldmarschall* Albert Kesselring had arrived to deliver the eulogy, and the attending men were assembled while almost every senior *Luftwaffe* and Army officer within driving or flying distance arrived to pay their respects, as did the Italians. The Me-109s took off in perfect formation. Following the eulogy and the fly over, they laid him to rest temporarily.

On this day the official *Oberkommando der Wehrmacht Kriegsbericht* dispatch stated:

> "*Hauptmann* Hans-Joachim Marseille, wearer of the highest German decoration for bravery, met a pilot's death in the North Africa theater unbeaten by the enemy. Filled with an insatiable spirit of attack, this young officer had vanquished

158 British enemies in air combat. The *Wehrmacht* mourns the loss of such a truly heroic warrior."[308] Ironically this message was intercepted by the British Ultra, the signals intelligence group managed by Alan Turing at Bletchley Park and sent to RAF Command in Cairo. The British were reading the German mail almost in real time.

Marseille's funeral on October 3, 1942 attended by German and Italian pilots. Generalfeldmarschall Albert Kesselring and Eduard Neumann gave eulogies. Later that day an unknown Allied P-40 pilot dropped the note of condolence over Neumann's airfield (Eduard Neumann)

Major and JG-27 *Geschwaderkommodore* Eduard Neumann provided his own memorandum addressed to the men of JG-27 who had served shoulder to shoulder with the brightest star in the sky over Africa:

ORDER OF THE DAY

On 30 Sep 1942 *Hauptmann* Marseille died a pilot's death, unvanquished by the enemy. It is difficult for us to accept that this bright, cheerful and brave fighter pilot of our *Geschwader* will no longer be with us.

His victories against our most bitter enemies, the English are one of a kind. We should both be happy and proud to have counted him among us.

These beautiful words cannot express what his loss means to us.

He leaves behind us our duty to emulate him as a person and a soldier. His spirit will forever be a model for this Geschwader.

The *Geschwaderkommodore* Neumann, *Major*

Marseille's death was well known news to the Allies. In fact, British intelligence had Ultra intercepts and decoded and translated the following two reports that were sent within hours of the crash:

Marseille's original grave marker at the German cemetery (Eduard Neumann)

MEDITERRANEAN
AIR PERSONALITIES

On 30/9 *Fliegerfuehrer* AFRIKA reported the death of *Hptm.* MARSEILLE, *Staffelkapitaen* in JG 27. He was not killed by enemy action. His engine caught fire and he baled out at 3,000 m. His parachute failed to open and he crashed at 0940/30/9 7 km south of the mosque at SIDI ABD EL RAHMAN, in his own territory. He was flying a Messerschmitt 109G.

TO: C.S.S. Personal
From: Duty Officer, Hut 3
Following neither reported in CX/MSS nor signaled abroad CX/MSS/C45

MEDITERRANEAN
AIR PERSONALITIES

AMSEL Ia to 5th Air Corps for *Feldmarshall*, on *Hptm.* MARSEILLE 2nd Report.

His engine began to smoke from unknown causes over the front area, at 6,000 metres. He then glided towards our territory, during which time the *Geschwader* control heard him speaking continuously. The enemy did not interfere. MARSEILLE's voice was perfectly clear. He supposed himself that his engine was on fire. He let his companion in the Schwarm guide him as the cockpit was full of smoke. Flames were first seen as he bailed out, which he did at 3,000 metres 7 km. S of SIDI ABD EL RAHMAN....(several sentences illegible)....The a/c was burnt out. Engine and parachute have been found. Funeral probably in the afternoon of 1/10 at DERNA. 0827/1/10/42 GMT[309]

Geoffrey Morley-Mower provided information from their perspective:

"Well, as you know we had these chaps who monitored German radio traffic, but we also had the crypto types who took the intercepted and decoded Enigma transmissions between various units and Berlin, and even among each other I suppose. We received the teletyped report on the first of October, so we knew that Marseille was dead.

"There was not the expected cheering and festive atmosphere one may expect when a hated and feared enemy was gone. Instead, there was actually some light discussion but a respectful tone. All of us remembered the German pilot who played deliveryman and to our astonishment informing us about our pilots. We also remembered the very lethal pilot who carved us up from time to time. But I would say that all of us knew that we had fought against a worthy opponent who was an honorable man. The more I learned about him after the war only reinforced this belief."³¹⁰

Likewise, Michael Judd had this to say: "When we had that report about Marseille, I must admit that I had this overwhelming sense of relief that he was dead. And being a professional I also had to remember that he was probably solely responsible for many of our losses. But, At the end of the day I did respect and I guess I can say that I even admired his gentlemanly approach towards us. Yes, there are enemies in war, and we fight them, but then you can also find something admirable even in your enemy. I guess that Marseille was that one man who also understood that. But to be honest I was glad he was gone."³¹¹

As the Germans returned to the airfield and their tasks on the evening of October 2, 1942, a thick shroud of depression fell upon the men of JG-27, especially the first *Gruppe*. Neumann realized that he had a great morale problem building up, and that he needed to do something:

"I called all three *Gruppenkommandeure* to have a meeting. I asked them how the men felt, and all said to me that the men were totally deflated. I understood what they were saying, I saw it in my headquarters also. Moral was at the lowest point that I had ever seen in a flying unit. I made the decision to stand the entire *Geschwader* down for a day at least. They needed time to process everything, but I wanted them all back in the air and focused on their work. Dwelling upon 'Seille's death was not healthy for any of them."³¹²

On October 3, 1942 an unknown Allied pilot in a P-40 Kittyhawk flew over the airfield that was home to I./JG-27, and dropped an object from his cockpit and banked away. The object was retrieved; a letter tied to a large stone. It was taken to Neumann, and after he read it, he called the men together, and he remembered this:

"This pilot probably remembering the flights Marseille had made over their airfields to deliver his messages had delivered one himself. I later sent that note to Marseille's mother along with the letter I wrote to her after his death. Once the men were around, I read it to them: 'Honoring a fallen enemy, who was also a chivalrous foe. Rest in Peace.' I think that says all that must be said about what our enemies thought of him."[313]

On October 1989 the Gemeinschaft der Jagdflieger traveled to Egypt to commemorate the pyramid memorial marker placed where Marseille had died so long ago. From left to right foreground Ambassador Franz Ellis, next three unknown, Colonel Eduard Neumann (second from right) General Anton 'Toni' Weiler (far right). In attendance were several former WW II German, British, Australian and South African pilots and their families (Eduard Neumann)

EPILOGUE

When we went back to Africa, the feelings, smells, even the faces of the men long dead came back. It was surreal really.
Emil Clade

Marseille's remains were brought from Derna and later reinterred in the Tobruk German War Cemetery, where they are now in a small clay coffin bearing the number 4133 once the construction of that monument was completed. It was there where Marseille's mother paid her one and only visit to her son's grave after the war. In later years she fell upon extremely hard times financially. There were no survivors' pensions for the vanquished or the relatives who survived them. Such a world, crumbling around her, would have broken a lesser woman. She had lost her two children and ex-husband, and she had seen her nation fall into ruin. She had outlived everyone. She was all alone, except for the support she received from the men of JG-27, especially from Eduard Neumann, as he explained:

"I stayed in contact with her during and after the war. I had written a personal letter to her, as I did for all the men I lost, but I let her know that 'Seille was special. She wrote back several times, and I knew she was having a difficult time. I lost contact with her for a few years because she moved I believe, but one day I had a letter from her that found me in 1954 or

1955. We started having gatherings of the old JG-27 men once every year when we could get together.

"I had been sending her a little money when I could, and I mentioned this to the other men. Many of my pilots, such as remained in the military and had good steady incomes, so they also helped her. I thought that was outstanding. And so that you know we also helped the families of others, such as Steinhausen, Stahlschmidt, Kugelbauer and others when we could. A few times I visited her and we had good discussions. She always wanted to know about what he did with his friends when not flying. I told her everything as I had no reason to withhold information.

"She laughed as I told her of the pranks her son played on the men, such as Schroer on the toilet, Clade with the scarecrow, and other crazy things for which he was famous. As I came to know her I felt even more sorry for her as she had no one, I mean no one at all. Her entire family was gone. She was very sad at not having grandchildren. That to me, being totally alone was the greatest tragedy of the war and my heart broke for her."[314]

Occasionally she would receive visits, and even more often money, usually anonymously on Jochen's birthday, which was around Christmas time. Frau Charlotte Marie Johanna Pauline Gertrud Riemer Marseille Reuter went to her grave as the matriarch of the Desert *Geschwader*. At her funeral service, those who survived the war and knew her son attended her graveside ceremony with a dignity and solemn honor befitting the mother of one of history's greatest pilots, aces, heroes, and humanitarians. She was, in a way, the mother of them all.

Those Germans who fell into and died in enemy hands were buried by the British and Commonwealth forces with complete respect and full military honors in their cemetery in Alexandria, Egypt, while many German graves are in the Tobruk and Benghazi cemeteries as well as Commonwealth dead. The men buried in British-held cemeteries included Wolfgang Burger, Karl Kugelbaur, Cay Carstensen, Friedrich Hoffmann, Werner Boden, Heinrich Prien, Wolfgang Lippert, Erwin Sawallisch, Heinrich Müller, Günther Zahn, Hans Würschinger, Hans Schirmer, Hermann Tangerding, Eberhard Schmidt, and others from JG-27, StG-2 and 3, ZG-26, and JG-53, and a number of Italians.

Marseille had flown 382 total sorties in his career, claimed 158 victories and an average of 2.4 victories per combat engagement. He had an unofficial score of 11 additional victories that were never confirmed, but at least 17 of his "victories" actually managed to return to their airfields, often heavily damaged and many with wounded pilots. Other claims were probably the result of mutual destruction also claimed by other pilots, which sometimes happened. My colleagues, historian and author Robert Tate and researcher Nick Hector who assisted with new additional information have independently worked to assess Marseille's actual victories given this knowledge.

It is believed that by factoring in at least those 17 enemies claimed as "victories" who made it back to base whose aircraft were repaired, his score would more accurately be around 136 to 142 confirmed victories at the most. Even that score is quite impressive. For the rest of the war no other German fighter pilot would score as many victories over the Western Allies, further securing his legend.

On October 24, 1975, the *Bundesluftwaffe* Non-Commissioned Officers Kaserne of Uetersen was renamed "Marseille Kaserne," mainly due to the continued efforts of *Oberst* Eduard Neumann and others, such as *Brigadegeneral* Gustav Rödel, and *Generalmajor* Friedrich Körner. Even *Generalleutnant* Adolf Galland (who started World War II in JG-27 under *Oberst* Max Ibel) joined the campaign, as did *Generalleutnant* Johannes Steinhoff and Dr. Ludwig Franzisket, to name but a few. This honor followed a long tradition of honoring fallen heroes as icons for the future generations to follow.

Today there is still great debate ongoing as the current German government is renaming all buildings and locations, removing the names of Germany's heroes during the Third Reich, whether or not they had any affiliation with the NSDAP or not. They are in effect erasing their own history.

Marseille's original grave in Africa was still listed where a temporary marker had been placed. Today, a permanent burial marker in the shape of a pyramid stands in his honor, placed there during the ceremony from October 21–22, 1989, by his surviving squadron mates, and his old commanding officer, Eduard Neumann and then-president of the *Gemeinschaft der Jagdflieger* Anton Weiler. Matthew Letuku (aka Mathias) had also been located in his native South Africa, and he was brought for the event as the special guest of honor.

Also joining the group to pay their respects were former JG-27 pilots Emil Clade, Friedrich Körner, Gustav Rödel, Ambassador Franz Elles, Fritz Keller, Sighart Dinkel, Gustav Holderle, Wolfgang Ewald (JG-53), and Ulrich Walk (JG-77). The German group and their former Italian comrades were welcomed by the Egyptian government, and Anton Weiler read the dedication of the Marseille Memorial, a pyramid structure befitting the rich history of the region. Eduard Neumann unveiled the special plaque on October 22.

Körner had a special memory of the location, as he had been shot down within a mile of the location of Marseille's Memorial while flying with 2 *Staffel* on July 4, 1942, and taken prisoner. "I never thought I would ever return, and to do so under those circumstances was very strange, but I would have not missed it for anything in the world."[315]

Emil Clade said of the event: "I could almost feel Marseille there. I keep remembering the scarecrow in my cockpit, the jokes he played on me and others. I recall the music blaring and his laugh, like a young boy at Christmas. I felt privileged to have known him."[316]

By the time of his death, Marseille would be awarded Italy's Gold Medal for Bravery by Benito Mussolini, and Germany's Iron Cross 2nd

and 1ˢᵗ Class, the German Cross in Gold, and Knight's Cross with Oak Leaves, Swords and Diamonds (posthumously). Only 27 of the latter were awarded, just ten of which were *Luftwaffe* recipients, nine of those fighter pilots. Adolf Hitler would personally decorate him on only one occasion: with the Oak Leaves and Swords.

Marseille the legend lives on among fighter pilots and historians and retains strong appeal in the popular imagination. He performed miracles in aerial combat, averaging 15 rounds of ammunition per kill. This must be placed into proper context: the average fighter pilot, regardless of nationality, averaged over 80–120 rounds per kill, with most rounds not striking the aircraft, but "walked" into the flight path in a deflection shot. Marseille's deflection shots required no extra rounds in leading the target, as almost all hit their mark.

Even other great fighter pilots like *Generalleutnant* Günther Rall and *Generalleutnant* Johannes Steinhoff, *Oberst* Erich Hartmann, and *Generalmajor* Dietrich Hrabak praised the wizardry of Hans-Joachim Marseille. Adolf Galland called him "the unrivalled virtuoso of the fighter pilots."

Marseille's marksmanship was extraordinary, and his piloting skill and chivalry were unprecedented. Even his enemies respected him, a throwback to World War I where professional airmen and soldiers had the utmost respect for their enemies and certain protocols were followed. Gentlemanly conduct was the order of the day.

Galland, upon becoming General of the Fighters, embodied and expected his men to follow that same code of conduct. Neumann, Woldenga and Rödel reinforced it, and Marseille embraced it. What those who knew him the best and remembered the most were his laugh, and his infectious sense of humor, and that smile that endeared him to women and broke the ice with even the most acerbic senior officers. He was a controversial role model, a sort of James Dean of his day.

It can be said that what a man's comrades and fellow countrymen say about him means more than what he could ever say about himself. The Germans interviewed who knew Marseille all had their personal impressions of the man outside of the cockpit. Their insights are quite revealing. Perhaps one of the greatest tributes to Marseille came from Knight's Cross recipient and Stuka legend *Oberst* (later *Generalmajor*) Kurt Kuhlmey:

"We knew that when JG-27 was with us, we had a great chance. When we saw Yellow 14 and his men, I always knew that I was coming home. They were a great life insurance for us, although in war there are no guarantees. Our losses would have been much greater if not for Marseille. If you have ever been in battle, you rely upon your comrades, those around you to keep you safe as much as they can.

"Of all the fighter pilots who protected me and my Stukas, I can only say that none were as dedicated as Marseille. It seemed that it was his personal mission to help me and my men whenever possible. I know that he had a lot of problems with higher ranking officers because of his attitude, but in my book, I only cared that whenever I was in trouble, and I heard him call me on the radio, that was a real friend. He was a hero to all of us, and what he did by giving the enemy the information on their pilots proves that he was indeed an extraordinary gentleman. I miss him."[317]

Franz Elles said this: "Marseille was a master prankster and as undisciplined as a man could be, believe me. But he was always worth a good laugh. He had a very great outlook on life. He hated the war and the killing, but he loved flying, and wanted to continue flying after the war, as most of us did. I think that his childish manner and generally cheerful outlook prevented him from becoming a hardened person. That was a benefit that he shared with us and many of us felt the same way."[318]

Franz Stigler also had thoughts: "I did not know Marseille well at all, I only met him twice, but he came across to me as a boy who was having a great adventure. Marseille was one of those people you only read about, or heard of, never really expecting to meet. When I met him, I knew who he was already, and I spoke with him and when I walked away, I forgot to ask for his autograph. Many years have passed, and I still remember him. He had a great smile, and I only knew him when he was happy. It would have been hard to remember him otherwise. When he died it really put a blanket over the entire unit. The more famous he became the more he craved the attention, but he was a good man from my experience."[319]

Hans Baur: "I was totally astonished at the man I met. I was expecting a straight and very professional type of officer, a poster boy if you will for the German military. In physical appearance he was all of that, but in his personal actions, he was a shocking and very entertaining person. I liked him, although I could see where others, especially his superiors would have had headaches dealing with him."[320]

Artur Axmann: "I could not understand where Marseille's mind was. Here was this great hero of Germany, one of the most famous faces in Europe, a real fighter, and then you meet him and here is this carefree child. Intellectually he was superior to most I would agree, but I was shocked at his lack of social skills and his desire to simply shock people at any given moment just to have a laugh was very upsetting. In fact, it was embarrassing."[321]

Karl Wolff: "I knew a lot about Marseille, as did most of us Germans. He was in all the newspapers and magazines. I have to say that when I met him briefly, he was not an impressive looking person. Not what I would consider the look of a great hero. He looked like a member of the Hitler Youth. When he played that piano and then lost his mind, I had every confidence that his career was over, and he would just disappear. But then again, he had great propaganda value."³²²

Leni Riefenstahl: "You must understand that men like Marseille were thought of the same as great movie stars today. They were larger than life, and Marseille was one of the greatest. I was very happy to get to know him for a few days, he was in fact one of the most sensual and interesting men I have ever known. When I heard that he had died, I was very sad, because I always thought that after the war, however it turned out, he would have had a lot to offer the world."³²³

Walter Krupinski said this: 'I wish I had been able to know him better. I learned more about him from the discussions about him at the reunions many years later. We all knew who he was during the war of course, but you cannot get an accurate picture of a man unless you meet him, speak with him, and get to know him. I think that he would have done Germany and the new *Luftwaffe* much good helping repair our image as a nation had he lived."³²⁴

Dr. Heinz-Georg Wilhelm Migeod: "When I flew with *Stukageschwader* 3 in Libya I spoke with Kuhlmey many times, and the others about Marseille. We had a few occasions to stay at one of their airfields. Seeing Marseille and his friend Mathias acting carefree as if there was no war made everyone feel lighthearted. We could forget the war for a while and just enjoy being alive. I think that was his greatest gift, other than saving us on many occasions. There was not a racial bone in his body, he hated no one, except for Homuth, and I know that story, but even then, he saved Homuth a few times when he could have let him get shot down. But he did his duty, but when we heard that he shot up Homuth's tent, Kuhlmey said to us, 'I think that is the end of our guardian angel.' Luckily, he was wrong. We all loved Marseille and his *Staffel*, they were just good men, all of them. I was proud to be their friend."[325]

Kurt Bühligen recalled Marseille from flight school: "He was not a serious person, and in fact I disliked him immensely. He always seemed to have this attitude that he was above regulations and ranks. I will admit that he was a gifted pilot, but he was a total disaster as a German officer. But I followed his success, it was hard not to with all of the propaganda. He did well for the *Luftwaffe* and became a national hero, but I really had no use for him as a person. Perhaps he changed and matured, if so, and I heard he had, then I was not a witness to that."[326]

Josef Kammhuber: "I only met Marseille once, but I knew many people who knew him, such as Baur, Kuhlmey and others. When I met him, I thought, 'Who is this child?' But after speaking with him, I saw his charm and I knew that he was not a typical warrior, but he did exhibit many of the attributes of the average fighter pilot. He was just far more gregarious than most, and I personally liked him."[327]

Bernhard Woldenga gave his impressions: "You must understand that the *Luftwaffe*, like any military group had to be professional, Discipline was strict, and the expectations of professional courtesy and respecting ranks were paramount. Marseille could have cared less about any of that. When he arrived, we already knew all about him, but Neumann and I decided to let this loose cannon go for a while and see what he could do.

"At first, he was not impressive, and I was ready to dismiss him, even maybe take him off flying and work with the mechanics, but Neumann talked me out if it. He saw something that I did not see, not at first anyway. I decided to let Neumann take charge of him, and as we all know that turned out to be the right decision. But Marseille was an infuriating subordinate. Neumann or I were always getting involved with him or covering for him for one insane thing or another.

"But I must say in all honesty I really did like the boy. He had a certain charm about him that was infectious, that devil may care attitude typical of fighter pilots, but with Marseille it was a lifestyle. When I heard he had died I did feel a sense of loss, especially when the manner of his death was revealed. He brought a certain humanity to the war, providing a sense of honor for all of us. He was a good young man."[328]

However, perhaps the best assessment of a man's character is best described by his enemies. Geoffrey Morley-Mower had this assessment:

"I wish I had been able to meet him [Marseille]. Even though he was an enemy, and a damned good fighter pilot who took a serious toll of us, I always thought of him as a gentleman knight, given his proclivity for letting us know about our chaps, at great risk to himself I might add. That took a special kind of bollocks, that did. But I think I understood his mind. He wanted to do the right thing. I would say that, despite the horrendous actions of the Nazis during the war, there were some good Germans who were just caught up in the mayhem, and Marseille was perhaps the most tragic figure in that group."[329]

Michael Judd had his thoughts: "This fellow Marseille really intrigued me. Once I learned his name and was able to gather some information from the captured newspapers and magazine articles I sort of felt that I knew him. We had discussions about him, and some others we knew of by name, or at the very least their aeroplane numbers. Those of us who had been in theater and saw him in combat knew what we were dealing with. He was a dangerous bloke, no doubt, one to be avoided unless you had some friends with you.

"We put a collective bounty on him for the man who shot him down, and the competition was keen. But then that proved to have been a very bad idea, because then we had some new pilots, not really aware of what to expect, start looking for Yellow 14. I warned all the new pilots in pre-flight briefings, and even in casual chat not to go looking for him, and if found make sure they had others with them. Many of them just laughed at our concern over this bloody Frankenstein. That was until after a few sorties they saw what we were talking about. I think that after a few post mission debriefings, these young wankers finally understood what we had been saying.

"I really wish I could have met him on the ground. I know that I went up against him a few times, and I was lucky, others were not. I know that there is a fascination with meeting the other guy, your enemy. And we did have a few Germans who were prisoners, some who knew Marseille, and we did get some good information. I would say that from what I know today, Marseille would have either been the most decorated British pilot in the RAF, or a former pilot doing prison time for his antics. Either way he seems to have been a most amazing young man. Sad that he ended up that way."[330]

Cecil Golding: "He was a bastard, as you know he shot me down. But I will say that he was obviously a great fighter pilot, and as I have learned from many people who knew him, he was pretty much like us; a young man doing his duty, effectively I would say, but the stories of his honorable intentions towards our chaps' sort of dampened the hatred I felt for him. The Germans I know who knew him all said the same things, that he was an undisciplined clown, on the ground and in the air, but he was also a pilot to be respected. The fact that he had honor says much about him. I always wanted another crack at him, you know? But I still think he was a bastard."[331]

Within a few days of his death the major newspapers in the Allied nations ran his obituary almost as if in tribute to a noble enemy who was simply on the wrong side. On October 3, 1942, his death was featured in such publications as the American *New York Times, London Times* and the Australian newspapers *Newcastle Herald, The Sun* (Sydney), *Melbourne Times,* and on October 6, 1942 in the *Kalgoolie Miner.* Almost as if in a final humorous gesture, Marseille still had the final laugh as he was still the star of the show even in death.

Hans-Joachim Marseille was hated by a few, loved by many, but respected by all. He had a deadly talent that made him a superior fighter pilot, a tragic personal life that he somehow managed, and a professional career that seemed to go off the rails on occasion, but it was his *bon vivant* approach to life, his belief in fair play and his humanity that secured his legend. Everyone who knew him called it the "Marseille Magic."

AFTER THE WAR

Professor Geoffrey Morley-Mower came to live in the United States after the war and was on faculty at George Mason University in Virginia as a professor of literature. He died on Dec. 16, 2005 (Geoffrey Morley-Mower)

Brigadegeneral Gustav Rödel ended WW II earning the Oak Leaves to the Knight's Cross and scored 98 victories. He later retired from the Bundesluftwaffe and died on February 6, 1995 (Gustav Rödel)

Generalleutnant Johannes Steinhoff ended WW II flying the Me-262 jet in both JG-7 and JV-44 commanded by Adolf Galland, earning the Knight's Cross, Oak Leaves and Swords and scoring 176 victories. He joined the post war Bundesluftwaffe and became the NATO Inspector of Fighters. He was also a very talented landscape artist. In this photo he shows one of his works. Steinhoff died on Feb. 21, 1994 (Johannes and Ursula Steinhoff)

Major Ludwig Franzisket ended the war with the Knight's Cross and 43 victories. He later became a world-renowned professor of natural biology and died on Nov. 23, 1988 (Ludwig Fransizket)

Michael Judd ended his career as a Group Captain and came to the United States working in the oil and investment business, living in Houston, Texas. He died on August 22, 2010 (George P. Judd)

Clive Caldwell transferred to Australia after North Africa to fight against the Japanese. He was tutored by American fighter ace and Medal of Honor recipient Captain Joseph Foss, United States Marine Corps. He was demoted from Group Captain to Flight Lieutenant for smuggling alcohol. He ended the war with 6.5 Japanese kills added to his 22 German victories becoming Australia's top ace in North Africa and the war with 28.5. After the war he went into the cloth import/export business. Caldwell died on August 5, 1994, in Sidney, Australia (Alcheron Free Encyclopdia)

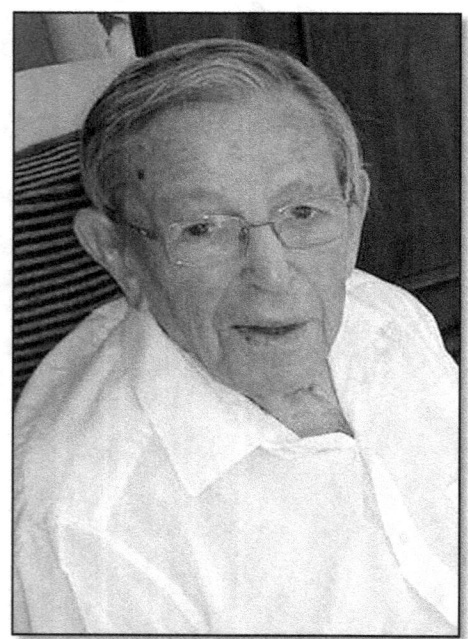

Major Cecil Golding retired from the SAAF and took up a career as an artist. Golding died on May 29, 2014 in Cape Town, South Africa (Military History Journal, Vol 16 No 3 - June 2014, Tinus Le Roux)

Stuka pilot Dr. Heinz-Georg Wilhelm Migeod studied Islamic history and economics in Munich and Göttingen receiving his PhD in 1956. He travelled throughout Africa and the Middle East as a corporate representative and emigrated to South Africa living in Somerset West and wrote a book about the war titled Der Kommandeur He died on November 10, 2010 (SAAF WW 2 Heritage Tinus Le Roux)

Generalleutnant Walter Krupinski finished the war with 197 victories in approximately 1,100 combat missions, also flying the Me-262 jet in Galland's JV-44 earning the Knight's Cross with Oak Leaves. After the war he joined Organization Gehlen, then later Amt Blank both working in military intelligence. He joined the new Bundesluftwaffe and retired on November 8, 1976 and died on October 7, 2000. (Walter Krupinski)

Colonel Charles Brown (left) and Franz Stigler at an event. Franz refused to shoot down Brown's B-17 "Ye Olde Pub" on December 20, 1943 which was the subject of Adam Makos' bestselling book A Higher Call. In 1990 the two pilots finally reunited and were close friends until their deaths. Stigler would end the war flying the Me-262 with JV-44 and scored 26 victories. Franz died on March 22, 2008 in Vancouver, British Columbia, Canada. Brown died on November 24, 2008 in Miami, Florida (Franz Stigler)

Generalmajor Friedrich Körner being promoted to Brigadegeneral in 1973. During the war he shot down 36 aircraft in approximately 250 combat missions, all scored over North Africa with JG-27. Like many others he joined the West German Air Force and retired in 1979. Friedrich Körner died on Sept. 3, 1998 (Robert Tate)

Generalleutnant Adolf Galland never joined the West German Air Force, but did take the job of building the Argentine Air Force for President Juan Peron after the war. After returning to Germany, he went into business with his old JG-26 wingman and trusted friend Major Gerhard Schöpfel who had 45 aerial victories in 700 combat missions, all on the Western Front. Schöpfel died on May 17, 2003. Galland became an author on the air war and was a worldwide favorite at aviation gatherings with his wife Heidi. Galland died on February 9, 1996 (Adolf Galland)

Major Werner Schroer ended the war with the Knight's Cross, Oak Leaves and Swords and credited with 114 enemy aircraft shot down in 197 combat missions. He was kept in British custody until February 7, 1946, and after returning home he worked as a taxi driver, later working in Rome, Italy for eleven years. He returned to Germany working as head of the central protocol department with Messerschmitt-Bölkow-Blohm. He died of cancer on February 10, 1985 (Ludwig Franzisket)

Tables

Synopsis of Marseille's Life and Milestones

December 13, 1919: Born in Charlottenburg, Berlin.
1937: Enlisted in the *Luftwaffe*.
April 1940: Completed fighter pilot training. Posted to 4./JG-52 on the Channel Coast under *Oberleutnant* Johannes Steinhoff. Later reassigned to I./JG-52.
August 1940: Awarded Iron Cross 2nd Class
September 1940: Awarded Iron Cross 1st Class.
April 1941: Arrived with I./JG-27 in Libya.
April 23, 1941: Scored first African victory (eighth of the war), a Hurricane II over Tobruk. On second mission he was shot down himself and landed in German territory.
September 24, 1941: Scored five victories, British-flown aircraft.
December 3, 1941: Awarded German Cross in Gold.
February 1942: Score reached 52 victories.
February 22, 1942: Awarded Knight's Cross for 40th victory, given medal February 24.
June 3, 1942: Shot down six P-40s in 11 minutes.
June 17, 1942: Shot down 35 additional aircraft that month, last mission in June. Went to Germany.
September 1, 1942: Mission 1: Shot down two Hurricanes and two Spitfires in 11 minutes.
Mission 2: Shot down eight P-40s.
Mission 3: Shot down five more aircraft for a total of 17 victories.
September 2, 1942: Shot down 126th aircraft, notified by *Generalfeldmarschall* Erwin Rommel that he was to be awarded the Diamonds, only the fourth person to be awarded by that time. Only 27 awarded during the war, with ten going to *Luftwaffe* pilots, and nine to fighter pilots.
September 3, 1942: Scored six victories.
September 15, 1942: Official victory score stood at 150.
September 16, 1942: Officially promoted to *Hauptmann*, the youngest in the Luftwaffe at that time.
September 26, 1942: Shot down a Spitfire, his score stood at 158 victories.
September 30, 1942: Killed when bailing out of Me-109G-2, struck by vertical stabilizer, body recovered by Ludwig Franzisket. He was 22 years old.

Marseille's Dates of Ranks/Promotions

November 7, 1938: *Flieger*
March 13, 1939: *Fahnenjunker*
May 1, 1939: *Fahnenjunker-Gefreiter*
July 1, 1939: *Fahnenjunker-Unteroffizier*
November 1, 1939: *Fähnrich*
March 1, 1941: *Oberfähnrich*
April 1, 1941: *Leutnant*
April 1, 1942: *Oberleutnant*
September 16, 1942: *Hauptmann*

Marseille's Assignments and Unit Postings

Ergänzungsjagdgruppe Merseburg
July 18, 1940–August 10, 1940, to Merseburg–West

I.(Jagd)/LG 2
August 10, 1940–September 30, 1940, to Calais–Marck

II./JG-52
September 30, 1940–November 5, 1940, Peuplingues
November 5, 1940–December 22, 1940, Mönchengladbach
December 22, 1940–January 15, 1941, Leeuwarden
January 15, 1941–February 10, 1941, Ypenburg
February 10, 1941–February 21, 1941, Berck sur Mer

I./JG-27
February 21, 1941–March 3, 1941, Döberitz
March 3, 1941–April 4, 1941, Ghedi
April 4, 1941–April 11, 1941, Graz–Thalerhof
April 11, 1941–April 14, 1941, Zagreb
April 14, 1941–April 16, 1941, München–Riem
April 18, 1941–April 22, 1941, Castel Benito–Tripoli
April 22, 1941–December 7, 1941, Ain el Gazala
December 7, 1941–December 12, 1941, Tmimi
December 12, 1941–December 17, 1941, Martuba
December 17, 1941–December 23, 1941, Magrum
December 23, 1941–December 26, 1941, Sirte
December 26, 1941–January 1, 1942, Acro Philaenorum
January 1, 1942–January 22, 1942, Agedabia
January 22, 1942–January 27, 1942, El Agheila

January 27, 1942–February 1, 1942, Agedabia
February 1, 1942–February 7, 1942, Benina
February 7, 1942–May 22, 1942, Martuba
May 22, 1942–June 14, 1942, Tmimi
June 14, 1942–June 16, 1942, Derna
June 16, 1942–June 22, 1942, Ain el Gazala
June 22, 1942–June 25, 1942, Gambut
June 25, 1942–June 27, 1942, Sidi Barrani
June 27, 1942–July 2, 1942, Bir el Astas
July 2, 1942–July 7, 1942, Mumin Busak
July 7, 1942–July 20, 1942, Turbiya
July 20, 1942–October 2, 1942, Quotaifiya

Marseille's Leaves and Temporary Orders

January 16, 1941–February 20, 1941: Vacation at home.
June 18, 1941–August 25, 1941: Vacation at home.
October 15, 1941–December 3, 1941: For *Staffel* transition from Me-109 E-7 Trop and familiarization to Me-109 F-4/Trop in München-Riem and Erdingen.
December 26, 1941–February 6, 1942: Medical examination in Athens. On leave in Berlin.
February 28, 1942–April 24, 1942: Home leave, including two weeks in *Luftwaffenkrankenhaus* in Munich. Engagement to fiancée Hannelies Küpper in Berlin. Layover in Rome to receive the Italian Silver Medal for bravery (*Medaglia d'Argento al Valor Militare*), Italian Pilots Badge and the German–Italian African Campaign Badge in Silver from Benito Mussolini.
June 19, 1942–August 21, 1942: Home leave after receiving Oak Leaves and Swords from Adolf Hitler, propaganda and recruitment tour. Also awarded the Combined Pilots-Observation Badge in Gold with Diamonds presented by Göring personally. The infamous piano concert followed. In Rome again upon return route to receive the Italian Medal for Bravery in Gold (Medaglia d'Oro al Valor Militare) personally from Benito Mussolini. Goes absent without leave and is found.

Marseille's Decorations and Dates of Awards

February 1, 1940: *Flugzeugführerabzeichen* (Pilots Badge) September 9, 1940 for action in August: Iron Cross Second Class for two victories September 17, 1940: Iron Cross First Class for four victories November 3, 1941: Silver Honor Goblet
November 21, 1941: German Cross in Gold awarded, but not presented until December 17, 1941, by *Generalfeldmarschall* Albert Kesselring

February 22, 1942: Awarded 416th Knight's Cross for 46 victories. Presented by Kesselring to Marseille on February 24.
February 23, 1942: News arrived of Italian Silver Medal for Bravery
June 6, 1942: Ninety-seventh recipient of the Oak Leaves for 75 victories.
June 18, 1942: Twelfth recipient of Swords for 100 victories. This and the Oak Leaves were presented to Marseille on June 28 by Hitler in the same ceremony at the *Führerhauptquartier* Wolfschanze in Rastenburg, due to the closeness of the award dates.
August 6, 1942: Awarded highest Italian decoration for bravery, the *Medaglia d'Oro* presented by Benito Mussolini in Rome on August 23.
August 12, 1942: Awarded Combined Pilots-Observation Badge in Gold with Diamonds
September 3, 1942: Fourth man to be awarded the Diamonds. Hitler had decided to present them to Marseille personally later in the year. However, Marseille died before the investiture, and the Diamonds were never presented to Marseille's mother. This would have been the protocol under the *Reichsgesetzblatt* I S. 1573 Article 7, which was the German Law of 1939 that authorized the awarding and requirements for the Knight's Cross. The requirements changed over time, especially for the *Luftwaffe* fighter pilots as the war progressed. What would have earned a pilot like Galland and Mölders the Diamonds in 1941 would only qualify a pilot for the Swords by 1943, and only the Oak Leaves by 1944.
September 16, 1942: Early promotion to *Hauptmann*, youngest in *Luftwaffe* up to that time. Awarded Front Flying Clasp of the *Luftwaffe* in Gold with Pennant for 300 missions.
November 30, 1962: Italian Minister of Defense Giulio Andreotti gave Marseille's mother and Joachim Müncheberg's widow 1,500 DM each.

Breakdown by Type of Marseille's Victories in North Africa

101 Curtiss P-40 Tomahawks
30 Hawker Hurricanes
16 Supermarine Spitfires
2 Martin A-30 Baltimores
1 Bristol Blenheim
1 Martin Maryland

Marseille's Personal Aircraft

Me-109E (W.Nr 3579): Sustained 50 percent damage on September 2, 1940 in aerial combat and crash-landed near Calais-Marck.

Me-109E (W.Nr 5597): Sustained 75 percent damage on September 11, 1940 in aerial combat and made an emergency landing near Wissant.
Me-109E (W.Nr 5094): Sustained 100 percent damage on September 23, 1940. Marseille bailed out after aerial combat near Dover.
Me-109E (W.Nr 4091): Sustained 35 percent damage Théville on September 28, 1940 following emergency landing after engine failure.
Me-109E (W.Nr 1259): Sustained 80 percent damage, April 20, 1941, during emergency landing after engine failure near Cahela.
Me-109E (W.Nr 5160): Sustained 100 percent damage on April 23, 1941, crash-landing near Tobruk.
Me-109E (W.Nr. 1567): Sustained 40 percent damage on May 21, 1941, following aerial combat and emergency landing near Tobruk.
Me-109F-4 (W.Nr. 12593): Scored 50th victory on February 23, 1942. Scored another 58 victories in this aircraft.
Me-109F-4 (W.Nr. 10059): September 15, 1942, lost a wing in a midair collision when *Leutnant* Friedrich Hoffmann of 3./JG-27 collided with *Unteroffizier* Heinrich Pein of 5./JG-27. Pein was killed outright, and Hoffmann bailed out at low altitude, but five weeks later died from the injuries he sustained.
Me-109F-4 (W.Nr. 10137): Probably the aircraft flown on September 1, 1942, when he flew three missions and scored 17 victories. Engine replaced.
Me-109F-4 (W.Nr. 8673): Scored last seven victories in this fighter on September 26, 1942.
Me-109G-2 (W.Nr. 14256): Destroyed on September 30, 1942, when Marseille was killed.

Marseille's Total Victory Claims

(Additional Data Courtesy of Nick Hector)
(Some victories were misidentified; see endnotes.)

	Date	Unit	Type	Time	Location
1	08/24/40	I. (Jagd)/LG 2	Spitfire	Unknown	Kent, England
2	09/08/40	I. (Jagd)/LG 2	Spitfire	09:40	Detling, Kent, England[332]
3	09/11/40	I. (Jagd)/LG 2	Spitfire	17:05	French Coast[333]
4	09/15/40	I. (Jagd)/LG 2	Hurricane	Unknown	Thames, England[334]
5	09/18/40	I. (Jagd)/LG 2	Spitfire	Unknown	Dover Coast, England[335]
6	09/27/40	I. (Jagd)/LG 2	Hurricane	Unknown	London, England[336]
7	09/28/40	I. (Jagd)/LG 2	Spitfire	Unknown	South Coast, England[337]
8	04/02/41	I./JG-27	Hurricane	12:50	Tobruk, Libya[338]

	Date	Unit	Type	Time	Location
9	04/28/41	I./JG-27	Blenheim	09:25	Offshore, Tobruk[339]
10–11	05/01/41	I./JG-27	Hurricane (2)	09:15, 09:25	Tobruk, Libya[340]
12–13	06/17/41	I./JG-27	Hurricane (2)	17:15, 18:45	Gambut/Sidi Omar, Libya[341]
14	08/27/41	I./JG-27	Hurricane	18:00	Sidi Barrani[342]
15–16	09/09/41	I./JG-27	Hurricane (2)	17:12, 17:18	Bardia, Libya[343]
17	09/13/41	I./JG-27	Hurricane	17:25	Bardia, Libya[344]
18	09/14/41	I./JG-27	Hurricane	17:46	El Sofafi, Libya[345]
19–23	09/24/41	I./JG-27	Hurricane (4) Maryland	16:45, 16:47, 16:51, 17:00 13:30	Buq Buq, Libya[346] Coast, Libya
24–25	10/12/41	I./JG-27	P-40 (2)	08:12, 08:15	Bir Sheferzan, Libya[347]
26	12/05/41	I./JG-27	Hurricane	15:25	S. of Bir el Gubi, Libya[348]
27–28	12/06/41	I./JG-27	Hurricane (2)	12:10, 12:25	El Adem, Libya[349]
29	12/07/41	I./JG-27	Hurricane	09:30	Sidi Omar, Libya[350]
30	12/08/41	I./JG-27	P-40	08:15	El Adem, Libya[351]
31	12/10/41	I./JG-27	P-40	08:50	El Adem, Libya[352]
32	12/11/41	I./JG-27	P-40	09:30	Tmimi, Libya[353]
33–34	12/13/41	I./JG-27	P-40 (2)	16:00, 16:10	Martuba, Libya[354]
35–36	12/17/41	I./JG-27	P-40 (2)	11:10, 11:28	Derna/Martuba[355]
37–40	02/08/42	I./JG-27	P-40 (4)	08:22, 08:25, 14:20, 14:30	Martuba Bomba Bay[356]
41–44	02/12/42	I./JG-27	Hurricane P-40 (3)	13:30 13:32, 13:33, 13:36	Tobruk, Libya[357]
45–46	02/13/42	I./JG-27	Hurricane (2)	09:20, 09:25	Tobruk, Libya[358]
47–48	02/15/42	I./JG-27	P-40 (2)	13:00, 13:03	Gambut, Libya[359]
49–50	02/21/42	I./JG-27	P-40 (2)	12:10, 12:18	Fort Acroma[360]
51–52	02/27/42	I./JG-27	P-40 (2)	12:00, 12:12	Fort Acroma, Gazala[361]
53–54	04/25/42	I./JG-27	P-40 (2)	10:06, 10:08	N. Gazala[362]
55–56	05/10/42	I./JG-27	Hurricane (2)	09:13, 09:15	SE of Martuba[363]
57–58	05/13/42	I./JG-27	P-40 (2)	10:10, 10:15	Ain el Gazala[364]
59–60	05/16/42	I./JG-27	P-40 (2)	18:05, 18:15	Fort Acroma, Gazala[365]
61–62	05/19/42	I./JG-27	P-40 (2)	07:20, 07:30	Fort Acroma[366]
63–64	05/23/42	I./JG-27	Baltimore (2)	11:05, 11:06	Tobruk[367]
65	05/30/42	I./JG-27	P-40	06:05	El Adem, Libya[368]
66–68	05/31/42	I./JG-27	P-40 (3)	07:34, 07:26, 07:28	El Acroma[369] Bir-el Harmat

	Date	Unit	Type	Time	Location
69	06/01/42	I./JG-27	P-40	19:15	Mteifel Chebir, Libya[370]
70–75	06/03/41	I./JG-27	P-40 (6)	12:22, 12:25, 12:27, 12:28, 12:29, 12:33	Bir Hacheim[371]
76–77	06/07/42	I./JG-27	P-40 (2)	16:10, 16:13	El Adem[372]
78–81	06/10/42	I./JG-27	P-40 (3) Hurricane	07:35, 07:41, 07:45 07:50	Mteifel Chebir[373] Mteifel Chebir, Libya
82–83	06/11/42	I./JG-27	Hurricane (2)	17:24, 17:34	Fort Acroma[374], El Adem
84–87	06/13/42	I./JG-27	Hurricane, P-40 (3)	08:10 08:11, 08:14, 08:15	El Adem[375] Gazala[376]
88–91	06/15/42	I./JG-27	P-40 (4)	18:01, 18:02, 18:04, 18:06	El Adem[377]
92–95	06/16/42	I./JG-27	P-40 (4)	18:02, 18:10, 18:11, 18:13	El Adem[378]
96–101	06/17/42	I./JG-27	P-40 Spitfire Hurricane (4)	12:09 12:12 12:02, 12:03, 12:05, 12:08	Gambut, Libya[379]
102–104	08/31/42	I./JG-27	Hurricane (2) Spitfire	10:03, 10:04 18:25	El Alamein, Egypt[380] Alam Halfa, Libya
105–121	09/01/42	I./JG-27	Hurricane (7) Spitfire (2) P-40 (8)	08:26, 08:28, 08:35 17:45, 17.48, 17:49, 17:50 08:39, 17:53 10:55, 10:56, 10:58 10:59, 11:01, 11:02, 11:03, 11:05	El Imayid[381] El Taqua Alam Halfa Deir el Raghat[382] El Imayid
122–126	09/02/42	I./JG-27	P-40 (4) Spitfire	09:16, 09:18, 09:24, 15:18 15:21	El Alamein[383] El Imayid
127–132	09/03/42	I./JG-27	Spitfire (2) P-40 (3) Hurricane	07:20, 15:10 07:23, 07:28, 15:08 15:42	SW Hammam El Imayid[384] SSE of El Alamein
133–136	09/05/42	I./JG-27	Spitfire (1)	10:48	Ruweisat, Libya[385]

	Date	Unit	Type	Time		Location
			P-40 (3)	10:49, 11:00	10:51,	El Taqua
137–140	09/06/42	I./JG-27	P-40 (3)	17:03, 17:16	17:14,	El Alamein[386]
			Spitfire	17:20		El Alamein, Egypt
141–142	09/07/42	I./JG-27	P-40 (2)	17:43, 17:45		El Alamein[387]
143–144	09/11/42	I./JG-27	Hurricane (2)	07:40, 07:42		El Imayid, Libya[388]
145–151	09/15/42	I./JG-27	P-40 (7)	16:51, 16:54, 16:59, 17:02	16:53, 16:57, 17:01,	SW of El Alamein[389]
152–158	09/26/42	I./JG-27	Spitfire (6)	09:10, 09:15, 16:59, 17:10	09:13, 16:56,	El Daba[390]
			Hurricane	09:10		

Examples of Hans-Joachim Marseille's Best Multiple Victory Missions

Victories	Date	Times of Victories
19–23	09/24/41	13:30, 16:45, 16:47, 16:51, 17:00
37–40	02/08/42	08:22, 08:25, 14:20, 14:30
41–44	02/12/42	13:30, 13:32, 13:33, 13:36
66–68	05/31/42	07:26, 07:28, 07:34
70–75	06/03/42	12:22, 12:25, 12:27, 12:28, 12:29, 12:33
88–91	06/15/42	19:02, 19:03, 19:04, 19:05
92–95	06/16/42	19:02, 19:10, 19:11, 19:13
96–101	06/17/42	12:02, 12:04, 12:05, 12:08, 12:09, 12:12
105–108	09/01/42	08:28, 08:30, 08:33, 08:39
109–116	09/01/42	10:55, 10:56, 10:58, 10:59, 11:01, 11:02, 11:03, 11:05
117–121	09/01/42	18:46, 18:47, 18:48, 18:49, 18:53
127–132	09/03/42	08:20, 08:23, 08:29, 16:08, 16:10, 16:11
137–140	09/06/42	18:03, 18:13, 18:14, 18:20
145–149	09/15/42	17:51, 17:53, 17:55, 17:57, 17:59
152–155	09/26/42	09:10, 09:13, 09:15, 09:16

Percentages of Marseille's Contributions in the Victory Count (Courtesy of Robert Tate)

	(1) 22 Apr 41 04 Dec 41	(2) 05 Dec 41 07 Jun 42	(3) 08 Jun 42 17 Jun 42	(4) 18 Jun 42 30 Aug 42	(5) 31 Aug 42 30 Sep 42	(6) 01 Oct 42 31 Dec 42
Marseille	18	52	24	0	57	0
Stab I	11 (5%)	8 (2%)	3 (4%)	8 (3%)	4 (3%)	6 (5%)
1	72 (33%)	33 (10%)	11 (15%)	26 (9%)	7 (5%)	8 (6%)
2	10 (5%)	50 (15%)	15 (20%)	57 (19%)	20 (14%)	6 (5%)
3*	39 (18%)	23 (8%)	1 (1%)	6 (2%)	1 (>1%)	3 (2%)
Gruppe I Total	150 (70%)	171 (51%)	54 (72%)	97 (33%)	89 (61%)	23 (18%)
Stab II	8 (4%)	16 (5%)	3 (4%)	11 (4%)	8 (6%)	16 (12%)
4	30 (14%)	51 (15%)	5 (7%)	91 (31%)	0 (0%)	13 (10%)
5	19 (9%)	46 (14%)	4 (5%)	20 (7%)	5 (3%)	29 (22%)
6	3 (1%)	20 (6%)	1 (1%)	27 (9%)	8 (6%)	2 (1%)
Gruppe II Total	60 (28%)	133 (39%)	13 (17%)	149 (51%)	21 (15%)	60 (47%)
Stab III	1 (>1%)	2 (>1%)	0 (0%)	0 (0%)	0 (0%)	2 (2%)
7	0 (0%)	19 (6%)	3 (4%)	12 (4%)	6 (4%)	9 (7%)
8	0 (0%)	6 (2%)	0 (0%)	21 (7%)	24 (17%)	29 (22%)
9	4 (2%)	7 (2%)	5 (7%)	14 (5%)	4 (3%)	7 (5%)
Gruppe III Total	5 (2%)	34 (10%)	8 (11%)	47 (16%)	34 (24%)	47 (36%)
JG 27 Wing Total Victories	215	338	75	294	145	130
Stab	1 (>1%)	0 (0%)	0 (0%)	1 (>1%)	1 (>1%)	0 (0%)

Marseille as % of 3./JG 27	18 of 57 31.5%	52 of 80 65%	24 of 25 96%	0 of 6 0%	57 of 58 98%	0 of 3 0%
Marseille as % of I Gruppe	18 of 150 12%	52 of 171 30%	24 of 54 44%	0 of 97 0%	57 of 89 64%	0 of 23 0%
Marseille as % of Entire JG 27 Wing	18 of 215 8%	52 of 338 15%	24 of 75 32%	0 of 294 0%	57 of 145 39%	0 of 130 0%

1) Percentages in each column are the Stab or Squadron's percentage of total Gruppe victories for the given period.
2) Must add Marseille's total percentage of JG27 Wing to each column to achieve 100%.
3) Does not consider the likelihood of Marseille's or any other pilot's overclaiming. For the purposes of this discussion, these small numbers are not critical, and the illustrative purpose thus remains intact.
4) Due to rounding up/down, some total percentages may not be exactly 100%.
5) List may not be exhaustive. Minor exclusion errors, although vigorously reviewed, may have unfortunately occurred.

Effects-Based Approach to Operations (EBAO) and Likely Marseille Overclaiming

(Courtesy of Robert Tate)

EBAO is an approach to planning, executing and assessing military operations with a focus on achieving desired effects as opposed to focusing solely on the observable destruction of enemy forces, personnel (i.e. Body Count), industries or infrastructure.

If Marseille's total desert victories "only" reached 120-135 confirmed, as some research may indicate, and if some of his claims limped back to base, the tactical level effect achieved was the same. Whether an enemy plane crashed or escaped, that formation was still reduced by Marseille's actions. Marseille unwittingly achieved what we call today in operational planning, the desired "Measure of Effectiveness" (MOE). This cannot be denied. Allowing for his documented proclivity for using ridiculously small amounts of ammunition, it is highly likely some of his "victories" fall into this category.

His likely overclaims, however few, were not figments of his or his squadron's imagination. He was clearly hitting his opponents but perhaps while trusting too much in his superior marksmanship, he was not finishing them all off. This is likely to have occurred more during the last two months of his combat career. This in no way diminishes his desert accomplishments,

THE STAR OF AFRICA   363

and regardless of his final tally, Marseille was clearly the superior pilot operating in the North African skies from April 1941 through September 1942.

Hans-Arnold Stahlschmidt Victories
(Courtesy of Nick Hector)

Victory: Date/Time, Type, Location, Unit
  Pilot Details

1: 15.6.41/1140, Hurricane II, Sollum, No. 6 Sqn.
   F/L John Easton McFall, DOW
2-4: 20.11.41/1220, 3 x Maryland II, No. 21 Sqn, SAAF. AH305/E of Lt. E. S. Corbett and crew all KIA, AH409/# of Capt. J. H. Eccles POW, but crew all KIA (recorded as 1st and 2nd lost respectively). Plus AH387 of Lt. M. C. E. MacDonald and crew all safe except one man WIA.
5: 27.11.41/1620, Hurricane, S of El Adem
   Day's only fighter losses were Hurricane I of No. 260 Sqn, P/O J M Wylie and Tomahawk of No. 2 Sqn SAAF, Lt. D A Hinde safe (latter attributed to an MC200)
6: 14.12.41/1120, P-40 Tomahawk, S. of Tmimi, No. 3 Sqn RAAF.
   They lost F/O Donald Erskine Knight KIA in AN285 and Sgt. Derek Scott bailed out and POW in AN270 (Josef Unterberger claimed the other)
7: 11.1.42/1248, P-40 Kittyhawk, NE of Agedabia, No. 3 Sqn RAAF.
   F/O R S Jones and AK617 of Sgt. Allan Cecil "Tiny" Cameron DFM, DFC, POW (betrayed by Arabs) (Körner claimed the other)
8: 22.1.42/1250, P-40 Kittyhawk I, E. of Gtafia, No. 3 Sqn RAAF.
   Underclaiming—both F/O Eric Bradbury (returned from Saunna) in AK599 (attributed to Ju-87 gunner) and F/O James Andrew McIntosh (KIA) in AK736 went down.
9: 22.5.42/0750, P-40, Kittyhawk, SW of Tmimi, No. 112 & 250 Sqns.
   Down in flames, 112 lost AK682/GA-U of P/O Henry Knapik (PAF) and AK908 of F/O Felix Knoll (PAF) damaged but got home. No. 250 lost AL116/V of P/O Rogerson (crash landed) (claims by Steinhausen and von Lieres und Wilkau)
10: 29.5.42/0749, P-40 Kittyhawk, N. of Fort Acroma, No. 450 Sqn RAAF.
   3 losses. AK973 of Sgt. John Nicholson Dean, AK998/O of P/O Raymond Shaw and AL613 of Sgt Thomas Edwin Packer all KIA (Maack and Körner claimed the other two)
11: 13.6.42/0652, Hurricane II, Tobruk, No. 213 Sqn.
   Z3507 of P/O P P Wilson and BE340 of F/S. Dick Halvorsen (acknowledged victim of Körner) bailed out, WIA (3 claims by Körner)
12: 14.6.42/1108, P-40 Tomahawk, NNW of Gambut, No. 5 Sqn SAAF.
   Overclaiming, only two losses: AK533/Y of Lt. Van der Spuy bailed out WIA and AN345/V of Lt. Kemsley force landed (Körner claimed two)

13: 16.6.42/1525, P-40 Kittyhawk, SW of Gambut. This day's combats were very confusing. RAF and SAAF both suffered losses. Benefit of the doubt.
14-15: 26.6.42/1220 and 1227, 2 x Hurricanes, Mersa Matruh sector, Possibly No. 238 Sqn.
Sgt. Lawrence-Smith.
16: 26.6.42/1230, Curtiss P-40, W. of Marsa Matruh. Losses at this time likely from No. 450 Sqn RAAF, No. 3 Sqn RAAF and No. 112 Sqn. 112 Sqn lost ET526 of P/O B A. F. Cuddon bailed out and returned safely. No. 450 Sqn lost AL107 of F/O T E Jones KIA. No. 3 Sqn lost S/L A W "Nicky" Barr POW (Franzisket claimed one, Körner claimed 3)
17: 26.6.42/1906, Curtiss P-40, SSW of Marsa Matruh, Possibly No. 4 or 5 Sqn SAAF.
18: 27.6.42/1305, Curtiss P-40, 10km SE of Fuka, No. 260 Sqn. Overclaiming, no losses.
19: 2.7.42/0625, Beaufighter, into sea N. of Fuka, No. 252 Sqn. Either T4888 of F/L A. S. Malcolm and P/O K. Sharp both KIA or serial unknown of P/O Abdulgani Ydlibi and F/S E. W. Spiller both KIA (the other was claimed by an Italian pilot).
20: 2.7.42/1823, P-40 Kittyhawk, Burg el Arab, No. 2 Sqn SAAF.
41-36260/ET906 of Capt. J. O. De Waal KIA and AK941/K of Lt. Rupert Alan Durose force landed. AK970/C of Capt. H.E.N. Wildsmith was damaged Cat.I (Körner claimed two).
21-22: 3.7.42/1509, 1515, 2 x Hurricane IIs, El Alamein sector No. 213, Sqn. BM981 of F/L Cyril Bernard Temlett ("A" Flight Commander).
BN537 of WO2 John David Ritchie RCAF and BN597 of Sgt. Gordon Stuart Bolton RNZAF all KIA, BN541 of P/O K N R Sissons WIA (Körner and von Lieres und Wilkau claimed one each too)
23-24: 4.7.42/0630, 0632, 2 x P-40 Kittyhawks, El Alamein sector, No. 450 Sqn. Slight overclaiming, only one aircraft the other damaged.
25: 4.7.42/0825, Hurricane II, El Alamein, No. 213 Sqn.
BN368/Z of P/O Don Ross Rehill and BN349/B of P/O W. H. Tomlinson both KIA (not sure who or what claimed the other one. Need to check for Flak claims or Italian fighters).
26: 4.7.42/1705, Hurricane II, SW of Burg el Arab, BG971/V of No. 1 Sqn SAAF. Maj. Gerald John "Major Lemmie" Le Mesurier force landed WIA and BE200 of Lt. W.F. Powell force landed unhurt.
27: 7.7.42/0602, Gladiator, 10km NE of El Daba, P/O Ahmed Saudi Hussein. Egyptian pilot, either defecting or photographing British lines for the Germans.
28-30: 8.7.42/1032, 1035, 1040, 3 x Hurricane IICs, No. 33 Sqn.
Two actual losses plus one damaged: BP181 of P/O Robert Edwin Wigle RCAF KIA and BN116 of Sgt. David Arthur Morris KIA. The damaged one was BN359 of S/L D C Cloete safe (cat II damaged).
31-33: 10.7.42/1325, 1333, 1335, Hurricane IIs (claimed as P-40s), El Alamein sector No. 80, 92, or 127. Sqn. Losses include Sgt. Ralph Stuart Sykes of No. 80 Sqn KIA, P/O Wales of No. 92 Sqn shot down and WIA

and F/S Moulden of 127 was WIA with slightly damaged plane (von Lieres und Wilkau claimed one as well).

34: 11.7.42/1610, Curtiss P-40, SW of El Alamein, No. 2 and 5 Sqns SAAF. No. 2 Sqn lost ET1020(?)/B of Lt. Rupert Alan Durose KIA and ET912/H "Pinkie IV of Lt. L.C.H. Hope slightly damaged. 5 Sqn lost AK392 of Capt. K.R. Coster WIA-POW and AK382 of 2/Lt. Lionel William Rapp KIA whilst AK439 of Lt. Lindbergh WIA, AN451 of 2/Lt. Hinton WIA and AN394 of Maj. D V D Lacey DFC were all badly damaged. 2 Sqn also had ET530/G of Maj. J.D.W. Human force landed in Allied lines on the return flight (2 claims each by Steis and Schroer, one each by Boerngen and Vavra).

35: 14.7.42/1829, Spitfire, El Alamein, No. 92, 145 or 601 Sqn? Appears to be overclaiming.

36: 16.7.42/1015, Hurricane II, SE of El Alamein, crash landed W. of Hammam, Z5235/H of No. 127 Sqn. F/S W P Benedict (American) bailed out WIA.

37: 17.7.42/1325, Hurricane II, SW of El Alamein, No. 80 Sqn.
4 losses: BM984/Z of W/O Mitchell POW, BP121/L of Sgt. Ralph Harrison Groom KIA and BP511/A of Sgt. I.H.S. Watson POW (from No. 92 Sqn). BN542/E of F/L L Crocker (also from No. 92 Sqn) bailed out WIA. (Franzisket, Stigler, claimed one each, Sinner claimed two)

38-39: 22.7.42/0825, 0840, Curtiss P-40s, El Alamein sector ET790/GA ? of No. 112 Sqn.
P/O John Satterehwaite Barrow KIA (also claimed by Flak) Possibly also claimed against 4 Sqn SAAF, no losses.

40: 22.7.42/1200, Hurricane II, S. of El Alamein, No. 73 Sqn.
BN165 of F/S Albert Alexander Carcary RCAF KIA and BP220 of P/O Hall (returned later), plus one other damaged (Max Winkler claimed the other).

41: 27.7.42/1226, Hurricane II, SE of El Hammam @ 500m, No. 33 or 213, Sqn. No. 33.
Sqn lost BP199/C of Sgt. J D Leicester KIA and BN342 of P/O D W McLarty damaged, pilot safe. No. 213 Sqn lost BN359 of Sgt. J.D. Newick KIA, BP231 of P/O T A McCann KIA, BP197 of F/S R. Griffiths KIA and BN180 of W/O R.J. Wallace bailed out safely and Homuth claimed 3, Berben claimed 1.

42: 27.7.42/1730, Hurricane, SW of El Alamein, Z5606/E of No. 1, Sqn SAAF. Lt. S M Hope KIA.

43: 27.7.42/1742 or 1746, P-40 Kittyhawk, W. of El Alamein, AK805 of No. 450 sqn RAAF. P/O Thomas Jeffery Forsyth KIA (slight over-claiming: it was also claimed by Unterberger).

44-45: 1.8.42/1640, 1645, Hurricane II, W. of El Alamein, No. 80 Sqn.
Two losses: BP379 of P/O Robert Peter Atkins and BP235 of F/S Michael Paynter Reece RCAF WIA (DOW 10 days later). Both pilots on loan from No. 92 Sqn.

46-47: 16.8.42/0815, 0825, P-40 Tomahawk, El Hammam-El-Alamein sector, AN329 of No. 5 Sqn SAAF.
Lt. C. Trenchard POW plus ET522/W of No. 2 Sqn SAAF. Capt. R. Clifton bailed out WIA.

48: 23.8.42/0803, P-40E-1 Kittyhawk, S. of El Hammam, ET875 of No. 450 Sqn RAAF.
F/S R N.B. Stevens WIA.

49-50: 1.9.42/1748, 1750, Hurricane IIs, SE of El Alamein, No. 213 Sqn.
Possibly BP409 of F/O Richard Francis Wollaston KIA, BP499 of Sgt. F.G. Potter MIA-KIA, BP342 of F/O J.E. Avise or HL704 of F/S P.D. Ross crash landed both unhurt (Steinhausen claimed one and Marseille claimed four).

51: 2.9.42/1612, Hurricane (P-46), SW of El Hammam, No. 274 Sqn.
BG966/N of Sgt. F.A. Carter and BP667/P of Sgt. B. Ott (Stahlschmidt's victim seen to bellyland, the other was claimed by Marseille)

52-55: 3.9.42/0722, Curtiss P-40, SW of El Hammam, No. 260 Sqn.
FL226 of W/O Joseph Stanislas Emile M. Bernier KIA or No. 2 Sqn SAAF, ET900/T of Lt. Ryneke force landed safely (attributed to flak by SAAF sources). No. 4 Sqn SAAF and 64th and 57th FGs (American) also Involved. 3.9.42/0724 Spitfire SW of El Hammam AB349/V of No. 145 Sqn. Sgt. Mac A. Powers Jr. bailed out WIA. 3.9.42/0729 Curtiss P-40 SW of El Hammam No. 260 Sqn, FL226 of W/O Joseph Stanislas Emile M. Bernier KIA or No. 2 Sqn SAAF, ET900/T of Lt. Ryneke force landed safely (attributed to flak by SAAF sources). No. 4 Sqn SAAF and 64th and 57th FGs (American) also involved. 3.9.42/1512 Hurricane SW of Imayid No. 145 Sqn (Spitfires) or No. 33 and 213 Sqns (Hurricanes) Sgt. Anderson crash landed near El Kanabish. While No. 33 Sqn also lost F/SM.J. Belleau, bailed out.

56: 3.9.42/1526, Curtiss P-40, S. of Imayid, No. 7 Sqn SAAF.
4 losses: BP918 of Lt. A.W. Meikle (returned 5.9.42), Z5312 of Lt. W.B. Pearce (bailed out) and BE678 of Lt. B.W. Small (bailed out, POW). Lt. H.E. Kirkby crash landed and returned (Remmer and Marseille also claimed).

57: 5.9.42/1049, Spitfire, VC Trop SW of Imayid, No. 145, Sqn.
AB468 of Sgt. Stewart bailed out WIA in leg or either of AR286 of Sgt. Thomas (crash landed) or Sgt. Small. Thomas and Small both had their aircraft badly damaged.

58: 5.9.42/1052, Curtiss P-40 (P-46), SE of Imayid, No. 450 Sqn RAAF.
Sgt Oakley, badly damaged.

59: 6.9.42/1725, Curtiss P-40, SE of El Hammam, 8 x Kittyhawks of 260 Sqn, Mk IIB Tomahawks of No. 5 Sqn SAAF (including parts of 57th FG). No. 260 Sqn lost one aircraft and one damaged, No. 5 Sqn lost three with one damaged beyond repair. No. 7 Sqn SAAF lost 5 Hurricanes (Very confusing engagement).

Disposition of North Africa Western Desert Air Force Units

Bomber Units as of June 10, 1940

HQ 202 Group located at Ma'aten Bagush
No. 250 Wing RAF at Ismailia
No. 30 Squadron RAF at Ismailia
No. 55 Squadron RAF at Fuka
No. 113 Squadron RAF at Ma'aten Bagush
No. 253 Wing RAF, HQ at Ma'aten Bagush
No. 45 Squadron RAF at Fuka
No. 211 Squadron RAF at Daba
No. 70 (Bomber-Transport) Squadron RAF at Helwan
No. 216 (Bomber-Transport) Squadron RAF at Heliopolis

April 19, 1941 RAF No. 204 Group was created under the command of Air Commodore Raymond Collishaw and consisted of:

Bomber Units

No. 14 Squadron (Blenheim IVs and Marauders) at Burg el Arab
Detachment of No. 39 Squadron (Marylands) at Maaten Baggash
Detachment of No. 24 Squadron SAAF (Marylands) at Fuka
No. 45 Squadron (Blenheim IVs) at Fuka
No. 55 Squadron (Blenheim IVs) at Zimla
Fighter Units
No. 73 Squadron (Hurricanes) at Tobruk
No. 274 Squadron (Hurricanes) at Gerawla
No. 6 Squadron (Hurricanes and Lysanders) at Tobruk

From November 18, 1941 to 19 May 19, 1942 the A.H.Q. Western Desert was organized as:

A.H.Q. Western Desert – Maaten Bagush
Fighter Units
No. 30 Squadron (Hurricanes)
No. 33 Squadron (Hurricanes)
No. 80 Squadron (Hurricanes)
Bomber Units
No. 60 Squadron SAAF (Marylands)
No. 113 Squadron (Blenheim Fighter)
No. 223 Squadron (Marylands)
No. 272 Squadron (Beaufighter)
No. 805 Squadron FAA (Martlets)

No. 815 Squadron FAA (Swordfish and Albacores)
No. 826 Squadron FAA (Albacores)
261 Wing (Bombers)
No. 11 Squadron (Blenheims)
No. 12 Squadron SAAF (Marylands)
No. 21 Squadron SAAF (Marylands)
No. 24 Squadron SAAF (Bostons)
270 Wing (Bombers)
No. 8 Squadron (Blenheims)
No. 14 Squadron (Blenheims)
No. 45 Squadron (Blenheims)
No. 55 Squadron (Blenheims)
No. 84 Squadron (Blenheims)
French Squadron Lorraine (Blenheims)
253 Wing (Fighters)
No. 208 Squadron (Hurricanes)
No. 237 (Rhodesia) Squadron (Hurricanes)
No. 451 Squadron RAAF (Hurricanes)
258 Wing (Fighters)
No. 2 Squadron SAAF (Tomahawks)
No. 3 Squadron RAAF (Tomahawks)
No. 4 Squadron SAAF (Tomahawks)
No. 112 Squadron (Tomahawks)
No. 250 Squadron (Tomahawks)
RN Squadron (Marine Tomahawks)
262 Wing (Fighters)
No. 1 Squadron SAAF (Hurricanes)
No. 94 Squadron SAAF (Hurricanes)
No. 229 Squadron (Hurricanes)
No. 238 Squadron (Hurricanes)
No. 260 Squadron (Hurricanes)
No. 274 Squadron (Hurricanes)

Western Desert Air Force reorganization as of October 27, 1942 subordinated to General Headquarters RAF Middle East (GHQ RAF Middle East)

Bomber Units

No. 3 South African Air Force (SAAF) Bomber Wing
12 Squadron SAAF (24 × Martin Marylands)
21 Squadron SAAF (24 × Martin Baltimores I,II & III)
24 Squadron SAAF (24 × Douglas Boston III)
No. 232 Bomber Wing
No. 55 Squadron RAF (24 × Baltimores I, II & III)
No. 223 Squadron RAF (24 × Baltimores I, II & III)

82nd Bombardment Squadron USAAF (12 × Mitchell B-25C)
83rd Bombardment Squadron USAAF (12 × Mitchell B-25C)
434th Bombardment Squadron USAAF (12 × Mitchell B-25C)
No. 285 Reconnaissance Wing
No. 2 PRU Squadron RAF (Photo Reconnaissance) (Spitfire VB)
40 Squadron SAAF (Tactical Reconnaissance) (18 × Hurricane I/II/A/B)
60 Squadron SAAF (Photo Reconnaissance) (12 × Marylands)
No. 208 Squadron RAF (Tactical Reconnaissance) (18 × Hurricane IIA/B)
No. 1437 Flight RAF (Strategic Reconnaissance) (8 × Baltimores I, II & III)
No. 211 Group (Fighter Wings and Squadrons)
No. 7 Wing (Fighters)
No. 80 Squadron RAF (16 × Hurricane IIc)
No. 127 Squadron RAF (16 × Hurricane IIb)
No. 335 (Greek) Squadron RAF (16 × Hurricane IIb)
No. 274 Squadron RAF (16 × Hurricane IIb)
7 Squadron SAAF (anti-tank) (16 × Hurricane IID)
No. 6 Squadron RAF (anti-tank) (16 × Hurricane IID)
64th Fighter Squadron USAAF (25 × P-40F Warhawks)
65th Fighter Squadron USAAF (25 × P-40F Warhawks)
No. 233 Wing (Fighters)
2 Squadron SAAF (16 × Kittyhawks I, II & III)
4 Squadron SAAF (16 × Kittyhawks I, II & III)
5 Squadron SAAF (16 × Tomahawks)
No. 260 Squadron RAF (16 × Kittyhawks I & IIb)
No. 239 Wing (Fighters)
No. 3 Squadron RAAF (16 × Kittyhawk I, II & III)
No. 112 Squadron RAF (16 × Kittyhawk IA)
No. 250 Squadron RAF (16 × Kittyhawk IIA)
No. 450 Squadron RAAF (16 × Kittyhawk)
66th Fighter Squadron USAAF (25 × P-40F Warhawks)
No. 244 Wing (Fighters)
No. 145 Squadron RAF (16 × Spitfires Vb)
No. 601 Squadron RAF (16 × Spitfires Vb)
No. 73 Squadron RAF (16 × Hurricane IIc)
No. 92 Squadron RAF (16 × Spitfires Vb/c)
No. 212 Group (Fighters)
No. 243 Wing units:
1 Squadron SAAF (16 × Hurricane IIc)
No. 33 Squadron RAF (16 × Hurricane IIc)
No. 213 Squadron RAF (16 × Hurricane IIc)
No. 238 Squadron RAF (16 × Hurricane IIc)
  Early in 1943 that squadron was renamed No. 462 Squadron RAAF (note Australian) despite mainly British personnel.
57th Fighter Group USAAF (American)
64th, 65th, and 66th Fighter Squadrons with P-40F Warhawks detached to RAF
12th Bombardment Group USAAF

82nd, 83rd, and 434th Bombardment Squadrons with B-25C Mitchells detached to RAF
81st Bombardment Squadron (not detached to RAF)
Air Ambulance Squadron
835th Aviation Engineer Battalion
No. 211 Group (Spitfires)
Fighter Wings and Subordinate Squadrons Including No. 244, 322, and 324 Wings
1 Squadron SAAF, No. 81 Squadron, No. 72 Squadron (RAF)
No. 92 Squadron (RAF), No. 154 Squadron (RAF), No. 93 Squadron (RAF)
No. 417 Squadron (RCAF), No. 232 Squadron (RAF), No. 111 Squadron (RAF)
No. 601 Squadron (RAF), No. 242 Squadron (RAF), No. 152 Squadron (RAF)
No. 145 Squadron (RAF), Polish Fighting Team P.F.T. (Flight "C" "Skalski Circus"), No. 43 Squadron (RAF), No. 243 Squadron (RAF)
40 Tactical Reconnaissance Squadron, SAAF (Spitfires)
1/2 No. 600 Squadron (TEF/N) operating on Malta under A.O.C. Malta (Beaufighters)
No. 325 Wing RAF (Beaufighters)
1/2 No. 600 Squadron
No. 153 Squadron (TEF/N) operating from North Africa
Rear Headquarters, Desert Air Force Operating from Tripoli Area Command
No. 239 Wing RAF (Kittyhawks), 57th Fighter Group USAAF (P-40s), 79th Fighter Group USAAF (P-40s)
No. 3 Squadron RAAF, 64th Squadron, 85th Squadron
No. 112 Squadron RAF, 65th Squadron, 86th Squadron
No. 450 Squadron RAAF, 66th Squadron, 87th Squadron
No. 250 Squadron RAF
No. 260 Squadron RAF
No. 285 Wing RAF (Reconnaissance)
No. 1437 Flight RAF (SR) (Baltimores)
60 Squadron SAAF
No. 682 Squadron RAF
(60 and 682 were Photographic Reconnaissance (PR) squadrons assigned from the Northwest African Photographic Reconnaissance Wing)
Supplemental RAF units
No. 6 Squadron (TD) (Hurricane IIDs) and No. 249 Air Transport Wing

BIBLIOGRAPHY

Alexander, Kristen. *Clive Caldwell: Air Ace*. Crows Nest, Australia: Allen & Unwin, 2006.

Brown, Russell. *Desert Warriors: Australian P-40 Pilots at War in the Middle East and North Africa, 1941–1943*. Maryborough, Queensland, Australia: Banner Books, 2000.

Clade, Emil. *Glück gehabt. Ein deutscher Jagdflieger berichtet*. Self-published, ca. 1996.

Die Wehrmachtberichte 1939–1945 Band 1, 1. September 1939 bis 31. Dezember 1941. München: *Deutscher Taschenbuch* Verlag GmbH & Co. KG. 1985.

Fellgiebel, Walther-Peer. *Die Träger des Ritterkreuzes des Eisernen Kreuzes 1939–1945*. Friedburg, Germany: Podzun-Pallas, 2000.

Guttman, Jon. "One-Oh-Nine: Messerschmitt's Killing Machine," *World War II*, ISSN 0898-4204 (May 1999), pp. 38–46.

Heaton, Colin D., and Anne-Marie Lewis. *The German Aces Speak: World War II Through the Eyes of Four of the Luftwaffe's Most Important Commanders*. Minneapolis, MN, Zenith Press, 2011.

———. *The German Aces Speak: World War II Through the Eyes of Four More of the Luftwaffe's Most Important Commanders*. Minneapolis, MN, Zenith Press, 2014.

Kurowski, Franz. *German Fighter Ace: Hans-Joachim Marseille: Star of Africa*. Atglen, Pennsylvania: Schiffer Military History, 1994.

Makos, Adam and Larry Alexander. *A Higher Call: An Incredible True Story of Combat and Chivalry in the War-Torn Skies of World War II*. Dutton Caliber; Illustrated edition, May 6, 2014.

Morley-Mower, Geoffrey. "Luftwaffe Ace's Act of Chivalry," *World War II*, ISSN 0898-4204, Primedia Publications (January 1999), pp. 38–44.

Musciano, Walter. "Killer Caldwell: Australia's Ace of Aces." *Air Progress*, Volume 19, No. 3, September 1966.

Odgers, George. *The Royal Australian Air Force: An Illustrated History*. Brookvale, Australia: Child & Henry, 1984.

Patzwall, Klaus D., and Veit Scherzer. *Das Deutsche Kreuz 1941– 1945 Geschichte und Inhaber Band II*. Norderstedt, Germany: Verlag Klaus D. Patzwall, 2001.

Pentland, Geoffrey. *The P-40 Kittyhawk in Service*. Melbourne, Victoria, Australia: Kookaburra Technical Publications Pty. Ltd., 1974.

Prien, Jochen, Peter Rodeike, and Gerhard Stemmer. *Messerschmitt Bf 109 im Einsatz bei Stab und I./Jagdgeschwader 27 1939– 1945*. Struve- Druck, Eutin, 1998.

Scherzer, Veit. *Ritterkreuzträger 1939–1945 Die Inhaber des Ritterkreuzes des Eisernen Kreuzes 1939 von Heer, Luftwaffe, Kriegsmarine, Waffen-SS, Volkssturm sowie mit Deutschland verbündeter Streitkräfte nach den Unterlagen des Bundesarchives*. Jena, Germany: Scherzers Miltär-Verlag, 2007.

Scutts, Jerry. *Bf 109 Aces of North Africa and the Mediterranean*. London: Osprey Publishing, 1994.

Shores, Christopher. *A History of the Mediterranean Air War, 1940–1945: Tunisia and the End in Africa, November 1942–1943*. Grub Street Publishing, August 5, 2016.

_____. *Aces High, Volume 2: A Further Tribute to the Most Notable Fighter Pilots of the British and Commonwealth Air Forces in WWII*. Grub Street Publishing, July 15, 2008.

Shores, Christopher and Clive Williams. *Aces High: Volume 1: A Tribute to the Most Notable Fighter Pilots of the British and Commonwealth Forces of WWII*. Grub Street Publishing; 1st edition, September 18, 2008.

Spick, Mike. *Luftwaffe Fighter Aces*. New York: Ivy Books, 1996.

Stephens, Alan. The Royal Australian Air Force: A History. London: Oxford University Press, 2006.

Tate, Robert: *Hans-Joachim Marseille: An Illustrated Tribute to the Luftwaffe"s Star of Africa*. Atglen, PA: Schiffer Publishing, 2008.

Watson, Jeffrey. *Killer Caldwell*. Sydney, Australia: Hodder, 2005.

Weal, John. *Jagdgeschwader 27 'Afrika.'* London: Osprey Publishing, 2003.

Wilkinson, Stephen. "The Star of Africa," *Aviation History*. Leesburg, VA: Weider History Group (November 2008), pp. 24–31. ISSN 1076-8858.

Index

115th *Panzergrenadier* Regiment, 322

15th Panzer Division, 110

15th Panzer Divisions, 99

2./JG-27, 45

20mm cannon, 54, 68, 77, 149, 169, 190, 192, 209, 263, 314

21st Panzer Division, 110

3./JG-27, 112, 193, 357

31st Fighter Group USAAC, 231

4./JG-27, 99, 100, 101

4./JG-52, 33, 40, 353

5./JG-27, 89, 357

57th Fighter Group USAAC, 245, 263, 277, 279, 369, 370

64th Fighter Squadron USAAC, 279, 369

7./JG-27, 45

Abu Dweis, 318

Afrika Korps, 45, 56, 125, 129, 258, 298, 299

Alam Halfa, 262, 276, 359

Alexandria, Egypt, 334

Altendorf, Oberleutnant, 112

Annoni, Emanuele, 299

Athens, 130, 132, 134, 135, 136, 139, 355

Augsburg, Germany, 53, 227

Auschwitz, 224

Axmann, Artur, xiv, 1, 8, 217, 218, 222, 339, 386

B-24, 229

Bardia, Libya, 99, 101, 358

Barnes, L.E., 258

Battle of Britain, 24, 53, 101, 177, 313

Baur, Hans, xiv, 107, 137, 168, 214, 217, 219, 221, 222, 223, 339, 341

Bay of Sollum, 99

Bayerlein, Fritz, 88, 89

Bee, Ken, 294

Bendert, Karl-Heinz, 232, 233, 234, 236, 244, 248

Benghazi, Libya, 45, 47, 138, 139, 213, 238, 239, 240, 334

Berlin, Germany, iii, ix, xiii, 1, 2, 3, 5, 10, 61, 74, 91, 135, 136, 137, 138, 139, 149, 152, 156, 167, 168, 210, 212, 213, 217, 219, 220, 223, 224, 228, 238, 255, 271, 272, 273, 274, 300, 312, 316, 317, 329, 353, 355

Berrangé, Leonard James Peter, 195

Bick, Dr., 322

Bir el Gubi, 165, 358

Bir Hacheim, 165, 179, 187, 191, 195, 359

Bir Sheferzan, 104, 358

Blenheim bomber, 61, 128, 148, 356, 358, 367

Boden, Werner, 335

Bofors anti-aircraft gun, 13, 14

Bomba Bay, 45, 149, 358

Botha, Louis C., 191

Bradley, Omar, 299

Braune, Erhard, 120

Braunschweig, Germany, 22

Briggs, P. J., 159

Bucharest, Romania, 44

Buckland, Graham George, ii, iii, iv, v, vi, 180, 181, 182

Buhl, Adolf, 29

Bühligen, Kurt, xiv, 20, 22, 341, 386

Bülowius, Alfred, 32

Burger, Wolfgang, 335

Byers, Patrick, 12, 101

Calais-Marck, France, 24, 356

Caldwell, Clive, 98, 111, 124, 126, 132, 160, 371

Canham, Flight Lieutenant, 277, 278

Canty, M.A., 120, 121

Carman, E. H. O., 276

Carstensen, Cay, 335

Castel Benito, 45, 354

Castelnau, Sergeant, 49

Channel Coast, 22, 43, 44, 53, 353

Chinchen, Geoff, 172

Ciano, Gian Galeazzo, 167

Clade, Emil, xiv, 80, 89, 105, 131, 142, 172, 196, 204, 230, 232, 235, 240, 333, 336

Crete, Greece, 44, 50, 54, 135, 168, 176

Cundy, Ronald, 246

Curtis P-40
Warhawk/Tomahawk/Kittyhawk, 11, 68, 100, 104, 105, 106, 108, 113, 117, 118, 119, 120, 147, 148, 149, 158, 159, 160, 168, 169, 170, 173, 174, 175, 177, 178, 179, 180, 181, 185, 186, 188, 189, 191, 194, 195, 196, 197, 198, 199, 201, 206, 208, 212, 233, 234, 243, 244, 245, 247, 248, 263, 264, 265, 266, 274, 275, 276, 279, 280, 292, 294, 330, 356, 358, 359, 360, 363, 364, 365, 366, 371, 372

Cyrenaica, Libya, 133

Daimler-Benz engine, 54

Davies, Hugh, 13

Deir el Raghat, 268, 359

Denham, R. C., 206

Derna, Libya, 12, 14, 45, 47, 87, 110, 120, 128, 129, 130, 138, 148, 236, 321, 326, 333, 355, 358

Diamonds (awards), 91, 217, 271, 272, 273, 276, 284, 296, 300, 303, 311, 312, 317, 337, 353, 355, 356

Douglas Boston bombers, 117

Dover, England, 29, 357

Driver, Kenneth, 71, 133

Eastern Front, x, 44, 53, 100, 116, 137, 193, 216, 227, 289, 296

Eder, Georg-Peter, 78, 289

Edwards, James, 126, 212, 281

Eighth Army (UK), 235, 276

El Adem, Libya, 116, 118, 123, 180, 195, 200, 201, 205, 206, 228, 358, 359, 363

El Alamein, 229, 233, 235, 242, 244, 245, 246, 247, 279, 281, 282, 359, 360, 364, 365, 366

El Daba, Egypt, 200, 230, 232, 245, 304, 360, 364

El Hammam, Algeria, 232, 233, 234, 242, 243, 244, 246, 247, 248, 305, 365, 366

El Imayid, Egypt, 244, 258, 268, 274, 291, 318, 359, 360

El Taqua, Egypt, 260, 278, 359, 360

Elles, Franz, xiv, 336, 338

Elwell, George Walton, 149

En Nofilia, Libya, 46

English Channel, 30

Espenlaub, Albert, 49, 111, 123

Ewald, Wolfgang, 336

Final Solution, 224

Förster, Hermann, 124

Fort Acroma, 159, 358, 359, 363

Franzisket, Ludwig, xiv, 9, 49, 50, 57, 62, 63, 70, 71, 72, 73, 75, 79, 84, 86, 87, 90, 93, 95, 96, 103, 106, 118, 124, 129, 130, 131, 133, 134, 135, 138, 139, 142, 145, 152, 166, 168, 178, 180, 181, 184, 185, 204, 211, 224, 238, 239, 240, 241, 253, 254, 256, 258, 265, 267, 272, 273, 274, 285, 288,

293, 295, 297, 298, 299, 300, 310, 312, 315, 317, 320, 321, 322, 323, 325, 326, 335, 353, 364, 365, 386

Free Polish Brigade, 165

Fw-190, 78

G-50, 100

Gadd el Ahmar, 186

Galland, Adolf, viii, xi, xiv, 8, 16, 40, 41, 43, 85, 89, 90, 91, 101, 127, 167, 171, 183, 212, 216, 217, 227, 237, 256, 271, 273, 284, 313, 314, 335, 337, 356, 386

Gambut Airfield, 116, 158, 159, 191, 355, 358, 359, 363, 364

Gazala, Libya, 10, 45, 46, 47, 52, 70, 71, 74, 111, 112, 116, 129, 174, 179, 201, 207, 230, 354, 355, 358, 359

Gerlitz, Erich, 44, 117, 119, 164, 171, 176

German Cross, 112, 337, 353, 355

Göbbels, Josef, 7, 137, 214, 215, 217, 218, 219, 220, 221, 222, 224, 284, 311, 316

Göbbels, Magda, 217

Göring, Hermann, 95, 137

Got el Bersis, Libya, 130, 131

Halfaya Pass, 69, 75

Hanbury, Osgood, 170

Hancock, A. J., 195, 199

Hawker Hurricane, 12, 13, 25, 26, 27, 29, 48, 49, 58, 60, 62, 68, 70, 71, 73, 74, 75, 76, 77, 100, 101, 102, 103, 107, 115, 117, 128, 142, 146, 147, 148, 149, 154, 156, 157, 168, 169, 172, 185, 195, 199, 200, 201, 231, 232, 233, 234, 243, 244, 248, 258, 261, 262, 269, 275, 278, 280, 281, 288, 291, 293, 295, 297, 304, 314, 353, 357, 358, 359, 360, 363, 364, 365, 366, 369, 370

He-111, 24

He-59, 28

Hess, Rudolf, 137

Heydrich, Reinhard, 138, 224

Hickam Field, 116

Himmler, Heinrich, 8, 10, 137, 138, 221, 222, 224

Hitler Youth, 2, 3, 217, 218, 339

Hitler, Adolf, 2, 7, 107, 163, 193, 212, 214, 337, 355

Hoffmann, Friedrich, 72, 75, 99, 100, 220, 292, 335, 357

Homuth, Gerhard, 42, 44, 45, 46, 47, 62, 71, 93, 95, 96, 97, 100, 102, 112, 118, 124, 130, 131, 137, 139, 140, 141, 142, 143, 144, 145, 146, 148, 149, 150, 151, 152, 153, 154, 155, 156, 158, 159, 160, 163, 165, 170, 171, 173, 179, 181, 191, 193, 194, 195, 203, 207, 208, 210, 211, 212, 214, 231, 233, 257, 280, 282, 296, 297, 298, 304, 325, 340, 365

Höss, Rudolf Franz Ferdinand, 224

I./JG-27, 44, 45, 99, 100, 101, 102, 104, 106, 108, 110, 111, 112, 118, 128, 130, 133, 139, 145, 147, 148, 150, 157, 158, 159, 170, 171, 184, 187, 193, 205, 206, 207, 231, 260, 277, 278, 280, 281, 282, 289, 305, 318, 330, 353, 354, 357, 358, 359, 360

I./JG-53, 62

Ihlefeld, Herbert, xii, xiv, 25, 26, 27, 28, 29, 30, 31, 32, 33, 34, 39, 85, 95, 96, 386

II./JG-27, 41, 42, 99, 106, 107, 110, 111, 115, 142, 168, 169, 176, 187, 230, 234, 235, 243, 244, 245, 247, 279, 280

III./JG-26, 116

III./JG-27, 116, 120, 168, 229, 261, 318

III./JG-53, 63, 112, 114, 120, 176, 179, 184, 187, 190, 195, 260, 279, 317, 318

III./ZG-76, 62

Iron Cross, 27, 37, 112, 163, 193, 215, 336, 353, 355

Jagdfliegerschule 5, 19, 23

JG-26, 63, 101, 313

JG-27, 9, 15, 21, 40, 43, 44, 53, 56, 57, 59, 60, 62, 63, 67, 69, 70, 71, 72, 77, 90, 97, 98, 100, 101, 104, 107, 108, 111, 116, 117, 120, 123, 125, 127, 129, 132, 133, 137, 138, 140, 158, 168, 170, 176, 179, 184, 186, 187, 193, 195, 198, 199, 206, 216, 228, 229, 231, 236, 249, 258, 261, 268, 270, 276, 278, 280, 281, 283, 289, 291, 297, 299, 301, 313, 314, 317, 318, 324, 326, 327, 330, 333, 334, 335, 336, 338

JG-51, 193

JG-52, 27, 36, 95, 296, 353, 354

JG-77, 62, 63, 296, 336

Ju-52, 91, 95, 135, 212, 217, 238

Ju-87, 24, 56, 75, 170, 185, 187, 363

Ju-88, 24, 102, 158

Keller, Fritz, 148, 336

Kent, UK, 25, 27, 357

Keppler, Feldwebel, 165, 279

Kesselring, Albert, 144, 163, 193, 210, 212, 236, 256, 271, 272, 276, 284, 302, 315, 316, 317, 326, 355, 356

KLG-1, 263

Knight's Cross, 10, 22, 25, 27, 41, 54, 57, 63, 95, 100, 112, 120, 128, 133, 148, 153, 158, 160, 163, 165, 193, 212, 227, 231, 250, 258, 272, 276, 283, 303, 316, 323, 337, 338, 353, 356

Knightsbridge War Cemetery, 174, 182, 200

Körner, Friedrich, xiv, 67, 146, 149, 206, 230, 335, 336

Kugelbaur, Karl, 102, 103, 106, 254, 255, 261, 335

Kuhlmey, Kurt, xiv, 57, 59, 75, 113, 114, 115, 116, 127, 156, 184, 186, 187, 188, 190, 194, 200, 255, 263, 268, 274, 287, 302, 305, 306, 318, 324, 338, 340, 341

Küpper, Hannelies, 167, 355

Kurowski, Franz, xii, 14, 59, 83, 287, 322, 326, 371, 386

Leander, Zarah Stina Hedberg, 240, 242

Letuku, Matthew "Mathias", 9, 16, 17, 253, 254, 255, 256, 257, 258, 259, 262, 266, 267, 268, 270, 272, 273, 274, 282, 284, 285, 286, 288, 295, 296, 309, 310, 311, 312, 321, 322, 323, 324, 325, 326, 336, 340

Lindbergh, J., 276, 365

Lippert, Wolfgang, 99, 100, 335

London, UK, 27, 29, 344, 357, 372

Lufbery Formation, 43, 75, 79, 80, 81, 98, 102, 103, 132, 189, 192, 194, 206, 208, 258, 264, 280, 292, 293, 294, 304

Marseille Memorial, 336

Marseille, Charlotte, x, 1

Marseille, Ingeborg, 137

Marseille, Siegfried, x, 1

Martin Maryland, 71, 102, 356

Martuba Air Base, 124, 138, 146, 155, 157, 160, 171, 172, 176, 179, 354, 355, 358

MC.202, 195

Me-109, 14, 27, 54, 60, 68, 73, 74, 104, 107, 111, 145, 157, 169, 176, 180, 184, 187, 189, 194, 198, 212, 236, 246, 265, 281, 307, 308, 355

Me-110, 24, 62

Mediterranean Sea, 56, 130, 231, 233, 372

Mentnich, Leutnant, 77, 179, 185

Mersa, Egypt, 97, 249, 364

Merseburg, Germany, 21, 22, 354

Messerschmitt, Willi, xiii, 221, 311, 314

MG 151, 198

MG 17, 198

Milch, Erhard, 212, 221, 222, 223, 284

Müncheberg, Joachim, 45, 63, 64, 67, 193, 304, 318, 356

Musaid, Libya, 69

Mussolini, Benito, 43, 167, 223, 237, 238, 239, 240, 284, 300, 301, 336, 355, 356

Naples, Italy, 132, 213, 223

Neumann, Eduard, vi, xi, xii, xiv, 12, 15, 39, 40, 41, 44, 45, 47, 49, 53, 72, 74, 76, 80, 83, 84, 85, 86, 88, 91, 92, 93, 96, 97, 100, 101, 104, 108, 109, 110, 112, 114, 115, 123, 124, 125, 130, 131, 132, 133, 134, 136, 139, 140, 141, 143, 144, 145, 146, 147, 148, 150, 151, 152, 153, 154, 155, 156, 157, 158, 163, 167, 168, 170, 171, 178, 181, 187, 190, 193, 203, 204, 205, 207, 210, 211, 212, 216, 224, 236, 237, 238, 239, 247, 249, 250, 254, 256, 258, 259, 263, 266, 267, 268, 270, 271, 272, 273, 274, 282, 283, 284, 285, 286, 287, 288, 295, 297, 298, 305, 307, 308, 309, 310,

312, 315, 316, 318, 319, 320, 321, 323, 324, 325, 326, 327, 330, 333, 335, 336, 337, 341, 342

No. 1 Squadron SAAF, 98, 102, 104, 113, 124, 128, 156, 230, 242, 243, 258, 261, 368

No. 112 Squadron RAF, 102, 104, 148, 154, 160, 186, 200, 208, 278, 294, 369, 370

No. 112 Squadron RNZAF (Royal New Zealand Air Force), 292

No. 127 Squadron RAF, 277, 365, 369

No. 145 Squadron RAF, 231, 232, 277, 278, 369, 370

No. 2 Squadron SAAF, 104, 119, 142, 170, 195, 243, 244, 247, 274, 278, 368

No. 203 Squadron RAF, 102

No. 204 Group RAF, 204, 367

No. 213 Squadron RAF, 195, 232, 233, 268, 291, 369

No. 216 Squadron RAF, 112, 235

No. 223 Squadron RAF, 179, 367, 368

No. 229 Squadron RAF, 77, 368

No. 238 Squadron RAF, 261, 262, 368, 369

No. 24 Squadron SAAF, 100, 101, 367, 368

No. 250 Squadron RAF, 98, 113, 120, 152, 165, 170, 180, 181, 206, 293, 294, 368, 369, 370

No. 260 Squadron RAF, 126, 170, 212, 245, 246, 275, 277, 278, 279, 280, 368, 369, 370

No. 274 Squadron RAF, 113, 116, 117, 145, 154, 156, 200, 212, 369

No. 274 Squadron SAAF, 62

No. 3 Squadron, 102, 104, 118, 148, 158, 160, 165, 172, 174, 292, 294, 368, 369, 370

No. 3 Squadron RAF, 158, 159

No. 3 Squadron SAAF, 118, 124, 160

No. 310 Squadron RAF, 27

No. 33 Squadron RAF, 99, 101, 276, 291, 369

No. 4 Squadron SAAF, 242, 244, 245, 368

No. 40 Squadron SAAF, 172

No. 45 Squadron RAF, 61, 367

No. 450 Squadron RAAF, 175, 176, 180, 201, 278, 294, 369, 370

No. 451 Squadron, 12, 101, 368

No. 5 Squadron SAAF, 184, 187, 206, 232, 247, 276, 280, 282

No. 601 Squadron RAF, 283, 369, 370

No. 7 Squadron SAAF, 280

No. 73 Squadron RAF, 49, 59, 148, 149, 206, 207, 208, 369

No. 92 Squadron RAF, 261, 304, 369

Oak Leaves and Swords, 10, 25, 54, 63, 153, 212, 217, 227, 239, 258, 312, 316, 323, 337, 355

Operation Barbarossa, 44, 53

Operation Battleaxe, 69

Operation Crusader, 117

Operation Reinhard, 224

Operation Tigercub, 69

P-38, 63

Pearl Harbor, 116

Pöttgen, Reiner, 52, 57, 97, 209, 325

Prien, Heinrich, 292, 335, 372

Propaganda Ministry, 2, 217, 273

Quotaifiya, 230, 282, 309, 355

RAAF (Royal Australian Air Force), iv, 68, 101, 102, 104, 148, 165, 172, 174, 175, 176, 179, 180, 201, 208, 278, 292, 294, 363, 364, 365, 366, 368, 369, 370

Rall, Günther, viii, xi, xiv, 54, 337

Redlich, Karl-Heinz, 44, 45, 47, 72, 100, 108, 111

Reich Labor Service, 5

Remmer, Hans, 116, 201, 234, 278, 366

Riefenstahl, Leni, xiv, 213, 218, 340

Rödel, Gustav, xiv, 41, 49, 51, 53, 81, 85, 99, 100, 124, 132, 142, 171, 226, 231, 236, 237, 256, 302, 325, 335, 336

Rome, Italy, ii, 130, 134, 167, 213, 223, 237, 238, 239, 355, 356

Rommel, Erwin, 45, 56, 88, 89, 110, 117, 138, 179, 227, 229, 238, 257, 272, 276, 284, 298, 299, 300, 301, 302, 303, 312, 353

Sahara Desert, 108

Sawallisch, Erwin, 232, 233, 234, 236, 237, 242, 244, 245, 248, 249, 250, 255, 335

Schlang, Jost, 261, 262, 265, 269, 272, 299, 304, 305, 306, 307, 308, 309, 319, 320, 321, 324, 325

Schneider, Bernd, 72, 118, 235

Schroer, Werner, xiv, 6, 7, 11, 15, 19, 20, 21, 22, 41, 42, 47, 48, 52, 57, 60, 64, 72, 78, 84, 85, 90, 93, 97, 98, 100, 106, 110, 111, 124, 125, 132, 133, 139, 142, 143, 147, 150, 153, 155, 163, 167, 196, 203, 204, 205, 224, 225, 229, 231, 240, 253, 254, 256, 259, 270, 272, 284, 286, 288, 289, 291, 295, 296, 299, 301, 302, 309, 310, 312, 318, 319, 320, 321, 334, 365, 386

Schulz, Otto, 99, 112, 116, 142, 149, 158, 163, 212, 281, 304

Schwechat, Austria, 19, 33

Scorpion Airfield, 46

Sidi Barrani, Egypt, 97, 230, 355, 358

Sidi Omar, Libya, 69, 358

Sidi Rezegh, 212

Sippel, Hans, 47, 48

Spitfire, 29, 30, 53, 54, 68, 168, 169, 208, 209, 230, 232, 233, 246, 258, 261, 262, 275, 277, 278, 280, 289, 304, 305, 306, 307, 308, 309, 312, 318, 353, 357, 359, 360, 365, 366, 369

Stab/LG-1, 24

Stahlschmidt, Hans-Arnold "Fifi", 52, 62, 64, 72, 83, 85, 97, 160, 163, 165, 166, 167, 179, 231, 240, 247, 248, 249, 250, 256, 272, 275, 277, 278, 281, 282, 283, 284, 285, 287, 296, 298, 311, 334, 366

Steinhausen, Günther, 97, 100, 170, 179, 185, 228, 231, 256, 272, 278, 279, 281, 283, 284, 285, 311, 334, 363, 366

Steinhoff, Johannes "Macky", xi, xii, xiv, 27, 28, 33, 34, 35, 39, 40, 41, 63, 85, 93, 95, 97, 289, 335, 337, 353

StG-2, 335

StG-3, 57, 113, 115, 138, 169, 187, 287, 289, 317

Stigler, Franz, xiv, 15, 123, 234, 235, 236, 237, 242, 243, 244, 248, 249, 250, 253, 289, 338, 365, 386

Strait of Gibraltar, 56

Supermarine Spitfire, 27

Tangerding, Hermann, 120, 335

Tmimi, Libya, 112, 116, 119, 120, 129, 230, 354, 355, 358, 363

Tobruk, Lubya, 9, 45, 56, 57, 58, 59, 61, 62, 73, 98, 102, 116, 117, 121, 142, 156, 165, 179, 180, 200, 207, 229, 249, 254, 333, 334, 353, 357, 358, 363, 367

Transvaal, 9, 288

Treblinka, 224

Tripoli, Libya, 44, 354, 370

Vickers Wellington, 47

Vienna, Austria, 19, 137, 138

Vögl, Ferdinand, 234, 236, 243, 248

von Below, Nicolaus, 137, 214, 216, 223

von Kageneck, Erbo Graf, 116, 120, 132

von Lieres und Wilkau, Karl, 170, 279, 282, 283, 363, 364, 365

Western Allies, 24, 126, 208, 335

Western Front, 53

Woldenga, Bernhard, xiv, 45, 63, 72, 93, 120, 124, 125, 130, 131, 132, 136, 140, 141, 144, 150, 151, 152, 153, 154, 155, 163, 166, 170, 171, 337, 341

Wolff, Karl, xiv, 10, 138, 221, 224, 339

ZG-26, 335

About the Author

COLIN D. HEATON earned BA and MA degrees in history as well as an MPhil degree in Europeans Studies, and he has taught history, academic writing, military history, and sociology in various universities. He has been interviewing military veterans, pilots in particular, for three decades. He has published 11 books in five languages and over 30 articles, many derived from his interviews. His articles have appeared in periodicals such as *Military History, Aviation History, World War II,* and *Vietnam Magazine.*

Notes

[1] The equivalent of an American high school, only far more academically rigorous.

[2] Lothar Löwe interview 1999.

[3] Ibid.

[4] Interview with Werner Schroer, 1984.

[5] Ibid.

[6] Artur Axmann interviews, 1984-85.

[7] Ludwig Franzisket interviews, 1984-85.

[8] Schroer interview.

[9] Franz Kurowski, *German Fighter Ace Hans-Joachim Marseille: The Life Story of the Star of Africa* (Schiffer Publishing, Ltd., Atglen, PA, 1994) pp. 19–20.

[10] Interviews with Geoffrey Morley-Mower 1989-90.

[11] Interview with Franz Stigler, 1998.

[12] Galland interview, see *The German Aces Speak*, vol 1, p, 101.

[13] Schroer interview, See also Kurowski, p. 14.

[14] Ibid.

[15] Ibid.

[16] Kurt Bühligen interview, 1984.

[17] Herbert Ihlefeld interview 1984

[18] Kurowski, p. 16

[19] Ibid.

[20] Herbert Ihlefeld interview 1984.

[21] Ibid.

[22] Ibid.

[23] Ibid.

[24] Ibid.

[25] Ibid.

[26] Ibid.

[27] Johannes Steinhoff interview 1984. See full interview in Colin D. Heaton and Anne Marie Lewis, *The German Aces Speak: WW II Through the Eyes of Four More of the Luftwaffe's Most Important Commanders* (Minneapolis, MN: Zenith Press, 2014), pp. 140–48.

[28] Ibid.

[29] Ibid.

[30] Ibid.

[31] Ibid.

[32] Walter Krupinski interview.

[33] Gustav Rödel interview 1984.

[34] Schroer interview 1984.

[35] Kurowski, p. 34. Neumann mentioned this event as did a few other JG-27 pilots.

[36] Ibid., pp. 34–35.

[37] Schroer interview 1984.

[38] Kurowski, p. 33.

[39] Franzisket interview 1984.

[40] Ibid.

[41] Ibid.

[42] Rödel interview, 1985.

[43] Schroer interview 1984.

[44] Rödel interview, 1985.

[45] Ibid.

[46] Josef Kammhuber interview 1984.

[47] Günther Rall interviews, 1984-2009.

[48] Kurt Kuhlmey interviews 1984-85.

[49] Kurowski, p. 51.

[50] Kurt Kuhlmey interviews 1984-85.

[51] Kurowski, p. 51.

[52] Robert Tate, *Hans-Joachim Marseille: An Illustrated Tribute to the Luftwaffe's "Star of Africa"* (Atglen, PA: Schiffer Publishing Ltd.; 1st edition July 28, 2008) p. 99.

[53] Schroer interview.

[54] Tate, p. 59.

[55] Franzisket interviews.

[56] Ibid.

[57] Schroer interview.

[58] Rödel interview, 1985.

[59] Kurowski, pp. 61–62.

[60] Franzisket interview.

[61] Bernhard Woldenga interview 1985.

62 Franzisket interviews

63 Kurowski, p. 74

64 Kulmey interview.

65 Schroer interview.

66 Georg-Peter Eder interview 1984.

67 Franzisket interview.

68 Emil Clade interview 1984.

69 Rödel interview.

70 Kurowski, pp. 68–70.

71 Franzisket interview

72 Kurowski, p. 72.

73 Schroer interview.

74 Kurowski, p. 64.

75 Franzisket interview.

76 Kurowski, p. 73.

77 Franzisket interview.

78 Hans Baur interview 1984.

79 Emil Clade interview.

80 Schroer interview.

81 Franzisket interview.

82 Galland interview, see *The German Aces Speak*, pp. 100-01.

83 Franzisket interview.

84 Kurowski, p. 72.

[85] Schorer interview.

[86] Nourse would later be killed in action on January 25, 1942.

[87] Franzisket interview.

[88] Clade interview.

[89] Franzisket interview.

[90] Schroer interview.

[91] Baur interview.

[92] Ibid.

[93] Kurowski, p. 110.

[94] Ibid., p. 111.

[95] Ibid., p. 112.

[96] See data at http://www.clubhyper.com/reference/jg27bookextractjw_1.htm.

[97] Kurt Kuhlmey interview.

[98] Ibid.

[99] Neumann interview.

[100] Kuhlmey interview.

[101] Kurowski, pp. 114–15.

[102] Franzisket interview.

[103] Ibid., p. 116.

[104] Rödel interview.

[105] Geoffrey Morley-Mower interview 1989.

[106] Michael Judd interview 1990.

107 Neumann interviews, and Espenlaub's fiancé and her child emigrated to Australia after the war.

108 Tate, p. 61.

109 Rödel interview. See also Tate, p. 61.

110 Schroer interview.

111 Morley-Mower interview.

112 Edwards interview.

113 Judd interview.

114 Franzisket interview.

115 Ibid.

116 Ibid.

117 Clade interview.

118 Franzisket interview

119 Rödel interview.

120 Woldenga interview.

121 Neumann interview.

122 Ibid.

123 Franzisket interview.

124 Ibid.

125 Kurowski, p. 127.

126 Woldenga interview.

127 Neumann interview.

128 Hans Baur interview, 1984.

[129] Schroer interview.

[130] Franzisket interview.

[131] Woldenga interview.

[132] Neumann interview.

[133] Ibid.

[134] Clade interview.

[135] Schroer interview.

[136] Woldenga interview.

[137] Neumann interview.

[138] Franzisket interview.

[139] Ibid.

[140] Körner interview

[141] Neumann interview.

[142] Schroer interview.

[143] On May 27 1942, Flight Sergeant Sands was detailed to fly BN282 from El Adem to Gambut West. He did not leave with the rest of the squadron as the aircraft was temporarily unserviceable. He left at a later time but BN282 did not arrive at its destination. Although initially reported as missing in action, Sands' remains were found in the Sollum-Tobruk area by the Second Cameroons, identified by a pay book and buried with the grave being marked by a cross. Following post war searches failed and the grave could not be located, so the search was abandoned in 1946. See RAAF Aviation Museum and https://aviationmuseumwa.org.au/afcraaf-roll/sands-alwyn-harold-402064/

[144] Körner interview. He was shot down by Lieutenant Lawrence Waugh of 1 Squadron SAAF on July 4, 1942 as he intercepted a RAF bomber formation near El Alamein in his Me-109 F-4/Trop (Werknummer 8696) "Red 11". He was captured and sent to a prisoner of war camp in Canada and was released in 1947.

[145] Neumann interview.

146 Schroer interview.

147 Woldenga interview.

148 Rödel interview.

149 Neumann interview

150 Schroer interview

151 Rödel interview.

152 Neumann interview

153 Schroer interview.

154 Woldenga interview.

155 Neumann interview.

156 Kurowski, p. 13.

157 Ibid., p. 138

158 Schroer interview.

159 Kurowski, p. 139.

160 Franzisket interview.

161 Schroer interview.

162 Baur interview.

163 Franzisket interview.

164 Tate, p. 62.

165 Clade interview.

166 Kurowski, p. 149.

167 Geoffrey Morely-Mower interview.

[168] Franzisket interview

[169] Tate, p. 48. See also the after-action report as recorded by Tate.

[170] Franzisket interview.

[171] Neumann interview.

[172] RAAF Fatalities in Second World War among RAAf Personnel Serving on Attachment in Royal Air Force Squadrons and Support Units: Commonwealth War Graves records AWM 237 (65) NAA : A705, 163/165/101.

[173] Geoffrey Morely-Mower interview.

[174] Michael Judd interview.

[175] Franzisket interview.

[176] Kuhlmey interview.

[177] Kurowski, pp. 150–51.

[178] Franzisket interview.

[179] Kuhlmey interview.

[180] Ibid.

[181] Ibid.

[182] Ibid.

[183] Cecil Golding interview.

[184] Schroer interview.

[185] Clade interview.

[186] Kuhlmey interview.

[187] Commonwealth War Graves Records. AWM 237 (65) NAA : A705, 163/145/124.

[188] Ibid. AWM 237 (65) NAA: A705, 163/150/116. Micro Film No. 463 OAFH.

[189] Ibid.

[190] Clade interview.

[191] Schroer interview.

[192] Franzisket interview.

[193] Neumann interview.

[194] Schroer interview.

[195] Neumann interview.

[196] Morley-Mower interview.

[197] Neumann interview.

[198] Franzisket interview.

[199] While with No. 260 Squadron, Edwards flew 195 sorties in North Africa, accumulating 261 hours of flight time. He was officially credited with 15 1/2 aircraft destroyed, 6 1/2 probables, and 13 damaged. He personally accounted for approximately 20 percent of No. 260 Squadron's victories.

[200] Kurowski, p. 172.

[201] Leni Riefenstahl interview.

[202] Löwe interview.

[203] Ibid., p. 176.

[204] Georg Ludwig Heinrich Nicolaus von Below was the *Luftwaffe* adjutant to Adolf Hitler. He was the liaison officer between Hitler and Göring.

[205] Baur interview.

[206] Heaton and Lewis, *The German Aces Speak*, Vol.1, pp. 152–153.

[207] Artur Axmann interview, 1985.

[208] Leni Riefenstahl interview.

[209] Baur interview.

[210] Axmann interview.

[211] Baur interview.

[212] Ibid.

[213] Karl Wolff interview.

[214] Franzisket interview.

[215] Schroer interview.

[216] Rödel interview.

[217] Schroer interview.

[218] Körner interview. He scored 36 victories in 250 sorties while in North Africa. He lived with his wife in Paris after retiring as a *Generalmajor* and passed away on September 3, 1998.

[219] Clade interview.

[220] Schroer interview.

[221] Stigler interview.

[222] Clade interview. In March 2005, the eighty-nine-year-old Clade and the eighty-one- year old Squadron Leader James met in Bonn for a reunion, as James was the sole survivor of this victory. Clade passed away in May 2010. He scored twenty-seven victories, including two four-engine USAAF bombers and was awarded the Iron Cross in both classes and the German Cross in Gold.

[223] Rödel interview.

[224] Franz Stigler interview.

[225] Rödel interview.

[226] Kappler would be tried and sentenced to life in prison after the war. It was he who gave *Hauptsturmführer* Erich Priebke the orders to kill approximately seventy-five civilians in retaliation for partisan attacks on German soldiers. This occurred in the Ardeatine Caves on March 24, 1944, the same area that Marseille was hiding in.

[227] Franzisket interview.

228 Neumann interview

229 Clade interview.

230 Schroer interview.

231 Franzisket interview.

232 Clade interview.

233 Franz Stigler interview. Stigler flew 487 combat missions with 28 victories. He was shot down 17 times and he bailed out six times and landed in damaged fighters 11 times.

234 Rudolf Sinner was credited with 39 victories in 305 missions. 36 of his victories were achieved over the Western Front, including three four-engine bombers and three flying the Me 262 jet fighter. Three victories were achieved over the Eastern front. He was shot down 12 times, bailing out on three occasions, and was wounded five times.

235 O'Neill's victories appear not to have been entered in the USAAF records, which is possibly due to him flying with a RAF formation. It is highly likely that he completed a RAF after action combat report.

236 Franz Stigler interview.

237 Neumann interview.

238 Franzisket interview.

239 Ibid.

240 Schroer interview.

241 Neumann interview.

242 Migeod interview. See also the YouTube interview where he discussed this and other issues at https://www.youtube.com/watch?v=ClJDdDP#1qc This is a series of episodes that are worth watching, by Tinus le Roux.

243 Clade interview.

244 Neumann interview.

245 Franzisket interview.

246 Rödel interview

247 Neumann interview.

248 Franzisket interview.

249 Schroer interview.

250 Neumann interview.

251 Franzisket interview.

252 Ibid.

253 Neumann interview.

254 Franzisket interview.

255 Kuhlmey interview.

256 Schroer interview.

257 Neumann interview.

258 Franzisket interview.

259 Ibid.

260 Franzisket interview.

261 Tate, pp. 63–64.

262 Ron Cundy interview.

263 See also the report located at the following website: http://www.century-of-flight.net/Aviation%20history/ WW2/aces/James%20F. Edwards.htm

264 James Edwards interview. According to Christopher Shores and Williams' *Aces High*, his final wartime score was 15 with 3 shared destroyed, with 9 more destroyed on the ground. Brown and Lavigne's Canadian Wing Commander credits him with 19 victories, 2 shared, 6.5 probable, 17 damaged and 12 destroyed on the ground. During an interview, Edwards himself specified that he had 19 confirmed victories during the war. Many who flew with him have said that he only reported those "kills" he was certain of

and that his real number of aerial victories was probably much higher than officially reported. Eighteen of Edwards' 19 victories, according to Brown and Lavigne, were enemy fighters (14 Me-109s, 3 Fw-190s and one Macchi 202). German losses compared to his claims show that Edwards probably had 24 victories.

[265] Rödel interview.

[266] Schroer interview.

[267] Franzisket interview.

[268] Neumann, Heaton and Lewis, *The German Aces Speak*, p. 156.

[269] Franzisket interview.

[270] Schroer interview.

[271] Neumann interview.

[272] Schroer interview.

[273] Marseille was credited with seven victories against P-40s in eleven minutes. JG-27 was up in full strength and engaged 36 P-40s: Eighteen Me-109s from I./JG-27 scored ten victories. Fifteen Me-109s from II./JG-27 claimed one kill, while ten Me-109s from III./JG-27 claimed eight P-40s and a Spitfire. Losses included Jack Donald of No. 3 Squadron RAAF, whose Kittyhawk lost the port aileron torn away and the engine burning as he bailed out. He landed on an Italian mess tent and became a POW; Sgt. Cedric Young of No. 112 Squadron RNZAF, went down, possibly due to flak. In addition, four other pilots: Thorpe of No. 250 Squadron and Strong of No. 450 Squadron were both shot down and captured. Sgt. Ken Bee of was wounded in action, but flew his damaged fighter back to base. Also of No. 3 Squadron RAAF was Pilot Officer Keith Kildey, who returned with his tail shot up, and Pilot Officer Donald, who bailed out and was captured. One of the P-40 pilots of No. 450 Squadron RAF shot down was Sgt. Peter Ewing. He bailed out and was captured. He was also the personal guest of Marseille until transferred to the POW auxiliary camp at Tobruk. Sgt. Gordon Scribner of No. 3 Squadron RAAF was killed in EV322 during this engagement. However, the records of the individual Allied squadrons involved conflict with the German claims. No. 3 Squadron RAAF, No. 112 Squadron RAF, No. 250 Squadron RAF, and No. 450 Squadron RAAF show that their total losses to enemy action that day were only five P-40s. It is highly possible that more than one pilot shot at the same aircraft, thinking he had scored the fatal shots. Marseille's timeline for his undisputed seven victories in eleven minutes was 16:51, 16:53, 16:54, 16:57, 16:59, 17:01, and 17:02. It would

also appear that two or three of Marseilles "kills" actually survived and returned as stated. Australian F/L Desmond "Des" Cormack was damaged.

[274] Franzisket interview.

[275] Judd interview by Jeffrey L. Ethell, provided by Ethell.

[276] Franzisket interview.

[277] Ernst Börngen interview.

[278] Franzisket interview.

[279] Ibid.

[280] Ernst Börngen interview.

[281] Ibid.

[282] Ibid

[283] Ibid.

[284] Franzisket interview.

[285] Kurowski, p. 94.

[286] Morley-Mower interview.

[287] Marseille's morning mission saw his *Schwarm* engage Hurricanes of No. 33 and No. 213 Squadrons RAF, plus eight Mk V Spitfires of No. 92 Squadron RAF. Marseille's first victory was a Hurricane flown by Pilot Officer Luxton of No. 213 Sqn, who crash-landed in BN186, and his last kill was a Spitfire VC flown by Pilot Officer Turvey, who bailed out of BR494. Marseille's enemies on his last mission included eleven Spitfires from both No. 145 and 601 Squadrons RAF. One loss was a Hurricane flown by Warrant Officer Kenwood. Marseille victories were overclaiming, damaged fighters but no losses.

[288] Kuhlmey interview.

[289] Tate, p. 66.

[290] Schroer interview.

[291] Ibid.

[292] Franzisket interview.

[293] Ibid.

[294] Neumann interview.

[295] Franzisket interview.

[296] Ibid.

[297] Ibid.

[298] Kuhlmey interview.

[299] Schroer interview.

[300] Neumann, *The German Aces Speak* vol 1, pp. 163-64.

[301] Franzisket interview.

[302] Kurowski, pp. 211–12.

[303] Franzisket interview.

[304] Rödel interview.

[305] Franzisket interview.

[306] Neumann interview.

[307] Kurowski, p. 213.

[308] Ibid, p. 215.

[309] See Public Record Office, UK National Archives, DEFE 3/573 – Intelligence from series of intercepted German, Italian and Japanese radio communications, WWII, CX/MSS/C 1-533, 1942 Sept 16-1945 May 15.

[310] Morley-Mower interview.

[311] Michael Judd interview.

[312] Neumann interview.

[313] Ibid.

[314] Ibid.

[315] Körner interview. Ironically, Emil Clade and Friedrich Körner had both retired and sometimes lived in Paris, France, where they came together several times per week to enjoy morning coffee and have dinners with their wives. They often spoke about the war and, in particular, Marseille.

[316] Clade interview.

[317] Kuhlmey interview.

[318] Franz Elles interview.

[319] Franz Stigler interview.

[320] Hans Baur interview.

[321] Artur Axmann interview.

[322] Karl Wolff interview.

[323] Leni Riefenstahl interview.

[324] Krupinski interview.

[325] Heinz-Georg Wilhelm Migeod interview. Migeod was shot down and made a prisoner of war. Golding shot down the Stuka flown by Hans Deible and right afterward Marseille shot Golding down. The two downed pilots spent some time together on wing of the Stuka that landed with a dead engine. Golding died in 2014.

[326] Kurt Bühligen interview.

[327] Josef Kammhuber interview.

[328] Woldenga interview.

[329] Geoffrey Morley-Mower interview.

[330] Michael Judd interview.

[331] Cecil Golding interview.

[332] Marseille, damaged, crash-landed on beach at Calais flying Me-109 E-7 W.Nr. 3579 White 13 with 50 percent damage. Enemy pilot unidentified.

[333] Marseille damaged by Hurricane flying Me-109 E-7 W.Nr. 5597 was 75 percent damaged in crash landing at Wissant. Pilot unidentified.

[334] There were only two Hurricanes lost over the Thames on this date. Fighters were from Nos. 310 Squadron RAF (Czech), one flown by Pilot Officer A. Hess in R4085 and the other by Sgt. J. Hubacek in R4087, and both pilots survived. The other Hurricane losses were from No. 303 Squadron (Polish), P3939 of Sgt. T. Andruszkow who bailed out over Dartford and P3577 of Sgt. M. Brzezowski KIA off Gravesend.

[335] Possibly Pilot Officer J.P Lloyd (WIA) in Spitfire P9368 No. 72 Squadron, or possibly from No. 603 Squadron which had two losses; K9803 flown by Sgt. G.J. Bailey who survived. Possibly No. 92 Squadron N3193 flown by Pilot Officer R. Mottram (WIA) and N3282 of Pilot Officer A.C. Bartley who safely crash landed.

[336] RAF Fighter Command lost 28 aircraft this day.

[337] Pilot unknown.

[338] Lost a/c from No. 73 Squadron, pilot KIA probably V7834 flown by Pilot Officer Peter Haldenby. Additional Allied fighter losses were most likely Hurricanes from No. 73 Squadron RAF. This unit lost three aircraft in aerial combat around midday. Another Hurricane was lost in combat by No. 6 Squadron RAF. Marseille's Me-109 E-7 (W. Nr. 5160) suffered 100 percent damage after combat, when he crash-landed at Tobruk.

[339] The Blenheim victory has a discrepancy. It was either Z5898 or T2429 of No. 45 Squadron with crew Pilot Officer Bruce Cartwright de Gardanne Allan, Flight Sergeant L.W. Morling, Wing Commander D.V. Johnson, Squadron Leader Rev. J.E. Cox, S/L D.P. Barclay, Pilot Officer S.E. Bledsoe and Capt. Ronald W. Plowright, all KIA.

[340] These were from No. 274 Squadron RAF and No. 6 Squadron RAF. I./JG-27 claimed four victories. Pilot Officer Stanley Godden, a seven-victory ace, was killed in action, probably by Marseille. The other victory was probably Pilot Officer H.V. Hutt who was damaged, but crash landed safely.

[341] The Italians of the *Regia Aeronautica* were also in combat and claimed three victories. Marseille's victories were from either No. 229 Squadron RAF and/or No. 274 Squadron RAF, since thirteen Hurricanes were claimed with eleven being confirmed, with seven of those victories being credited to I./JG-27. At midday seven Hurricanes of No. 1 Squadron SAAF

engaged Me-109s losing four fighters, one of which was lost to ground fire. Later in the afternoon a Hurricane from No. 73 Squadron RAF was also lost due to ground fire, and No. 229 Squadron RAF lost two Hurricanes in aerial combat. No. 274 Squadron RAF lost two also to Me-109s. No. 33 Squadron RAF lost one Hurricane to both an Italian Fiat G.50 and a Ju-87 Stuka, probably Kurt Kuhlmey's rear gunner.

[342] Marseille's *Schwarm* engaged twelve Hurricanes of No. 1 Squadron SAAF. Marseille's victory was Lt. V. F. Williams, who crashed into the sea, suffering injuries, but he was rescued. Victory confirmed the following day while 2nd Lt. Herbert's fighter was damaged.

[343] The Germans with their Italian allies engaged Hurricanes from No. 33 Squadron RAF during an escort mission for Martin Marylands from No. 24 Squadron SAAF. Marseille shot down Sgt. Nourse, who bailed out. The other may have been Z4505 flown by Squadron Leader James Marsden of No. 33 Squadron. The Commonwealth forces lost three Hurricanes against twelve Bf 109s and six Fiat G.50s.

[344] This victory was Hurricane V7775 of South African Flight Lieutenant Patrick Joseph Anthony Byers with No. 451 Squadron RAAF. No. 451 had the only reconnaissance camera equipped fighter in the Group, and he did the recon flight for No. 250 Squadron whose camera equipped Hurricane was inoperable. This was the day that Byers took off alone late in the afternoon and did not return. It was two days later when Marseille and his wingman flew to No. 451 Squadron's base and dropped the note informing them that Byers had been shot down. It was two weeks later that they informed the unit that Byers had died of his wounds in Derna Hospital.

[345] The Germans engaged a total of eighteen enemy fighters, nine Hurricanes from No. 1 Squadron SAAF and nine were probably from No. 112 Squadron RAF, as well as fighters from No. 33 Sqn. The South Africans lost a total of three Hurricanes. Captain C. A. van Vliet and 2nd Lieutenant J. MacRobert were recovered uninjured, although Lieutenant B. E. Dold remains missing in action. I./JG-27 claimed six victories. No. 112 Squadron was bounced by a Me-109 after a shipping escort mission. New Zealander Pilot Officer D. F. "Jerry" Westenra bailed out safely. Possible that Sgt. Nourse from No. 33 Squadron was again shot down by Marseille and bailed out and returned to his unit.

[346] This bomber claimed may have been from No. 203 Squadron RAF, which did not register a lost aircraft, but one was damaged. Possibly legitimate overclaiming. No. 1 Squadron SAAF had 2nd Lieutenant J. MacRobert and Captain C.A. van Vliet shot down but both returned to unit. Lieutenant B.E. Dold was MIA. One of the aircraft serial numbers was Z4241 but to date which pilot was flying that aircraft is unknown.

[347] JG-27 was operating at nearly full strength when they encountered 24 Mk IIB Tomahawks from No. 2 Squadron SAAF and No. 3 Squadron RAAF. The Australians lost three aircraft, while the South Africans reported one loss plus one severely damaged. I./JG-27 claimed four aerial victories in this engagement. Flying Officer H. G. "Robbie" Roberts and Sergeant Derek Scott, both of No. 3 Squadron RAAF were Marseille's victories. Roberts made a forced landing inside Allied lines and his aircraft was repaired. Scott made it back to his base and crash-landed his badly damaged fighter. It was a total loss.

[348] I./JG-27 engaged twenty Hurricanes of No. 274 Squadron RAF and No. 1 Squadron SAAF, with both squadrons reporting damage of and a loss of one aircraft each respectively. Lt. N.M. Sandilands of No. 1 Squadron was KIA. Homuth also claimed his 29th victory. It would seem that either Marseille's or Homuth's victory made it back.

[349] I./JG-27 and II./JG-27 engaged twenty-four Hurricanes from No. 229 Squadron RAF and No. 238 Squadron RAF and the Germans claimed four Hurricanes. These Allied units actually lost five Hurricanes. Incidentally, Hurricanes from No. 274 Squadron RAF were also involved although no losses were reported. Pilot Officer Ruffhead of No. 229 Squadron was shot down but returned to base, as did Sergeant Roy. No. 238 Squadron lost Flying Officer Zabaiski, with P/O Omerod WIA and Sergeant Matthews who all returned to base. Horst Reuter of II./.JG-27 also claimed a victory.

[350] No. 274 Squadron RAF lost three fighters in combat with fifteen Ju-87 Stukas, six Me-109s, twelve Italian MC 202s and MC 200s. The Italians and Germans claimed three victories each. It was possibly Flight Lieutenant Hobbs who fell victim to Marseille. Another possible victim was F/O B.D. White, and there is a claim that flak got him, but the location and time match exactly.

[351] Marseille had misidentified his kill (P-40) as a Hurricane, from either of No. 274, 94 or 260 Squadrons RAF, in which No. 274 lost three fighters against 30 Me-109s and Italian flown MC 200s and MC 202s. Other JG-27 men claimed probables or damaged.

[352] The pilot of the Tomahawk IIB was from No. 2 Squadron SAAF, and Lt. B. G. S. Enslin bailed out uninjured. He was picked up and "piggybacked' home by Lt. Lipawsky.

[353] This was a Tomahawk IIB of No. 250 Squadron RAF. Canadian born Flight Sgt. Malcom Allen Canty. It may have been his body found by British ground forces, still trapped in his fighter with a single bullet in his forehead. He is buried in Sollum, Tobruk Grave R 62966.

[354] One kill was a Tomahawk IIB of No. 3 Squadron RAAF. Flying Officer Tommy Trimble in AM384 was wounded and crash-landed and returned to unit. His second opponent was either 2nd Lieutenant Connel or Lieutenant Meek, both from No. 1 Squadron SAAF, as both went down that day.

[355] I./JG-27 claimed five aerial victories in this engagement. The enemy were eight misidentified Hurricanes of No. 1 Squadron SAAF on an escort missions for eight Bristol Blenheims from No. 14 Squadron RAF and No. 84 Squadron RAF. The South Africans suffered heavy losses to 12 Me-109s. The result: three Hurricanes missing; a fourth shot down, a fifth crash-landed, a sixth sustained heavy damage but returned to base. Pilots KIA were Lieutenant C.G. Hojen in Z5156, Lt. K.H. O'Reilley in Z5456, and Lieutenant J. Mac R. Barclay in BD619. Captain C.A. van Vliet in Z5304 and Lieutenant A.J. Biden in BD779 were damaged but returned. Franzisket claimed a victory.

[356] The airfield at Martuba was the first engagement. The first victory was a Flight Sergeant Hargreaves and was Marseille's first kill when he belly landed his smoking fighter. Marseille's third victory was mistakenly identified as a P-40, which was actually a Hurricane IIB of No. 73 Squadron RAF, when Flight Sergeant Alwyn Sands (RAAF) crash-landed. Marseille's last kill was Sergeant A. Tait Donkin of No. 112 Squadron, who was killed. Marseille flew another solo mission later to inform the enemy as to what had happened to their comrades, informing them that Hargreaves was a POW and alive. No. 112 Sqn had three losses: Sergeant Brian Patrick Hoare in AK585 (RNZAF) who was KIA; Sgt. George Walton Elwell also KIA in AK593, and Sgt. Tait in AK852. Both Homuth and Körner made claims.

[357] Nos. 73 (no losses) and 274 Squadron RAF were involved, 274 lost four Hurricanes. Sgt. R. W. Henderson crash-landed and Sgt. Parbury bailed out, both uninjured. Pilot Officer S. E. van der Kuhle's Hurricane IIA crashed into the sea. Flight Lieutenant Smith remains missing in action. Henderson and Parbury thought they were shot by flak as they never saw Marseille. Danish pilot P/O Sven Erik van der Aa Kuehle of No. 274 was KIA. Also from No. 274 was F/L Smith listed as MIA.

[358] Marseille's adversaries were seven Hurricanes from No. 1 Squadron SAAF and No. 274 Squadron RAF. These units lost in aerial combat with three fighters from I./JG-27, which claimed three aerial victories were South African Lieutenant Le Roux of No. 1 Sqn crashed-landed his burning Hurricane Z2317 but was injured and was a guest of Marseille, his victor. Also of No. 1 Sqn was Lt. Herbert KIA.

[359] The P-40s of No. 3 Squadron RAAF were bounced during takeoff at Gambut airfield by Marseille and his wingman. Marseille's first victory was

a Kittyhawk I flown by Pilot Officer P. J. "Tommy" Briggs, who was forced to bail out at three hundred feet and was injured on impact. The second victory was the Kittyhawk I flown by Flight Sgt. Frank Blunden Reid, who died in the crash.

[360] Six Germans engaged eleven Kittyhawks from No. 112 Squadron RAF, which lost three aircraft in aerial combat. I./JG-27 reported three victories. Sgt. Phillip Thornton Elliot (RAAF) crash landed at El Adem and POW on March 9, 1942. Marseille's other victim was Lt. Witold Jander WIA ordered back to England, later killed in a hospital bombing.

[361] No. 3 Squadron RAAF lost two Kittyhawks. Sgt. Roger Maurice Herbert Jennings was killed in a crash landing (his 4th mission); Pilot Officer Richard C. Hart bailed out of AK689 near friendly lines with a dead engine and returned to his unit.

[362] Engaged were Kittyhawks from No. 260 Squadron RAF and Tomahawks IIB from No. 2 Squadron SAAF and No. 4 Squadron SAAF. I./JG-27 claimed five P-40s, II./JG-27 shot down three P-40s. Marseille's victories were from No. 260 Squadron RAF: Squadron Leader Osgood Villiers "Pedro" Hanbury, who crash-landed near Gazala, and South African Sergeant John William Wareham in AK808 was listed as MIA presumed KIA. The Allied units had the following losses in this engagement: three Tomahawks and one Kittyhawk missing, with one pilot later recovered wounded, two Kittyhawks and two Tomahawks that crash-landed, one heavily damaged and one lightly damaged Kittyhawk.

[363] Both Captain Cobbledick and Lieutenant Flesker of No. 40 Squadron SAAF were on a patrol mission and both reported MIA. The two aircraft call numbers were Z4377 and V7780 but it is not certain which pilot flew which aircraft. Cobbledick may have been one of the pilots Marseille tried to guide down knowing he was wounded and too low to bailout, since this did occur on this day.

[354] 12 Mk I Kittyhawks from No. 3 Squadron RAAF were bounced from higher altitude by two Me-109s diving out of the sun. Flying Officer Harold Graham Pace in AL172 was killed with a bullet in his head that penetrated the canopy. Sgt. Colin Shaw McDiarmid was injured and bailed out of AK855. Marseille's Me-109 was damaged, with hits on his propeller and a leak in the oil cooler. Flying Officer Geoff Chinchen reported that he damaged a Messerschmitt, hence explaining Marseille's aircraft.

[365] The first engagement saw Sergeant E. V. Teede of No. 3 Squadron RAAF uninjured despite crash-landing AL120 on fire and returned to his unit. The second engagement saw No. 450 Squadron RAAF lose four Kittyhawks. Pilot Officer Dudley Parker bailed out of AK697 uninjured, but his fighter

then crashed into the Kittyhawk of Sgt. W.J.K. Metherall. Both aircraft were lost, and Metherall was killed. Marseille only claimed only two victories, as he only saw Parker bail out. Unclaimed victory.

366 Sgt. E.P. Oakley crash landed on Gambut airfield in AK993. The Kittyhawk I of Flight Sgt. Ivan C. Young in AK842, No. 450 Squadron RAAF was hit in the engine. He safely crash-landed his fighter unharmed, but the plane burned. Young managed to make it back to Allied lines.

367 I./JG-27 claimed four aerial victories that day. These were mistakenly reported as Bostons and belonged to No. 223 Squadron RAF. Four bombers attacked the airport at Derna, without fighter escort and three were shot down. The fourth bomber crash-landed on its return flight. Crew of AG703 P/O D.G.W. Leakem and another uninjured, two crewmen WIA. Crew of AG708 were all KIA with P/O L.W. Bangley. Sgt. H. Chorsfield and his crew in AG717 were all KIA. (Mentnich and Homuth both claimed a kill each).

368 Marseille's *Schwarm* attacked a combined force of twenty Kittyhawks of both No. 250 Squadron RAF and No. 450 Squadron RAAF between Tobruk and El Adem. Sgt. Graham Buckland (No. 250 Sqn. RAAF) bailed out of AK705, but the parachute failed to open after he struck the tail. Marseille personally recovered the body and then later notified the enemy over their airfield. Marseille dropped his personal effects on No. 250 Sqn airfield.

369 No. 4 Sqn SAAF lost the following P-40s: Lt. Neal Washington Hancock in AH914 who returned to unit, Lt. Ronald Ford Marillier in AN360 KIA, Lt. Rowan Edgar Jackson listed MIA presumed KIA in AK509, Capt. Gordon Goodenough Bayly who crash landed in Allied lines possibly due to flak or Stukas, and Lt. Woodcliffe WIA and had a damaged aircraft. Steinhausen claimed 2 and von Lieres und Wilkau claimed 1 as did Mentnich. fighters involved belonged to No. 5 Squadron SAAF; one of the pilots killed was an ace with 5.5 victories, Maj. Andrew Duncan who was the son of the Governor-General of South Africa, Sir Patrick Duncan.

370 These were Kittyhawks from No. 112 Squadron RAF. One confirmed death was Pilot Officer Collet. I./JG-27 scored two victories. The other was P/O R.K. Wilson. One of these fighters was marked AL196, unsure which pilot was flying that aircraft. Rainer Pöttgen scored one victory.

371 Marseille scored six victories in eleven minutes against nine Mk IIB Tomahawks of No.4 and 5 Squadrons SAAF, and three of these "kills" were aces: 2nd Lt. Cecil Alexander Douglas Golding of No. 4 Sqn (wounded), Lt. Robin Pare in AK384 (killed), Capt. R.L. Morrison WIA in AK421, and Louis C. Botha (emergency landing at Gambut uninjured). The South Africans were already engaged in combat with Ju-87s and Me-109s at Bir

Hacheim when Marseille's *Schwarm* sliced through them from higher altitude. Also killed was 2nd Lt. Mike Martin of No. 5 Squadron SAAF.

372 The enemy were from No. 2 Squadron SAAF who lost two fighters. Lieutenant P.R. Frewen (flying either AL193 or AK611) bailed out and was uninjured. Lt. Leonard James Peter Berrangé in AK628 was claimed by both Marseille and Helmut Belser of 8. *Staffel* III/JG-53 and he was killed in the crash. Both Marseille and Belser may have honestly claimed the same pilot.

373 I./JG-27 claimed seven P-40s and II./JG-27 claimed one Hurricane after they engaged twenty-four Hurricanes from No. 73 and No. 213 Squadrons RAF, which had also lost four Hurricanes near Bir Hacheim. II./JG-27 alone engaged forty to fifty 50 P-40s, meaning that additional Allied units may have been involved, as No. 145 Squadron is also recorded, and they flew Spitfires. Marseille's fourth kill was not a P-40 as claimed, but was actually a Hurricane IIB No. 213 Squadron, after Pilot Officer A. J. Hancock in BM966, which Marseille had pursued for twenty miles, and finally shot down. It crash-landed near El Gubbi. Tate has No. 145 Squadron RAF listed as the unit suffering all three losses due to Marseille, however, this is in dispute to some degree. They may have been shot down by another pilot. This author tends to agree with Tate. No. 73 Sqn. F/L T.P.K. Scade in BN370 WIA and later received the DFC. Other No. 213 losses include Sgt. D.H. Jackson in BN159 KIA, and F/O J.A. Sowrey in BN562 who was safe.

374 Sgt. D.F. Greaves of No. 112 Sqn bailed out of AK937 and evaded capture. No. 112 Squadron RAF lost two Kittyhawks. Sergeant Greaves bailed out. One Hurricane was mistakenly claimed as a P-40 BE864 of No. 274 Sqn, flown by P/O Charles William Parry Persse KIA.

375 The Allied unit remains unidentified. I./JG-27 claimed six victories against 12 P-40s. The intelligence report for No. 204 Group RAF reported four aircraft lost. Marseille scored four victories in five minutes near El Adem. One was No. 122 Sqn P/O Felix Francis Joseph Edwards KIA.

376 During the battle only four aircraft were shot down outright, but another sustained heavy damage and was written off after limping away and crash-landing at base. Allied casualties were from No. 450 Sqn: Flight Sgt. William John "Bubba" Halliday (AL127) and Flight Sgt. Roy Stone, both killed, while Pilot Officer Osborne crash-landed safely and was recovered by the British Army. Marseille claimed four and *Leutnant* Hans Remmer one victory for I./JG-27 when engaged against No. 450 Squadron RAAF; yet despite the misidentified claims no Hurricanes were present.

377 No. 5 Squadron SAAF losses included Lt. R. C. Denham, who was killed. and Maj. John "Jack" Frost, missing in action. One victory was misidentified

and was actually a Hurricane. Other units involved were No. 73 Squadron RAF and No. 208 Squadron RAF.

[378] The enemy aircraft consisted of several different aircraft types: Kittyhawk Is of No. 112 Squadron RAF and No. 250 Squadron RAF, twelve Hurricane IIc in No. 73 Squadron RAF. Pilot Officer Stone (BN121) and Flight Sergeant Goodwin (BN157) borh from No. 73 Squadron bailed out safely. Another two victories were also Hurricane IIc types from No. 73 Squadron, and both pilots, New Zealanders Squadron Leader Derek Harland war (BN277) and Pilot Officer Gerald John Wooley (BN456) both died. South African Flight Sergeant Roy Arthur Drew, RAAF of No. 112 Squadron (AK856) was listed as missing in action. Marseille's final victory was the Spitfire IV on reconnaissance duty flown by Pilot Officer Squires (BP916). The other lost pilot was Flight Lieutenant Guy Robin (BN560) of No. 73 Squadron who was killed.

[379] One kill was Pilot Officer L. E. Barnes in BP451 who bailed out of his Hurricane IIC severely wounded. He died in a field hospital on September 12, 1942. Marseille later informed his squadron mates. The other was Flt. Sgt. W.H. Stephenson who crash landed.

[380] I./JG-27 engaged over a dozen Mk II Hurricanes from No. 1 Squadron SAAF and a like number from No. 238 Squadron RAF, and perhaps ten to twelve Mk V Spitfires of No. 92 Sqn RAF. F.O. Ian W. Matthews of No. 238 Squadron was killed, Pilot Officer Bradley- Smith of No. 92 Squadron bailed out uninjured from his burning Spitfire VC. Lieutenant D.G. Bailey was injured in a crash landing. Maj. P. R. C. Metelerkamp WIA flew his smoking fighter BH283 back to base. Marseille's four victories on this first mission were at 08:26, 08:28, 08:35, and 08:39. Also No. 601 Sqn lost Sgt. K.J. Lusty in BR363 listed MIA, and Sinner and Rödel also had claims. F/O Ian Walter Matthews in Z5666 No. 238 Sqn is MIA.

[381] Marseille's eight victories on the second mission were Mk IIB P-40s of No. 2 Squadron SAAF and No. 5 Squadron SAAF. No. 2 Squadron had U.S. pilots of the 57th Fighter Group attached. Lieutenant Stearns was wounded when he crash-landed. Lt. W. L. O. Moon bailed out of his Kittyhawk I, EV366 and was uninjured and captured. Morrison (EV366) and G. B. Jack (AM390) were both captured. The timeline for these victories is: 10:55, 10:56, 10:58, 10:59, 11:01, 11:02, 11:03, and 11:05.

[382] Marseille's five victories on the last mission were Hurricanes from No. 213 Squadron RAF. Marseille's 117th kill was a Hurricane Mk IIB, flown by Sgt. A. Garrod (BN273), who was not wounded and bailed out. F/O Richard Francis Wollaston of No. 213 Sqn in BP409 was KIA; Sgt. F.G. Potter in BP499 MIA, F/O J.E. Avise survived uninjured, as did Flt. Sgt. P.D. Ross in HL704. The timeline for the last mission kills was 17:47, 17:48, 17:49, 17:50,

and 17:53. Marseille's single-day score was equaled once by *Luftwaffe* ace August Lambert and exceeded by ace Emil Lang (18 victories), both on the Eastern Front. Marseille still holds the record for the most victories against the Western Allies in a single day. One Hurricane was misidentified as a Spitfire.

383 Units engaged were No. 2 Squadron SAAF (including U.S. 57th Fighter Group pilots) and No. 33 Squadron RAF. One of Marseille's victories was Lt. Mac M. McMarrell (USAAF), who was wounded and crash-landed in LG172. Another identified kill was Pilot Officer George Robert Dibbs (BN908) of No. 33 Sqn was MIA. I./JG-27 also engaged No. 5 Squadron SAAF, and the USAAF 64th Fighter Squadron. Marseille shot down both Lt. E. H. O. Carman (AN238) and Lt. J. V. Lindbergh (AK349), both listed as missing in action. Also shot down were a Lieutenant D.D. Stuart (AL181) of No. 2 Squadron SAAF, who bailed out while Lt. Ryneke crash landed and returned to unit. One of the P-40s was initially claimed as a Spitfire.

384 Marseille's I *Gruppe* engaged twenty-four Hurricanes of No. 7, No. 127, No. 145, No. 33 and No. 274 Squadrons SAAF and RAF, along with fifteen Kittyhawks of No. 260 Squadron RAF, No. 2 Squadron SAAF, and No. 4 Squadron SAAF. They also tangled with eight Spitfires of No. 145 Squadron RAF. The U.S. 57th Fighter Group had pilots attached to some of the units. Marseille's first victim was Sgt. M. Powers of No. 145 Squadron who was wounded and bailed out of his Spitfire V. Two P-40 pilots were Warrant Officer Stanislas Emile M. Bernier (FL226) of No. 260 Squadron, who was killed, and Lieutenant Ryneke of No. 2 Squadron again crash landed unhurt. Sgt. Anderson crash landed near El Kanabish and Flt. Sgt. M.J. Belleau in BE334 bailed out. Lieutenant A.W. Meikle bailed out of BP918 but returned to his unit two days later. Lieutenant W.B. Pearce in Z5312 bailed out as did Lieutenant B.W. Small in BE678 who was captured. Lieutenant H.E. Kirkby crash landed and returned to unit. Stahlschmidt and Remmer also claimed victories.

385 Marseille claimed all P-40s, but actually was probably responsible for either Bicksler or Canham. Sergeant Stewart of No. 145 Squadron in AB468 bailed out wounded, Sergeant Thomas in AR286 crash landed and Sergeant Small also landed damaged. Stahlschmidt also claimed a victory. Also hit was RNZAF Sergeant H.G.E. Thomas of No. 112 Squadron.

386 Flight Lieutenant Canham and Pilot Officer Bicksler (both of No. 145 Squadron RAF) both bailed out of their Spitfire Vs. It seems that one of them was Marseille's first victory. Marseille's other victories were two Kittyhawks of No. 112 Squadron RAF and No. 450 Squadron RAAF respectively. Marseille's cannon jammed after a few rounds, so all kills were made with this two 7.92mm cowl-mounted guns. Two *Geschwadern* were engaged on this mission. I./JG-27 claimed five 20 P-40s; II./JG-27 reported engaging

23 P-40s, claiming one victory. III./JG-53 claimed one P-40 when in combat with 12 P-40s and six Spitfires. Marseille's 137th victim was Pilot Officer Dick Dunbar of No. 260 Sqn KIA, who was reported as missing. Marseille's *Schwarm* engaged eight P-40s of No. 260 Squadron RAF and P-40s of No. 5 Squadron SAAF which lost three fighters and another scrapped upon return. On this mission as in previous sorties, American pilots of the U.S. 64th Fighter Squadron, 57th Fighter Group, were attached. No. 260 Squadron lost one P-40 with a second heavily damaged. No. 5 Squadron SAAF lost four fighters, while No. 7 Squadron SAAF lost five Hurricanes.

[387] I./JG-27 claimed four aerial victories in this engagement. Marseille shot down a P-40 southeast of El Alamein from No. 4 Squadron SAAF and a P-40 from No. 5 Squadron SAAF. One of his claimed victories actually made it back to base but was a loss. No. 5 Squadron SAAF lost Lieutenants Cowan (who safely crash landed in AN399) and Lt. R.A. McCarthy in AN394 also uninjured.

[388] I./JG-27 engaged twenty fighter bombers. Marseille's kills were misidentified as P-40s and were actually Hurricane IIs from No. 33 and No. 213 Squadrons RAF, and Spitfires from No. 145 and 601 Squadron. Flight Sgt. S. R. Fry in BP381 was a known victim, with F/L Lance C. Wade damaged but returned to base.

www.ingramcontent.com/pod-product-compliance
Lightning Source LLC
Chambersburg PA
CBHW070124080526
44586CB00015B/1546